The Best of
BAKING

The Best of
BAKING

Includes more than 400 easy and delicious recipes
for bread, cakes, cookies, pies, and pastries

With 200 full-color photographs

International Culinary Society
New York

Copyright © 1989 Ottenheimer Publishers, Inc.

This 1989 edition published by arrangement
with Ottenheimer Publishers, Inc., for the
International Culinary Society, distributed by
Crown Publishers, Inc., 225 Park Avenue South,
New York, New York 10003

Title of the original German edition:
BACKEN LEICHT UND GUT DAS GANZE JAHR
© 1983 BLV Verlagsgesellschaft mbH, Munchen

Photographs by C. P. Fischer, Baldham
Text by Mechthild Piepenbrock, Munchen

Translated by Judith Geerke

All rights reserved.
Printed in Hong Kong

ISBN: 0-517-65591-8
h g f e d c b a

Contents

Tarts

Pineapple Cream Boats

3¼ cups sifted cake flour	7 tablespoons butter
1 egg	Flour for rolling out
Pinch of salt	Butter for greasing
Grated rind of ½ lemon	Ground almonds for sprinkling
⅓ cup sugar	

For the filling:

¼ cup cold milk	2 tablespoons crème fraîche
2 tablespoons sugar	4 canned pineapple rings
Pinch of salt	⅔ cup pineapple or apricot
2 teaspoons cornstarch or	jam
vanilla pudding mix	¼ cup slivered almonds
3 egg yolks	Powdered sugar for dusting
1 egg white	

For the dough, place flour on a smooth work surface and make a well in the middle. Place egg, salt and lemon rind into it.

Sprinkle sugar over dry ingredients and distribute butter in flakes around the edges. Cut all the ingredients with a knife to a crumb-like consistency. Then quickly knead into a smooth dough. Refrigerate covered for 30 minutes.

In the meantime prepare the filling. Place milk (retaining a small amount), together with sugar and salt in a saucepan and bring to a boil. Whisk together cornstarch or vanilla pudding mix with egg yolks and remaining milk. Stir into the boiling milk mixture. Bring to a boil again stirring constantly, then remove from heat and allow to cool. Stir occasionally to avoid the creation of a skin. Whip egg white until stiff; fold into the cream mixture together with the crème fraîche and the well-drained pineapple which has been cut into pieces.

Roll out the dough on a work surface that has been dusted with flour. Grease 10-12 boat shaped forms, sprinkle them with ground almonds and line the forms with the dough. Prick the dough several times with a fork. Pour the cream into the forms, smooth out the surfaces and place the boats on a cookie sheet. Bake for 30 minutes on the middle or lower rack of an oven preheated to 400°. After half the baking time, cover the boats or bake on low heat.

Stir pineapple or apricot jam until smooth. When ready, take the boats from the oven and remove them from their forms. Coat the surface of the boats with jam and sprinkle with slivered almonds. Dust the boats lightly with powdered sugar and allow them to cool on a rack.

Grape Torte

2½ cups sifted cake flour	⅔ cup cottage or ricotta
Pinch of salt	cheese
Pinch of grated nutmeg	½ cup butter
1 teaspoon vanilla	Butter for greasing the form
¼ cup sugar	Bread crumbs

For the filling:

1¼ pounds each red and	Sugar to taste
white grapes	Piece of lemon rind 1 inch
½ cup dry white wine	long
½ cup water	1 ¼-ounce package gelatin

For the dough, combine flour, salt, nutmeg, vanilla and sugar. Place the mixture on a smooth work surface and make a well in the middle. Put the cottage or ricotta cheese into it and distribute the butter in flakes over the surface. Quickly knead all the ingredients together; form into a ball, refrigerate covered for 1-2 hours. Grease a fruit tart form, sprinkle it with bread crumbs, roll out the dough and line the form with it. Pierce the bottom repeatedly with a fork. Bake for 20-25 minutes on the middle rack of an oven preheated to 400°. Turn the tart shell out onto a rack and allow to cool. Wash the grapes and allow them to dry well. Remove stems, halve grapes and remove seeds. They may also be peeled if desired. Place the grapes onto the cooled tart shell as shown in the picture. Or begin by placing a large red grape in the middle and alternating red and white grapes in a circular pattern until the cake is full. Bring the wine, water (retaining a small amount), sugar and lemon rind to a boil. Whisk the gelatin together with the remaining water and stir into the liquid mixture. Bring to a boil, remove lemon rind and pour glaze evenly over the grapes. Allow to gel before cutting.

Kiwi and Raspberry Tarts

1¾ cups sifted cake flour	1 egg
⅔ cup ground almonds	⅓ cup sugar
Pinch of salt	½ cup butter

For the filling:

½ package frozen raspberries	Water
(about 1 cup)	1 tablespoon raspberry
⅓ cup sugar	schnapps
Juice of 1 lemon	1 ¼-ounce package gelatin
4 kiwis	

Combine flour, almonds and salt. Knead the dry ingredients together with egg, sugar and butter. Refrigerate for 30 minutes, then line 8 tart forms with the dough and pierce the bottoms. Bake on the middle rack of an oven preheated to 400°-425°. Allow to cool on a rack. Mix the thawed raspberries with sugar and lemon juice. Drain in a sieve and retain the drained-off liquid. Peel and halve the kiwis. Place one half in the middle of each tart. Place a circle of raspberries around each kiwi half. Combine the drained-off raspberry juice with the raspberry schnapps and add enough water to obtain 1 cup of liquid. Using this liquid prepare the torte gelatin-glaze according to package directions. Pour evenly over the tarts and allow to gel.

Nut Triangles

2 cups flour	⅔ cup butter
Pinch of salt	¾ cup plus 2 tablespoons
½ cup hazelnuts	sugar
⅓ cup sugar	3 tablespoons honey
1 egg	1⅔ cups slivered hazelnuts
½ cup chilled butter	3 ounces bittersweet chocolate
3 tablespoons heavy cream	

On a smooth work surface, combine flour, salt, hazelnuts and sugar. Make a well in the middle and add the egg. Distribute butter in flakes around the edges. Cut all the ingredients with a knife until they have a crumb-like consistency. Knead into a dough and refrigerate for 30 minutes. Roll out onto a baking sheet and spread the cream over the dough. While stirring constantly, heat the butter with the sugar and honey until melted. Fold in the hazelnuts and bring to a boil. Remove from heat immediately and allow to cool slightly before spreading evenly onto the dough. Bake for 15-20 minutes in an oven preheated to 400°-425°. While still hot, cut into triangles. Cool them on a rack. Melt the chocolate and dip the corners of the triangles in it.

Nut Rings

2½ cups flour	Flour for rolling out
½ cup sugar	½ cup sugar
Pinch of salt	1 tablespoon honey
1 teaspoon vanilla	1 tablespoon cognac or
1 egg	brandy
7 tablespoons chilled butter	½ cup melted bittersweet
1 pound shelled hazelnuts	chocolate
Butter for greasing	

Knead flour together with sugar, salt, vanilla, egg and butter and refrigerate.

Roast the shelled hazelnuts on a dry baking sheet for approximately 10 minutes in an oven that has been preheated to 400°. Then drop them into a cloth and rub off the brown skins. Grease and lightly flour a baking sheet then roll out the dough to a thickness of 1¼ inches. Cut rings out of the dough. The rings should have an outside diameter of 7 inches and an inside diameter of 3 inches. Lay the rings on a baking sheet that has been lined with aluminum foil.

While stirring constantly, melt together sugar, honey and brandy. Allow to cool slightly and then brush onto the dough rings. Place nuts close together on the rings and brush again with the sugar mixture (if it has become hard, place it in a warm water bath). Bake on the middle rack of an oven preheated to 400° for 10-15 minutes. Loosen from aluminum foil and allow to cool.

Melt the chocolate in a double boiler and brush onto the bottoms of the nut rings.

Note

In order to avoid having the nuts roll off during baking, place metal forms around the rings.

Glazed Knots

4 cups flour	½ cup sugar
⅓ cup ground almonds	7 tablespoons chilled butter
Pinch of salt	Flour for rolling out
1 egg	1¾ cups powdered sugar
1 egg yolk	3 teaspoons lemon juice
4 tablespoons sour cream	2 tablespoons white rum
1 teaspoon almond extract	

Combine flour, almonds and salt on a smooth surface and make a well in the middle. Put egg together with egg yolk, sour cream and almond extract into the well, sprinkle with sugar and flakes of butter. With a knife, cut all the ingredients together to a crumb-like consistency, then knead into a smooth dough.

Refrigerate covered for 1 hour. On a lightly floured surface, roll out to a thickness of ½ inch. Cut into 1 x 8-inch strips. Carefully tie a knot with each strip and place onto a baking sheet lined with aluminum foil. Bake for 10-15 minutes on the middle rack of an oven preheated to 400°.

Cool the knots on a rack. Stir together the powdered sugar, lemon juice and rum to make a glaze. Cover the knots with the glaze and allow to harden.

Black Forest Tartlets

½ cup dried pears	½ cup hazelnuts
3¾ cups sifted cake flour	⅛ teaspoon almond extract
Pinch of salt	Butter for greasing
1 egg	Flour for rolling out
6 tablespoons sugar	1 tablespoon cornstarch
⅔ cup butter	½ cup milk
4 tablespoons pear schnapps	½ cup heavy cream
¼ cup sugar	½ cup crème fraîche
1 teaspoon vanilla	1 egg
⅛ teaspoon cinnamon	

Cover pears with water and soak overnight.

The next day knead a tart dough out of flour, salt, egg, sugar and butter as previously described and refrigerate for 10 minutes.

Meanwhile drain the pears well and chop them to a fine consistency or puree in a blender. Mix 2 tablespoons of the pear schnapps together with sugar, vanilla, cinnamon, nuts and almond extract. Grease 15 cupcake or brioche forms and divide the dough into 15 portions. Flatten slightly and press into the forms. Pierce bottoms with a fork and fill with pear filling about three-quarters full.

Combine cornstarch with the remaining pear schnapps, milk, cream, crème fraîche and egg. Pour over the filling. Bake the tartlets on the middle rack of an oven preheated to 400° for 15-20 minutes. Carefully remove the tartlets from the forms and allow to cool.

Almond Crumb Cake with Cherries

3¾ cups sifted cake flour	1 cup plus 2 tablespoons
⅔ cup ground almonds	butter
Pinch of salt	1½ cups pitted sour cherries
Grated rind of ½ lemon	Powdered sugar for dusting
⅔ cup sugar	

Mix flour with almonds, salt, lemon rind and sugar. Sprinkle butter in flakes over the mixture. Cut all the ingredients together with a knife until they have a crumb-like consistency, and then knead the dough with hands that are as cool as possible (rinse them in cold water and dry them), only until the dough is crumbly and all the ingredients are evenly mixed. In doing this, always work quickly so that the butter does not become warm. Refrigerate half the dough. Line a 10-inch springform pan with the other half and form a small edge on the sides. Spread well-drained sour cherries evenly onto the bottom. Take the remaining dough out of the refrigerator. Sprinkle it over the fruit as crumbs. Place on the middle rack of an oven preheated to 350°-400° and bake for 60-70 minutes. Remove onto a rack, dust with powdered sugar and allow to cool. If desired, the cake may be served with whipped cream flavored with vanilla or crème fraîche.

> **Tip:** *For a very sweet cake, sweeten the sour cherries with sugar before use. First, however, drain them well before sugaring, otherwise the crust will become soggy. To avoid this, place a thin layer of bread crumbs between the dough and the fruit.*

Variations

Crumb Cake on a Cookie Sheet: Double all the ingredients. Roll out half of the dough onto the cookie sheet and continue as indicated above.

Crumb Cake with Chocolate: A few minutes before the cake is done sprinkle coarsely grated chocolate over the upper crust. The chocolate should just barely melt and not become runny.

Crumb Cake with a Fruit Mixture: Instead of cherries, use a mixture of strawberries, sweet or sour cherries, apricots and raspberries, or apples and pears. If fresh fruit is not available, use frozen or canned fruit. The fruits must, however, be well-drained. Frozen fruit must be thawed.

Latticed Fruit Tart

3¼ cups sifted cake flour	Butter for greasing
Pinch of salt	Flour for rolling out
Pinch of cinnamon	Bread crumbs for sprinkling
1 egg	¾ cup apricot jam
Grated rind of ½ lemon	1 pound gooseberries
½ cup sugar	1 egg yolk
½ cup butter	2 tablespoons whipping cream

Mix flour, salt and cinnamon on a smooth work surface. Make a well in the middle and put the egg and grated lemon rind into it. Sprinkle with the sugar and place the butter in flakes around the edges. With a knife, cut all ingredients to a crumb-like consistency and then with cool hands quickly knead into a smooth dough. Refrigerate covered for about 1 hour. Then roll out about ⅔ of the dough into a well-greased, 10-inch spring-form pan. Take some of the remaining dough and make a roll ½ inch thick. Use it to make the sides of the tart by pressing it against the sides of the springform pan to a height of 1 inch. Stir the apricot jam until smooth and spread over the dough, then place the gooseberries (see note on preparation) into the pan.

Roll out the remaining dough and cut into eight strips, or make long rolls by hand. Weave a lattice over the gooseberries. Press the lattice firmly to the sides of the tart.

Whisk together egg yolk and whipping cream and brush the lattice with the mixture. Bake the tart on the middle rack of an oven preheated to 400° for 35-45 minutes. Allow to cool on a rack. Serve with sweetened whipping cream or with vanilla ice cream. Or serve it with crème fraîche lightly flavored with sugar and vanilla.

> **Tip:** *For a change, mix the apricot jam with a bit of apricot liqueur. Or instead of apricot jam, use raspberry jam with some raspberry schnapps added to it.*

Note

Use either fresh or canned gooseberries for this tart. Fresh berries must be washed, stems and any dried flowers removed. Pierce them a few times with a needle so that they won't split. For canned gooseberries be especially careful to drain them well, otherwise the dough will become soggy.

Variations

Of course other types of fruit can be used for this Latticed Fruit Tart. Try, for example, apples, pears, cherries or rhubarb.

Cheese Cake

3¼ cups sifted cake flour
Pinch of salt
⅛ teaspoon baking powder
4 hard-boiled egg yolks
1 egg yolk
⅔ cup chilled butter

⅓ cup sugar
⅓ cup ground almonds
Rind of ½ lemon
4-5 tablespoons white wine
Butter for greasing
Bread crumbs for sprinkling

For the filling:
⅓ cup flour
1 cup milk
Pinch of salt
1 vanilla bean
½ cup raisins
4-6 tablespoons rum
⅓ cup butter
½ cup sugar

6 egg yolks
4 cups ricotta or cottage
  cheese
¾ cup crème fraîche
1 teaspoon almond extract
Juice of 1 lemon
Grated rind of ½ lemon
6 egg whites

For the dough, combine flour, salt and baking powder, on a smooth work surface and make a well in the middle. Press the hard-boiled egg yolks through a sieve, place in the well together will the raw egg yolk, distribute butter in flakes around the edges. Sprinkle sugar, almonds and lemon rind over the surface. With a knife cut all ingredients to a crumb-like consistency, then knead into a smooth dough. While kneading add wine drop by drop. Form the dough into a ball and refrigerate for half an hour. Then press onto a 10-inch springform pan that has been greased with butter and sprinkled with bread crumbs. Cover the bottom of the form with the dough and make the sides about 1½ inches high. While the dough is resting, prepare the filling. Whisk the flour together with some of the cold milk. In a saucepan, combine the remaining milk with salt, the marrow of the vanilla bean as well as the "empty" bean pod and bring to a boil. Stir in the flour and milk mixture and bring to a boil again. Allow to cool slightly and remove the vanilla bean.

Wash the raisins in hot water and rub them dry in a kitchen towel. Combine raisins with rum, cover and allow to soak. Beat together butter, sugar and egg yolks until foamy, then slowly fold in the ricotta or cottage cheese and crème fraîche. Add the flour mixture by the spoonful. Beat until a loose and light batter is obtained. Fold in the almond extract, lemon juice and lemon rind, and the drained raisins. Whip the egg whites until stiff and fold in.

Pour the filling into the tart shell and smooth out the surface. Bake on the lower rack of an oven preheated to 425° for 60-70 minutes. If necessary cover loosely with aluminum foil after half the baking time in order to keep the surface from becoming too dark. After removing allow the cake to settle for a few minutes, then remove from form onto a rack and allow to cool completely.

Dutch Pear Squares

6¼ cups sifted cake flour
Pinch of salt
2 small eggs
Grated rind of ½ lemon
⅛ teaspoon cinnamon
¾ cup plus 2 tablespoons
  sugar

1 cup plus 2 tablespoons
  butter
Butter for greasing
Bread crumbs for sprinkling

For the filling:
4 pounds ripe pears
3 tablespoons butter
½ cup water
1 cup sugar
1 tablespoon ground
  cinnamon

1 cup grated Gouda or
  Edamer cheese
Flour for rolling out
2 egg yolks

For the dough, combine flour and salt, place on a smooth work surface and make a well in the middle. Place the eggs together with the lemon rind and cinnamon into the well, sprinkle with sugar and place butter in flakes on the edges. With a knife, cut all the ingredients to a crumb-like consistency, then quickly knead into a smooth dough working from the outside to the inside. Refrigerate for 1 hour.

Grease a baking sheet with an edge about ½-inch high and coat it with bread crumbs. Roll out about ⅔ of the dough onto the baking sheet and prebake on the middle rack of an oven preheated to 400° for about 10 minutes. Take care not to allow the dough to get too dark.

Meanwhile prepare the filling. Peel, core and slice the pears. Stew them together with butter, water and 3 tablespoons of sugar until soft. Subsequently puree in a blender or by pressing through a sieve. Stir in remaining sugar (retaining 3 tablespoons), cinnamon and cheese. Remove from heat and allow this mixture to cool.

Remove the prebaked crust from the oven, spread the pear mixture onto it and smooth out evenly. On a work surface that has been lightly dusted with flour, roll out the remaining dough and cut into strips. Lay these close to each other on the pear mixture (as shown in picture).

Brush the surface with whisked egg yolks and sprinkle with the remaining sugar. Place on the middle rack of the preheated oven and bake for another 45 minutes. Allow to cool and then cut into squares or rectangles.

> **Tip:** *Talented "bakers" can lay the dough cover on in one piece. To attempt this, use only half the dough for the bottom. However, using the strips of dough to make the cover is the easier method.*

Brandied Fruit and Marzipan Cake

4½ cups sifted cake flour
2 eggs
Pinch of salt
⅔ cup sugar
⅔ cup butter

Flour for rolling out
Butter or margarine for
    greasing
Bread crumbs for sprinkling

For the filling:
1¼ cups crushed macaroons
1 cup brandied fruit with
    liquid
1 cup marzipan
3 tablespoons butter
½ cup sugar

2 egg yolks
Pinch of salt
½ teaspoon almond extract
2 egg whites
⅓ cup sifted cake flour

For the glaze:
3¾ cups powdered sugar
1 teaspoon lemon juice
Water to thicken

1-2 drops of red food
    coloring

Make a well in the flour, put eggs and salt into it, then sprinkle with sugar and distribute the butter in flakes around the edges. With a knife, cut all ingredients to a crumb-like consistency, then quickly knead into a dough working from outside to inside. Form into a ball and refrigerate covered for about 30 minutes.

Roll out dough onto a lightly floured work surface and pat into a 10-inch loaf form that has been greased and coated with bread crumbs.

While the dough is resting, crush the macaroons by placing them in a plastic bag and rolling them with a rolling pin.

Drain the brandied fruit retaining the liquid. Drip 4-5 tablespoons of the liquid onto the crushed macaroons. Beat the marzipan together with the butter until foamy. Slowly add sugar, egg yolks, salt and almond extract. Beat until the sugar is dissolved, then fold in the moist macaroon crumbs. Beat egg whites until stiff, slide them into the marzipan batter and then sift the flour on top. Gently fold all the ingredients together including the brandied fruit (be sure to remove pits from the cherries), and fill into the prepared form. Lay the remaining dough on top as a cover, press edges together firmly. Bake on the lower rack of an oven preheated to 425°. After about 15 minutes reduce temperature to 350°. Bake for a total of 50 minutes. Remove cake from oven. Allow to settle for a few minutes, then turn onto a rack.

For the glaze, stir together powdered sugar and lemon juice, add water drop by drop until a thick glaze is formed. Continue to stir until it is foamy and gleaming white. Spread about ⅘ of this thick glaze onto the cooled cake. Color the remaining glaze with red food coloring and place in a pastry bag made of bakery paper (see page 318). At regular intervals of ½ inch draw lines across the width of the cake. Allow to dry only a second. With a knife, draw three lines perpendicular to these in alternating directions to make the design shown in the picture. Allow the cake to dry before slicing.

Lemon Tart

2½ cups sifted cake flour
Grated rind of 1 lemon
Pinch of salt
1 egg
⅔ cup sugar

½ cup butter
Butter for greasing
Bread crumbs for sprinkling
4 cups dry peas or beans for
   baking blind

For the filling:
1 ¼-ounce package gelatin
¾ cup plus 2 tablespoons
   butter
1⅔ cups sugar

5 eggs
Juice of 4 lemons
Grated rind of 2 lemons

For the trimming:
1-2 lemons
½ cup plus 2 tablespoons
   sugar
4 tablespoons water

For the dough, knead flour, lemon rind, salt, egg, sugar and chilled butter, which has been distributed over the other ingredients in flakes, into a smooth tart dough and refrigerate covered for about 1 hour.

Then pat dough into a 10-inch springform pan that has been greased and coated with bread crumbs. Pierce the bottom several times with a fork and weight it with dry peas or beans (see page 311). Bake on the middle rack of an oven preheated to 400° for 25 minutes. Pour out peas or beans and cool the tart shell on a rack.

For the filling, mix the gelatin with cold water according to package directions. Whisk together the butter, sugar, eggs, lemon juice and rind in a metal bowl and place in a hot, but not boiling, water bath. Beat with an electric mixer until the sugar is dissolved and the batter is foamy and light. Be sure to avoid boiling the mixture. Continue beating and add the gelatin to the cream mixture. Beat the cream occasionally as it cools and, just before it stiffens, pour it into the tart shell and allow it to gel in the refrigerator for about 3 hours.

Scrub the lemons with a brush under hot water, dry them and slice thinly.

In a saucepan, heat sugar and water. Drop in lemon slices and boil briefly, then remove them. Continue to boil the sugar and water mixture until it is reduced to a syrup.

Lay out the lemon slices on the surface of the tart and cover with the slightly cooled syrup. Allow to gel before cutting the tart.

> **Tip:** *Make an orange tart by replacing the lemons (juice and rind) with oranges. In this case enhance the filling with some orange liqueur. And of course, use this recipe to make lemon or orange tartlets by using small forms.*

Vanilla Crescents

2¾ cups flour	4 teaspoons vanilla
⅔ cup ground almonds	¾ cup plus 2 tablespoons
Pinch of salt	butter
1 vanilla bean	Flour for forming
1 egg yolk	1-2 tablespoons sugar for
½ cup powdered sugar	dusting

Combine flour, almonds, salt and vanilla marrow. Add egg yolk, powdered sugar, vanilla and the chilled butter in flakes and cut all the ingredients together with a knife until they have a crumb-like consistency. Then quickly knead into a smooth dough and refrigerate for 2-3 hours.

On a lightly floured work surface, divide into smaller portions and form into crescents, that is, form little ½-inch by 2-inch "sausages" with pointed ends and turn both ends in the same direction. Place on an ungreased baking sheet. Bake on the middle rack of an oven preheated to 350° for 15 minutes.

Remove the baked crescents from the baking sheet immediately. Carefully turn the warm crescents in the sugar and allow to cool on a rack.

Note

As an additional trimming dip the ends of the crescents into melted chocolate after they have cooled.

Jam Tarts

1¾ cups sifted cake flour	Flour for rolling out
1 cup almonds	Butter for greasing
1 egg	6 tablespoons powdered sugar
2 teaspoons vanilla	4 tablespoons raspberry jelly
Pinch of salt	2 tablespoons raspberry
6 tablespoons sugar	schnapps
¾ cup butter	

Combine flour with almonds, make a well in the middle and put in egg, vanilla and salt. Sprinkle with sugar and distribute the butter in flakes around the edges. Knead everything together into a tart dough.

Refrigerate for 1 hour, then roll out onto a lightly floured work surface to a 1-inch thickness. Cut into rounds with scalloped edges having a 1½ inch diameter. Then cut out rings for the tops, the dough for the rings should be ½-inch thick with a hole in the middle. Place dough rounds and rings on a baking sheet. Bake on the middle rack of an oven preheated to 400° for 15-20 minutes.

Remove immediately. Dip the top side of the rings into powdered sugar.

Stir together raspberry jelly and schnapps until smooth. Spread onto cookies. Place rings on top, sugar side facing up, and press lightly.

Crispy Marzipan Cookies

2½ cups flour	3 tablespoons sugar
¼ cup marzipan	Flour for forming
¾ cup plus 2 tablespoons	Sugar for sprinkling
chilled butter	Butter for greasing

Place flour on a work surface and crumble marzipan over it. Distribute flakes of well-chilled butter over the surface and sprinkle with sugar. With a knife, cut to a crumb-like consistency and then quickly knead into a smooth dough. Refrigerate for about 30 minutes. Then, on a lightly floured work surface, roll out half the dough to a thickness of ½-¾ inch and cut into 1 x 2-inch strips. Pierce diagonally three times with a fork to make a design, sprinkle with sugar and place on a greased cookie sheet. Refrigerate another 20 minutes, then bake on the middle rack of an oven preheated to 300° for 25 minutes. Be sure not to let the cookies get too dark.

Roll out the remaining dough and cut out rounds with a cookie cutter or a glass (see picture on preceding page). Score a cross on them with the back of a knife but don't cut through. Pierce the surface with a fork. By doing this, the edges may be indented or notched slightly. Sprinkle these cookies with sugar as well, place on a cookie sheet, refrigerate and then bake as indicated above. Remove all of the marzipan cookies immediately and place on a rack.

Almond Loaves

2 cups flour	½ cup butter
½ cup ground almonds	Flour for forming
Pinch of salt	1 egg yolk for brushing
Pinch of cinnamon	¾ cup almonds (skins
¾ cup powdered sugar	removed)
1 egg yolk	

Combine flour, ground almonds, salt, cinnamon, sugar and knead together with egg and chilled butter into a smooth dough. Refrigerate covered for 2-3 hours. Then on a lightly floured work surface roll walnut-sized balls and form these into a somewhat ovular shape. Brush with whisked egg yolk. Make a small cut in the middle and press an almond into it. Place the little loaves on a ungreased cookie sheet and bake on the middle rack of an oven preheated to 400° for 20 minutes. Remove from the cookie sheet immediately.

Black-and-White Cookies

2½ cups flour	2 teaspoons cocoa
Pinch of salt	Flour for forming
1¼ cups powdered sugar	1 egg white
⅔ cup chilled butter	

Combine flour, salt and powdered sugar. Distribute well-chilled butter cut into flakes over the flour mixture. With a knife cut all the ingredients into a crumb-like consistency. Then very quickly knead together into a smooth dough. Mix one half of the dough with the cocoa. Refrigerate both halves for 2 hours because the dough is very delicate and soft. Then roll out both halves on a lightly floured work surface to a thickness of ¼ inch and lay together to make various designs. For example:

Snails:

For this, a light-colored (or a dark-colored) sheet of dough is laid on the work surface, brushed with a thin layer of egg white, and a second sheet of dark (or light) dough is lightly pressed onto it. Both sheets of dough are rolled up together and then cut into slices ¼ inch thick.

Checkerboard Pattern:

Three light and three dark dough strips are alternately layered on top of each other into the pattern, then wrapped in a light or dark dough layer. Here, too, all the layers of dough used must be brushed with egg white so that they do not separate during baking.

Wrapped Dough Blocks:

These are very simple. Either form light or dark dough into a round or square bar and then, after brushing with egg white, wrap it in a sheet of dough of the opposite color. Cut into slices and bake on an ungreased cookie sheet.

Marbled Cookies:

Press together any remaining bits of dark and light dough and knead gently so that a marbled effect is obtained. Form this into a roll and cut into slices. All of these black and white cookies are baked on an ungreased baking sheet on the middle rack of an oven preheated to 350°-400° for 15-20 minutes. They must be carefully removed immediately after baking and allowed to cool.

Note

This very rich dough must always be kept cool while it is being formed.

Cream Crescents

1½ cups flour	1 egg yolk
Pinch of salt	2 tablespoons whipping cream
⅛ teaspoon baking powder	or milk
5 tablespoons sour cream	½ cup shredded almonds
¾ cup plus 2 tablespoons	¼ cup sugar
chilled butter	Butter for greasing
Flour for rolling out	

Combine flour with salt and baking powder, pour sour cream into the middle and distribute the butter in flakes over the other ingredients. Knead very quickly into a smooth dough and refrige-

rate for 2-3 hours. Remove from the refrigerator in smaller portions and roll out to a thickness of ⅛ inch. Cut out small crescents and brush with the egg yolk that has been whisked together with milk or cream. Try to keep the edges of the dough as free of the egg and milk mixture as possible otherwise the dough will not be "flaky" enough. Combine the almonds and sugar. Either sprinkle on the surface of the crescents or dip them into the sugar and almond mixture. Lay the crescents on a greased baking sheet and bake on the middle rack of an oven preheated to 400° for about 15 minutes. Remove from the baking sheet immediately and allow to cool on a rack.

Ginger Stars

3 cups flour	½ cup sugar
1 cup very finely chopped or	⅓ cup gingered plum
ground walnuts	preserves
1 egg	¾ cup plus 2 tablespoons
Pinch of salt	butter
Pinch of ginger	Flour for rolling out
Pinch of nutmeg	Butter for greasing

For the trimming:

6 ounces semi-sweet chocolate	Preserved or candied gingered
2 tablespoons coconut butter	plums

Combine flour, nuts, egg, salt, spices and sugar. Drain the gingered plums and chop very finely. Knead plums and butter into the flour mixture. Refrigerate dough for 1 hour, then roll out to ⅛-inch thickness on a lightly floured work surface. Cut small stars out of the dough with a cookie cutter. Place onto a greased cookie sheet and bake on the middle rack of an oven preheated to 425° for 10-15 minutes. Remove from the cookie sheet immediately and allow to cool on a rack.

Cut gingered plums into thin strips. Crumble the chocolate and melt with the coconut butter in a double boiler. Coat the stars with the chocolate mixture and sprinkle gingered plums over them. Allow the glaze to harden.

Vanilla Braids

5 cups flour	Flour for forming
⅓ cup sugar	Butter for greasing
3 hard-boiled egg yolks	1 egg yolk
1 egg	2 tablespoons heavy cream
5-6 tablespoons cognac or	¾ tablespoon vanilla
brandy	Sugar for sprinkling
⅔ cup butter	

Combine flour and sugar and place on a smooth work surface, make a well in the middle. Press hard-boiled egg yolks through a fine sieve and place them together with fresh egg and cognac or brandy into the well. Distribute the butter in flakes over the other ingredients. Knead everything together into a smooth dough; refrigerate covered for 30 minutes.

Take out the dough in small portions and, on a lightly floured work surface, roll out and cut into strips the thickness of macaroni. Using three strips, weave braids about 2 inches in length. Lay them on a greased cookie sheet. Whisk egg yolk, cream and vanilla together. Brush the braids with this mixture and sprinkle with granulated sugar.

Bake on the middle rack of an oven preheated to 400° for 15 minutes. Immediately remove from the cookie sheet and allow to cool on a rack.

French Plum Torte

2½ cups sifted cake flour	1 tablespoon raspberry
Pinch of ground cinnamon	schnapps
Pinch of salt	7 tablespoons chilled butter
1 egg	Flour for rolling out
1 tablespoon cold water	

For the filling:

2-3 pounds fresh blue plums	½ cup sugar
⅔ cup crushed almond	1 cup ground almonds
macaroons	½ cup red currant jelly
2 egg whites	1-2 tablespoons raspberry
Pinch of salt	schnapps
1 teaspoon lemon juice	

For the dough, combine flour, cinnamon and salt; place on a smooth work surface. Make a well in the middle and place egg, water and raspberry schnapps into it. Distribute the butter in flakes around the edges. With a knife, cut all the ingredients to a crumb-like consistency and then quickly knead into a smooth dough. Refrigerate covered for at least 1 hour. Then, on a lightly floured work surface, roll the dough out evenly and place in a 10-inch springform pan. In doing this make an edge that is about 1-inch high and pierce the bottom frequently with a fork. Bake on the middle rack of an oven preheated to 400° for 20 minutes.

In the meantime, wash and dry the plums. Remove stems and slit lengthwise in order to remove the pit. Then cut the halves lengthwise again so that they can't shrivel up while baking.

Put the macaroons in a plastic bag and crush them into fine crumbs with a rolling pin. Whip together egg whites, salt and lemon juice until stiff while slowly adding sugar. Gently fold in almonds together with macaroon crumbs and spread the batter onto the prepared torte shell. Smooth out batter and press the plum quarters into it in a cobblestone fashion.

Place the torte into the oven again at the same temperature and bake for another 20-25 minutes. Shortly before the torte is done, stir together the red currant jelly and raspberry schnapps.

Take the torte out of the oven and while it is still very hot spread the jelly over it.

Allow to cool and stiffen. Then cut into 12 pieces.

Variation

Instead of ground almonds, substitute ground hazelnuts. In this case flavor the filling with orange juice instead of lemon juice. Also add some grated orange rind.

Apple Torte with Cream Topping

3¼ cups sifted cake flour	½ cup butter or margarine
1 egg	Flour for rolling out
Pinch of salt	¼ cup bread crumbs
⅔ cup sugar	1½ pounds tart apples

For the topping:

4 egg yolks	1 cup heavy cream
1¼ cups powdered sugar	2 tablespoons butter
4 egg whites	½ cup ground walnuts or
Pinch of salt	hazelnuts
Grated rind of ½ lemon	

Place the flour on a work surface and make a well in the middle. Place egg and salt into it, sprinkle with sugar and distribute the butter in flakes around the edges. With a knife, cut all ingredients to a crumb-like consistency, then quickly knead into a smooth dough working from the outside to the inside. Form into a ball and refrigerate for 30 minutes.

Roll out on a lightly floured work surface and press into a 10-inch springform pan making an edge about 1 inch high. Pierce the bottom repeatedly with a fork and sprinkle with bread crumbs. Peel, quarter and core the apples. Lay them close to each other on top of the bread-crumb layer.

For the topping, beat the egg yolks with half the powdered sugar until foamy, then set aside. Beat the egg whites with the remaining powdered sugar until stiff, season with salt and grated lemon rind. Slide egg white mixture into egg yolk cream. Whip the heavy cream until stiff and gently fold into the egg mixture. Gently mix together.

Melt butter, avoid overheating. Cool until lukewarm, and pour slowly into the cream mixture while stirring. Stir as little as possible in order to retain the cream batter's light composition. Fold in ground nuts and pour batter evenly onto the apples. Smooth out the surface and bake on the middle rack of an oven preheated to 400° for 45 minutes. Allow to cool in the pan for 10 minutes before placing on a rack to cool completely. Serve with whipping cream or crème fraîche.

Note

Choose the variety of apple according to the season. The tarter aromatic varieties taste especially good.

> **Tip:** For a change, mix the apples with carefully washed and dried raisins or add coarsely chopped or slices of candied cherries. This not only looks good, it tastes delicious too.

Grape Torte

3¾ cups sifted cake flour	1 cup milk
Pinch of salt	Pinch of salt
⅓ cup sour cream	1 pound seedless grapes
½ cup sugar	3 eggs
⅔ cup butter	¾ cup sugar
Flour for rolling out	⅔ cup ground almonds
1 package vanilla pudding mix	¼ cup marzipan

For the dough, place the flour on a work surface and make a well in the middle. Put salt and sour cream into it. Sprinkle with sugar and distribute the butter in flakes over it. Cut all the ingredients to a crumb-like consistency and knead into a smooth dough. Form into a ball and refrigerate covered for 1 hour. Then roll out on a lightly floured work surface and line a 10-inch springform pan with the dough making a 1-inch edge. Pierce the bottom repeatedly with a fork. Bake on the middle rack of an oven preheated to 400° for 20 minutes.

In the meantime, whisk together the pudding mix with some cold milk. In a saucepan, bring the remaining milk with a pinch of salt to a boil. Remove from heat and stir in pudding mixture. Return to heat and bring to a boil again while stirring constantly. Remove the pan from the heat and allow to cool, stirring occasionally.

Remove the torte shell from the oven; reduce oven temperature to 350°.

Wash and dry grapes, remove from stems. Beat eggs together with sugar until foamy, fold in ground almonds and crumbled marzipan. Spoon into the cooled pudding; pour into the pre-baked shell and smooth out the surface. Distribute the grapes over the surface evenly. Bake on the middle rack, or one placed slightly lower, for about 80 minutes. Remove the torte from the oven and allow to cool slightly while still in the pan. Remove on a rack and allow to cool completely.

Tip: *If seedless grapes are unavailable, it is advisable to remove the seeds since they have a slightly bitter taste and would ruin the torte's delicate flavor. Of course, other fruit besides grapes can be used. Berries, pitted cherries and yellow plums are especially good.*

Cranberry Torte

3¼ cups sifted cake flour	7 tablespoons butter
1 egg	Butter or margarine for
Pinch of salt	greasing
1 teaspoon vanilla	Bread crumbs for coating
6 tablespoons sugar	

For the filling:

1 pound cranberries	1 teaspoon lemon juice
5 egg whites	1 cup chopped almonds
Pinch of salt	1 tablespoon cornstarch
1½ cups plus 2 tablespoons	Pinch of cinnamon
sugar	Powdered sugar for dusting

Make a well in the sifted flour. Place egg, salt and vanilla into it and sprinkle with sugar. Distribute the butter in flakes around the edges and, with a knife, cut all ingredients until they are well-mixed and have a crumb-like consistency. Then working from the outside to the inside, quickly knead into a smooth tart dough. Form into a ball and refrigerate for 30 minutes.

Meanwhile grease a 10-inch springform pan and coat it with bread crumbs.

Roll out the dough and line the pan with it making an edge about 1 inch high. Bake on the middle rack of an oven preheated to 400° for 10 minutes.

In the meantime, wash the cranberries in cold water, allow them to drain well or, better yet, dry them in a kitchen towel. Whip egg whites with salt until stiff while slowly pouring in sugar. At the very end, add lemon juice. Combine almonds, cornstarch and ground cinnamon. Together with the berries, gently fold into the egg whites. Pour into the tart shell and smooth out the surface. Dust with powdered sugar. Bake immediately on the middle or lower rack for 30 minutes.

Note

Cranberries are usually available in the winter and their tart aroma harmonizes well with the almond meringue batter and the crispy tart dough. To bake this tart in the summer, use red currants or blueberries. The amount of sugar used always depends on the ripeness and sweetness of the fruit.

Variations

Almond-Berry Torte: Merely replace ¾ to 1 cup of the sifted cake flour with finely ground almonds and proceed as above.

Hazelnut-Berry Torte: The dough is the same as in the first recipe. For the filling, beat 3 egg yolks together with about ½ cup sugar and the juice of ½ lemon until very foamy. Beat 3 egg whites with about ¼ cup sugar and 1 teaspoon vanilla until stiff. Fold the egg whites together with 1 cup ground hazelnuts and 1 pound prepared cranberries into the egg yolk cream and bake as described in the recipe.

Butter
Cakes

Marzipan Bundt Cake with Marsala

1⅓ cups soft butter
⅔ cup marzipan
2-4 tablespoons Marsala
⅔ cup sugar
1 teaspoon vanilla
5 egg yolks
1 teaspoon almond extract
1½ cups sifted cake flour

⅓ cup cornstarch
1 teaspoon baking powder
⅔ cup finely chopped
  almonds
5 egg whites
1 teaspoon salt
Butter for greasing
Bread crumbs for sprinkling

For the glaze:
1 egg white
3¾ cups powdered sugar
4 teaspoons Marsala

Cream the butter until soft. Gradually add the crumbled marzipan. Pour in a few drops of Marsala to make the batter smoother. Continue to cream until the butter mixture becomes very light. Then slowly add the sugar alternating with the vanilla and egg yolks. Continue creaming until the sugar is dissolved and the batter is very light. Flavor with almond extract.

Combine flour, cornstarch and baking powder and fold into the batter together with the chopped almonds and remaining Marsala. Combine the egg whites and salt and beat until stiff. Gently fold into the batter.

Grease a bundt form and coat with bread crumbs. Pour in the batter and smooth out the surface. Bake in an oven preheated to 350°-400° for 60-70 minutes. Remove from the oven and allow to settle a few minutes before turning out onto a rack.

For the glaze, beat together egg white, powdered sugar and Marsala with an electric mixer. Coat the cake with it and allow to dry.

Note

Finely ground zwieback crumbs (instead of bread crumbs), are an excellent substitute for coating the cake form.

Sour Cream Bundt Cake with Chocolate

4 ounces bittersweet chocolate
Butter for greasing
Bread crumbs for sprinkling
¾ cup plus 2 tablespoons soft
  butter
1 cup sugar
Grated rind of 1 lemon
1 teaspoon salt
5 eggs

1 teaspoon instant coffee
2½ cups sifted cake flour
1 teaspoon baking powder
¼ cup sour cream
1 tablespoon crème fraîche
2 tablespoons rum
2 tablespoons cocoa
½ cup slivered almonds
Powdered sugar for dusting

Coarsely chop or grind the chocolate. Grease an 8-inch bundt form with butter and coat with bread crumbs.

Cream the butter in a bowl until light. Gradually add sugar, lemon rind, salt and eggs. Cream until the sugar is dissolved and the batter is light. Mix in the instant coffee. Combine flour and baking powder and add to the batter, add sour cream and crème

fraîche. Beat together all the ingredients. Then divide the batter into two halves. To one half, mix in rum, cocoa and the ground chocolate; to the other, add the slivered almonds.

Put half the light-colored batter into the form, cover evenly with all of the dark-colored batter, then fill in the remaining light-colored batter. Using a fork, pull through the three layers of batter with a spiraling motion in order to obtain a marbled effect.

Bake the cake on the lower rack of an oven preheated to 350°-400° for 50-60 minutes. Allow the cake to settle for a few minutes before turning out onto a rack. Allow to cool before dusting with powdered sugar. Serve with hot chocolate and whipped cream.

Spiced Bundt Cake with Fruit

¾ cup plus 2 tablespoons soft
  butter
1 cup sugar
Pinch of salt
3 eggs
Pinch of ground nutmeg
Pinch of ground cardamom
Pinch of cinnamon
Juice and grated rind of
  1 lemon
½ cup whipping cream

⅔ cup raisins
⅔ cup currants
⅓ cup candied lemon rind
6¼ cups sifted cake flour
3 teaspoons baking powder
1½ tablespoons cognac or
  brandy
Butter for greasing
Bread crumbs for sprinkling
Powdered sugar for dusting

Cream butter, gradually add sugar, salt, eggs and spices. Stir in lemon juice and rind. As soon as all the ingredients are well-mixed and the sugar has begun to dissolve, gradually pour in the whipping cream. Continue to cream until the sugar is completely dissolved and the batter is very creamy.

Wash the raisins and currants in a sieve under hot water and rub dry in a towel. Chop candied lemon rind into very small cubes and combine with the other fruit. Stir the fruit, flour, baking powder, and cognac or brandy into the batter.

Grease a large bundt form and sprinkle with bread crumbs. Fill it with the batter, smooth out the surface and bake on the lower rack of an oven preheated to 350°-400° for 50-60 minutes. Allow to settle for a few minutes before turning out onto a rack to cool completely. Then dust with powdered sugar.

Tip: *Instead of dusting with powdered sugar, this cake can also be glazed with melted chocolate. A glaze made of powdered sugar and cognac is also a delicious finishing touch.*

Sunken Apple Torte

⅔ cup butter or margarine
¾ cup sugar
1 teaspoon vanilla
Pinch of salt
¼ teaspoon almond extract
2 eggs
2½ cups sifted cake flour
1 teaspoon baking powder
1 cup ground almonds

Butter or margarine for
    greasing
Bread crumbs for sprinkling
6-8 tart apples (2-3 pounds
    depending on size)
Juice of 1 lemon
½ cup currants
¼ cup slivered almonds
Powdered sugar for dusting

Cream butter or margarine with a wooden spoon or an electric mixer until creamed. Gradually add sugar, vanilla, salt and almond extract alternating with the eggs. Stir the dough until it is light and the sugar is dissolved. Combine flour and baking powder, add to the batter; add ground almonds and mix together quickly.

Grease a 10-inch springform pan with butter or margarine and sprinkle with bread crumbs. Fill with the batter and smooth out the surface.

Peel apples, halve lengthwise and core. Make several deep lengthwise slits into the outer surface without cutting through completely and brush with lemon juice. Lay the apples close together face down onto the batter.

Quickly, but thoroughly, wash the currants in hot water and rub dry in a kitchen towel. Distribute them over the apples together with the slivered almonds. Bake the cake on the lower rack of an oven preheated to 350° for 75-80 minutes until

golden brown. Remove from the oven, slide onto a rack and dust generously with powdered sugar.

Note

Serve with lightly sweetened whipped cream or ice-cold crème fraîche flavored with vanilla.

Variations

For a change, use ground hazelnuts or walnuts instead of ground almonds and slivered hazelnuts or coarsely chopped walnuts instead of the slivered almonds. This torte also tastes delicious when pears are substituted for the apples.

Tip: *This Sunken Apple Torte keeps especially well. Bake as usual but use aluminum foil pans if possible. After baking, allow the torte to cool completely, then wrap in aluminum foil and freeze. Before serving, thaw and bake briefly.*

Linzer Torte

1 cup plus 2 tablespoons
  butter
¾ cup sugar
1 teaspoon vanilla
Pinch of salt
2 egg yolks
1 cup ground almonds
Grated rind of ½ lemon

1¾ cups sifted cake flour
Butter or margarine for
  greasing
Flour for rolling out and
  dusting
2 cups raspberry or red
  currant jam
1 egg yolk for brushing

Cream butter in a bowl until smooth. Then gradually add sugar, vanilla, salt and egg yolks.

Continue to beat until the batter is very light and the sugar has dissolved. Stir in almonds together with lemon rind. Quickly work the flour into the batter, first stirring, then kneading. Divide the dough into two halves.

Line a springform pan with parchment paper, grease with butter or margarine and dust with flour. Press or roll out half the dough into the pan.

Place the remaining dough on a work surface that has been dusted with flour. Use about ⅓ of it to form a roll with which to line the sides of the springform pan.

Stir the jam until smooth and spread it out evenly on the bottom of the torte. Roll out the remaining dough. Cut strips and lay these on top of the jam in lattice fashion. Press lightly to attach strips to the sides of the torte. Brush all of the dough surfaces with the whisked egg yolk and bake on the lower rack of

an oven preheated to 350° for 60-65 minutes. Slide onto a rack and allow to cool.

Variation

In Vienna, the bakers make a slightly different Linzer Torte: Combine 1½ cups of finely crushed dry sponge cake crumbs with ¾ cup butter, powdered sugar, ground almonds and 2¼–2½ cups flour and place on a work surface. Make a well in the middle; place 2 eggs, the rind of 1 lemon, a pinch of salt, a pinch of cinnamon, a pinch of ground cloves and 2 teaspoons of baking powder into the center and knead together. Roll out as above, fill with jam and cover with a dough lattice. Brush with a whisked egg and sprinkle with slivered almonds as a finishing touch.

> **Tip:** *To bake Linzer Bars, roll the dough out onto a cookie sheet and continue as above. Care should be taken that the dough is not too soft. Before rolling out, it can be stiffened by refrigeration or, if necessary, knead in more flour.*

Fruit Fritters

3 tablespoons soft butter	1 pound prepared fruit (for
1 teaspoon vanilla	example, apple or
1 egg yolk	pineapple rings, pear or
⅔ cup whipping cream	peach quarters,
2½ cups flour	strawberries, etc.)
½ cup milk	Vegetable oil for deep frying
2 egg whites	Sugar and cinnamon for
Pinch of salt	coating

Cream butter, vanilla, egg yolk and whipping cream until foamy. Beat in flour and milk. Then allow the batter to rest for 15 minutes. Combine egg whites and salt and whip until stiff. At the same time, heat the oil to 325°-350°. Gently fold egg whites into the batter and dip the prepared pieces of fruit into it so that they are well covered. Carefully drop them into the hot oil and fry 5-8 minutes until golden brown. Drain the pieces on a paper towel and then turn lightly in cinnamon sugar.

Americans

7 tablespoons butter	3 teaspoons baking powder
½ cup sugar	4 tablespoons milk
Pinch of salt	Butter or margarine for
1 teaspoon vanilla	greasing
2 eggs	⅔ cup powdered sugar
4 teaspoons rum	2 tablespoons lemon juice or
3½ cups flour	rum

Cream butter and gradually add sugar, salt, vanilla, eggs and rum. Combine flour and baking powder, stir into the batter alternating with the milk. The batter should remain quite firm.

Grease a cookie sheet. Using two tablespoons or a pastry bag (without a spout), drop 16-20 mounds of dough onto it. Bake immediately on the middle rack of an oven preheated to 350°-400° for 10-15 minutes until golden brown. Allow to cool on a rack. Stir together the sifted powdered sugar and lemon juice or rum to make a glaze. Brush the bottoms of the Americans with it and allow to dry.

Note

For deep fried pastries, alter the "Americans" recipe accordingly. Increase the amount of flour to 5 cups. Beat well over half the flour into the batter as above, the remainder must be kneaded in. Furthermore, reduce the baking powder to 1 teaspoon and omit the milk. After kneading the dough, allow it to rest for about 30 minutes. Then, on a work surface that has been dusted with flour, roll out the dough to a thickness of 1½ inches. Cut into 10 strips about 1½ inches wide. Make a 3-inch slit down the middle and pull one end through to make a twisted effect. Heat shortening or vegetable oil to 325°-350° and deep-fry for about 5 minutes until golden brown. Drain on a paper towel and dust generously with powdered sugar.

Deer's Back

3 ounces bittersweet chocolate
⅔ cup butter
¾ cup sugar
Pinch of salt
6 egg yolks
6 egg whites
⅔ cup ground almonds
⅔ cup dried sponge cake
   crumbs

⅓ cup sifted cake flour
Butter or margarine for
   greasing
Bread crumbs for sprinkling
1½ tablespoons marzipan
6 tablespoons powdered sugar
1 tablespoon cognac
⅓ cup slivered almonds
4 ounces chocolate for glazing

Crumble chocolate and melt over a warm, but not hot, water bath. Allow to cool until lukewarm.

Cream butter, sugar, salt and egg yolks. Add chocolate gradually. Whip egg whites until stiff and slide into the batter. Gently fold in almonds, sponge cake crumbs and flour.

Grease a "deer's-back form" (see picture above: the ideal baking form has a "backbone groove" at the height of the arch), and sprinkle it with bread crumbs. Fill with batter and smooth out the surface. Bake on the lower rack of an oven preheated to 400° for 55-60 minutes.

Turn out onto a rack. Knead together marzipan, powdered sugar and cognac. Form a long pencil-thick roll, lay into the groove and press gently. Stick slivered almonds into the deer's back so that they stick up like spines. Melt chocolate over a warm water bath and glaze the cake.

Hollow Wafers

½ cup butter
⅔ cup sugar
Pinch of salt
Grated rind of ½ lemon
2 eggs

2½ cups flour
½ cup milk
Butter or margarine for
   greasing

Cream butter, sugar, salt, grated lemon rind and eggs. While beating constantly, add flour and milk alternating the two ingredients. The batter should not become too firm and should be similar to a pancake or omelette batter. Cover and allow to rest for 30 minutes so that the flour can swell. Line a cookie sheet with parchment paper and, using a cookie cutter or a glass (with a diameter of 2 inches), draw 5-6 circles a good distance apart since the batter runs. Spread small quantities of the batter in these circles and bake on the middle rack of an oven that has been preheated to 400° for 4-6 minutes.

Remove the wafers immediately and—while still hot!—curve them over the broad handle of a wooden spoon or a similar piece of curved wood. As soon as the wafers have taken on their new form, slide them off and stand them on end in glasses until they have cooled completely.

> **Tip:** *In the making of Hollow Wafers it is important to remember that only small quantities of batter can be worked at one time, since the curvature can only be formed while the wafers are still hot and soft.*

Gooseberry Cake with Macaroon Cap

⅔ cup butter or margarine	2 tablespoons cornstarch
¾ cup sugar	1 teaspoon baking powder
Pinch of salt	Butter for greasing
Grated rind of ½ lemon	½ cup bread crumbs
½ teaspoon ground cinnamon	¼ cup ground hazelnuts or
3 eggs	almonds
3¼ cups sifted cake flour	

For the meringue:

1½ pounds fresh or 2 pounds canned gooseberries	2 teaspoons vanilla
	1 teaspoon lemon juice
6 egg whites	2 generous pinches of ground cinnamon
2 pinches of salt	
1⅓ cups plus 4 tablespoons sugar	5 cups ground hazelnuts or almonds

For the dough, allow the butter or margarine to reach room temperature, then cream in a bowl until white and foamy. While creaming, gradually add sugar, salt, lemon rind, cinnamon and eggs. Cream until the batter is foamy and the sugar is completely dissolved.

Combine flour, cornstarch and baking powder and add to the batter. Mix together quickly, but thoroughly, and smooth the dough out on a greased baking sheet. (If the baking sheet has no edges, make edges with aluminum foil in order to keep the dough from running over.) Combine bread crumbs with ground hazelnuts or almonds and sprinkle over the dough.

Wash the gooseberries in cold water and drain well. Cut off the stems and any remaining flowers with scissors. Dry the berries with a cloth. Then either pierce a few times with a fork or with a thick needle to keep the berries from splitting open too much during the baking process. Spread the berries evenly on the bread crumb and nut mixture.

Bake on the middle rack of an oven preheated to 400° for about 20 minutes.

In the meantime, whip the egg whites and salt in a completely greaseless bowl. While beating, sprinkle in ⅔ of the sugar and the vanilla. Continue to beat until the mixture is firm and tough. Add lemon juice and beat once more. Then gently fold remaining sugar together with cinnamon and ground nuts into the meringue mixture.

Remove the prebaked cake from the oven and evenly spread the nut-meringue mixture over it. Raise the oven temperature to 425° and bake for an additional 10-15 minutes.

Allow the cake to cool on the baking sheet, during this time the meringue will dry.

Then cut into squares or rectangles and remove from the baking sheet.

This cake should be served fresh since the fruit is very moist and meringue "easily attracts moisture," that is, it becomes somewhat tough.

Variations

Gooseberry Cake with Nut Cream: Instead of a meringue mixture, whip until stiff, 1 cup whipping cream sweetened with ½ cup sugar and 2 teaspoons vanilla. Fold in 1 egg yolk and ⅔ cup ground almonds mixed with 2 tablespoons cornstarch. Then beat egg whites until they form peaks, gently fold in and spread mixture (as described above), over the berries. Bake this mixture 5 minutes less than above or lay parchment paper over the cake to keep the topping from becoming too dark. In any case it is advisable to make higher edges around the cake with aluminum foil to keep the topping from running off.

Gooseberry Cake with Coconut Meringue: Instead of ground nuts, add grated coconut to the meringue mixture. In this case, replace the vanilla with ½ teaspoon almond extract or some ground cinnamon.

Gooseberry Cake with Nut Meringue: Halve the ingredients and fill everything (as described above), into a greased springform pan that has been coated with bread crumbs or finely ground nuts or almonds.

Instead of gooseberries, substitute other tart fruits and "cap" them with a macaroon topping. Depending on the season, use rhubarb, sour cherries, red currants, cranberries as well as tart apples or pears that are not overly sweet (the latter two should be peeled and cored).

Note

The meringue will taste especially piquant if a portion of the nuts or almonds are substituted with finely chopped candied lemon or orange rind, or add a few very finely chopped raisins that have been soaked in rum or cognac.

Tip: *When butter-cake batter is baked with a fruit topping, it frequently sticks to the baking sheet. To avoid this the sheet can be lined with parchment paper or aluminum foil. This makes removal from the pan easier.*

Mandarin Cheese Tart

½ cup butter	1½ cups less 2 tablespoons
⅔ cup sugar	sifted cake flour
2 eggs	1 teaspoon baking powder
Pinch of salt	Butter or margarine for
Grated rind of ½ lemon	greasing
½ cup whipping cream	Bread crumbs for sprinkling

For the filling:

3 egg yolks	1 can mandarin orange
¾ cup sugar	segments (about 10
2 teaspoons vanilla	ounces)
Juice of ½ lemon	2 ¼-ounce packages gelatin
2 cups ricotta or cottage	1 cup whipping cream
cheese	3 egg whites
	Powdered sugar for dusting

For the dough, cream the butter in a bowl. Gradually add sugar, eggs, salt, lemon rind and whipping cream until the batter is very foamy and the sugar is dissolved.

Combine flour and baking powder and add to the batter. Mix thoroughly. Grease a 10-inch springform pan and coat bottom and sides with bread crumbs. Fill with batter, smooth out the surface and bake on the middle rack of an oven preheated to 350°-400° for 35 minutes. Turn out onto a rack and allow to cool.

Cut the thin cake into two layers and divide one of the layers into 12 to 16 pieces. Place the cake that is still in one piece on a cake plate. Put the springform rim which has been lined with parchment paper around it again.

Combine egg yolks, sugar, vanilla and lemon juice. Press the ricotta or cottage cheese through a sieve, add to the batter above and mix well. Drain the mandarin segments in a sieve, retaining the liquid. Using this liquid, prepare gelatin according to package directions. Allow to cool to the same temperature as the cheese batter. Then stir the gelatin into the batter and refrigerate.

Beat whipping cream and egg whites separately until firm. Fold gently into the cheese batter only after it has begun to gel.

The mandarin segments can be halved, if desired, and then folded into the topping. Fill cheese mixture into the springform pan, smooth out surface and then place the cake pieces one after the other on top of the filling. This cake should be served within three hours of completion and refrigerated until that time.

Before serving, dust with powdered sugar. Then remove rim and parchment paper.

Note

Before filling any cream or cheese cake like this one, it is advisable to cut the upper layer into pieces. This way the cake can later be divided without applying undue pressure and the filling is never squeezed out of the sides.

Fruit Cake

1 cup sultanas	Pinch of cinnamon
1 cup currants	Pinch of clove
1 cup dried figs	⅔ cup chopped almonds
½ cup candied lemon rind	1 cup chopped hazelnuts
½ cup candied orange rind	1½ cups less 2 tablespoons
3-4 tablespoons rum	sifted cake flour
3 eggs	1½ teaspoons baking powder
⅔ cup sugar	Butter or margarine for
Grated rind of ½ lemon	greasing

Wash sultanas and currants under hot running water and dry in a kitchen towel. Chop figs, candied lemon and orange rind into very small cubes and combine with the washed fruit. Pour rum onto the fruit, cover and allow to soak.

Beat the eggs until foamy, gradually add sugar, lemon rind, spices, almonds and nuts. Combine flour and baking powder, and fold in together with the fruit soaked in rum.

Line a 12-inch loaf pan with parchment paper and grease the sides. Pour the dough into the form and smooth out the surface. Bake on the lower rack of an oven preheated to 350° for about 50 minutes. Turn out of the form, remove the paper and allow to cool.

Round Almond Bread

2½ cups sultanas	1 teaspoon baking powder
⅔ cup candied lemon rind	Pinch of salt
3-4 tablespoons cognac or	½ cup ground almonds
brandy	Butter or margarine for
1 cup plus 2 tablespoons	greasing
butter	⅔ cup whole almonds (skins
1 cup brown sugar	removed)
6 eggs	3 tablespoons sugar
3½ cups wheat flour	2 tablespoons water

Wash the sultanas under hot running water and dry in a kitchen towel. Dice the candied lemon rind into very small cubes and combine with the cognac and sultanas.

Cream the butter, gradually adding sugar and eggs. Continue beating until sugar is dissolved and the batter is very light. Combine flour, baking powder and salt; fold into the batter. Fold in the ground almonds together with the fruit soaked in alcohol. Grease a 9-inch springform pan, pour in the dough and smooth out the surface. Decorate with the skinless almonds. Bake on the lower rack of an oven preheated to 350° for about 80 minutes. Shortly before the cake is fully baked, combine sugar and water in a small saucepan and boil until the syrup is clear. Take the cake out of the oven, carefully remove it from the pan, place on a rack and brush with the sugar glaze.

Note

Fruit cakes and almond breads can be stored up to four weeks if wrapped in aluminum foil after they have completely cooled.

Sachertorte

²⁄₃ cup almonds (skins removed)	8 egg yolks
3 ounces bittersweet chocolate	2¾ cups sifted cake flour
¾ cup soft butter	8 egg whites
¾ cup plus 2 tablespoons sugar	Pinch of salt
	Butter for greasing
	Bread crumbs for sprinkling

For the glaze:

1 cup apricot jam	½ cup plus 2 tablespoons sugar
3 cups bittersweet chocolate	
½ cup water	

Grind the almonds twice in a grinder. Crumble chocolate and melt over a hot, but not boiling, water bath while stirring constantly. Remove from the water bath and allow to cool until lukewarm, stirring occasionally.

Cream butter in a bowl until very light and airy. Gradually add sugar and egg yolks. Continue to cream until the sugar is completely dissolved and the batter is very light.

Combine flour with almonds and fold into the dough. Whip egg whites and salt until firm and gently fold in taking care not to stir the batter too much.

Grease a 10-inch springform pan and dust with bread crumbs. Fill with the batter, smooth out the surface and bake on the lower rack of an oven preheated to 350° for 80-90 minutes. Take out of the oven and remove from the springform pan immediately. Turn the torte out onto a rack and allow to cool over night.

The next day, cut the cake into three layers. Heat the jam in a small saucepan. Stir constantly until smooth. Allow to cool slightly, then spread ⅓ on the bottom layer. Lay the next cake layer on top, again spread ⅓ of the jam on this layer, and cover with the third cake layer. Spread the remaining jam on the sides and top and allow to dry.

In the meantime, crumble the chocolate and melt together with the water and sugar while stirring constantly. Allow to boil for 5-10 minutes so that the glaze becomes quite thick. It is important to continue stirring constantly since chocolate burns easily.

While still stirring, allow the glaze to cool until it begins to become firm and a skin forms. Glaze the top and the sides of the Sachertorte and allow the glaze to become firm.

Note

Very slightly sweetened whipped cream, crème fraîche or vanilla ice cream taste delicious with Sachertorte.

> **Tip:** *For a stronger almond flavor, coat the springform pan with ground almonds instead of bread crumbs, or add ground almonds to the bread crumbs.*

Frankfurt Wreath

4 eggs
1 cup plus 2 tablespoons
  butter
1⅓ cups sugar
1 teaspoon almond extract

3¼ cups sifted cake flour
Butter or margarine for
  greasing
Bread crumbs for sprinkling

For the filling and decoration:
3 egg whites
¾ cup sugar
1 cup plus 2 tablespoons
  butter

1 tablespoon coconut butter
1 tablespoon pectin
⅔ cup crumbled croquettes
16 candied cocktail cherries

For the dough, first weigh the eggs (with their shells), then weigh out exactly the same amount of butter, sugar and flour.

Cream the butter in a bowl. Gradually add sugar and eggs. Continue to cream until the sugar is dissolved and the batter is very light. Flavor with almond extract. Stir the flour into the batter until smooth.

Grease a wreath form carefully with butter or margarine and coat with bread crumbs. Pour in the batter and smooth out the surface. Bake on the lower rack of an oven preheated to 325°-350° for 60-70 minutes. Turn out onto a rack and allow to cool.

For the filling, put egg whites into a bowl. Whip until firm. Gradually sprinkle in ⅔ of the sugar. Beat well and fold remaining sugar in gently. Cream butter together with coconut butter, that has been softened at room temperature, and pectin. Gradually fold into the egg-white mixture.

Cut the wreath cake into three layers. Spread ⅓ of the cream on each layer and place on top of each other. Remove a small portion of the remaining cream and fill into a pastry bag with a star spout. Spread the remaining cream smoothly over the surface of the cake. Sprinkle all of the surface with the croquettes and score the cake for 16 pieces. Decorate each piece with a cream star with a cherry in the middle. Refrigerate until ready to serve.

Note

For a more piquant cake, flavor the butter cream with a few drops of rum or cognac.

> **Tip:** *Fill the Frankfurt Wreath—just like its classical prototype—with real butter cream (made out of the equal amounts of butter and sugar) or out of a butter cream consisting of half vanilla custard and half sweetened creamed butter. However, the recipe given here is not quite as rich in calories. Furthermore, this very light cream with greater volume has the advantage of remaining fresh longer.*

Tree-Ring Cake

1 cup plus 2 tablespoons butter	1¾ cups sifted cake flour
1 cup sugar	½ cup finely ground, skinless almonds
2 teaspoons vanilla	2 tablespoons rum
5 eggs	Butter or margarine for greasing
⅔ cup cornstarch	

For the filling and trimming:

½ cup marzipan	6 ounces chocolate
¾ cup plus 2 tablespoons powdered sugar	2 tablespoons chopped pistachios
2 tablespoons rum	

Cream the butter. Gradually add sugar, vanilla and eggs. Then beat all these ingredients together for two minutes with an electric mixer set at the highest speed. Sift together cornstarch and flour. Fold into the batter along with the almonds. Then stir in the rum.

Grease a 10-inch springform pan well and spread 3 table-spoons of batter on the bottom. Bake on the middle rack of an oven preheated to 350° for about 7 minutes until golden brown. Remove and spread a new, thin layer on the previously baked one. Bake again. This process is repeated until half the dough is used up. The batter must be spread so thin that 7-9 layers can be baked with half of the batter. After all of the layers have been baked, loosen the rim with a knife and remove the cake from the form. With a glass having a diameter of approximately 2 inches, cut a chimney out of the center of the warm cake.

Clean the form and dry it well. Then grease again and proceed as previously for the remainder of the dough. Also cut out a chimney from this cake.

For the filling, put the marzipan and powdered sugar into a bowl, add the rum and knead into a smooth dough. Roll out on a work surface that has been lightly dusted with powdered sugar. Form into a strip the width of the cake and lay it on the bottom cake. Place the second cake on top of it and press gently.

Melt the chocolate over a hot water bath. Glaze the cake with it. Allow to harden somewhat before sprinkling with pistachios.

Note

This cake can also easily be baked in forms for small cakes or tartlets, in which case two or more forms can be baked at once. Divide the marzipan mixture in such a way that a layer of marzipan is put between two "complete" cakes in order to hold them together. For a more sophisticated taste, spread apricot jam over the surface before glazing.

Tip: *Cut the "chimney" into triangles. Similarly glaze it with chocolate and serve as a tartlet after it has hardened.*

Apricot Tartlets

⅓ cup butter or margarine	Butter or margarine for
6 tablespoons sugar	greasing
Pinch of salt	Bread crumbs for sprinkling
2 eggs	3 tablespoons apricot jam
Grated rind of ½ lemon	1 28-ounce can of apricots
3¼ cups sifted cake flour	1 ¼-ounce package gelatin
1½ teaspoons baking powder	3 tablespoons grated coconut
4 tablespoons cold milk	

For the dough, cream the butter. Gradually add sugar, salt and eggs. Mix in lemon rind and beat until sugar is dissolved and the batter is light and airy. Combine flour and baking powder and add to the batter. Continue to beat while slowly adding milk. Grease small tartlet forms and coat with bread crumbs. Fill in the batter ½ inch high. Smooth out the surfaces with a lightly moistened knife. Place the tartlet forms on an oven rack or baking sheet and bake on the middle rack of an oven preheated to 350° for 15-20 minutes. Immediately turn the tartlets out onto a rack and allow to cool.

In a saucepan, stir the apricot jam over low heat until smooth. Then brush the insides of the tartlets with it. Drain the apricots in a sieve, retaining the liquid. If desired, the fruit may be cut into smaller pieces and then generously laid in the tartlets. Measure the juice. Then, using it as the liquid, prepare the gelatin according to package directions. Pour carefully over the fruit taking care not to spill any of the glaze over the edges. As soon as the surface begins to gel, sprinkle evenly with grated coconut. Then allow to gel completely.

Variations

This butter cake batter is even more delicious if the flour is reduced to 2½ cups and ½ cup ground almonds or hazelnuts is added. In this case the surfaces should also be sprinkled with almonds or nuts. Instead of apricots, use any fruit. Be sure to drain canned fruit well and use the liquid for the glaze. If fresh fruit is used, make the glaze out of a wine-water-sugar mixture bound with gelatin.

Tip: *If, by accident, the tartlet forms have not been carefully greased and coated, the tartlets might "stick." Turn them out onto a rack and moisten the bottoms of the forms with cold water to loosen the cake more easily.*

Sponge
Cakes

Sponge Roll with Chestnut Cream

5 egg yolks
5 tablespoons cold water
⅔ cup sugar
1 teaspoon vanilla
5 egg whites

Pinch of salt
1¾ cups sifted cake flour
Butter for greasing
Sugar for sprinkling

For the filling and trimming:
1½ ¼-ounce packages gelatin
1 8-ounce can peeled
  chestnuts
1 16-ounce can chestnut
  puree
3-5 tablespoons cognac or
  brandy

1½ cups whipping cream
Pinch of salt
½ cup sugar
1 vanilla bean
1 tablespoon cocoa
3 ounces chocolate
½ cup slivered almonds

Put egg yolks and water in a bowl and beat with an electric mixer until very foamy. Gradually add about ⅔ of the sugar and the vanilla and continue to beat until the sugar is completely dissolved and the batter is thick and whitish in color.

Combine egg whites and salt and beat until peaks form, then slowly sprinkle in the remaining sugar. Slide into the egg-yolk cream and add flour. Fold in gently, but do not stir.

Line a baking sheet with parchment paper which extends over the ends of the pan. Grease it and the sides of the baking sheet with butter. Smooth the batter into it and bake on the middle rack of an oven preheated to 400°-425° for 10-12 minutes until golden yellow.

Sprinkle a kitchen towel with sugar. Turn the sponge cake out onto it. Brush the paper with cold water and peel off. Roll up the cake with the kitchen towel. Allow to cool.

Drain the chestnuts and retain 12 for decoration. Puree the remaining nuts in a blender and combine with the canned chestnut puree, cognac or brandy and about ½ cup cream. Stir in salt, sugar, vanilla bean marrow and cocoa.

Prepare gelatin with a little water according to package directions. While stirring, add gelatin to the chestnut cream and allow to gel in the refrigerator.

Whip the remaining cream until stiff. Melt the chocolate in a double boiler and glaze the whole chestnuts with it. Allow the glaze to harden.

As soon as the chestnut cream begins to gel, fold in the cream and unroll the sponge cake. Spread about ⅔ of the cream on it and roll the cake up again. Spread the remaining cream on the outside of the roll and place the chestnuts in a row on top. Roast the almonds in a dry pan until golden, cool slightly and sprinkle over the cake.

Note

Very little chocolate is needed to glaze the chestnuts. Nevertheless, melt more than needed because it will make the coating more even. Use the leftover chocolate at another time.

Chocolate Sponge Roll with Mandarin Oranges

5 egg yolks
6 tablespoons cold water
¾ cup sugar
1 teaspoon vanilla
1 tablespoon instant coffee
6 egg whites
Pinch of salt

¾ cup sifted cake flour
¼ cup cornstarch
2 tablespoons cocoa
Pinch of baking powder (if desired)
Butter for greasing
Sugar for sprinkling

For the filling and trimming:
1 can mandarin orange sections
White wine
3 egg yolks
⅔ cup sugar
Juice of 1 lemon
1 ¼-ounce package gelatin

3 egg whites
Pinch of salt
1 cup whipping cream
¼-½ teaspoon cream of tartar
2 tablespoons mandarin or orange liqueur

Combine egg yolks with water and beat with an electric mixer. Gradually add about ⅔ of the sugar, all of the vanilla and sprinkle in the coffee. Beat until sugar is dissolved and the batter is thick and whitish.

Whip egg whites and salt until peaks form, sprinkle in the remaining sugar and slide into the egg-yolk cream. Combine flour, cornstarch, cocoa and baking powder (if desired), and add to the egg whites. Fold in gently. Then spread onto a buttered baking sheet that has been lined with a piece of parchment paper long enough to extend over the ends. Immediately bake on the middle rack of an oven that has been preheated to 400°-425° for about 12 minutes.

Turn the cake out onto a towel that has been generously sprinkled with sugar. Brush the paper with water and peel off. Roll the cake up in the towel. Allow to cool completely.

For the filling, retain 12 or 16 whole mandarin sections. In a blender, puree the remainder together with the juice. Add enough white wine to the puree to make 1½ cups of liquid.

Beat the egg yolks, sugar and lemon juice until light and foamy. Gradually add the puree. Continue to beat until the sugar is well-dissolved. Dissolve gelatin according to package directions, stir into the mixture and allow to gel in the refrigerator.

Meanwhile, beat egg whites and salt until peaks form. Whip the whipping cream and the cream of tartar until stiff.

As soon as the egg-yolk cream has begun to gel, fold in ⅔ of the whipped cream together with the egg whites and flavor with the liqueur. Unroll the sponge cake, fill with the egg-yolk cream mixture and roll up again. With the remaining whipped cream, decorate the top of the roll with 12 or 16 dots of cream topped with a mandarin section.

Note

Also dust this cake roll with powdered sugar before serving. Retain a portion of the whipped cream and decorate the cake platter with it.

Carrot Cake

1 cup carrots	1 teaspoon baking powder
6 egg yolks	6 egg whites
¾ cup sugar	Pinch of salt
½ lemon	3 tablespoons Kirsch
4 oranges	Butter or margarine for
Pinch of ground cloves	greasing
Pinch of ground cinnamon	Bread crumbs for sprinkling
2 cups ground hazelnuts	1 cup apricot jam
1⅓ cups ground almonds	1 egg white
⅓ cup flour	3 cups powdered sugar

Peel and rinse carrots or brush them thoroughly with a hard brush under cold running water. Dry and grate coarsely. Beat egg yolks until light and airy. Gradually sprinkle in about ⅔ of the sugar. Continue to beat until the batter is a whitish foam and very creamy.

Wash lemon and oranges under hot water, dry them and grate the rind of half a lemon and half an orange. Add to the batter together with cloves and cinnamon. Combine nuts, almonds, flour and baking powder. Whip egg whites and salt to firm peaks while gradually adding the remaining sugar. Add the egg whites, the carrots and the nut mixture to the egg-yolk cream together with 1 tablespoon of Kirsch. Quickly and gently stir all ingredients together.

Grease a 10-inch springform pan and coat with bread crumbs. Fill in the dough, smooth out the surface and immediately bake on the lower rack of an oven preheated to 350° for 60-70 minutes.

Turn out onto a rack, remove the springform pan and allow the cake to cool.

Stir the apricot jam until smooth and flavor with 1 tablespoon of Kirsch. Brush the surface and edges of the cake with the jam and allow to dry.

Beat the egg white in a bowl and gradually add the powdered sugar and remaining Kirsch. Continue beating until the glaze is thick and gleaming. Frost the carrot cake with it evenly and allow glaze to drip over the edges. Allow to dry.

Just before the surface has dried completely, use a potato peeler to cut very thin slices of orange rind from the remaining oranges. Sprinkle these on the outside edge of the cake and allow glaze to harden completely.

> **Tip:** *Instead of orange peel, decorate the cake surface with tiny marzipan carrots. These are sometimes available in fine delicatessens. Furthermore, this cake tastes especially delicious if allowed to stand for a day or two.*

Chocolate Butter Cream Cake with Walnuts

6 egg yolks	6 egg whites
6 tablespoons water	Pinch of salt
¾ cup sugar	1¾ cups sifted cake flour
1 teaspoon vanilla	1 cup ground walnuts
¼ teaspoon almond extract	Butter for greasing

For the filling and trimming:

2 ounces bittersweet or milk chocolate	1 tablespoon coconut butter
3 egg whites	1 tablespoon pectin
¾ cup sugar	1-2 tablespoons cognac
1 cup plus 2 tablespoons butter	12 walnuts

For the dough, combine egg yolks and water in a bowl and beat until foamy. Gradually add ⅔ of the sugar, as well as the vanilla and almond extract. Continue beating until the batter is thick and creamy and the sugar is completely dissolved.

Beat the egg whites, salt and remaining sugar until stiff. Slide into the egg-yolk cream. Combine flour and walnuts and add to the batter. Gently stir together; pour batter into a 10-inch springform pan that has been greased with butter and lined with parchment paper. Bake on the lower rack of an oven that has been preheated to 350° for 50-60 minutes. Turn out onto a rack and allow to cool (if possible until the next day).

For the filling and trimming, crumble the chocolate into a double boiler. While stirring constantly, melt over hot, but not boiling, water. Allow to cool until lukewarm.

Put the egg whites in a bowl. Beat until stiff. Continue beating while gradually adding sugar.

Stir together butter, coconut butter and pectin until creamy, then slowly fold in egg whites and finally the liquid chocolate. Flavor with cognac and refrigerate until needed. Cut the cooled cake into two or three layers and fill with about ⅔ of the cream. Smoothly spread half of the remaining cream on the surface and sides of the cake. Put the remainder in a pastry bag with a star spout and decorate the surface with twelve dots of butter cream each topped off with a walnut.

> **Tip:** *For a dark sponge cake, substitute 1½ tablespoons of cocoa for the same amount of flour. Or, fold in melted chocolate instead.*

Charlotte Royal

4 egg whites	1¾ cups sifted cake flour
Pinch of salt	Pinch of baking powder
⅔ cup sugar	Butter for greasing
1 teaspoon vanilla	Sugar for sprinkling
4 egg yolks	

For the filling:

2 cups red currant, raspberry or cherry jelly	2 ¼-ounce packages gelatin
Juice of 2 lemons	2 tablespoons Armagnac or rum
Juice of 1 orange	3 egg whites
White wine	Pinch of salt
3 egg yolks	1½ cups whipping cream
½ cup sugar	Cocktail cherries

Combine egg whites and salt and beat until stiff peaks form. Then gradually sprinkle in sugar. Continue to beat until the batter is very smooth and has a gleaming sheen. Whisk together egg yolks and vanilla. Pour over the egg whites. Combine flour and baking powder and add to the batter. Gently fold these ingredients together and spread onto a cookie sheet that has been greased and lined with parchment paper. Immediately bake on the middle rack of an oven preheated to 400°-425° for 12 minutes. Then turn out onto a towel that has been sprinkled with sugar, moisten the paper and peel off. Stir jelly until smooth and spread onto the hot cake. With the help of the towel, roll up the cake and allow to cool.

Combine the lemon and orange juice with enough white wine to make 1 cup of liquid. Combine egg yolks, sugar and a portion of the wine-liquid in a bowl and beat until the sugar is dissolved and the batter is light and foamy. Prepare the gelatin according to package instructions using the wine mixture and Armagnac or rum as the liquid. Allow to gel in the refrigerator. Meanwhile combine egg whites and salt, beat to firm peaks. Whip the cream until stiff.

As soon as the gelatin-cream has begun to stiffen, that is, has begun to "streak" (see page 326), fold in ¾ of the whipped cream and the egg whites. Put this batter in the refrigerator again. Now, quickly cut the cooled sponge cake roll into thin slices and line a round bowl with a smooth surface with the cake pieces. Pour in the cream, smooth out the surface and cover with the remaining cake pieces. Refrigerate again for 4-5 hours and allow to stiffen.

Before serving, turn the Charlotte out onto a round platter (in order to do this, dip the form into hot water for a few seconds). Place the remaining whipped cream in a pastry bag and decorate the top with a circle of cream. Drain the cocktail cherries and place at intervals on the cream.

Chocolate and Pear Charlotte

3 ounces milk chocolate	1 small can pears
3 ounces bittersweet chocolate	4 egg whites
4 egg yolks	Pinch of salt
⅓ cup sugar	1½ cups whipping cream
1-2 tablespoons instant coffee	30-35 lady finger-shaped wafers
1 cup milk	1 tablespoon powdered sugar
2 ¼-ounce packages gelatin	Chocolate logs for decoration
4 tablespoons pear schnapps	

Grate the chocolate or chop finely.

Whisk the egg yolks in a bowl, add sugar, instant coffee and milk. Place the bowl over, but not in, a double boiler with hot water. With an electric mixer set at the highest speed, beat until the batter is foamy white and creamy, and the sugar is dissolved. Prepare gelatin according to package directions using this hot cream as the liquid. Dissolve in the hot cream while beating continually. Remove the bowl from the hot water bath and place in a cold one. Continue to beat until the cream has cooled to lukewarm. Add the pear schnapps and allow the cream to gel in the refrigerator.

Drain the pears well, then cut into very small pieces and drain again on a paper towel. Place egg whites and salt in one bowl, in another add half the whipping cream, beat each until very stiff. As soon as the gelatin-cream begins to "streak" (see page 326), fold in egg whites, whipped cream and pears.

Cut the wafers until they are exactly as long as the sides of a round and have a completely smooth form. Spread out the cut off pieces on the bottom of the form and place the long wafers vertically along the rounded side. Pour in the cream and refrigerate the Charlotte for 3 hours.

Shortly before serving, whip remaining whipping cream, sweeten with powdered sugar, and put in a pastry bag with a star spout.

Turn the Charlotte out of the form onto a platter, and cover the surface with whipping cream stars. Decorate with chocolate logs.

Note

Filling the cake with cream requires a great deal of concentration: First of all, it must be done before the cream has fully gelled; and secondly, the wafers must not slide down. Here is a little trick: Allow the cream to gel in a smooth bowl, hold the bowl in hot water for a few seconds, and then turn the Charlotte cream onto a platter. Shorten the wafers and dip the smooth side of each one in pear schnapps, this way it will stick to the side of the cream. Distribute the cut-off pieces of wafer over the surface, and decorate everything with cream and chocolate logs.

Black Forest Cherry Cake

6 egg yolks	1¼ cups sifted cake flour
4 tablespoons water	1 tablespoon cornstarch
¾ cup plus 2 tablespoons sugar	2 tablespoons cocoa
	⅔ cup ground almonds
6 egg whites	Butter for greasing
Pinch of salt	Flour for dusting

For the filling and decoration:

2 cups canned sour cherries	2-3 cups whipping cream
½ cup cherry juice	1 teaspoon vanilla
2 teaspoons cornstarch	1 tablespoon powdered sugar
4-6 tablespoons Kirsch schnapps	Coarsley grated chocolate

For the dough, beat egg yolks together with water until foamy. Gradually add about ⅔ of the sugar. Beat until the sugar is completely dissolved and the batter is thick, foamy and whitish.

Beat egg whites and salt until they form peaks. Sprinkle in the remaining sugar. Then slide the egg whites into the egg-yolk cream.

Combine flour, cornstarch and cocoa; add to the egg-yolk cream. Then add the almonds and gently fold all ingredients together.

Grease only the bottom of a 10-inch springform pan. Pour in the dough and smooth out the surface. Bake immediately on the lower rack of an oven preheated to 350° for 50-60 minutes.

Remove the rim of the form, turn out onto a rack and then remove the bottom of the form. If possible, allow the cake to cool until the next day.

Drain the cherries retaining the liquid. Retain 12 or 16 of the cherries for decoration. Place ½ cup of the retained liquid in a saucepan and bring to a boil. Combine the cornstarch with a little more of the cherry juice and pour into the boiling juice while stirring constantly. Allow to boil for 1 minute, then add the cherries and remove the pan from the heat.

Cut the cake into three layers. Sprinkle about 2 tablespoons of Kirsch schnapps on the bottom layer. As soon as the cherries have cooled off and the glaze begins to thicken, spread them out on the bottom.

Combine whipping cream and vanilla. Whip until stiff and sprinkle in the powdered sugar while still beating. Spread some of the whipped cream onto the cherry layer, lay the second layer of cake on it. Also sprinkle this layer with 2 tablespoons of Kirsch schnapps, then spread cream over it thickly, and lay the final cake layer on top of the cream. Press gently and sprinkle with the remaining Kirsch schnapps. Remove some of the remaining whipped cream and put it in a pastry bag with a star spout. Spread the remaining cream over the surface and sides of the cake and carefully smooth out the surfaces. Sprinkle everything with chocolate.

Score the surface for 12 or 16 pieces. On each of these, place a large cream star topped off with a cherry.

Punch Torte

⅔ cup butter
9 eggs
1⅓ cups sugar
Pinch of salt
Juice and grated rind of ½
    lemon

1¾ cups sifted cake flour
2 tablespoons cornstarch
Butter for greasing
Flour for dusting

For the filling and decoration:
1 orange
Juice of ½ lemon
⅓ cup sugar
3 tablespoons water
6 tablespoons white wine or
    Madeira
5 tablespoons arrack or rum
⅔ cup marzipan
4½ cups powdered sugar

1 cup orange marmalade or
    apricot jam
1 egg white
1½ ounces bittersweet
    chocolate
12 candied violets or other
    sugared flowers
½ cup slivered almonds

Melt butter over low heat and allow to cool until lukewarm.

Whisk the eggs in a bowl and place over a hot, not boiling, water bath. While beating constantly, sprinkle in sugar, salt, lemon juice and rind. Beat until very creamy and light. Remove the bowl from the water bath and beat until the sponge-cake batter is cold.

Combine flour and cornstarch, fold in to the batter gently while simultaneously pouring in a thin stream of melted butter. Line the bottom of a 10-inch springform pan, grease with butter and dust with flour. Pour in the batter and bake immediately on the lower rack of an oven preheated to 350° for about 60 minutes. Then turn out onto a rack and, if possible, allow to cool until the next day.

Wash the orange under hot water, dry, and thinly peel half of it with a potato peeler. In a saucepan, combine the orange rind and the juice of the entire orange together with lemon juice, sugar, water, wine and arrack or rum. Boil until sugar is completely dissolved and the liquid is clear. Remove the orange rind and allow the punch to cool.

Knead together marzipan and ½ cup powdered sugar, roll out and cut out two torte-sized rounds. Cut the torte into 3 layers and sprinkle each layer with punch. Lay a marzipan round on the first layer, brush it with marmalade that has been stirred until smooth. Lay the second layer on top and brush it with marmalade, cover with marzipan, and lay the third layer on top of it. Press gently.

Combine the egg white and remaining powder sugar, beat into a very thick glaze and spread over the upper surface. Melt the bittersweet chocolate, place in a parchment-paper bag (see page 318) and, starting at the middle, draw a spiral on the hardening white glaze from the middle to the outside edge. With a knife, draw 12 straight lines from the center to the circumference of the cake making the design shown in the picture. Decorate each piece with a flower. Press the slivered almonds on the sides.

Spanish Vanilla Torte

7 tablespoons butter
1⅓ cups marzipan
5 egg yolks
1 egg
¾ cup sugar
2 vanilla beans
5 egg whites
Pinch of salt
1¼ cups sifted cake flour
⅔ cup cornstarch
1½ ounces coarsely grated or
  chopped bittersweet
  chocolate

⅓ cup chopped almonds
¼ cup finely diced candied
  lemon rind
Butter for greasing
Ground almonds for sprinkling
2 cups apricot jam
6 ounces milk chocolate
4 tablespoons whipping cream
2 tablespoons chopped
  pistachios

Melt butter over low heat, then allow to cool until lukewarm without letting it harden again. Crumble marzipan and beat together with egg yolks, the egg and sugar until very light. Slit the vanilla beans lengthwise, remove the marrow and add to the egg-yolk cream. Continue beating until the sugar is dissolved and a very thick and foamy batter is obtained.

Whip egg whites and salt until peaks form and slide into the egg-yolk cream. Combine flour and cornstarch, fold into the egg-yolk cream gently. Then, finally, fold in the melted butter, chocolate, almonds and candied lemon rind.

Use a conical form (or substitute a daisy or rosette form), grease it and sprinkle with almonds. Smooth the batter into it and bake for 45 minutes on the lower rack of an oven preheated to 350°. Turn out onto a rack to cool.

Stir apricot jam until smooth, if necessary it can be heated. Spread over the torte and allow to dry.

Heat about 5 ounces of the chocolate for the glaze over hot, but not boiling, water. Allow to cool slightly before spreading over the surface and sides of the torte. Allow to harden.

Chop the remaining chocolate. Place the whipping cream in a saucepan and bring to a boil. While stirring constantly, melt the chocolate in it and then allow to cool completely. Whip the chocolate-cream mixture and fill into a pastry bag with a star spout. Dot the edge of the surface with cream stars and sprinkle these with pistachios. Refrigerate until ready to serve.

> **Tip:** *This Spanish Vanilla Torte freezes very well. In order to freeze, allow to cool completely, then wrap in aluminum foil or a freezing bag and place in the freezer. Before serving, the torte should be allowed to slowly thaw at room temperature, since its flavor does not develop fully when it is cold. Then, after it has thawed, it can be covered with apricot jam and chocolate, and decorated with the chocolate-cream. It is advisable to wait with glazing, because chocolate glazes often get water spots and crumble when they have been frozen and allowed to thaw.*

Imitation Almond Torte

1 pound dried navy beans
Cold water for soaking
1 vanilla bean
½ cup raisins
Flour for dusting
5 egg yolks
1 teaspoon vanilla
3 tablespoons almond or
   vanilla liqueur
1⅓ cups sugar

1 tablespoon baking powder
5 egg whites
Pinch of salt
⅓ cup chopped almonds
Butter or margarine for
   greasing
Bread crumbs for sprinkling
1 egg yolk
1-2 tablespoons whipping
   cream

Sort the beans if necessary. Place them in a large bowl and cover with water. Allow to soak over night. The next day put them in a saucepan together with the water they were soaked in. Slit open the vanilla bean, place the marrow and the pod in the saucepan and simmer for 45 minutes until soft. Or, cook the beans, water and vanilla in a pressure cooker for about 15 minutes (consult the manufacturer's instructions), until tender. Remove the vanilla bean and drain the beans in a sieve. Allow them to stand a moment before pressing the beans through the sieve.

Wash the raisins in hot water, then rub dry in a cloth. Dust them with some flour. Whisk together egg yolks, vanilla and liqueur. Then, while beating constantly with an electric mixer, gradually add the sugar. Beat until the sugar is dissolved and the batter is foamy and quite thick.

Fold in the pureed beans and the baking powder. Combine egg whites and salt and beat until firm. Gently fold into the dough. Finally, add the raisins and almonds.

Carefully grease a 10-inch springform pan and sprinkle with bread crumbs. Pour in the batter, smooth out the surface and bake immediately on the middle rack of an oven preheated to 400° for 90 minutes.

Whisk together the egg yolk and whipping cream. Starting about 15 minutes before the cake is finished, brush the surface with this mixture several times so that it will become golden brown.

After removing from the oven, let the torte settle in the pan for about 3 minutes, then slide it onto a rack and allow to cool completely.

Note

In this recipe it is necessary to dry the raisins extremely well and dust them with flour, otherwise they will all drop to the bottom of the torte during the baking process. This way they remain well distributed.

> **Tip:** *For a stronger almond flavor, add almond extract to the dough.*

Chocolate Sponge Cookies with Hazelnut Butter

3 egg yolks
1 tablespoon cold water
¾ cup plus 1 tablespoon
  sugar
1 teaspoon vanilla
3 egg whites
Pinch of salt
⅔ cup flour

¼ cup cornstarch
¼ cup cocoa
¼ teaspoon instant coffee
Butter for greasing
Flour for dusting
1 cup hazelnut butter
Powdered sugar for dusting

Combine egg yolks and water and whisk together. With an electric mixer set at the highest speed, beat until very foamy. Gradually add half the sugar and the vanilla. Continue beating until the sugar is dissolved and the batter is thick and creamy. In a second bowl, combine egg whites and salt. Beat until stiff peaks form, then add the remaining sugar. Slide the egg whites into the egg-yolk cream.

Combine flour, cornstarch, cocoa and coffee. Gently fold into the eggs.

Put the dough through a cookie press onto a prepared cookie sheet lined with parchment paper which has been greased and dusted with flour. Bake for 18-20 minutes at 350°. Allow to cool on a rack.

Stir the hazelnut butter until it is spreadable. Thickly brush it onto the smooth underside of half the cookies. Place the underside of a second cookie against the filling and press gently. Refrigerate for about 10 minutes (or place in the freezer for 5 minutes), so that the hazelnut butter can stiffen, then dust the surface lightly with powdered sugar.

Anise Sponge Cookies

1 tablespoon anise seeds
2 eggs
1 tablespoon cold water
1 teaspoon lemon juice
¾ cup sugar
1½ cups plus 3 tablespoons
  flour

Butter for greasing
Flour for dusting
Sugar and anise seeds for
  sprinkling

Coarsely grind anise seeds with a mortar.

Place the eggs in a metal bowl. Whisk together with the water and lemon juice, then place the bowl in a hot, but not boiling, water bath. With an electric mixer set at the highest speed, beat this mixture until it is thick, foamy and whitish in color. While beating, add sugar gradually. During this process the water bath must not become too hot, otherwise the egg will begin to coddle. Remove the bowl from the water and continue to beat until the batter is lukewarm. Combine the flour and the ground anise and fold gently and thoroughly into the batter.

Line a baking sheet with parchment paper, grease and dust with flour.

Place the cookie dough into a cookie press with a smooth spout having a diameter of ¾ inch and place walnut-sized dots of dough on the baking sheet 2-3 inches apart. Sprinkle sparingly with anise seeds and a bit more generously with sugar, then hold the baking sheet at an angle so that the excess rolls off.

Allow the cookies to dry at room temperature for about 1 hour, during which time they may melt a bit but they will also get a slight crust on the surface. Then bake in an oven preheated to 350° for 15 minutes.

Remove from the baking sheet and paper immediately and allow to cool on a rack.

Variation

Allspice Sponge Cookies with Poppy Seed: Prepare the dough according to the above recipe replacing the anise with ½ teaspoon ground allspice. Put the dough through a cookie press onto the cookie sheet and then sprinkle a mixture of poppy seed and sugar instead of anise seed and sugar. Bake as above and allow to cool on a rack.

Sponge Cookies

3 egg yolks
1 tablespoon cold water
¾ cup plus 1 tablespoon
  sugar
1 teaspoon vanilla
3 egg whites

Pinch of salt
1 cup flour
¼ cup cornstarch
Butter for greasing
Flour for dusting
Powdered sugar for sifting

Combine egg yolks and water in a bowl and whisk together. With an electric mixer set at the highest speed, beat until very foamy and gradually add half the sugar as well as the vanilla. Continue beating until the sugar is dissolved and the batter is foamy white and quite thick and creamy.

In a second bowl, combine egg whites and a pinch of salt. Beat until peaks form before sprinkling in the remaining sugar.

Slide the egg whites into the egg-yolk cream. Add flour combined with the cornstarch. Very gently but thoroughly, fold together and put the dough into a cookie press with a spout about ½ inch in diameter.

Line a cookie sheet with parchment paper, grease it, and dust lightly with flour. At a distance of 2-3 inches, press out a 3-inch long cookie that is a bit thicker at each end. Make the thick ends by waiting a moment at the start before pressing out the length of the cookie, and at the end by lifting off with a slight turn of the hand. Dust the cookies lightly with sugar and allow to dry for about 2 minutes. Then hold the cookie sheet at an angle to allow the excess to roll off. Dip a brush in cold water, shake off excess water, then spray the still remaining, tiny water drops onto the sugared cookies. In this way, some of the sugar will stick during the baking process and, because of this procedure, will form very delicate blisters.

Bake the sponge cookies for 18-20 minutes in an oven preheated to 350°. Immediately remove from the paper and place one next to the other (never one on top of the other) on a rack and allow to cool.

Variations

Sponge Cookies dipped in Chocolate: Melt 3 ounces of milk chocolate over a double boiler. Then dip both ends of the sponge cookies into the chocolate and allow to dry.

Filled Sponge Cookies: Again melt 3 ounces of milk chocolate and chop about ⅓ cup of pistachios. Thickly brush the smooth underside of all the cookies with the chocolate and generously sprinkle with chopped pistachios. When the chocolate begins to harden, press two cookies together.

Sprinkled Sponge Cookies: Make the sponge cookies as above and place on a prepared cookie sheet. Instead of dusting with sugar, sprinkle with colored sugar sprinkles (mixed decor) and bake as above.

Sponge Omelettes with Berries

3 egg yolks	½ cup flour
2 tablespoons water	2 teaspoons cornstarch
⅓ cup sugar	Butter for greasing
1 egg white	Flour for dusting
Pinch of salt	

For the filling and trimming:

½ package frozen blueberries (about 5 ounces)	1-2 teaspoons vanilla
1 cup whipping cream	2 teaspoons sugar
3-4 tablespoons Crème de Cassis (black currant liquer)	Powdered sugar for dusting

Combine egg yolks and water in a bowl and beat until foamy. Continue beating while sprinkling in ½ of the sugar.

In a separate bowl whip egg white and salt until firm peaks are formed, then continue whipping while sprinkling in the remaining sugar. Slide the egg white into the egg-yolk cream. Combine flour and cornstarch, then gently fold into the eggs.

Line a cookie sheet with parchment paper. Draw circles about 6 inches in diameter on it, butter these and dust with flour.

Divide the sponge batter equally among these circles and spread it out evenly with a spoon or a pastry bag with a smooth spout. Bake in an oven preheated to 425° for 8-10 minutes until golden.

Immediately remove the cakes from the paper, fold them in half and place on a rack. This procedure must be carried out very quickly, because the dough breaks as soon as it hardens.

Allow the folded cakes to cool while the blueberries are thawing.

In the meantime, prepare the filling. Whip cream until stiff. Gradually pour in the Crème de Cassis and the vanilla. Continue whipping while sprinkling in sugar. Place this mixture into a pastry bag with a large star spout.

Carefully unfold the omelettes and squirt in the cream in large spirals. Drain the berries, distribute among the cakes and then close the omelettes again. Dust with powdered sugar and serve immediately.

Variations

Sponge Omelettes with Orange-Chocolate: Prepare the filling before baking the omelettes as described above. Crumble 3 ounces of fine bittersweet chocolate, then combine with 1½ cups whipping cream and melt over low heat while stirring constantly. Refrigerate for at least 2 hours. Bake the omelettes as above, fold together and allow to cool.

Carefully peel two oranges, being sure to remove the white skin completely. Now with a very sharp knife remove the individual sections from their skins, remove seeds and set aside the sections. Remove the chocolate cream from the refrigerator and whip until stiff. Flavor with 1-2 tablespoons of orange liqueur and fill into a pastry bag with a large star spout.

Squirt into the opened omelettes in large spirals and place orange sections (which can be halved, if desired), on the cream. Fold the cakes together again. Cut a piece of waxed paper into ½-inch strips and place these diagonally across the omelettes so that some of the cake is still visible. Dust the omelettes with cocoa and remove some of the paper strips. Now dust with powdered sugar; in doing this try to avoid dusting the cocoa surfaces too heavily. Finally, remove the paper strips and serve the cakes immediately.

Sponge Omelettes with Kiwi Ice Cream: Bake the omelettes as above, fold together and allow to cool. Thaw a pint of vanilla ice cream slightly. Peel 2 kiwis and cut into small pieces. Place in a blender, flavor with 1-2 teaspoons of white rum and whip to a smooth consistency. Place in a pastry bag with a large star spout. Either place the bag in the freezer for a while or fill the carefully opened omelettes immediately. Peel another kiwi, slice, quarter and decorate the ice cream with these. Dust the surfaces of the omelettes with powdered sugar. Serve immediately before the cakes become soggy and the ice cream melts.

Nut-Sponge Squares

6 egg yolks
1 cup sugar
⅛ teaspoon cinnamon
6 egg whites
Pinch of salt

1 teaspoon lemon juice
2 cups ground hazelnuts
3 ounces grated bittersweet
    chocolate
Butter for greasing

For the filling and trimming:

36 hazelnuts
7½ ounces bittersweet
    chocolate

1 tablespoon coconut butter
2 cups whipping cream
2 teaspoons vanilla

For the dough, combine egg yolks, ⅔ of the sugar and cinnamon. Beat until creamy. Combine egg whites, salt and remaining sugar and beat until stiff, then mix in the lemon juice. Slide into the egg-yolk cream, add the hazelnuts and grated chocolate. Then very gently fold all ingredients together.

Line a baking sheet with parchment paper; if the sheet has no edges, be sure to fold the paper so that the dough cannot drip over the edge during baking. Grease the paper and spread the dough onto it. Bake on the middle rack of an oven preheated to 400° for about 25 minutes. Turn out on a rack, remove the paper and allow to cool.

Then cut off the edges so that they are straight and cut the dough into 24 squares.

While the sponge cake is cooling, bake the hazelnuts on a dry baking sheet for about 10 minutes at 400°. Drop them into a towel and rub off the skins. Then allow the nuts to cool.

Crumble the chocolate and melt in a hot water bath together with the coconut butter. Dip the nuts into the chocolate and allow to cool until the glaze hardens. Pour the remaining chocolate onto half of the cake squares, smooth out and allow to drip over the edges.

Combine whipping cream and vanilla, whip until stiff, place in a pastry bag with a star spout and squirt about ¾ of it onto the unglazed squares as a filling. Lay the glazed squares on top. With the remaining cream, place 3 small stars diagonally across each square and top these with a chocolate-coated hazelnut. Serve the squares as soon as possible.

Pineapple Wine-Cream Tartlets

4 egg whites
Pinch of salt
¾ cup plus 2 tablespoons
    sugar
Juice and grated rind of ½
    lemon

4 egg yolks
1½ cups sifted cake flour
½ cup cornstarch
Butter or margarine for
    greasing
Sugar for sprinkling

For the filling and trimming:

1½ ¼-ounce packages gelatin
½ cup pineapple juice (from
    the can)
2 eggs
5 tablespoons sugar
1 cup dry white wine
1-2 tablespoons white rum

½ cup whipping cream
1 teaspoon vanilla
1 16-ounce can pineapple
1 ¼-ounce package gelatin
16 cocktail cherries
Chopped pistachios for
    sprinkling

For the dough, combine egg whites and salt. Beat until stiff. Gradually add sugar, followed by lemon juice and rind. Beat in whisked egg yolks. Combine cornstarch and flour and add to the egg mixture. Gently fold all ingredients together.

Line a baking sheet with parchment paper and grease with butter or margarine. If necessary, make higher edges with the paper. Spread the dough out onto the cookie sheet and bake in an oven preheated to 400° for about 15 minutes.

Sprinkle a towel with sugar and turn the cake out onto it. Moisten the paper and remove immediately. Allow the cake to cool. As soon as it no longer emits steam, but while it is still soft, cut as many pineapple-ring-sized rounds (about 3 inches in diameter), out of the cake as possible. In doing this, care should be taken to waste as little cake as possible. Collect all the leftover cake, crumble it and bake again at 400° for 10-15 minutes, cool, place in a plastic bag and crush with a rolling pin into fine crumbs.

For the cream, prepare gelatin according to package directions using some of the pineapple juice as the liquid. Combine eggs, sugar, ½ cup of pineapple juice and white wine in a bowl. Place in a hot, not boiling, water bath and beat until a thick, white cream is obtained. Remove from the heat. Add gelatin and continue beating until well mixed. Add rum. Then refrigerate the cream until gelled. As soon as it begins to "streak" (see page 326), whip cream with vanilla until stiff, then gently fold it into the wine cream.

Spread the cream onto the round cakes and allow to stiffen slightly. Then immediately place a well-drained and blotted pineapple ring on top. Prepare gelatin according to package directions using either the remaining pineapple juice from the can, water or white wine. After allowing to cool slightly, coat the pineapple rings with the gelatin. Also brush the sides of the cakes with gelatin and then coat the sides with the cake crumbs.

Place a well-drained cocktail cherry in the middle of each pineapple slice and surround it with a delicate wreath of pistachios. Refrigerate the tartlets until ready to serve.

Prince Pueckler's Checkered Cake

For the light-colored dough:

⅓ cup butter	4 egg whites
4 egg yolks	Pinch of salt
3 tablespoons water	1¾ cups sifted cake flour
⅔ cup sugar	Butter for greasing

For the dark-colored dough:

1½ ounces bittersweet chocolate	4 egg whites
2 teaspoons butter	Pinch of salt
4 egg yolks	1¾ cups sifted cake flour
3 tablespoons water	2½ tablespoons cocoa
⅔ cup sugar	¼ teaspoon baking powder
	Butter for greasing

For the filling and trimming:

2 cups butter	Red food coloring
3¾ cups powdered sugar	1½ ounces bittersweet chocolate
Pinch of salt	
2 egg yolks	½ cup sliced almonds
2 tablespoons raspberry schnapps	8 fresh strawberries (all the same size)
2 tablespoons strawberry jam	

For the light-colored cake, melt the butter and allow to cool until lukewarm.

Cream egg yolks together with water and about ⅔ of the sugar. Whip egg whites, salt and remaining sugar until stiff. Add the flour to the egg-yolk cream and fold in together with the egg whites. Finally, carefully stir in butter. Line a 10-inch springform pan with parchment paper, grease the bottom, and bake the cake on the middle rack of an oven preheated to 400° for 25 minutes.

For the dark cake, melt butter together with chocolate and allow to cool. Prepare egg yolks and egg whites as above. Combine flour with cocoa and baking powder. The chocolate-butter mixture should also be gently folded in. Bake as above and turn both cakes out onto racks and allow to cool (if possible over night).

Cut each cake into two layers. With the aid of large stencils cut out four rings, each one smaller than the previous one.

Cream butter, powdered sugar and salt until sugar is completely dissolved. Add egg yolks and raspberry schnapps. Stir jam until smooth and press through a sieve. Take half of the butter-cream and color it with the jam and 1-2 drops of red food coloring.

Place 2 light and 2 dark cake rings into each other, alternating the colors. Coat the top with the jam-butter cream and place the next layer of rings on the previous layer alternating colors vertically and horizontally. Continue until all rings and jam-butter cream are used. Spread about ⅔ of the retained butter cream smoothly over the surface and edges of the torte.

Melt the chocolate, cool it slightly, then stir into the remaining cream and refrigerate again.

Cover the edges and surface of the cake with sliced almonds, score 16 pieces with a knife. On each place a chocolate-cream star. Halve the washed and dried strawberries lengthwise and place ½ on each chocolate star. Refrigerate the cake until ready to serve.

Coil Cake

For the bottom cake layer:
1¼ cups sifted cake flour
⅓ cup ground almonds

3 tablespoons sugar
⅓ cup butter

For the sponge cake:
5 egg yolks
5 tablespoons water
1 teaspoon vanilla
⅔ cup sugar
5 egg whites
Pinch of salt

¾ cup sifted cake flour
¼ cup cornstarch
4 tablespoons cocoa
Butter for greasing
Sugar for sprinkling

For the filling and trimming:
3 cups whipping cream
2 teaspoons vanilla
1 tablespoon sugar

1 small jar of cranberry or
   whortleberry jam
3 tablespoons canned
   cranberries

For the bottom layer, quickly knead all ingredients together and refrigerate covered for 30 minutes.

Line a 10-inch springform pan with parchment or waxed paper, roll out the dough and line the bottom of the form with it without making a raised edge. Pierce the bottom repeatedly with a fork, then bake on the middle rack of an oven preheated to 400° for 15-20 minutes. Allow to cool on a rack.

For the sponge cake, cream egg yolks together with water and vanilla until light and foamy, then gradually sprinkle in ⅔ of the sugar and whip together until batter is very light and the sugar

completely dissolved. Beat the egg whites with salt and the remaining sugar until stiff, then slide egg-white mixture into the egg-yolk mixture. Combine flour, cornstarch and cocoa and gently fold into the egg-mixture. Gently fold all ingredients together. Line a baking sheet with parchment paper, grease it with butter and spread with batter. Bake on the middle rack at the same temperature for 10-15 minutes.

Immediately turn out the cake onto a towel that has been sprinkled with sugar. Moisten the paper and peel off. Roll the dough in the towel and allow to cool.

Whip the cream, vanilla and sugar until stiff. Mix about ⅔ of it with the cranberry jam (see note below).

Unroll the sponge-cake roll, spread with the cream and cut lengthwise in 2-inch wide strips. Roll up one strip again and place it vertically in the middle of the bottom cookie-crust layer. Carefully coil the remaining strips of cake around it. Spread a portion of the cream around the outside edge. Place the remainder in a pastry bag and generously cover the top of the cake with tiny dots of cream. Carefully blot the cranberries or whortleberries dry, sprinkle over the cake and serve as soon as possible.

Note

To avoid having the whipped cream lose its consistency when adding the jam, it is advisable to first stir the jam until smooth and then fold it in by the spoonful.

Fritters and Beignets

Eberswald Beignets

1 cup water	5-6 eggs
1 tablespoon sugar	Oil for brushing
Pinch of salt	Vegetable oil or shortening for
1 teaspoon vanilla	deep frying
1/3 cup butter or margarine	2 cups powdered sugar
2½ cups flour	3-4 tablespoons rum

Tip: *To test the temperature of the oil without a thermometer, stick the handle of a wooden spoon (not plastic!) spoon into the hot oil. As soon as small bubbles appear on it, begin frying. Or drop in a piece of dry bread. If it browns quickly, then the oil is the correct temperature.*

For the batter, place the water, sugar, salt and vanilla in a saucepan. Add the butter or margarine in flakes. Melt the butter and bring liquid to a boil. Just as it begins to boil, remove the pan from the heat and add the flour in one fell swoop. Then stir very quickly with a wooden spoon until a thick dough is obtained. Place the pan on the stove again. While stirring constantly and vigorously, heat the dough until a completely smooth clump of dough and a delicate white skin begins to show on the bottom of the pan. Now place the dough in a bowl and immediately stir in 1 egg. At this stage, it is important to work very quickly, otherwise the egg white may coagulate leaving small white spots in the dough.

Allow the dough to rest and cool off until it is lukewarm. Then blend in the eggs one at a time. The next egg should be added when the previous one is fully incorporated into the dough. As soon as the fifth egg has been worked in, examine the consistency of the dough: With the wooden spoon, lift up a spoonful of dough to see whether it hangs down from the spoon in long, gleaming ribbons. If it already has this consistency you can omit the entire sixth egg or half of it. If you need to add half an egg, the egg yolk and white should be whisked together and then the amount needed added by the spoonful. As soon as a sufficient amount of egg is added, stop stirring the dough, otherwise it will lose its airiness and not rise as well. Now place the dough into a pastry bag with a large star spout. Cut 5-inch squares out of parchment paper and brush with oil.

With a pastry bag, press out circles that have an inside diameter of 1½ inch.

In the meantime, heat the oil to 350°. Drop in 2-4 beignets at a time. To drop them in, pick up the parchment paper by the ends and slide the beignet into the hot oil. As soon as the bottom is golden brown, turn it over with a slotted spoon and fry the other side. When removing allow excess oil to drip off before placing on a thick layer of paper towel. Continue until all the beignets are fried. Be sure never to have too many pieces in the oil at once since they will expand.

Finally, sift the powdered sugar, add rum and stir to a thick glaze. Glaze the beignets.

Variations

Instead of vanilla, add the rind of ½ lemon to the dough. To do this, also add lemon juice to the glaze.

To make *Viennese-Style Beignets* use milk instead of water and dust the finished product with powdered sugar.

Raisin and Almond Fritters

1 cup water	3-4 tablespoons rum, port or
Pinch of salt	cognac
1/3 cup butter or margarine	½ cup chopped almonds
1⅔ cups flour	Oil or shortening for frying
4-5 eggs	Powdered sugar for dusting
¾ cup raisins	

Prepare a fritter dough as in the previous recipe out of water, salt, butter and flour. Place the dough in a bowl and immediately stir in the first egg. Allow the dough to rest and cool as usual. In the meantime, wash the raisins in hot water, rub dry in a towel, combine with rum, port or cognac and soak while the remaining eggs are being incorporated into the dough.

Then stir in the raisins with any remaining alcohol and the chopped almonds. Heat the oil to 350°.

Using a spoon that has been dipped into the hot oil, cut out the fritters and fry in the hot oil turning them only once. Remove with a slotted spoon and drain on a paper towel. Shortly before they have cooled completely, dust them generously with powdered sugar or turn them in sugar. After they have cooled, serve immediately.

Variations

Instead of dusting with powdered sugar, use vanilla sugar (sugar that has been stored with a vanilla bean), or cinnamon sugar. For "fruitier" fritters, mix in thinly sliced apples. Or, substitute the raisins with finely diced pitted prunes soaked in plum brandy.

Flake Torte with Exotic Fruits and Cream

½ cup water	2-3 eggs (depending on size)
Pinch of salt	Butter or margarine for
3 tablespoons butter	greasing
1¼ cups sifted cake flour	Flour for dusting

For the filling and trimming:

1 cup whipping cream	1 small cantalope
1 teaspoon vanilla	2 kiwis
1 can guavas (smallest size	1 orange
available)	Powdered sugar for dusting
2 slices pineapple (fresh or	
canned)	

Combine water, salt and butter in a saucepan and bring to a boil. Remove from heat and add the flour in one fell swoop. Return to the stove and heat, while stirring constantly, until the dough becomes one large clump and a delicate white skin begins to develop on the bottom of the pan. Remove the pan from the heat, put the dough in a bowl and immediately blend in 1 egg. Allow to cool until lukewarm and then incorporate the remaining eggs one after the other. Stir, until the dough hangs from a spoon in a long, thick, gleaming ribbon. Then stop stirring.

Grease a 10-inch spring-form pan and dust with flour. Spread out ⅓ of the dough and bake on the middle rack of an oven preheated to 425° for about 20 minutes. Cool on a rack and then bake two more cake layers. Allow to cool in the same way.

Whip the cream until stiff, add vanilla and place a portion of the cream in a pastry bag with a star spout.

Drain the canned fruits well. Cut the guavas into thin slices and the pineapple into small pieces. Halve the melon and remove the seeds. With a melon baller cut out small balls. Peel the kiwis and slice. Peel the orange, separate into sections and remove seeds.

Cover one of the cake layers with ¼ of the cream, distribute ½ of the fruit onto it, except for the orange sections and some of the melon balls. Cover again with cream, lay the second layer on top of this, repeat the process with cream, fruit and cream. Top with the third layer and sift powdered sugar over it. Place generous dots of whipping cream on the outer edge and decorate these with a melon ball and an orange section. Serve the torte as soon as possible since the bottom gets soggy if it is allowed to stand too long.

Note

Instead of topping the cake with the third layer, crumble it over the top layer of cream. When this is done, the torte is easier to cut; nevertheless, it is still best to cut it with an electric knife or a knife with a very sharp, serrated edge so that the filling will not be squeezed out the sides.

Filled Puff Ring with Almonds

1 cup water	3-4 eggs (depending on size)
⅓ cup butter	Butter or margarine for
Pinch of salt	greasing
1¾ cups sifted cake flour	Flour for dusting
1 teaspoon baking powder	

For the filling and trimming:

1 10-ounce package frozen raspberries	1 cup whipping cream
	2 teaspoons vanilla
3-4 tablespoons rum or cognac	½ cup sliced almonds
	1½ cups powdered sugar

In a saucepan combine water, butter and salt and bring to a boil. Remove from heat and add flour combined with baking powder in one fell swoop. Return to the stove and heat while stirring constantly until the dough forms a large clump and a delicate, white skin becomes visible on the bottom of the pan. Place the dough in a bowl and blend in the first egg. Allow to cool until lukewarm. Add the remaining eggs one after the other. The dough has the correct consistency when it hangs from a spoon in long, thick, gleaming ribbons. Grease a baking sheet and dust with flour. Press the dough through a pastry bag with a large, smooth spout to make a thick ring with a diameter of about 10 inches. Bake until golden brown on the middle rack of an oven preheated to 425° for 30-40 minutes. Remove from the oven and immediately cut the ring through horizontally with a pair of scissors. Allow both halves to cool.

In the meantime, pour rum or cognac over the raspberries and allow them to thaw in a covered bowl. Drain in a sieve and retain the liquid. Whip the cream until stiff, sweeten it with vanilla and gently fold in the drained raspberries. Fill the ring with this cream. In a dry pan, quickly brown the almonds, then allow to cool on a plate. Stir together the retained raspberry juice and powdered sugar into a thick glaze. Distribute over the surface of the ring and sprinkle with almonds.

Tip: *For a change, fill the puff ring with chocolate cream. While stirring constantly, melt 3 ounces of fine milk chocolate, 1½ ounces of bittersweet chocolate and 2 tablespoons of butter over low heat. Allow to cool slightly. Combine 3 egg yolks, ½ cup sugar and a few drops of hot water. Cream until thick and white. Stir into the chocolate and allow to cool. Whip 3 egg whites with salt until stiff. In a separate bowl, whip 1 cup of whipping cream until very stiff. Fold both into the chocolate mixture as soon as it begins to solidify again. Fill the puff ring with this cream, dust the surface with powdered sugar or cocoa.*

Orange and Ricotta Cheese Torte

1 cup water	4-5 eggs (depending on size)
Pinch of salt	Butter or margarine for
3 tablespoons butter	greasing
1¾ cups sifted cake flour	Flour for dusting

For the filling and trimming:

1½ ¼-ounce packages gelatin	1 teaspoon vanilla
1 cup ricotta or cottage	Orange liqueur for flavoring
cheese	1 cup whipping cream
½ cup freshly squeezed	Pinch of salt
orange juice	2 teaspoons vanilla
1 separated egg	1 orange
½ cup sugar (more or less, if	Dark chocolate for sprinkling
desired)	

In a saucepan, bring water, salt and butter to a boil. Remove pan from heat and add flour in one fell swoop. Return to stove and stir until a large clump of dough forms and the bottom of the pan begins to show a delicate, white skin. Immediately place the dough in a bowl and blend in 1 egg. Allow to cool until lukewarm. Then incorporate eggs one after the other, being sure to only add the next egg when the previous one has been blended in fully. Before adding the fifth egg, test the dough by lifting some of it out with a spoon. If it flows off the spoon lethargically in long, gleaming ribbons, omit the last egg. If this is not the case, either add the entire egg or part of it. When a sufficient amount of egg has been added, stop stirring immediately, otherwise the dough will lose its lightness and will not rise as much while baking. Grease a baking sheet and dust with flour. Draw a circle in the middle with the help of a spring-form pan having a diameter of 10-11 inches. Place the puff dough in a pastry bag with a large star spout. Following the circumference of the circle, press out cream puffs quite close to each other at regular intervals; they should touch each other when they rise in baking.

Bake on the middle rack of an oven preheated to 400°-425° for 25-30 minutes being sure not to open the oven during the first 15-20 minutes of baking. Remove and cut the cake through horizontally while still hot.

For the filling stir cheese, orange juice, egg yolk, sugar and vanilla until it is creamy and the sugar is dissolved. Flavor with orange liqueur and allow to cool slightly. Stir in a few spoonfuls of the orange cream, then mix in all of the gelatin mixture into the cheese mixture. Refrigerate and allow to gel.

Combine egg white and salt and whip until stiff. As soon as the cheese-cream begins to gel, fold in the egg white.

Spread onto the lower layer of the torte wreath and cover with the upper layer. Whip cream together with vanilla until stiff, place in a pastry bag with a star spout. Peel oranges, divide into sections and remove seeds. The section may be halved, if desired. Dot each cream puff with whipping cream and top with an orange section. Crumble dark chocolate on top.

Cream Puffs

1 cup water	4-5 eggs (depending on size)
Pinch of salt	Butter or margarine for
⅓ cup butter	greasing
1⅔ cups flour	Flour for dusting

For the filling and trimming:
2-3 cups whipping cream
2-3 teaspoons vanilla
Powdered sugar for dusting

In a saucepan, bring water, salt and butter to a boil. Remove from heat and add flour in one fell swoop. Return to heat and stir until dough forms a large clump and a delicate, white skin forms on the bottom of the pan. Immediately place the dough in a bowl, stir in 1 egg and allow to cool until lukewarm. Then incorporate the remaining eggs one after the other. Fill the dough into a pastry bag with a large star spout. Grease a baking sheet and thinly dust with flour. With the pastry bag, press out egg-sized dollops of dough onto the baking sheet leaving sufficient space between them to allow for expansion during baking. Bake on the middle rack of an oven preheated to 425° for 20-25 minutes. Remove from the baking sheet, immediately cut through horizontally with a pair of scissors and allow to cool completely on a rack. Then fill them.

For the filling, whip cream and vanilla until stiff. Fill into a pastry bag with a star spout and generously fill the bottom part of each cream puff. Cover with the lid and dust evenly with powdered sugar.

Puffed Swans

1 cup water	4-5 eggs (depending on size)
Pinch of salt	Butter or margarine for
⅓ cup butter	greasing
1⅔ cups flour	Flour for dusting

For the filling and trimming:
2-3 cups whipping cream
2-3 teaspoons vanilla
Powdered sugar for dusting

Prepare a puff pastry as in the recipe for cream puffs. Place about ¾ of this dough in a pastry bag with a large star spout. Grease a baking sheet and dust with flour. Leaving sufficient space between each puff, press elongated puffs that come to a point at one end onto the baking sheet. Then put the remaining puff pastry into a pastry bag with a smooth, thin spout and press necks and heads out onto the baking sheet. In order to do this, while again leaving sufficient space, "write" a slightly elongated question mark. The upper end (the beginning of the question mark), can be a little thicker than the lower end, thus making the head. Be sure that you end up with the same number of torsos as heads. It is best to bake the torsos and heads, with their necks, separately since they require different amounts of baking time.

The torsos need 20-25 minutes, while the necks, depending on their thickness, need 15-20 minutes. Both are baked on the middle rack of an oven preheated to 425°. After baking, remove from the baking sheet and allow to cool on a rack. Before placing on rack, cut the torsos once horizontally and the necks once vertically.

Shortly before serving, whip cream and vanilla until stiff. Place in a pastry bag with a star spout and generously fill the torsos of the swans. Press the wings into the cream at a slight angle, then insert the necks in the cream at the rounded end of the torso. Finally dust the birds with powdered sugar and serve as soon as possible.

Eclairs

1 cup water	4-5 eggs (depending on size)
Pinch of salt	Butter or margarine for
⅓ cup butter	greasing
1½ cups flour	Flour for dusting

For the filling and trimming:

1 ¼-ounce package gelatin	½ cup milk
4 egg yolks	1-2 tablespoons white rum
1 teaspoon vanilla	1¾ cups powdered sugar
½ cup sugar	2-3 tablespoons water
Pinch of salt	2 teaspoons instant coffee
1½ cups whipping cream	

Prepare a puff pastry out of the water, salt, butter and flour as described in the recipe for cream puffs above. Place in a pastry bag with a large star spout. Grease a baking sheet and dust with flour. Press out finger-length strips of dough leaving some distance between each one. Bake on the middle rack of an oven preheated to 425° for 20-25 minutes. Immediately remove from the baking sheet, cut through horizontally with scissors and allow to cool completely on a rack.

For the filling, cream egg yolks, vanilla, sugar, salt, ½ cup whipping cream and milk until slightly foamy. Place the bowl over a hot, but not boiling, water bath. Continue to beat until the sugar is dissolved and the cream is white and has become somewhat thicker. Press out the gelatin and add to the hot cream while continuing to beat the mixture. Then allow to cool and gel. Whip the remaining whipping cream until stiff, add the rum and fold into the egg-cream mixture as soon as it has begun to "streak." Refrigerate briefly again, then place into a pastry bag with a star spout and fill the bottom halves of the eclairs. Top with the upper halves.

Stir together powdered sugar, water and coffee to make a thick glaze. Frost the eclairs with it and allow to dry.

Hazelnut Tartlets made of Puff Pastry

For the filling:

1 package chocolate pudding mix	3 tablespoons sugar
1½ cups milk	1 vanilla bean
½ cup whipping cream	1 egg yolk
Pinch of salt	2-3 tablespoons cognac or brandy

For the pastry:

1 cup water	1 cup ground hazelnuts
Pinch of salt	Butter or margarine for
⅓ cup butter	greasing
⅔ cup less 1 tablespoon flour	Flour for dusting
⅓ cup cornstarch	1 egg yolk for brushing
4-5 eggs (depending on size)	Powdered sugar for dusting

For the filling, stir a small amount of milk into the chocolate pudding powder. Combine the remaining milk, whipping cream, salt, sugar and the marrow of the vanilla bean in a saucepan and bring to a boil. Stir in the pudding mixture according to package directions and allow to boil briefly. Remove pan from heat. Whisk together egg yolk, cognac or brandy and a small amount of the pudding. (This is actually a custard). While stirring vigorously, pour into the custard. Heat again, but do not allow to boil. Remove from heat; cool to a lukewarm but still liquid state.

Meanwhile, in a saucepan bring water, salt and butter to a boil. Sift together flour and cornstarch. In one fell swoop, add flour mixture to the boiling liquid which has just been removed from the heat. Return pan to heat and stir until a large clump of dough forms and a delicate white skin begins to appear on the bottom of the pan. Immediately place the dough in a bowl and stir in 1 egg. Allow to cool until lukewarm, then add the remaining eggs one after the other. After the third egg, alternate the eggs with the ground hazelnuts. Here, too, the dough must hang from a spoon in long, gleaming strands. Place the dough in a pastry bag with a large star spout. Grease a baking sheet and dust with flour. With the pastry bag, press out saucer-sized rings. Place chocolate custard in the middle of each. Brush the rings with the egg yolk and bake on the middle rack of an oven preheated to 425° for 20-25 minutes. Allow the tartlets to settle briefly, then, while still hot, remove from the baking sheet and place on a rack. Shortly before completely cooled, dust with powdered sugar.

Cream Puff Torte with Nut Cream

For the bottom crust:
1¼ cups sifted cake flour
2 tablespoons sugar
3 tablespoons butter

2 tablespoons ground hazelnuts
Butter or margarine for
   greasing

For the puff pastry:
1 cup water
⅓ cup butter
Pinch of salt
1¾ cups flour
4-5 eggs

Grated rind of 1 lemon
Butter or margarine for
   greasing
Flour for dusting

For the filling and trimming:
2 cups whipping cream
1 tablespoon sugar
1 teaspoon vanilla
⅛-¼ teaspoon ground
   cinnamon

1 cup ground hazelnuts
Powdered sugar for dusting

For the bottom crust, pour the flour onto a work surface. Add sugar, butter in flakes and ground nuts. Quickly knead all ingredients together into a smooth dough. Roll out into a greased 10-inch spring-form pan, pierce repeatedly with a fork and bake on the middle rack of an oven preheated to 400° for about 15 minutes. Allow to cool.

For the puff pastry, combine water, butter and salt in a saucepan and bring to a boil. Remove pan from heat and add flour in one fell swoop. Return to heat and stir until a clump forms and a delicate white skin begins to develop on the bottom of the pan. Place the dough in a bowl and immediately stir in the first egg. Cool until lukewarm, then add remaining eggs one after the other. Stir in grated lemon rind. Place half the dough into a pastry bag with a large, smooth spout and the other half in a pastry bag with a smaller, smooth spout. Grease a baking sheet and dust with flour. In the middle draw a circle having a diameter of 10-10½ inches. Through the thick spout, press a ring of dough out onto the baking sheet. Using the bag with the small spout, press 13 small balls onto the baking sheet. Bake on the middle rack of an oven preheated to 425°. Bake the small balls 15-20 minutes, and the ring 20-25 minutes. Allow to cool.

Whip cream, sugar, vanilla and cinnamon until stiff. Spread a thin layer onto the bottom crust and place the puff ring onto it. Place the remaining whipped cream into a pastry bag with a star spout, fill the inside of the ring with it and place 12 dots on the pastry ring itself. Place a tiny puff ball on each of the 12 dots of cream, and the 13th ball in the middle. Dust with powdered sugar.

Note

Decorate this torte even more intricately by cutting open the little puffs after baking and filling them with a flavored whipping cream or by topping the torte with a chocolate glaze.

Puff Cluster

½ cup water
Pinch of salt
2½ tablespoons butter
¼ cup cornstarch
½ cup flour

2-3 eggs (depending on size)
Butter or margarine for
  greasing
Flour for dusting

For the filling:
1 ¼-ounce package gelatin
2 egg yolks
⅓ cup sugar
½ cup freshly squeezed
  orange juice
Juice and grated rind of ½
  lemon

3-4 tablespoons orange
  liqueur or cognac
2 egg whites
Pinch of salt
½ cup whipping cream

For the glaze:
1⅓ cups sugar
½ cup water
Oil for brushing

In a saucepan, bring water, salt and butter to a boil. Combine flour and cornstarch. As soon as the liquid boils and the butter is melted, remove the pan from the heat and add the flour mixture in one fell swoop. Return the pan to the stove and stir until a clump of dough forms and a delicate white skin appears on the bottom of the pan. Immediately place the dough into a bowl, blend in one egg and allow to cool until lukewarm. Then incorporate the remaining eggs one after the other. Place the dough into a pastry bag with a small, smooth spout. Grease a baking sheet and dust with flour. Press out walnut-sized balls leaving sufficient space between them for expansion. Bake on the middle rack of an oven preheated to 400°-425° for 10-12 minutes until light brown. Remove the little puffs from the baking sheet, cut open and allow to cool on a rack.

For the filling, prepare the gelatin according to package instructions. Whip together egg yolks, sugar, orange juice and orange liqueur or cognac. Grate lemon and then squeeze out the juice. Add rind and juice to the liquid and beat until sugar is dissolved and the liquid is creamy white. Mix in gelatin. Refrigerate and allow to gel. Whip egg whites and salt until stiff. Whip cream separately until stiff. Fold both into the orange cream as soon as it begins to "streak." Place in a pastry bag with a very small spout and fill the puffs.

In a saucepan, melt about ½ of the sugar over low heat while stirring constantly. Add ¼ cup of water, place in a hot water bath to keep the caramel in liquid form. Glaze the cream puffs with it. On oiled aluminum foil, arrange the filled puffs into a cluster. As the caramel hardens, it will hold the puffs in place. Make more caramel out of the remaining sugar and water and glaze more puffs. Depending on their size, 3-5 clusters of puffs can be made.

Puff Pastry Ring with Orange Filling

1 cup water	Grated rind of ½ orange
1⅓ cups butter	Butter or margarine for
Pinch of salt	greasing
1¾ cups sifted cake flour	Flour for dusting
4-5 eggs (depending on size)	

For the filling and trimming:

1 package orange pudding	Juice of 1 orange
mix	1 cup whipping cream
1 cup water	3 oranges
½ cup sugar	Powdered sugar for dusting

Place water, butter and salt in a saucepan and bring to a boil. Remove the pan from the heat and add flour in one fell swoop. Return pan to heat and stir until a clump of dough forms and a delicate, white skin begins to form on the bottom of the pan. Immediately remove the pan from the stove, place the puff pastry in a bowl and blend in the first egg. Allow the dough to cool until lukewarm. Then add the remaining eggs, one after the other, and the grated orange rind. Test the dough: when lifted with a wooden spoon, the dough should hang down in long, gleaming ribbons. Immediately discontinue stirring, otherwise the dough will lose its airiness and the rings will not attain sufficient volume during baking. Grease a baking sheet and dust with flour. Place the dough in a pastry bag with a large star spout and press out into the shape of rings about the size of cream puffs. Be sure to leave sufficient space between each ring for expansion during baking. Bake on the middle rack of an oven preheated to 425° for 20-25 minutes. Do not open the oven during the first 10-15 minutes of baking, otherwise the rings will collapse. Remove from the baking sheet and immediately cut the rings through once horizontally. Then allow to cool on a rack.

For the filling, mix the pudding powder with some water. Combine the remaining water with sugar and orange juice and bring to a boil. Stir in the pudding powder and prepare according to package directions. Remove from heat and allow to cool in a cold water bath. Stir frequently so that no skin forms.

Whip cream until stiff. Peel oranges, divide into sections and remove seeds. Cut the sections once or twice and fold into the orange pudding together with the whipped cream. Generously fill the bottoms of the rings, cover with tops and dust thickly with powdered sugar. Serve immediately.

Profiteroles

½ cup water	2-3 eggs (depending on size)
3 tablespoons butter	Butter or margarine for
Pinch of salt	greasing
1 cup flour	Flour for dusting

For the filling and trimming:

1 ¼-ounce package gelatin	2 egg whites
2 egg yolks	Pinch of salt
3 tablespoons sugar	6 ounces bittersweet chocolate
1 cup milk	1 tablespoon butter
1 teaspoon vanilla	

Prepare the puff pastry as in the previous recipe. Place in a pastry bag with a large star spout. On a greased baking sheet that has been dusted with flour, press out walnut-sized balls of dough. Bake on the middle rack of an oven preheated to 400°-425° for 10-12 minutes. Remove the profiteroles from the baking sheet and immediately cut through horizontally. Place them next to each other on a rack and allow to cool.

In the meantime, prepare the gelatin according to package directions. Cream egg yolks with sugar until foamy and the sugar has dissolved completely. Combine milk and vanilla and bring to a boil. While beating continuously, add milk-mixture to the egg-sugar mixture, then stir in gelatin until dissolved. Refrigerate and allow to gel. Combine egg whites and salt and beat until stiff. As soon as the pudding begins to ''streak,'' fold in the egg whites. Refrigerate again briefly before filling the profiteroles.

Crumble the chocolate and melt with the butter over a hot, but not boiling, water bath. Stir until it becomes liquid, then allow to cool somewhat. Pour over the profiteroles and allow the chocolate glaze to harden.

Note

Filling profiteroles with fruit sherbets or ice cream is an excellent idea; these can then be topped off with vanilla-flavored whipping cream. Or, fill with whipping cream alone or any other flavored cream.

Snowballs with Pears and Almonds

1 cup milk	2 small pears
⅓ cup butter	⅓ cup sliced almonds
Pinch of salt	Oil or shortening for deep
2½ cups flour	frying
6-7 eggs (depending on size)	Powdered sugar for dusting
⅓ cup raisins	

Bring milk, butter and salt to a boil. Remove saucepan from heat and add flour in one fell swoop. Return to heat and stir until the dough forms a clump and the bottom of the pan begins to show a delicate, white skin. Place the dough in a bowl and blend in 1 egg. Allow to cool slightly. Then add the remaining eggs one after the other. Test the dough: It should hang from a wooden spoon in long, gleaming ribbons. Wash raisins in hot water and dry. Peel, core and dice pears. Stir raisins, pears and almonds into the puff pastry. Heat oil or shortening to 325°-250°. Dip a tablespoon into the hot oil and cut out small fritters with it. Fry them in the hot oil until golden brown. Drain on a paper towel. Immediately turn in powdered sugar and serve.

Yeast Doughs

Brioche Apostle Cakes

1 package dry yeast	Flour for dusting and forming
3 tablespoons lukewarm milk	¾ cup plus 2 tablespoons
2 cups wheat flour	softened butter
2½ cups flour	Butter for greasing
¼ cup sugar	1 egg yolk
1 teaspoon salt	2 tablespoons whipping cream
5 eggs	

Combine yeast with some lukewarm milk and allow to stand for about 10 minutes so that it can dissolve. Place flour in a bowl, thoroughly mix in sugar and salt and make a well in the middle. Whisk the eggs and pour them, together with the yeast-milk mixture, into the well. Starting in the middle and working to the outside, stir all ingredients together. Place this very soft and sticky dough onto a surface that has been dusted with flour and knead until it becomes elastic. It is advisable to knead the dough with one hand, while using a dough scraper in the other hand to constantly scrape the dough off the work surface. At the beginning the dough will stick a lot, but this tendency decreases the more the dough is kneaded. It may also help to repeatedly dust the work surface lightly with flour. As soon as the dough is smooth, gradually work in the butter in flakes. This process should be completed quickly so that the butter has no chance of becoming too warm or melting.

Form the dough into a ball. Place in a lightly-floured bowl, cover with aluminum foil and allow to rise for 3-4 hours. After the dough has expanded to 2 or 3 times its original size, knead it again. Then cover with aluminum foil and refrigerate, overnight if possible. Thoroughly grease about 20 brioche or tartlet forms with very high rims. Knead the dough with floured hands and divide into 20 equal pieces. From each piece, set aside ⅓. Form the larger pieces into balls, place in the forms and, using both thumbs, press a well into the middle of each ball. Form the smaller pieces of dough into balls as well and place into the wells. Cover with a towel and allow to rise for 15 minutes.

Whisk egg yolk with whipping cream and brush on the brioches. Bake immediately on the middle rack of an oven preheated to 425° for 12-15 minutes. Carefully turn the brioches out of their forms and allow to cool on a rack until they cease steaming. Serve as soon as possible.

Note

For breakfast or afternoon tea, serve brioches with butter, jam and honey. At other times "behead" the brioches and fill with fruit, puddings or ice cream.

Raisin Rolls made with Ricotta Cheese

3 cups flour
1 package dry yeast
⅓ cup sugar
3 tablespoons lukewarm milk
1 cup ricotta or cottage
  cheese
2 eggs
⅓ cup soften butter

Pinch of salt
Grated rind of ½ lemon
1 cup raisins
Flour for dusting and forming
Butter or margarine for
  greasing
1 egg yolk for brushing

Place flour in a bowl and make a well in the middle. Add yeast to the well and stir it together with some sugar, some milk and a little flour to make a starter. Cover with a towel and allow to rise for about 15 minutes until it bubbles. Add ricotta or cottage cheese, eggs, butter (in flakes), salt and grated lemon rind and mix thoroughly. Beat the dough until bubbles appear and no longer sticks to the sides of the bowl. Cover again with a towel and allow to rise in a warm place for 20-25 minutes. By then it should have doubled its volume. Meanwhile wash raisins in hot water and dry well with a towel. Knead the dough. Dust raisins with flour and knead into the dough. With lightly floured hands, divide dough into small rolls (about 2 inches in diameter) and place on a greased baking sheet leaving sufficient space between them for expansion during baking. Allow to rise once more, then brush the surfaces with the whisked egg yolk and bake on the middle rack of an oven preheated to 400° for 20-25 minutes. Allow to cool on a rack.

Note

Be sure to serve these rolls with lots of fresh butter. Jam and honey taste delicious with them, too. Or try this: Halve the rolls, butter both sides, sprinkle with grated chocolate and put together again.

> **Tip:** *There are numerous other possibilities for these very light rolls. Substitute sultanas or currants for the raisins. Or add ⅓ cup finely chopped or grated almonds or nuts (together with diced dried fruit). Of course, they can also be augmented with all sorts of flavors, like rum, arrack or almond extract, the marrow of vanilla bean or vanilla extract, or by adding cinnamon, nutmeg or orange rind. Add additional flour to the dough to make it more firm and form it into pretzels, crescents, braids or rings.*

Savarin with Raspberries

3¾ cups sifted cake flour	3 tablespoons sugar
1 package dry yeast	⅛ teaspoon salt
8 tablespoons lukewarm milk	Flour for dusting
½ cup butter	Butter for greasing
4 eggs	

For the glaze:

1 cup water	2 cups fresh raspberries (or
¾ cup sugar	10-ounces frozen
4-6 tablespoons raspberry	raspberries)
schnapps	Chopped pistachios for
1 cup apricot marmalade	sprinkling
1 cup whipping cream	

Place flour in a bowl, make a well in the middle and add the yeast. Pour milk into the well and, stirring constantly, dissolve the yeast. Dust this starter with some flour, cover with a towel and allow to rise for 15 minutes.

During this time, melt the butter and allow to cool until lukewarm. Combine with whisked eggs, sugar, salt and add to starter. Mix all ingredients thoroughly. Beat dough vigorously until it begins to show bubbles and no longer sticks to the side of the bowl. It should not, however, become too stiff.

Dust with flour again, cover with a towel and allow to rise for 15-20 minutes. Grease a 10-inch savarin (or ring-mold) form and dust with flour. Knead the dough again and fill into the form, which should then only be half full. Cover with a towel once more and allow the dough to rise until its height has doubled; the form should be almost full now. Depending on the temperature, this will make 10-15 minutes. Bake in an oven preheated to 400°-425° for 25-30 minutes. Shortly before the cake is finished, combine water and ⅔ cup sugar in a saucepan and boil until sugar is dissolved and the liquid is clear. Remove from heat and cool until lukewarm.

Remove the savarin from the oven, turn out onto a rack and allow to cool for 10-15 minutes.

Then place the cake, together with the rack, on top of a bowl. Flavor the sugar syrup well with raspberry schnapps and gradually pour or brush over the savarin until all the liquid has been soaked in. Any liquid that falls into the bowl should also be poured back onto the cake.

Combine apricot jam with a few drops of water and heat while stirring constantly. Press through a sieve. Glaze the savarin with this and allow to cool on a platter.

Whip cream until stiff and flavor with remaining sugar. Fill into a pastry bag with a star spout. Sort the raspberries, rinse under cold water, dry well and remove stems. (If using frozen berries, allow them to thaw.)

Press the cream into the savarin and simultaneously sprinkle in raspberries. Or gently fold raspberries into cream and spoon into the savarin. Decorate with a few berries and chopped pistachios.

Variations

Cardinal's Savarin: Bake as described above and flavor the refined sugar with Maraschino liqueur instead of raspberry schnapps. Soak the savarin with it and then allow to cool.

Meanwhile, thaw 2, 10-ounce packages of frozen strawberries, or clean and wash fresh strawberries. Place in a blender and puree with 1-2 teaspoons of lemon juice and about ¼ cup sugar. While stirring constantly, boil this liquid until thick. Place the soaked and cooled savarin on a platter, empty a small can of finely sliced peaches into the middle. Then pour the strawberry puree over the savarin and sprinkle with sliced almonds.

Babas au Rhum

1¾ cups sifted cake flour	Pinch of salt
1 teaspoon dry yeast	¼ cup raisins
4 tablespoons lukewarm milk	¼ cup currants
¼ cup butter	Flour for dusting
2 eggs	Butter for greasing
2 tablespoons sugar	

For the glaze:

1 cup water	1-2 teaspoons lemon juice
½ cup sugar	1-2 tablespoons apricot
3-5 tablespoons Jamaican rum	brandy
1 cup apricot jam	

Prepare yeast dough as previously described and allow to rise a second time. Meanwhile, wash raisins and currants in hot water, rub dry in a towel and dust with flour. Punch down the dough and work in the fruit.

Grease 12 small 10-inch savarin (ring-mold) forms and dust with flour. Fill in dough so that forms are half full. Cover with a cloth and allow to double in size. Bake on the middle rack of an oven preheated to 400°-425° for 15-18 minutes. Turn out onto a rack and allow to cool for 10 minutes.

In the meantime, bring water and sugar to a boil, allow to cool until lukewarm, flavor with rum. Soak the Babas with the syrup just as in the Savarin recipe, or the Babas can be placed in the syrup until it is completely soaked in.

While stirring constantly, combine apricot jam, a few drops of water and lemon juice and bring to a boil. Then press through a sieve and flavor with apricot brandy. Glaze the Babas with this and allow glaze to dry.

Rosette Coffee Cake

6¼ cups sifted cake flour
1 package dry yeast
6 tablespoons sugar
1 cup lukewarm milk
3 tablespoons softened butter
  or margarine
½ cup raisins
1 cup red-colored jam or jelly
  (any flavor)

Flour for dusting and shaping
⅓ cup slivered almonds
Butter or margarine for
  greasing
1¼ cups powdered sugar
1 tablespoon lemon juice
1 tablespoon water

Place flour in a bowl and make a well in the middle. Add the yeast and stir in 1 teaspoon sugar, some milk and a little flour from the sides to make a starter. Cover with a cloth and allow to rise for about 20 minutes.

Add remaining sugar with all the milk and butter or margarine in flakes. Stir all ingredients into a smooth dough. Beat the dough until bubbles appear and it no longer sticks to the side of the bowl. Cover with a cloth and allow to rise again until the volume doubles.

Meanwhile, wash raisins thoroughly in hot water and dry completely with a cloth. Stir jam or jelly until smooth. Then punch down the dough and knead thoroughly. On a lightly floured work surface, roll out a rectangle 12 × 32 inches in size. Spread jam or jelly evenly over the surface. Sprinkle raisins and almonds over it and cut the dough in half lengthwise. Then cut each half perpendicularly 16 times to have 32 2-inch strips.

Roll these up and place vertically next to each other in a 10-inch greased springform pan. The individual rolls should not touch each other since they will expand during baking.

Cover the rosette cake once more with a cloth and allow to rise for about 20 minutes. Bake at 350°-400° in a preheated oven for about 40 minutes. Allow the cake to settle briefly before turning out onto a rack. Stir together powdered sugar, lemon juice and water to make a glaze and frost the surface with it. Allow the cake to cool completely.

Note

There are numerous variations of the rosette cake recipe: Sprinkle chopped walnuts and pistachios over the dough onto which a very thin layer of honey should be spread. Or, sprinkle grated apples or pears onto the dough. They can additionally be mixed with cinnamon, nuts, almonds, lemon rind or raisins. To get a more delicate dough, add an egg or egg yolk and also mix in grated almonds or nuts. The frosting can also be varied: Add a liqueur or brandy to the powdered sugar, or glaze the cake with chocolate.

Braided Coffee Cake with Fig Filling

5 cups sifted cake flour	2 eggs
1 package dry yeast	Pinch of salt
3 tablespoons water	Flour for rolling out
7 tablespoons softened butter	Butter or margarine for
½ cup lukewarm milk	greasing
⅓ cup sugar	

For the filling and trimming:

⅓ cup currants	Grated rind of ½ lemon
1⅓ cups dried figs	½ cup chopped almonds
4-6 tablespoons rum	Butter for spreading
1 cup marzipan	1 egg yolk
1 cup powdered sugar	¼ cup sliced almonds for
⅛ teaspoon cinnamon	sprinkling

Add 3¾ cups of the flour to a bowl and make a well in the middle. Pour the yeast into the well. Stir together with about 3 tablespoons of lukewarm water, then work in the butter in flakes. Shape the dough into a clump and place it in a large bowl or bucket filled with cold water. After 40 to 60 minutes the risen clump of dough will float to the surface, then it is ready to be worked again. Take the dough out of the water, allow excess water to drip off or, even better, blot off the excess water with a towel. Add remaining flour, milk, sugar, eggs and salt and knead in thoroughly.

Divide the dough into 3 pieces of equal size. On a lightly floured work surface roll out each piece into a rectangle measuring 8 × 20 inches.

While the dough is rising, prepare the filling. Wash currants in hot water and dry thoroughly with a towel. Dice figs. Combine both in a bowl together with rum, cover and allow to soak. Knead together marzipan, powdered sugar, cinnamon and lemon rind. Add these ingredients together with almonds to the rum-soaked fruit. Mix all ingredients thoroughly and form into a paste. If necessary, add additional water or rum.

Brush the 3 pieces of dough with melted butter and place equal portions of filling lengthwise along the middle of each strip. Carefully roll up the dough around the filling and press the edges together well. Then braid the 3 filled strands and press the ends together firmly. Lay on a greased baking sheet and allow to rise again. Finally brush the braid with the whisked egg yolk and sprinkle with almonds. Bake on the middle rack of an oven preheated to 400°-425° for 30-35 minutes. Immediately remove the braid from the baking sheet and slide onto a rack. Allow to cool completely, and serve as soon as possible.

Sugared Pretzels

5 cups flour
1 package dry yeast
½ cup sugar
⅔ cup lukewarm milk
2 eggs
7 tablespoons butter or
  margarine

⅔ cup ground almonds or
  nuts
Pinch of salt
Flour for shaping
Butter or margarine for
  greasing

For the glaze:
1 egg yolk
3 tablespoons milk
⅓ cup chopped almonds

½ cup rock candy sugar for
  sprinkling

Pour flour into a bowl and make a well in the middle. Add the yeast and mix with some sugar, a little milk and some flour to make a starter. Cover with a cloth and allow to rise for about 20 minutes. Add sugar with remaining milk, eggs, butter in flakes, almonds or nuts and salt. Work all ingredients into an elastic dough, then beat until bubbles appear and dough no longer sticks to the side of the bowl. Cover again with a cloth and allow to rise for another 20 minutes. Then, on a lightly floured surface, make 12-inch long strips and shape into pretzels. Place them a sufficient distance apart on a greased baking sheet. Whisk together egg yolk and milk and brush on the pretzels. Sprinkle generously with almonds and rock candy sugar. Allow to rise briefly before baking on the middle rack of an oven preheated to 400° for 20 minutes.

Variations

Apples or Pears in a Jacket: With the same dough "wrap up" 6 to 8 apples or pears. Peel and core the fruit. then steam in red wine until half tender. Drain, cool and, if desired, fill with raisins soaked in alcohol, marzipan or a mixture of both. Or fill with alcohol-soaked macaroons. Roll out the dough very thinly, cut out rounds of dough having the diameter of each piece of fruit. Cut remaining dough into ½-inch wide strips. Wrap these around the fruit starting at the top and overlapping slightly working your way down. (This is necessary in order to make the dough stick together during baking.)

Finally, place the pieces onto the cut out rounds, press gently, and brush with a whisked egg yolk. Stand fruit upright and bake on a greased baking sheet on the middle rack of an oven preheated to 400° for 20-30 minutes.

Piquant Pretzels: Use 1 package of yeast and 1 tablespoon of sugar for the starter. Omit additional sugar and almonds. After the pretzels have been shaped and brushed with an egg yolk, sprinkle with coarse salt and/or caraway seeds. Additional salt and/or caraway seeds (ground, if desired) should also be used in the dough.

Kolatchen

8 cups sifted cake flour
1 package dry yeast
1 cup plus 1 tablespoon sugar
1 cup lukewarm milk
⅔ cup butter
Grated rind of ½ lemon
⅛ teaspoon ground cinnamon

Pinch of salt
1 egg
1 egg yolk
Flour for shaping
Butter or margarine for
  greasing

For the poppy-seed filling:
½ cup milk
2 tablespoons butter
1 cup ground poppy seed
1 tablespoon semolina

¼ cup sugar
2 tablespoons rum
⅛ teaspoon ground cinnamon

For the cheese filling:
½ cup raisins
1-3 tablespoons rum
1 cup ricotta or cottage
  cheese
1 egg yolk

3 tablespoons whipping cream
1 teaspoon vanilla
⅓ cup sugar
1 egg white

For the glaze:
1 egg yolk
2 tablespoons whipping cream
1 cup plum butter

⅓ cup chopped almonds
Rock candy sugar for
  sprinkling

Pour flour into a bowl and make a well in the middle. Add the yeast and stir together with 1 teaspoon sugar, some milk and some flour from the sides of the well. Cover with a cloth and allow to rise for 15 minutes. Melt butter and cool until lukewarm. Add it, together with all the other dough ingredients, to the starter and knead into a smooth yeast dough. Beat until bubbles appear and until dough no longer sticks to the side of the bowl. Allow to rise again for 20-25 minutes.

Punch the dough down and knead thoroughly. Using lightly floured hands, divide the dough into egg-sized pieces. Form these into somewhat flattened balls and place a sufficient distance apart on a greased baking sheet. Allow to rise again.

In the meantime, bring milk and butter to a boil, sprinkle in poppy seed, semolina and sugar. Allow mixture to boil vigorously for a few minutes while stirring constantly. Flavor with rum and cinnamon. Remove from heat and allow to steep well.

For the cheese filling, wash raisins in hot water, rub them dry and soak them in rum. Stir ricotta or cottage cheese, egg yolk, cream, vanilla and sugar until smooth. Beat the egg white until stiff and fold in. Drain raisins. Add the retained rum to the cheese mixture.

Make a depression in the middle of the raised dough rounds so that the outside rim is higher. Brush the rim with whisked cream and egg yolk and fill the kolatchen with the prepared fillings. Sprinkle the poppy seed filling with chipped almonds and the cheese filling with the rum-soaked raisins. Also fill some kolatchen with plum butter. Bake on the middle rack of an oven preheated to 425° for 15-20 minutes. Sprinkle the plum-butter kolatchen with rock candy sugar.

Sheet Coffee Cakes

These belong to the "evergreens" of cake baking and, even though they are "old as the hills," they are still in fashion. It is assumed that they were invented in agricultural regions in order to fully utilize the heat of the ovens after bread baking had been completed. The fillings always depend on what is "naturally" available: If Damson plums are in season they are used, if it happens to be apples or cherries, rhubarb or pears then they are used. If there is absolutely nothing to harvest at the moment, then the baker turns to the good old butter cake, crumb cake or a Bienenstich with a honey glaze. The almond-topped apple cake and a dappled egg tart (see pages 96 and 97) also belong in this category. The basic recipe, given here below, is the same for all of these cakes. But it can be varied at will. Let's start with the "normal recipe" that is always calculated for one baking sheet measuring about 12 × 16 inches. For especially thin dough, use about ⅓ of the dough for ½ of a second baking sheet. To do this, however, build a border with a strip of aluminum foil folded double at the edge of the dough.

6¼ cups sifted cake flour	7 tablespoons softened butter
1 package dry yeast	or margarine
¼ cup sugar	Flour for dusting
1 cup lukewarm milk	Butter, margarine, or
1 egg	vegetable oil for greasing
Pinch of salt	
1 teaspoon vanilla	
Either a grated rind of ½	
lemon or ⅛ teaspoon	
ground cinnamon	
(depending on the type of	
filling)	

Pour flour in a bowl and make a well in the middle. Add the yeast and stir in some sugar, some lukewarm milk and a little flour from the edges to make a starter. Cover and allow to rise in a warm place for about 15 minutes until the starter has risen substantially and begins to show bubbles as well as cracks. Add the remaining sugar, milk, egg, salt, vanilla and spices. Sprinkle butter in small flakes on the edges (or it can also be melted together with the milk, cooled until lukewarm and poured in; it should not be too hot).

Then, using either a wooden spoon or by hand, work from the inside to the outside and stir all the ingredients together. (The kneading attachment of an electric mixer can be used, but this method often lacks the subtle intuition necessary for judging the readiness of the dough.) Finally, beat the dough until bubbles appear and it no longer sticks to the side of the bowl. Cover for about 20 minutes and allow to double in size, punch down and knead well. Roll out on a greased baking sheet and allow dough to rise once more. In the meantime prepare one of the fillings.

The cake is then usually baked on the middle rack of an oven preheated to 400°-425°.

Butter Coffee Cake

1 basic coffee cake dough recipe	⅔ cup sugar
1 cup sweet or sour cream	2 teaspoons ground cinnamon or 1-2 teaspoons vanilla
7 tablespoons butter	

The dough is rolled out on a greased baking sheet as usual. If vanilla is used, it should be stirred into the cream. If cinnamon is used, it should be added to the sugar. Brush dough with cream. Allow to rise, then make small depressions in the dough at regular intervals and place flakes of butter in them. Sprinkle with sugar. Bake in a preheated oven for 25 minutes.

Note

For an even more "buttery," cake, remove the cake from the oven when half done, make additional depressions, fill them with butter and sprinkle again with sugar. However, to do this, it is advisable to use a baking sheet with a higher rim, or place a doubled strip of aluminum around the edge, so that no butter drips over the edge.

> **Tip:** *The butter cake is even more refined by combining sliced almonds or nuts with the sugar.*

Crumb Coffee Cake

1 basic coffee cake dough recipe	2 teaspoons ground cinnamon
¾ cup plus 2 tablespoons butter	1-2 teaspoons vanilla or the grated rind of 1 lemon
1 cup sugar	4½ cups sifted cake flour
	4 tablespoons lukewarm milk

Roll out the coffee cake dough onto a greased baking sheet and allow to rise. Meanwhile place the butter in flakes in a bowl, add sugar and spices and sift flour on top. Using 2 knives, cut all the ingredients into crumbs.

Brush milk on the raised dough and sprinkle it generously with the crumbs. Bake in a preheated oven for 25-30 minutes. Serve while it is still fresh.

Bienenstich or Honey-Glazed Filled Coffee Cake

1 basic coffee cake dough recipe	1 cup sliced almonds
1 cup butter	½ cup chopped almonds
1 cup plus 2 tablespoons sugar	½ cup whipping cream
	Marrow of one vanilla bean

For the filling:

2 cups milk	1 egg yolk
Pinch of salt	¾ cup plus 2 tablespoons
¼ cup sugar	butter
1 teaspoon vanilla	½ cup plus 2 tablespoons
1 package vanilla pudding	powdered sugar

Roll out the coffee cake dough on a baking sheet as usual and allow to rise. Meanwhile combine butter, sugar, sliced and chopped almonds, cream and vanilla marrow in a saucepan and bring to a boil while stirring constantly. Remove from heat immediately, allow to cool briefly, then brush on the dough. Allow to rise once again before baking in a preheated oven for about 25 minutes. Remove the Bienenstich from the oven and allow to cool.

For the filling, combine milk, salt, sugar and vanilla in a saucepan and bring to a boil. Whisk together pudding powder, egg yolk and some cold water. Add to the boiling milk while stirring constantly and bring this mixture to a boil again. Place the pan in a cold water bath. Stir frequently as the custard cools.

Cream butter and powdered sugar thoroughly. Mix into the custard by the spoonful as soon as the custard has reached the same temperature as the butter. Allow to cool for 1 hour.

Cut the Bienenstich into two layers, brush custard-cream on the lower half and place the upper half on top.

> **Tip:** Go ahead and cut the Bienenstich into strips before filling, making the cutting of the cake into two layers easier. Then by cutting the upper half into one portion servings, no cream will be squeezed out when the lower layer is cut through.

Apple Coffee Cake from the Baking Sheet

1 basic coffee cake dough	1 cup currants or raisins
recipe	⅔ cup chopped almonds
3-4 pounds apples	3 tablespoons butter
(depending on the size)	¾ cup sugar
Juice of 1 lemon	2 teaspoons ground cinnamon

Roll out dough on a greased baking sheet as usual and allow to rise. Meanwhile peel, quarter, core apples and cut into thin slices. Immediately sprinkle with lemon juice to avoid discoloration. Wash currants or raisins in hot water, drain and rub dry with a cloth.

Blot the apples dry with a towel and lay them close to each other on the dough so that they look like the scales of a fish. Combine currants or raisins with almonds and sprinkle over apples. Melt butter and drip into the filling. Combine sugar and cinnamon, sprinkle well over half onto the cake and then allow it to rise for another 15-20 minutes. Bake in a preheated oven for 25-30 minutes. Immediately sprinkle with remaining cinnamon-sugar mixture upon removal.

> **Tip:** Instead of apples, this cake can be covered with pitted plums or prunes, cherries, pear or peach slices or any other fruit. By using extremely tart fruit, an increased amount of sugar required will be necessary. Of course, vanilla for the cinnamon can be substituted. If using canned fruit, 2 to 2½ pounds of each type of fruit will suffice.

Crumb Cake with Fruit

1 basic coffee cake dough	1 crumb recipe (see Crumb
recipe	Cake on preceding page)
3-4 pounds of fresh fruit (or	
3-4 cups canned fruit)	

Roll out coffee cake dough as usual and allow to rise. Cover with fruit (if canned fruit is used, be sure to drain it well). Sprinkle with crumbs. Allow to rise again and bake for 30-35 minutes.

Note

By using this recipe it is possible to bake a fruit-filled cake covered with chocolate sprinkles or grated chocolate. About 10 minutes before the baking is finished, sprinkle ½ cup of chocolate sprinkles or coarsely grated chocolate on top of the crumbs. Allow it to melt during subsequent baking.

Coconut-Fruit Coffee Cake

1 basic coffee cake dough	1 teaspoon vanilla
recipe	1 teaspoon almond extract
⅓ cup butter	3 cups grated coconut
1 cup sugar	4 cups prepared fruit (pitted
1 teaspoon ground cinnamon	and finely sliced cherries,
4 egg yolks	grated apples, orange
5 tablespoons crème fraîche	sections cut into strips,
3 egg whites	cleaned berries, or similar
Pinch of salt	fruit)
½ cup whipping cream	

Roll out coffee cake dough on a greased baking sheet as previously described and allow to rise.

Meanwhile, combine butter, sugar, cinnamon, egg yolks and crème fraîche in a bowl and beat with an electric mixer until sugar is dissolved and mixture is well creamed. Whip egg whites and salt in a bowl until firm. Combine whipping cream and vanilla in another bowl and whip until peaks form. Gently fold both into the egg-yolk cream together with almond extract, fruit and coconut. Spread onto dough and bake about 40 minutes.

Rich Bundt Cake

6¼ cups sifted cake flour
1 package dry yeast
6 tablespoons sugar
3-5 tablespoons lukewarm
  milk
½ cup sour cream
1 teaspoon vanilla
¾ cup plus 2 tablespoons
  softened butter
2 eggs
2 egg yolks
Pinch of salt
½ cup raisins
3-4 tablespoons rum or
  cognac

Flour for dusting
½ cup chopped almonds
1½ ounces coarsely grated
  semisweet chocolate
Butter or margarine for
  greasing
Bread crumbs for sprinkling
1 tablespoon butter for
  spreading
2 tablespoons sugar for
  sprinkling
Powdered sugar for dusting

Pour flour into a bowl, make a well in the middle and add the yeast. Sprinkle with some sugar and a little milk. Stir together with some flour from the edge of the well to make a starter. Dust very lightly with flour, cover with a towel and allow to rise in a warm place for 15 minutes. The starter should then have markedly expanded and bubbles should be visible on the surface. Mix in sour cream, remaining sugar, vanilla, and butter in flakes. Then add eggs, egg yolks and salt and work all the ingredients into a smooth dough. Beat until bubbles appear and the dough no longer sticks to the side of the bowl. Then form into a ball, again cover with a towel, and allow to rise in a warm place for

20-25 minutes. Its volume should double and the surface should appear "woolly."

Meanwhile, wash raisins in hot water, rub dry with a towel. Place in a bowl, cover with rum and allow to soak for 20 minutes. Drain, blot dry and dust lightly with flour. Retain the drained-off rum. Punch down dough, mix in retained rum and knead vigorously. At the very end, quickly knead in raisins, almonds and chocolate. Grease a Gugelhupf form well and dust with bread crumbs. Fill the dough into the form, allow to rise for 15 minutes in a warm place. Melt butter, brush half on the surface of the cake before baking. Bake on the lower rack of an oven preheated to 400° for 50-60 minutes. About 5 minutes before done, brush remaining butter on surface and sprinkle with sugar. Allow to caramelize; this gives the cake a very special flavor.

Turn the cake out onto a rack and allow to cool. Dust with powdered sugar before serving.

Danzig Poppy-Seed Cake

1 package dry yeast	2 eggs
½ cup sugar	Pinch of salt
3-5 tablespoons lukewarm milk	Flour for kneading and rolling out
6¼ cups sifted cake flour	Butter or margarine for greasing
⅔ cup softened butter	
½ cup lukewarm buttermilk	Milk for brushing

For the filling:

1 cup whipping cream	1½ cups ground poppy seed
4 tablespoons honey	2 egg yolks
1 vanilla bean	1 teaspoon lemon juice

For the glaze:

1 egg yolk	1½ cups powdered sugar
2 tablespoons whipping cream	3-4 tablespoons rum

Stir together yeast with 2 teaspoons sugar and the lukewarm milk. Allow to rise in a warm place until bubbles appear in the starter. Pour flour into a bowl, make a depression in the middle and pour in the starter. Sprinkle remaining sugar over it, place butter in flakes on the rim, add buttermilk, eggs and salt. Work all ingredients into a smooth dough. Beat until bubbles appear and dough no longer sticks to sides. Cover with a cloth, allow to rise in a warm place for 20 minutes.

Meanwhile, heat the cream over low heat, add honey and melt while stirring constantly. Slit open vanilla bean lengthwise, scrape out marrow and add marrow and pod to the cream. While stirring constantly, bring to a boil and sprinkle in poppy seed. Remove from heat, take out pod, and allow to cool slightly. Whisk together egg yolk and lemon juice and stir into poppy-seed mixture. Punch down dough and knead thoroughly on a lightly floured work surface. Halve the dough and roll out two long rectangles. Place one half on a greased baking sheet and brush the surface with milk. Evenly spread poppy-seed mixture over the surface. Place the second layer of dough on top and carefully press edges together. Cover cake with a cloth and allow to rise for 20 minutes. Then using a new razor blade or a very sharp knife (preferably with the thinnest blade possible) score the surface several times lengthwise. Whisk egg yolk together with cream and brush onto surface. Bake the cake on the middle rack of an oven preheated to 400° for 40-50 minutes. Then slide onto rack and allow to cool. Stir powdered sugar together with rum and glaze cake with this mixture.

Berlin Doughnuts

5 cups flour	⅓ cup softened butter
1 package dry yeast	1 tablespoon shortening
6 tablespoons sugar	Flour for shaping
½ cup lukewarm milk	1⅓ cups firm jam (any
Pinch of salt	flavor)
Grated rind of ½ lemon	Oil for frying
1 egg	Sugar for sprinkling or turning
2 egg yolks	

Pour flour into a bowl, make a depression in the middle and add the yeast. Stir in 1 teaspoon sugar, some milk and a little flour from the edges to make a starter. Cover with a towel and allow to rise for 15 minutes. Stir in milk, sugar, salt, lemon rind, egg, egg yolks and butter in flakes as well as shortening. Work into a smooth dough. Beat until bubbles appear and dough no longer sticks to sides. Cover again with a towel and allow to rise 25-30 minutes. It should double its volume.

Punch down dough and knead thoroughly. Divide into two halves. On a lightly floured work surface, roll out each half to ½-inch thickness. With a round cookie cutter measuring about 2½ inches in diameter, mark out as many rounds as possible. Place a thick dot of jam in the middle of each round. Lay the second layer of dough on top, gently press around each mound of jam and then press out the round with the cookie cutter. Press edges together again and allow the doughnuts to rise on a floured baking sheet until they are round and woolly.

Heat fat for frying. Drop only a few doughnuts into the hot fat at a time so that they do not touch each other. Fry for 5-7 minutes, turning once when the bottom has become nicely browned. Remove with a slotted spoon, drain well and turn in sugar while still hot.

Variation

Plum Fritters: Prepare dough as for Berlin Doughnuts and allow to rise twice. During this time prepare the plum filling: Wash and dry plums (Damson plums are preferred). Slit lengthwise on one side and remove pit. Knead together ⅓ cup marzipan with ¼ cup powdered sugar. Fill each plum with a small ball of marzipan. Press closed.

Knead dough, roll out and, as for Berlin Doughnuts, mark out rounds. Instead of the jam, place a filled plum in the middle of each round. Cover with second dough layer and proceed as above. After frying turn in cinnamon-sugar instead of sugar.

Fried Braids and Carnival Pretzels

5 cups flour
1 package dry yeast
⅓ cup sugar
½ cup lukewarm milk
Grated rind of ½ lemon
Pinch of salt
2 eggs

⅓ cup softened butter
Flour for shaping
Shortening for frying
Powdered sugar for dusting
1 cup whipping cream
1 teaspoon vanilla sugar

Pour flour into a bowl, make a well in the middle and add the yeast. Stir in some sugar, some milk and a little flour from the edges to make a starter. Cover with a towel and allow to rise in a warm place for 15 minutes. Stir in remaining sugar, milk, grated lemon rind, salt, eggs and butter in flakes. Work all ingredients into a smooth dough. Beat until bubbles appear and dough no longer sticks to the sides. Again allow to rise in a warm place for 30 minutes until volume has doubled. Knead thoroughly on a floured work surface. The dough should be quite soft, but no longer sticky. If necessary, additional flour can be worked in. Halve the dough and form one half into 5-inch strands that narrow toward the ends. Weave these strands into braids. Place on a floured baking sheet. Roll out remaining dough, cut out thin 12-inch long strands and fold these into pretzels. Press ends gently. Also place on floured baking sheet. Heat shortening to 325°-350° and drop in a few braids and pretzels at a time. Fry until golden brown. Drain well on a paper towel. Allow to cool in a rack. Shortly before completely cooled, dust braids gener-ously with powdered sugar. Before the pretzels are completely cooled, halve them horizontally and then allow to cool completely. Meanwhile, flavor cream with vanilla and whip until stiff. Place in a pastry bag with star spout and fill bottoms of pretzels. Replace tops and dust with powdered sugar.

> **Tip:** *Fried Braids as well as Carnival Pretzels may be turned in granulated sugar instead of dusting with powdered sugar. In this case, the sugar can be flavored with cinnamon. The braids can also be halved and filled. Whipped cream is certainly appropriate, but a layer of jam, or a mixture of jam or pureed fruit and whipped cream, are delicious as well.*

Panettone (Italian Holiday Cake)

1 package dry yeast	2/3 cup seedless raisins
3/4 cup sugar	1/3 cup finely chopped candied
1/2 cup lukewarm milk	orange rind
5 cups flour	1/3 cup finely chopped candied
Marrow of 1 vanilla bean	lemon rind
2/3 cup butter	Butter or margarine for
6-7 egg yolks	greasing
Pinch of salt	1 egg for brushing
Grated rind of 1/2 lemon	

Combine yeast, 2 teaspoons sugar and 4 tablespoons milk. Allow to rise for 15 minutes. Pour flour (setting aside 2 tablespoons) into a bowl and make a well in the middle. Pour in starter, milk, sugar, marrow of vanilla bean, butter in flakes, egg yolks, salt and grated lemon rind. Stir all ingredients into a smooth dough. Beat until blisters appear and dough no longer sticks to the side of the bowl. Form dough into a ball, cover with a towel and allow to rise for 20 minutes by which time its volume should have doubled.

In the meantime wash the raisins in hot water, rub dry with a towel. Combine with candied lemon and orange rind. Dust fruit with retained flour. Punch down dough and knead vigorously. Work in fruit. Then place dough in a high, narrow well-greased form. Allow to rise once more. Then brush with whisked egg and, using a razor blade or very sharp knife, slit the surface several times crosswise. Bake on the lower rack of an oven preheated to 425° for 60-65 minutes.

> **Tip:** *If a high, narrow form is not available, a small springform pan can be substituted and a collar made for it with waxed paper or aluminum foil. A coffee can will also work, as will a new flower pot. In all cases, fill form only 3/4 full.*

Highland Loaf

2 1/2 cups wheat flour	1 egg yolk
3 1/2 cups flour	2/3 cup softened butter
1 package dry yeast	1 1/3 cups seedless raisins
1 cup lukewarm milk	Flour for dusting and
3/4 cup sugar	sprinkling
1 teaspoon vanilla	Butter or margarine for
Pinch of salt	greasing
1 egg	1/4 cup butter for brushing

Pour flour into a bowl and make a well in the middle. Add the yeast and stir in 3 tablespoons milk and 2 teaspoons sugar to make a starter. Set in a warm place, cover with a towel and allow to rise for 15 minutes until bubbles appear. Add remaining milk, sugar, vanilla, salt, egg, egg yolk and butter in flakes and knead into an elastic dough. Beat until blisters appear and dough no longer sticks to the side of the bowl. Once again allow to rise.

Meanwhile wash the raisins thoroughly in hot water and rub dry with a towel. Dust with flour. Punch down dough, knead well and fold in raisins. Grease a loaf pan well and dust with flour. Fill in dough, allow to rise one last time, brush with melted butter that has cooled until lukewarm. Bake on the middle rack of an oven preheated to 400° for about 60 minutes.

Vanilla Cloverleaf Rolls

1 package dry yeast	1/2 cup whipping cream
1/2 cup sugar	Butter or margarine for
3 tablespoons lukewarm milk	greasing
5 cups flour	1 egg
Pinch of salt	3 tablespoons milk for
1/3 cup softened butter	brushing
Marrow of 2 vanilla beans	Rock candy sugar for
2 egg yolks	sprinkling

Combine yeast with 2 teaspoons sugar and milk to make a starter. Set in a warm place, cover with a towel and allow to rise for 15 minutes until bubbles appear in the starter. Pour flour into a bowl, make a well in the middle and pour in the starter after it has risen. Add remaining sugar, salt, butter in flakes, vanilla marrow, egg yolks and whipping cream and knead into an elastic dough. Beat the dough until blisters appear and it no longer sticks to the sides. Cover with a towel, allow to rise another 20 minutes. During this time the dough should double in volume. Punch it down, knead well and then, with floured hands, form walnut-sized balls of dough. On a well-greased baking sheet arrange 3 balls in the form of cloverleaves so that they will stick together during baking. Cover with a towel and allow to rise for about 20 minutes. Meanwhile whisk together egg and milk. After rolls have risen, brush them with this mixture and sprinkle with rock candy sugar. Bake on the middle rack of an oven preheated to 450° until golden brown.

Note

A salty version of the cloverleaf rolls can also be made. Use sugar only for the starter, omit remaining sugar as well as vanilla marrow. Instead, increase amount of salt to 1-2 teaspoons. Instead of rock candy sugar, the rolls should be sprinkled with coarse salt, caraway seeds or poppy seeds.

Apple Cake with Almond Glaze

4½ cups sifted cake flour
1 package dry yeast
2 tablespoons sugar
1 cup lukewarm milk
1 egg

Pinch of salt
Grated rind of ½ lemon
3 tablespoons softened butter
Butter for greasing

For the filling:
1 pound apples
Juice of 1 lemon
7 tablespoons butter
1 cup sugar

2 egg yolks
2 cups whipping cream
2 egg whites
1⅓ cups slivered almonds

For the dough, pour flour into a bowl, make a well in the middle and add the yeast. Stir together with some sugar, a little milk and some flour from the edge, set in a warm place and cover with a towel for about 15 minutes. Add remaining sugar, remaining milk, egg, salt, lemon rind and butter in flakes. Work all ingredients into a smooth dough. Then beat the dough until bubbles appear and it no longer sticks to the sides. Roll out onto a greased baking sheet, cover again with a cloth, set in a warm place and allow to rise for 20 minutes.

Meanwhile, prepare the filling. Peel, core and coarsely grate the apples. Immediately sprinkle with lemon juice so that they do not discolor.

Cream butter. Gradually add sugar and egg yolks. As soon as the sugar is dissolved, whip egg whites and whipping cream in separate bowls. Gently fold each into the butter mixture together with grated apples and slivered almonds. Spread evenly onto raised dough and allow to rise again for 10 minutes.

Then bake on the middle rack of an oven preheated to 425° for 35-40 minutes.

Allow cake to cool and cut into strips. Serve as fresh as possible, since old yeast cakes taste only half as good. In time apples will moisten the dough.

Whipped cream flavored with vanilla extract tastes delicious with this cake. It can also be served with vanilla ice cream.

> **Tip:** *For a change, substitute grated pears that are not too sweet for the apples. Or replace slivered almonds completely or in part with grated coconut.*

Dappled Egg Tart

6¼ cups sifted cake flour
1 package dry yeast
⅓ cup sugar
1 cup lukewarm milk

⅓ cup softened butter
Pinch of salt
Butter for greasing

For the filling:
2 cups ricotta or cottage
   cheese
⅔ cup sugar
Pinch of salt
2 eggs

Grated rind of 1 lemon
1 vanilla bean
⅔ cup raisins
½ cup sliced almonds

For the topping:
¾ cup plus 2 tablespoons
   butter
1 teaspoon vanilla

1 cup sugar
4 eggs
½ cup sliced almonds

For the dough, make a well in the flour, add the yeast together with some sugar, some milk and a little flour from the edges and stir to make a starter. Cover with a towel for about 15 minutes, set in a warm place and allow to rise. Then add remaining sugar, milk, butter in flakes and salt and mix well. Beat and knead the dough until bubbles appear and it no longer sticks to the side of the bowl. Allow to rise for another 20 minutes until its volume doubles. Then roll out onto a greased baking sheet (about 14 × 16 inches in size) with high edges.

For the filling, cream together cheese, sugar, salt, eggs, lemon rind and vanilla bean marrow until sugar is dissolved and mixture is somewhat foamy. Spread onto dough.

Wash raisins in hot water, rub dry with a towel. Sprinkle over the cheese mixture together with the sliced almonds. For the topping, cream butter with vanilla. Gradually add sugar alternating with eggs. Cream until the batter is quite foamy and sugar is dissolved. Carefully spread over filling and sprinkle with sliced almonds. Bake on the middle rack of an oven preheated to 350° for 30-40 minutes. Allow to cool before cutting into squares.

Tip: *Since this dough rises very well and since both filling and topping are very rich and light, the cake must be baked in a pan with high edges. Otherwise some of the delicious topping could run off and burn on the surface of the oven. If no appropriate pan is available, it is advisable to halve all ingredients and bake the cake in a greased springform pan. Although this won't correspond to the appearance of the traditional cake, the taste will remain just as scrumptious.*

Filled Yeast Rolls

3 cups flour
2 cups wheat flour
1 package dry yeast
1 cup lukewarm milk
½ cup sugar

½ cup butter
1 egg
1 egg yolk
Pinch of salt
Grated rind of ½ lemon

For the filling:
½ cup whipping cream
3 tablespoons flour
1 tablespoon sugar
1 teaspoon vanilla
1 vanilla bean
2 egg yolks
2-3 tablespoons almond
   liqueur

Flour for rolling out
1 egg white
Butter for greasing and
   brushing
Sugar for turning

For the dough, pour flour into a bowl, make a well in the middle and add the yeast. Stir in some milk and sugar, cover with a towel and allow to rise for 15 minutes.

Heat remaining milk together with sugar and butter until butter is melted and sugar dissolved. Cool until lukewarm. Add to starter together with egg, egg yolk, salt and grated lemon rind. Knead all ingredients well. Beat the dough until bubbles appear and it no longer sticks to the sides of the bowl. Allow to rise another 20 minutes.

Meanwhile, prepare the filling. In a saucepan, combine whipping cream with flour, sugar, vanilla, the scraped out marrow of the vanilla bean. Add egg yolks and beat over very low heat (or in a hot-water bath) until the batter is thick, creamy and well homogenized. The mixture should not boil. Remove from heat, stir in almond liqueur and allow cream to cool. Stir frequently to avoid the creation of a skin on the surface. Punch down dough and knead again, then roll out on a floured work surface to ¼-inch thickness. Cut out 2½-inch rounds and place mounds of the cream on half the rounds. Brush the edges of the rounds with whisked egg white and place a second dough round on top. Press edges together firmly. Place on a greased baking sheet leaving sufficient distance between each roll. Cover with a cloth and allow to rise for 20 minutes. Then bake immediately on the middle rack of an oven preheated to 500° for about 20 minutes. Remove rolls while still hot, brush with butter and turn in sugar. Then allow to cool.

> **Tip:** *To vary the filling, flavor it with cocoa, grated chocolate or a generous pinch of ground cinnamon. To make it more extravagant and also richer in calories, add a few spoonfuls of ground nuts or almonds.*

Hazelnut Butter Crescents

1 package dry yeast
⅔ cup sugar
3 tablespoons milk
5 cups flour
½ cup whipping cream
2 eggs
¼ cup softened butter
Pinch of salt

½ cup chopped almonds
Butter or margarine for
  greasing
Flour for rolling out and
  shaping
Milk or cream for brushing
Powdered sugar for dusting

For the filling:
½ cup hazelnut butter
1⅓ cups slivered almonds
1-2 teaspoons rum

Add yeast to a cup or small bowl and stir together with 2 teaspoons of sugar and the lukewarm milk to make a starter. Cover with a cloth, set in a warm place and allow to rise until bubbles appear on the starter, that is, until it "puffs." Pour flour into a bowl, make a well in the middle and pour in starter. Add remaining sugar together with cream, eggs, butter in flakes, salt, and almonds and work into a smooth, elastic dough. Beat the dough until bubbles appear and it no longer sticks to the sides. Form into a ball, place in a bowl, dust with flour, cover with a towel, set in a warm place and allow to rise for 20 minutes until it has doubled in size.

Meanwhile, prepare the filling. Divide hazelnut butter into small pieces and place in a saucepan. Melt over a warm, but not too hot, water bath. Fold in almonds and flavor with rum. Grease a large piece of waxed paper and spread thinly with hazelnut butter. Allow to cool and harden. Punch down dough and knead vigorously. On a floured work surface, roll out to ¼-inch thickness and cut out 6-inch squares. Cut these squares once diagonally. Cut cooled hazelnut butter into appropriately sized pieces and lay on the triangles. Roll up dough toward one point and bend both ends in one direction to make crescents. Place on a greased baking sheet leaving sufficient room for expansion. Cover with a towel and allow to rise for 20 minutes. Brush with milk or cream and bake on the middle rack of an oven preheated to 400° for 20-25 minutes until golden brown. Remove on a rack and allow to cool. Dust with powdered sugar before serving. The crescents taste best when still warm.

Meringues and Macaroons

Vacherin with Chestnut Cream

9 egg whites
Pinch of salt
2¼ cups plus 2 tablespoons
    sugar

1 teaspoon lemon juice
Butter for greasing
Flour for dusting

For the filling and trimming:
1½ cans chestnuts (about 20
    ounces)
½ cup milk
2 tablespoons sugar
1 vanilla bean
1 ¼-ounce package gelatin
2-3 tablespoons rum

1½ cups whipping cream
1 teaspoon vanilla
1 small can pineapple (about
    4 slices)
Chopped pistachios for
    sprinkling

Combine 8 egg whites with salt and beat until stiff. Then gradually sprinkle in 2¼ cups less 2 tablespoons of sugar in a thin stream while beating constantly. Continue to beat until very firm and shiny. Mix in lemon juice, retaining a few drops. Then place the meringue mixture in a pastry bag with a large star spout.

Line two or three baking sheets (depending on the size) with parchment paper. Grease with butter and dust with flour. On the paper, mark five circles with a diameter of 6 inches and three circles with a diameter 4½ inches.

Press out a thin ring of meringue around each of the circles. Also press out a lattice in two of the 6-inch circles as well as in one of the 4½-inch circles. Place the baking sheets in an oven preheated to 225° and dry, more than bake, the rings for 3-4 hours.

Combine the remaining egg white with a pinch of salt and beat until firm. Sprinkle in remaining sugar and mix in a little lemon juice. Also place this meringue in a pastry bag with a star spout.

Again line a baking sheet with new parchment paper, grease and dust with flour. Place one of the 6-inch meringue rings with lattice on the baking sheet. Very thinly press out some of the meringue onto the rim and place another 6-inch ring on top of it. Continue for the remaining 6-inch rings in the same way. For the second tier of the torte, place the second 6-inch ring with lattice on the baking sheet and place the two 4½-inch rings (without lattice), on top similarly held together with meringue. Press out dots or lines of meringue around the sides and again place this in a 225° oven for 2-3 hours and allow to bake together, or rather dry. Remove from the oven and allow both parts to cool on a rack.

For the filling, drain the chestnuts, dice or crush them. Then combine with milk and sugar in a saucepan. Slit the vanilla bean lengthwise, remove marrow and add to the chestnuts together with the pod. Bring to a boil in order to reduce the amount of liquid, stir occasionally so that the chestnuts do not burn. Prepare gelatin according to package directions with some water. Remove bean pod. Puree chestnuts with remaining liquid in a blender or press through a sieve.

Add gelatin to the still hot chestnut batter, stir constantly until dissolved. (If the batter has become too cool, it will have to be reheated.) As soon as the gelatin has dissolved, flavor the batter with rum, allow to cool and gel. Whip cream with vanilla. Drain

pineapple and cut three rings into small pieces. As soon as the chestnut mixture begins to gel (when "streaks" appear), fold in ⅔ of the cream and the pineapple pieces.

Place the lower portion of the torte (the 6-inch lattice with 6-inch rings), on a platter and fill with the chestnut-pineapple mixture. Place the second construction, the 6-inch lattice with the 4½-inch rings, on top and similarly fill with cream.

Finally, lay the remaining 4½-inch lattice on top. Fill the remaining whipped cream into a pastry bag and decorate the Vacherin with it. Cut the pineapple ring into pieces and decorate with them as well. Sparingly sprinkle the surface with pistachios and serve immediately.

Tip: *The Vacherin should always be served immediately after it has been filled because the delicate meringue mixture quickly becomes soft and moist which makes the taste a bit dull. Nevertheless it is a good idea to bake and construct the individual rings and lattices a day ahead of time. Or, bake the rings ahead of time and place them in an airtight container, so that only the construction remains before filling and decorating.*

Variations

A Vacherin may be served with various filling. Use whatever fruit is in season. Tart berries taste exceptionally good; try red currants, cranberries, whortleberries, blueberries or a mixture of a variety of fruits. Furthermore, cherries, citrus fruits and apricots go well with this light and sweet pastry. Of course, a Vacherin shouldn't be without whipping cream. It should be flavored with an appropriate fruit brandy depending on the type of fruit used. It should never be too sweet.

Pineapple wine cream can also be used (see page 58), or the cream for the wedding cake (see page 216), or the filling for the Charlottes (see page 48), or the mango champagne cream (see page 135).

Ice cream, of course, goes well with the Vacherin, too. Use any flavor desired or mix it with fruit and whipped cream.

Italian Almond Macaroons

1¾ cups skinned, ground almonds	Pinch of salt
1⅓ cups sugar	1 teaspoon almond extract
3 egg whites	Powdered sugar for dusting

Combine ground almonds with about half of the sugar. Combine egg whites with a pinch of salt and beat until stiff. Then gradually sprinkle in remaining sugar while beating continuously. Continue beating until the mixture is firm and gleams. Fold in almond extract. Spoon in the almond-sugar mixture. Then fill into a pastry bag with a large smooth spout. Line a baking sheet with parchment paper and press out walnut-sized balls leaving sufficient space between each one. Dust generously with powdered sugar.

Allow to dry for about 3 hours at room temperature, then place on the middle rack of an oven preheated to 250°-300°. For 30 minutes allow to dry more than bake. They should only become light brown during this time. Immediately remove from the baking sheet. Dust again with powdered sugar and allow to cool.

Note

Frequently only unskinned ground almonds are available. These are not as suitable for these delicate cookies. It is better to use whole almonds and remove their skins. Cover them briefly with boiling water leaving them in it for only 1-2 minutes. Fish them out with a slotted spoon and then, using thumb and index finger, rub off the brown skin. (If they are still too hot, quickly rinse them in cold water.) Rub the almonds in a towel until well dried or lay them on a dry baking sheet and let them dry in a warm oven being sure to avoid browning them. As soon as they have cooled, grind them in an almond mill.

Variation

Chocolate Amaretti are similarly prepared. Mix 4 tablespoons of flour into the almond-sugar mixture. Melt 1½ ounces of chocolate over low heat, then allow to cool until lukewarm. Continue as in the above recipe and fold in the liquid chocolate at the end.

Meringue Tartlets

4 egg whites
Pinch of salt
1 cup sugar
1½ teaspoons lemon juice
1 pound mixed berries or
    sour cherries (fresh or
    preserved)

1 10-ounce jar apple jelly
1 tablespoon sugar

Place egg whites in a bowl, add salt and beat with an electric mixer at the highest speed until completely firm. Then gradually sprinkle in sugar and continue to beat until the meringue pastry is stiff and gleaming. Finally mix in the lemon juice and fill into a pastry bag with a large star spout.

Line a baking sheet with parchment paper or aluminum foil and draw 3-inch circles on it. Using the pastry bag press out stars of meringue following the circumference of the circles. Place a large dot of meringue in the middle of each circle and smooth out.

Place the baking sheet into an oven preheated to 225°-250°. Leave the oven door slighty ajar (keep it pried open with a wooden, not plastic, handle). Allow meringue tartlets to dry for 3-4 hours, avoid browning.

Carefully remove the tartlets from the paper or foil. Allow to cool and dry further on a rack.

Drain fruit in a sieve and generously fill into the tartlets. Gently heat jelly and stir smooth. Glaze the fruit with it.

Note

Meringue tartlets quickly get soggy and then become sticky and tough. They must always be served immediately after filling! To give them additional protection against moisture, thinly coat the bottoms with liquid chocolate before filling with fruit. Or, sprinkle in crumbled macaroons or ground almonds mixed with zwieback crumbs as a "protective sheet."

Meringue-Ice Cream Torte with Fruit

3 egg whites
¾ cup plus 2 tablespoons
  sugar
1 teaspoon lemon juice

For the filling:

1 ¼-ounce package gelatin	¾ cup plus 2 tablespoons
10 ounces fresh or frozen	sugar
raspberries	½ cup dry white wine
2 tablespoons raspberry	5 kiwis
schnapps	3 cups whipping cream
5 egg yolks	

For the meringue bottom, place egg whites in a bowl and beat until very stiff. Gradually sprinkle in ⅔ of the sugar and beat until it is dissolved. Then add the lemon juice and beat vigorously once more. Gently fold in remaining sugar. Line a baking sheet with parchment paper and using the rim of a 10-inch springform pan draw a circle on the paper.

Fill the meringue pastry into a pastry bag with a smooth spout. Then fill the bottom by pressing out the mixture in spiral-form and covering the area within the drawn circle.

Place on the middle rack of an oven preheated to no higher than 225° and allow to dry, more than bake, for 3½ hours. During this process the oven should be kept slightly open so that the steam can escape. Remove the torte bottom from the oven, carefully turn it over, moisten the parchment paper slightly and peel off. Place the bottom on a rack and allow to dry again.

Prepare gelatin according to package directions with a little water. For the filling, wash raspberries, remove stems and drain well. If frozen berries are used, cover with schnapps and allow to thaw. Combine egg yolks, sugar and white wine in a bowl and beat well, then place in a hot, but not boiling, water bath. Beat until the sugar is dissolved and the mixture is thick and foamy. Be careful not to boil it. Remove from the hot water, add the prepared gelatin and dissolve while stirring constantly. Beat in a cold water bath until the mixture has cooled.

Press raspberries (retaining a few for decoration), through a sieve and then separately press 4 peeled kiwis through the sieve. Any raspberry seeds remaining in the sieve should be removed, kiwi seeds should not. Whip 2½ cups of cream until stiff and gently fold into the egg mixture. Divide this into three portions. Mix the first with raspberry puree and spread onto the meringue bottom around the enclosed rim of the springform pan.

Allow to stiffen somewhat in the freezer, just until the cream surface has become hard. Then fill in the light-colored cream (without fruit) and allow it to stiffen. Fold the kiwi puree into the third portion of cream and fill in to make the third layer. Freeze the torte for about 6 hours. Decorate the torte using the remaining whipped cream and fruit.

Frozen Chocolate Meringue Torte with Walnut Croquant

4 egg whites	2 teaspoons cocoa
Pinch of salt	1 teaspoon cognac
1⅓ cups sugar	1 teaspoon lemon juice
1 teaspoon instant coffee	

For the walnut croquant:

Oil for greasing	13 walnut halves
⅔ cup sugar	1½ cups chopped walnuts

For the cream:

2 eggs	2 tablespoons cognac
2 egg yolks	2 tablespoons Crème de
1 teaspoon vanilla	Cacao
3 tablespoons water	3 cups whipping cream
½ cup sugar	Dark chocolate

In a bowl, combine egg whites with salt and beat until firm. Then gradually sprinkle in sugar. When sufficiently beaten the egg whites should be quite thick and shiny. Dissolve coffee and cocoa in cognac and fold in with lemon juice. Line 1-2 baking sheets (depending on size), with parchment paper and draw two 10-inch circles on them.

Fill the meringue into a pastry bag with a large star spout and press out in a spiral-form into the circles to make the torte bottoms.

Place bottoms in an oven preheated to 225° for 4-5 hours and allow to dry more than bake. Moisten paper and peel off, place on a rack and allow to cool.

For the walnut croquant, brush a piece of aluminum foil with oil. Then line a baking sheet with aluminum foil and brush it with oil as well. Melt sugar in a frying pan and, as soon as it becomes light yellow, drop in the 13 walnut halves. Turn them once and immediately remove one after the other. Allow to cool on aluminum foil.

Immediately drop chopped walnuts into the pan. Stir vigorously. Then spread this mixture out onto the large piece of aluminum foil. Allow to harden. Then remove croquant from foil, place in a plastic bag and crush with a rolling pin.

For the cream, combine eggs, egg yolks, vanilla and water in a bowl and beat until light and foamy. Place in a hot, not boiling, water bath and sprinkle in sugar while continuing to beat.

As soon as the mixture is thick and very creamy, remove from the hot water bath and place in a cold one. Continue to beat until mixture has cooled off but is still thick. Flavor with cognac and Crème de Cacoa.

Whip 2 cups of whipping cream until stiff and fold into the egg-cream mixture together with the croquant crumbs. Enclose the meringue bottom in the rim of the springform pan. Fill in the cream. Place the second meringue layer on top and freeze the torte for about 6 hours. Remove the springform rim. Using a pastry bag with the remaining whipped cream, decorate the torte by pressing out whipped cream following the spiral of the meringue layer. Then trim with walnuts and crumbled dark chocolate.

Meringues

4 egg whites
Pinch of salt
3 cups plus 2 tablespoons
   powdered sugar
2 teaspoons lemon juice

Combine egg whites and salt in a bowl. Whisk together and beat until firm. Continue beating while gradually sprinkling in sugar. Only add a small quantity of sugar at a time so that the meringue does not liquify. It should be very firm and shiny. Beat in lemon juice: lemon juice provides additional stability on the one hand, on the other it tempers the sweetness a bit and gives the meringues a fresh aroma.

Fill the meringue into a pastry bag with a star spout and line a baking sheet with aluminum foil. With the pastry bag, press out egg-sized, round dots of meringue onto the aluminum foil. Place on the middle rack of an oven preheated to 225° and allow to dry, more than bake, for 4-5 hours. Avoid allowing the temperature to rise since the meringues will already begin to brown at 250°. Furthermore, it takes quite a while before the centers have dried out and become light and airy. Carefully remove the meringues from the foil, they break easily, and allow to "steam off" on a rack. If desired, they can be placed in the lukewarm oven again. Then allow them to cool completely. Store in a cool and very dry place until serving.

Pink Meringue Shells

4 very fresh egg whites   1¼ cups powdered sugar
Pinch of salt   2 teaspoons lemon juice
¾ cup sugar
Several drops of red food
   coloring

Combine egg whites with salt and beat until firm. Gradually sprinkle in the sugar. It is essential to continue beating until the sugar is completely dissolved. Add the food coloring and blend until the meringue is an even pink color throughout. Gradually sprinkle in the powdered sugar while beating constantly. Beat until the meringue is firm and gleaming. Mix in the lemon juice. Place the meringue in a pastry bag with a large star spout. Line a baking sheet with aluminum foil and press out in the form of spirals 2 inches wide and 4 inches long. Place on the middle rack on an oven preheated to 225° for 4-5 hours and allow to dry more than bake. Immediately remove the meringues from the foil and carefully press in the undersides with a tablespoon. Then allow the shells to cool on a rack. Fill just before serving.

As a filling, various flavors of ice cream can be used (either homemade or commercial) and, if desired, top it with whipped cream. Meringue shells also taste delicious with fruit and whipped cream.

> **Tip:** *Try glazing these meringue shells with melted chocolate. In order to do this, the shells must have cooled completely and the chocolate must also have cooled to such a point that it is just barely a liquid, since chocolate that is too warm will melt the meringue's surface. In order to glaze the shells, lay them on a rack, pour the chocolate over them and allow the excess to drip off onto a piece of parchment paper or aluminum foil that has been placed underneath. The excess chocolate can be removed from the paper after it has hardened and be reused.*

Saffron Meringues

4 egg whites   3 cups plus 2 tablespoons
Pinch of salt   powdered sugar
Pinch of saffron   2 teaspoons lemon juice
1 teaspoon water

Combine egg whites with salt in a large bowl. Dissolve saffron in water, add to egg-white mixture and stir. Beat until completely firm and then sprinkle in sugar in small quantities while beating constantly so that the meringue does not liquify. As soon as it is firm and shiny, beat in the lemon juice and fill the meringue into a pastry bag with a star spout. Line a baking sheet with aluminum foil and press out ping-pong-ball-sized dots of meringue. Place on the middle rack of an oven preheated to 225° and allow to dry, more than bake, for 4-5 hours. Immediately remove the saffron meringues from the foil and cool on a rack.

Variation

Lemon-Saffron Meringues: Together with the lemon juice beat in the grated rind of a lemon or sprinkle the surfaces of the meringues with some thin slivers of lemon rind. These meringues are wonderfully delicious when served together with lemon sherbert adorned with only very slightly sweetened or completely unsweetened whipped cream.

Coconut Macaroons glazed with Chocolate

2 egg whites
Pinch of salt
½ cup sugar
2 teaspoons vanilla

3½ cups grated coconut
1½ ounces bittersweet
   chocolate

In a bowl, combine egg whites with salt and beat until firm. Gradually sprinkle in sugar and beat until it is quite firm and has a healthy shine. Gently but thoroughly fold in vanilla and then coconut. Line a baking sheet with aluminum foil. Using two teaspoons, drop small dollops of meringue with a curl on the top onto the foil. Place on the middle rack of an oven preheated to 250° and bake for 35-40 minutes until golden and crispy. Remove from foil and place on a rack to cool. Melt chocolate in a double boiler over low heat. Place in a parchment-paper pastry bag and decorate the macaroons with very thin ribbons of chocolate. Leave macaroons on the rack until the chocolate has cooled and solidified completely.

Cinnamon-Hazelnut Macaroons

2½ cups shelled hazelnuts
¼-½ teaspoon ground
   cinnamon
3 egg whites

Pinch of salt
1⅓ cups sugar
1 teaspoon lemon juice

Spread hazelnuts onto a dry baking sheet and roast on the middle rack of an oven preheated to 400°-425° for 10-15 minutes until the brown skins can be rubbed off effortlessly. Drop the nuts into a towel and rub until all of the skins are removed. Cool and then grind in an almond mill. (The nuts must have cooled completely before grinding otherwise they will clog the grating surface.) Then combine ground nuts with cinnamon.

In a bowl, combine egg whites with salt and beat until firm. Gradually sprinkle in sugar. Then subsequently mix in lemon juice and gently fold in hazelnuts. Line a baking sheet with aluminum foil and, using two teaspoons, drop small round dollops onto the foil. Place on the middle rack of an oven preheated to 250°-275° and dry, more than bake, for about 60 minutes. Remove from foil and cool on a rack.

> **Tip:** *The macaroon mixture can be made stiffer by adding additional ground hazelnuts. This will enable balls to be formed rather than dollops. Place these on foil and top each with a whole hazelnut.*

Mocha Meringues

4 egg whites
Pinch of salt
3 cups plus 2 tablespoons
   powdered sugar

2-3 tablespoons cocoa
1 tablespoon instant coffee
2 teaspoons lemon juice

In a bowl, whisk together egg whites and salt. Gradually sprinkle in sugar while beating constantly. Continue beating until meringue is shiny and quite firm. Sift cocoa over mix and gently but thoroughly fold in. Dissolve instant coffee in lemon juice, then beat into the meringue. Fill into a pastry bag with a medium star spout and line a baking sheet with aluminum foil. Press out dots of meringue having a 1½-inch diameter. Place on the middle rack of an oven preheated to 225° and dry, more than bake, for 4-5 hours. Remove from foil and cool on a rack. Allow them to dry more thoroughly before serving or before storing in a dry and spacious canister.

Variations

Mocha Meringues flavored with rum are a true delicacy. Dissolve instant coffee in lemon juice as described above and then mix in 1 teaspoon of rum extract. Continue as in the recipe above.

Almond extract or arrack extract can similarly be added if these aromas are preferred. If an intensive chocolate flavor is desired, glaze the meringues with melted bittersweet chocolate that has been allowed to cool or serve with chocolate-flavored whipping cream or ice cream.

If meringues are baked in advance, that is, if they are to be stored for a longer period of time, adding cornstarch can insure their keeping. When cornstarch is added they are less likely to be prone to softening because of high humidity; however, they will never be as delicate as "true" meringues. The addition of starch is often used when meringues are made for Christmas tree decorations, pressed out of a pastry bag in various decorative forms. Stars, hearts and wreaths are very popular since these are forms that can easily be hung on a string or ribbon without having to pierce the meringue.

Almond Meringue Torte with Exotic Fruits

5 egg whites
Pinch of salt
3-3½ cups powdered sugar
1 teaspoon vanilla
1 teaspoon lemon juice

1⅔-2 cups skinless, ground
  almonds
Butter for greasing
Flour for dusting

For the filling and trimming:
½ pound fresh kumquats
½ cup water
¼ cup sugar
3 tablespoons white rum

2 kiwis
1 ¼-ounce package gelatin
½ cup whipping cream
1 teaspoon vanilla

For the meringue, combine egg whites with salt in a bowl and beat until firm. Gradually sprinkle in about ⅔ of the sugar while beating constantly. As soon as this mixture is very firm and shiny, mix in vanilla and lemon juice.

Combine ground almonds with remaining sugar and gently but thoroughly fold into the meringue. Line a baking sheet with parchment paper, draw a circle measuring 10-inches in diameter in the middle, then grease and lightly flour this area. Fill the almond-meringue mixture into a pastry bag with a large, smooth spout and press out the pastry in spiral form filling the circle. Smooth out the surface with a knife or a spatula and with the remaining meringue press out dots around the rim.

Place on the middle rack of an oven preheated to 225° for 3½-4 hours and allow to dry, more than bake. If baking in a conventional oven, leave the door slightly ajar (simply leave it pried open with a wooden spoon handle); if a convector oven is used this is not necessary since the bottom will dry faster anyway.

Remove the cake from the oven, carefully turn over and very quickly brush the paper with cold water. Peel off paper, then place the cake bottom upright on a rack to dry and cool.

Quickly brush off kumquats under hot water, dry and halve. In a saucepan, bring water, sugar and rum to a boil. Add kumquats, cover and bring to a boil again. As soon as the liquid bubbles again, remove from the heat and allow the kumquats to stew for another 5 minutes. Then remove them with a slotted spoon, drain briefly, place them on a plate and very briefly allow them to cool.

Peel the kiwis and slice them to the same thickness as the kumquats. Lay fruit out on the cake bottom in a circular form alternating kumquats and kiwis. Be sure to retain a few pieces of each for decorating.

Dissolve gelatin in a small amount of water. Combine the syrup used for the kumquats with enough water (or, if desired, white wine or white rum) to make 1 cup of liquid. Bring to a boil and pour in the dissolved gelatin. Bring to a boil while stirring constantly, then allow to cool briefly. Shortly before the liquid is completely stiff, evenly pour out a smooth layer over the fruit and allow to stiffen completely.

Whip cream with vanilla until stiff. Place into a pastry bag with a star spout and decorate the rim of the torte with it. Cut the remaining fruit into small pieces and place these on the peaks of cream. Serve the torte immediately.

Meringue Tartlets with Hazelnut Ice Cream

5 egg whites
Pinch of salt
3-3½ cups powdered sugar
1 teaspoon lemon juice

2½-3 cups ground hazelnuts
Butter for greasing
Flour for dusting

For the filling and trimming:
4½ ounces bittersweet
  chocolate
1 cup whipping cream
2 tablespoons cocoa liqueur
  or cognac
3 scoops vanilla ice cream
Powdered sugar for dusting

For the meringue, prepare all ingredients as in the previous recipe using hazelnuts instead of almonds. Line a baking sheet with parchment paper, grease and flour lightly. Draw 3-inch circles on it. Fill the meringue-nut mixture into a pastry bag with a small, smooth spout and press out a spiral filling each circle. If desired, the surface can be smoothed out and the remaining meringue pressed out onto the rims of the tartlets.

Place the tartlets on the middle rack of an oven preheated to 225° for about 2 hours to dry more than bake.

Carefully turn the tartlets out onto a towel, brush the paper with cold water and peel off. Turn the tartlets right side up and carefully lay on a rack to cool and dry further.

While the tartlets are in the oven, crumble the chocolate into the whipping cream and melt over very low heat. Then refrigerate for 3 hours until ice cold. Before serving, add liqueur or cognac to chocolate cream and whip until stiff. Place ⅓ of the cream in a pastry bag with a star spout and smooth out the rest onto the tartlets. Place one scoop of vanilla ice cream in the middle of each tartlet and decorate with peaks of chocolate-cream. Very lightly dust with powdered sugar and serve immediately.

> **Tip:** *For the torte as well as the tartlets fill the cream into the drawn circles with a spoon and then smooth it out; however, it is then much more difficult to distribute the meringue evenly. Thus, it is possible that the tartlets will dry out unevenly.*

Champagne Meringue Torte with Pureed Fruit

4 egg whites
Pinch of salt
1⅓ cups sugar
2 teaspoons lemon juice

For the filling and trimming:

1½ ¼-ounce packages gelatin	Pinch of salt
4 egg yolks	1 cup whipping cream
½ cup sugar	3 canned peach halves
1 teaspoon vanilla	2 cups raspberries (fresh or
1 cup champagne	frozen)
Juice of 1 lemon	2 kiwis
2 egg whites	

Combine egg whites and salt in a bowl and beat until stiff. Then, while beating constantly, gradually sprinkle in sugar. In doing this the egg-white foam must remain very firm. Finally add in lemon juice. Line a baking sheet with parchment paper. Draw a circle on it measuring 10-inches in diameter. Place the meringue into a pastry bag with a smooth spout and press out ⅔ of it in spiral form into the circle starting from the outside and working to the middle. If desired, the meringue bottom can be smoothed out with a knife. Using the remaining meringue, press out dollops around the outer edge to make an outside rim. Be sure to place the dollops of meringue close enough to each other so that the filling cannot leak out later. Place the meringue torte on the middle rack of an oven preheated to 225° and allow to

dry, more than bake, for 3½-5 hours depending on the humidity. Leave the door pried open with the handle of a wooden spoon. Remove the torte, peel off the paper and allow the torte to cool.

Dissolve the gelatin according to package directions. Whisk together egg yolks, sugar, vanilla, champagne and lemon juice. Beat in a hot, but not boiling, water bath until the cream is thick and white. Add the gelatin to the mixture and beat until well dissolved. Then remove from the hot bath and place in a cold one. Allow to cool while stirring frequently. Then place in the refrigerator and allow to gel.

In separate bowls, beat egg whites with salt until stiff and whipping cream until firm. Fold both into the cream as soon as it begins to "streak." Cool briefly, then spread out onto the bottom of the torte. Puree each of the fruits, peaches, raspberries and peeled kiwis separately and distribute them onto the cream in large splotches. Using a spoon, spread these out in spiral form so that the individual purees run into one another and so that the cream is also stirred into the fruit purees. Refrigerate until the cream stiffens.

Curved Almond Wafers

1 cup ground almonds
1½ tablespoons flour
⅓ cup sliced almonds
3 egg whites
Pinch of salt

1¾ cups powdered sugar
Pinch of ground cinnamon
1 small egg yolk
1 teaspoon vanilla
Butter for greasing

Gently combine ground almonds and flour. Chop the sliced almonds slightly so that the pieces become smaller. Combine egg whites and salt and beat until half firm. Sprinkle in sugar and cinnamon. Fold in almond-flour mixture, egg yolk and vanilla and stir until a very soft and runny mixture is created. Place into a pastry bag with a smooth spout measuring ½ inch or less. Generously grease a baking sheet with butter and press out walnut-sized balls of dough onto the sheet leaving a distance of 3 inches between each one. Sprinkle with the chopped, sliced almonds. Bake in an oven preheated to 350° for 8-10 minutes. The cookies should be light brown on the edges when done.

Remove the baking sheet from the oven and lift the cookies off with a spatula. Wrap the cookie around a rolling pin, the neck of a bottle or a high, narrow glass, and allow to cool. It is essential to work very quickly at this stage. As soon as the cookies have cooled off they will break if any effort is made to shape them. In order to curve them, they should be taken directly from the baking sheet without having had a chance to cool off.

Almond Sticks

2 egg whites
Pinch of salt
1½ cups powdered sugar
1 teaspoon vanilla

1 cup ground almonds
½ cup chopped almonds
3 ounces milk chocolate

Beat egg whites with salt until stiff. Add sugar by the spoonful while beating constantly. Then add vanilla. Gently fold in ground almonds with a wooden spoon. Place in a pastry bag with a smooth spout measuring 1 inch in diameter. Line a baking sheet with parchment paper and press out rods about 1½ inches long. Sprinkle with chopped almonds. Place in an oven preheated to 225°-250° for 40 minutes and dry more than bake the cookies. Cool on a rack.

Melt the chocolate in a double boiler and dip each end of the "sticks" into it.

Strudels

Cheese Strudel

2½ cups sifted cake flour
Pinch of salt
2 tablespoons butter

½ cup water
½ teaspoon vinegar

For the filling and topping:
1 cup bread crumbs
⅓ cup plus 1 tablespoon
   butter
½ cup sugar
1 teaspoon vanilla
2 egg yolks
Grated rind of ½ lemon
1 cup ricotta or cottage
   cheese

⅔ cup crème fraîche
½ cup finely ground almonds
⅔ cup raisins
Flour for rolling out
Butter for greasing and
   brushing
½ cup whipping cream
2 tablespoons sugar

Put flour into a bowl, make a well in the middle and pour in salt and butter. Gradually add water and vinegar and knead into a very smooth and pliable dough. Form into a ball and continue to throw it onto the work surface until no more lumps of flour or bubbles can be seen. The dough must be completely smooth, homogeneous and elastic. Place in a dry, hot pan (boil a large quantity of water in the pan before using), cover and allow to rest for 60 minutes.

In the meantime, while stirring constantly, roast the bread crumbs in 2 tablespoons of butter until golden. Then remove from heat and allow to cool. Cream the remaining softened butter, sugar, vanilla, egg yolks and lemon rind. Gradually add ricotta or cottage cheese and crème fraîche and continue to cream until the sugar has dissolved. Finally sprinkle the ground almonds over the cheese mixture. Wash the raisins in hot water and rub dry with a towel. Sprinkle them over the cheese mixture as well, then fold in almonds and raisins.

On a large, lightly floured cloth (a tablecloth works best), roll out the dough as thin as possible. Then, using both hands, pull it until it is almost transparent. In order to do this, place both hands, palms open, under the dough and extend it as far as possible. Cut off the thick rim that remains on the outside edges since it will become too hard during baking. Distribute the roasted bread crumbs over the dough leaving the outer edges free of crumbs. Then spread the cheese mixture over the crumbs; here, too, refrain from covering the outer 2 inches with filling. Fold the outside edges over the filling and then, with the aid of the tablecloth, roll up the strudel. Finally, press the ends of the dough together well. Grease a frying pan or a broiling pan with butter. With the aid of the cloth, slide the strudel into the pan bending it into a horseshoe shape. Place low in the oven, on the second rack from the bottom, and bake at a preheated temperature of 350°-400° for 45-50 minutes. After 30-40 minutes of baking time, stir together whipping cream and sugar. Repeatedly brush this mixture over the surface of the strudel and allow to caramelize. Remove strudel from the oven and serve immediately. Though it tastes best while still warm, it is also delicious cold.

Cherry and Rice Strudel

For the filling and topping:
1 cup milk
1 vanilla bean
6 tablespoons sugar
2 tablespoons butter
Grated rind of ½ lemon
½ cup short- or medium-
   grain rice
2 egg yolks
3-4 tablespoons Kirsch

⅔ cup sliced almonds
1 egg white
Pinch of salt
1 12-ounce jar or can sour
   cherries
5 tablespoons whipping cream
¼ cup sugar
½-1 teaspoon ground
   cinnamon

For the dough:
2½ cups sifted cake flour
Pinch of salt
3 tablespoons oil
½ cup water

½ teaspoon vinegar
¼ cup butter for brushing and
   greasing
Flour for rolling out

For the filling, bring the milk, the marrow of the vanilla bean and the empty pod, the sugar, butter and grated lemon rind to a boil. Meanwhile, in a sieve wash rice under cold running water until the drained-off water runs clear. Drain, then pour into the milk mixture. Again bring to a boil while stirring constantly, then simmer over very low heat for 45 minutes until almost tender. Remove from heat. Combine egg yolks and Kirsch with some of the rice, then mix together with remaining rice. Allow to cool. In a frying pan, roast almonds until golden and allow to cool.

Prepare the dough. Place flour into a bowl, make a well in the middle and pour salt, oil, water and vinegar into it. Work the dough as in the previous recipe and allow to rest for 60 minutes so that the flour can swell. Then, as above, pull out the dough until it is paper-thin and brush with melted butter. Sprinkle with almonds.

Whip egg white and salt until stiff and fold into the rice pudding together with the well-drained cherries. Spread out onto the dough leaving a 2-inch wide margin around the edge free of filling. Fold the edges over the filling and roll up the strudel as above. Slide into a well-greased frying or broiling pan and brush the surface with butter. Bake on the middle rack of an oven preheated to 425° for 30-35 minutes. Stir together cream, sugar and cinnamon and brush onto the strudel 10 minutes before the baking time is finished. Serve warm or cold.

Baklava

4½ cups sifted cake flour
Pinch of salt
4 eggs

3 tablespoons oil
½ cup water
½ teaspoon vinegar

For the filling and topping:
¾ cup walnuts
½ cup skinless almonds
¾ cup pistachios
6 tablespoons sugar
1 teaspoon ground cinnamon
⅓ cup butter
Flour for rolling out

Butter for greasing
⅓ cup butter
½ cup honey
Juice of 1 lemon
Grated rind of ½ lemon
Grated rind of ½ orange

For the dough, place flour into a bowl, make a well in the middle and pour in salt, eggs, oil, water and vinegar. Knead all ingredients into a smooth dough and form into a ball. Vigorously throw it onto the work surface until no more air bubbles or lumps of flour are visible when it is cut through with a knife.

Form the dough into a ball again and place in a dry, hot pan (boil water in it beforehand). Allow to rest for 60 minutes so that the flour can swell.

Meanwhile, prepare the filling. Coarsely chop each of the different kinds of nuts separately. Combine sugar with cinnamon and cut the butter into flakes. Halve the dough. Roll out one half on a large, floured tablecloth until it is as thin as possible. Then, with palms of hands extended, pull out the dough as far as

possible until it is transparent. The design on the tablecloth should be seen through it; or, better yet, a newspaper should be able to be read through it. Cut the dough into 8 squares of equal size that are somewhat larger than the flat, rectangular roasting pan in which the strudel is to be baked. Prepare the second half of dough in the same way.

Grease the pan well with butter and place 4 layers of dough into it so that the ends overlap slightly. Distribute the chopped walnuts evenly over the dough and sprinkle with ⅓ of the cinnamon-sugar and butter flakes. Cover again with 4 layers of dough and sprinkle with almonds, cinnamon-sugar and butter flakes. Sprinkle the next 4 layers of dough with pistachios, cinnamon-sugar and butter flakes and then cover with the remaining layers of dough. Cut the cake into 16 pieces with a sharp, pointed knife and pour melted butter over it. Bake on the middle rack of an oven preheated to 425° for 45 minutes. Remove from the oven, carefully pour off excess butter and mix it with heated honey, lemon juice and grated orange and lemon rind. Repeatedly pour over the strudel until it is saturated.

Fig and Raisin Strudel

2½ cups sifted cake flour
Pinch of salt
3 tablespoons oil
½ cup water

½ teaspoon vinegar
Flour for rolling out
Butter for greasing

For the filling and topping:
1 cup dried figs
⅔ cup raisins
½ cup rum
⅔ cup honey
5 tablespoons whipping cream
2 egg yolks
Pinch of salt

Pinch of ground cinnamon
Pinch of ground mace
Butter for greasing
1-2 tablespoons bread crumbs
⅔ cup ground almonds
Powdered sugar for dusting

For the dough, make a well in the flour and pour in salt and oil. Gradually pour in water together with vinegar and knead all ingredients into a smooth dough. Then "throw" it vigorously onto the work surface until air bubbles and lumps of flour are no longer visible when it is cut open. Form into a ball and place on a piece of parchment paper. Cover with a hot, dry pan (boil a large quantity of water in the pan beforehand and then dry it well), and allow it to rest so that the flour can swell. Roll it out on a lightly floured tablecloth and then pull it out further with the back of outstretched hands until it is almost transparent.

While the dough is resting, prepare the filling. Dice the figs finely. Wash raisins in hot water and rub dry with a towel. Combine figs and raisins with rum, cover and allow to soak. Heat the honey until it becomes liquid. Remove from heat and allow to cool slightly. Then stir in cream, egg yolks and spices. Drain figs and raisins, retain the excess rum and mix it with the honey mixture. Brush the strudel dough thinly with melted butter and evenly sprinkle with bread crumbs. Brush the honey mixture over it leaving the edges free of filling. Mix raisins, figs and ground almonds and distribute evenly over the strudel. Now, fold in the edges of the dough and roll up the strudel with the aid of the tablecloth. Slide onto a greased baking sheet and bake on the middle rack of an oven preheated to 400° for 30 minutes. Remove and immediately dust with powdered sugar.

Tip: *Instead of figs, try dried dates for the filling. Or make a mixture of various dried fruits, like raisins, dates, candied lemon and orange rind, candied cherries and pineapple. Other dried fruit, like apples, appricots, pears and prunes will also produce an exquisite strudel.*

Apple Strudel

3¼ cups sifted cake flour
Generous pinch of salt
3 tablespoons oil
½ cup water

½-1 teaspoon vinegar
Flour for rolling out
Butter for brushing and
  greasing

For the filling and trimming:
⅓ cup plus 1 tablespoon
  butter
¾ cup bread crumbs
⅔ cup raisins
2½ pounds tart apples
Juice of 1 lemon

½-⅓ cup sugar (depending
  on the tartness of the
  apples)
1-2 teaspoons ground
  cinnamon
Powdered sugar for dusting

Place flour on a work surface or into a large, flat bowl. Make a well in the middle and pour in salt together with oil, water and vinegar. Starting in the middle and working outward, stir all the ingredients together. With the other hand, press the flour into a high wall so that none of the liquid can run out. Then knead the dough thoroughly working from the outside to the inside. It must be completely smooth and soft, but may no longer be sticky. Form into a ball and vigorously throw the dough onto the table top. Now and again test it by cutting the ball with a sharp knife to see whether lumps of flour or air bubbles are visible. If none are apparent, the dough has reached the correct consistency. Knead it into a ball again and allow it to rest. For this, boil water in a pot, empty the pot, dry it and place it upside down over the dough. Allow to rest for 30 minutes, so that the flour can swell and the dough becomes elastic.

Meanwhile, prepare the filling. Melt ⅔ of the butter in a pan and, stirring constantly, roast the bread crumbs in it until golden brown. Remove from heat and allow to cool.

Wash the raisins in hot water and dry well with a towel. Peel, quarter, core apples and cut into thin slices. Immediately sprinkle with lemon juice to avoid discoloration. Combine sugar and cinnamon and set aside.

Place a cloth, preferably a tablecloth, on an open surface. Flatten the dough and roll it out in all directions as thin as possible. Then rub hands with flour and place them close to each other under the dough. Starting at the middle, pull the dough toward body until fingers are clearly visible. (An old saying has it that a good strudel dough is one in which a newspaper can be read through.) The dough may thus hang over the sides of the work surface if necessary. Finally, use scissors to cut off any remaining thick edges that can not extend any further.

Brush the dough with melted butter and evenly sprinkle with roasted bread crumbs. Mix the raisins and apples, similarly distribute over the dough and finally sprinkle with cinnamon-sugar. A 2-inch edge all around the strudel should remain free of all filling. Fold the side edges over the filling and press gently. Fold the nearest edge onto the filling and then, using the cloth underneath, gently lift and pull up at an angle so that the dough slowly slides down rolling over the filling. Hold the cloth by the

sides and allow the strudel to roll off of it onto a greased baking sheet. Brush the surface with melted butter and bake the strudel on the middle rack of an oven preheated to 400° for 40-45 minutes. Frequently brush with butter during baking so that it becomes golden brown and crispy.

Remove from the oven and dust with powdered sugar. Serve warm or cold.

Note

Warm apple strudel tastes delicious with a vanilla sauce. A cold strudel, however, tastes better with sweetened whipped cream flavored with vanilla extract. But, whether cold or warm, apple strudel tastes heavenly with crème fraîche.

Variations

Apple Strudel with Nuts: Combine chopped or sliced hazelnuts or almonds with the apples and distribute over the dough. Or use coarsely chopped walnuts. Instead of bread crumbs, crumbled almond macaroons can be used. Since they don't have to be roasted in butter, the dough can more generously be brushed with butter.

Old Viennese Apple Strudel: Before rolling up the dough, spread lightly whipped cream or up to 1 cup of stirred sour cream onto the apples and then sprinkle ½-⅔ cup of coarsely grated nuts over it.

Bavarian Apple Strudel: Place the strudel in a long narrow baking pan or in a broiling pan instead of on a baking sheet. Then pour up to 1 cup of milk or cream over it and bake as usual.

Tip: *Of course, other fruits can be "strudeled" in using this recipe. Try blue plums, sour cherries, apricots or tart pears.*

Prune Strudel

3¼ cups sifted cake flour
Generous pinch of salt
3 tablespoons oil
½ cup water

½-1 teaspoon vinegar
Flour for rolling out
Butter for brushing and
   greasing

For the filling:
½ pound prunes
2 cups tepid water
Rind of ½ lemon
4-6 tablespoons plum
   schnapps
⅔ cup ricotta or cottage
   cheese
3 egg yolks
Pinch of salt

6 tablespoons sugar
½ teaspoon ground cinnamon
½ teaspoon almond extract
3 egg whites
½ cup butter
½ cup sliced or chopped
   almonds
1¾ cups powdered sugar

About 1 hour before baking this strudel, place the prunes in water to soak and swell.

Make a well in the middle of the flour. Pour in salt, oil, water, and vinegar and mix, working from the middle to the outside. Then working from the outside to the inside, knead into a completely smooth dough. After all ingredients have been mixed together evenly, throw the ball of dough repeatedly onto the work surface so that all the air bubbles and lumps of flour are removed. Form the dough into a ball again and cover with a hot pot. Allow the dough to rest for 30 minutes.

Stew the prunes in their soaking water. Add washed, thinly peeled or grated lemon rind and briefly bring to a boil. Remove from heat, allow the stewed prunes to cool slightly and then drain in a sieve. Cut the prunes into strips and cover with 3-4 tablespoons of plum schnapps. Cover the bowl or pan with a lid and allow to soak. Combine ricotta or cottage cheese with egg yolks, salt, sugar, cinnamon and almond extract and stir thoroughly. Also set this mixture aside so that the sugar can dissolve completely.

Cover a table with a large tablecloth. Dust the cloth lightly with flour and roll out the strudel dough as thinly as possible. Then, with lightly floured hands, pull the dough out in all directions so that it becomes transparent. Cut off the thicker dough edges with scissors.

Beat egg whites until stiff and add to the cheese mixture together with the butter, almonds and stewed prunes. Any excess alcohol should also be added and all ingredients folded in gently. Brush the dough with melted butter and spread the filling onto it leaving a 2-inch outside edge free of filling. Fold the edges over the filling and press lightly. Lift up the edge of dough nearest the body and fold it over the filling as well. Then roll up the strudel with the aid of the cloth.

Grease a baking sheet and, with the aid of the cloth, lay the strudel on it in the form of a horseshoe. Brush the strudel with butter and bake on the middle rack of an oven preheated to 400° for about 40 minutes. During that time brush the surface once or twice with butter. Remove from the oven and cool slightly. Stir together powdered sugar and remaining plum schnapps and glaze the cake with it.

Poppy Seed Strudel

3 tablespoons shortening
3¼ cups sifted cake flour
Generous pinch of salt
1 egg yolk
4-5 tablespoons water

1 teaspoon vinegar
Flour for rolling out
Butter for brushing and
   greasing

For the filling and decoration:
2 cups ground poppy seeds
1 cup milk
¼ cup semolina
6 tablespoons sugar
1 teaspoon vanilla
Pinch of ground cloves
Pinch of ground nutmeg
¼ teaspoon almond extract

⅔ cup raisins
⅔ cup chopped almonds
2 egg yolks
2 egg whites
Pinch of salt
¾ cup whipping cream
Powdered sugar for dusting

Melt shortening and cool until lukewarm. Place flour and salt on a work surface or into a large, flat bowl. Make a well in the middle. In a separate bowl, combine egg yolk with water and the lukewarm shortening and beat with a fork until a homogeneous mixture is obtained. Stir in vinegar. Pour this liquid into the well and work all the ingredients into a smooth dough as above. Similarly throw the dough and then allow it to rest.

For the filling, place the poppy seeds in a bowl and cover with boiling water. Allow to soak for 5 minutes. Then stretch a cloth over the bowl, pour the poppy seeds into it and gently press out excess water. In a saucepan, bring the milk to a boil, sprinkle in semolina while stirring constantly. Simmer for 30 minutes, adding the poppy seeds after 15-20 minutes. Also stir in sugar, vanilla, spices and flavors. Wash the raisins in hot water and rub dry with a towel. Allow them to soak briefly in the poppy-seed mixture. Finally stir in the chopped almonds and egg yolks. Remove pan from heat and cool mixture slightly. Roll out the dough as far as possible, until it becomes transparent. Brush with melted butter. Beat egg whites and salt until firm, fold into poppy-seed mixture and spread filling onto the dough. Fold in the four edges and form the strudel as usual. Place in a greased frying or roasting pan, brush with melted butter, and bake on the middle rack of an oven preheated to 400° for about 50 minutes. Spread the whipping cream onto the strudel after about 35 minutes.

Dust with powdered sugar.

Apricot Strudel

3¼ cups sifted cake flour
Pinch of salt
1 egg yolk
3 tablespoons butter

1 teaspoon vanilla
4-5 tablespoons lukewarm
    water
½ teaspoon vinegar

For the filling and topping:
¾ pound fresh apricots or 2,
    15-ounce cans of apricots
½ cup white wine
1 7-ounce package marzipan
1 cup powdered sugar
Juice of 1 lemon
½ cup apricot jam

Flour for rolling
⅓ cup butter
3 tablespoons bread crumbs
Butter or margarine for
    greasing
5 tablespoons whipping cream
2 tablespoons apricot jam

For the dough, combine salt with flour in a bowl. Make a well in the middle and place egg yolk, butter in flakes, vanilla, water and vinegar in it. Knead all ingredients into a smooth dough. Repeatedly throw it onto a work surface until no more air bubbles or lumps of flour are visible. Form into a ball, lay it on a piece of parchment paper and cover with a hot dry bowl. Allow to rest for about 60 minutes.

For the filling, wash, dry, halve and pit apricots. Bring wine to a boil in a saucepan and drop in apricot halves. Simmer gently for 5 minutes. Drain in a sieve, retaining the liquid, and allow to cool. If canned apricots are used, simply drain them and retain the liquid.

Combine the marzipan with powdered sugar, lemon juice, apricot jam and some white-wine brew or apricot juice out of the can and mix into a spreadable batter.

Cover a work surface with a large cloth and lightly flour it. Roll out the strudel dough until it is as thin as possible, then extend it even further by hand. Cut off any thick edges with scissors.

Melt butter over low heat, cool until lukewarm, then brush some of it onto the dough. Sprinkle with bread crumbs, then spread dough with marzipan batter and the well-drained apricots, which can be chopped if desired. Leave the outer edges of dough free of filling and fold them in over the filling. Roll up the strudel with the aid of the cloth and slide it onto a well-greased baking sheet. Bend it into a horseshoe form. Brush generously with remaining butter and bake on the middle rack of an oven preheated to 400° for 45-55 minutes. After 10 minutes of baking time spread the whipping cream over the strudel. Meanwhile stir the apricot jam until smooth, if necessary add a few drops of hot water. About 10 minutes before the strudel is done, brush the jam onto the surface and allow to caramelize slightly. Remove the strudel from the oven, allow to cool and then serve as soon as possible.

Strudel Pockets with Plum-Butter Filling

2½ cups sifted cake flour
Pinch of salt
3 tablespoons oil
4-6 tablespoons lukewarm
    water
½ teaspoon vinegar

For the filling:
3 tablespoons butter
1⅓ cups slivered almonds
2⅔ cups plum butter
3-4 tablespoons almond
    liqueur
Juice of 1 lemon
2 ounces sponge cookies

Flour for rolling
Butter or margarine for
    greasing and brushing
1 egg white
3-5 tablespoons whipping
    cream
Powdered sugar for dusting

Combine flour with salt in a bowl. Make a well in the middle and pour in oil, water and vinegar. Knead all ingredients into a smooth dough. Repeatedly throw the dough onto a work surface until air bubbles and lumps of flour are no longer visible. Form into a ball and place in a hot, dry pot, cover and leave to rest for 60 minutes so that the flour can swell.

Meanwhile, prepare the filling. Heat butter in a pan and roast almonds in it until golden brown. Remove from heat and allow to cool. Stir together plum butter, almond liqueur and lemon juice; then fold in cooled almonds. Place sponge cookies in a plastic bag and crumble them with a rolling pin. Divide the dough into portions and, on a lightly floured work surface, roll out 3-inch squares having a thickness of ¹⁄₁₆th of an inch. Sprinkle them first with crushed sponge cookies, then spread out the filling always leaving the outside edges free. Whisk the egg white and brush onto the dough edges. Fold into triangles. Place the strudel pockets on a greased baking sheet and brush with the cooled, melted butter. Bake on the middle rack of an oven preheated to 400° for 15-18 minutes. Shortly before the pockets are done brush them with whipping cream. Allow to cool on a rack and dust with powdered sugar.

Pear Strudel made of Puff Pastry

2 10-ounce packages frozen puff pastry	3 tablespoons sugar
2 ounces sponge cookies	1-2 tablespoons pear schnapps
2 ounces almond macaroons	⅛ teaspoon ground cinnamon
½ cup hot milk	3 tablespoons crumbled croquant
1½ pounds (ripe, but not too soft) pears	Flour for rolling
Juice of 1 lemon	Milk for brushing
1 cup ground almonds	Sugar for sprinkling

Remove puff pastry from package and thaw at room temperature. Meanwhile crumble sponge cookies and macaroons. Place in a bowl, cover with milk and allow to soak. Peel, core and slice pears. Immediately sprinkle with lemon juice. Add almonds, sugar, pear schnapps and cinnamon to the softened sponge-cookie mixture and mix well. Finally, gently fold in pear slices with the croquant.

Place all the layers of puff pastry on top of each other on a floured work surface and, while applying light but even pressure, press it out in waves to the size of a baking sheet. Spread the pear mixture onto it leaving all edges free. Then fold edges onto the filling. Carefully, but quickly, roll the puff paste into a strudel and form into a U-shape. Slide it onto a baking sheet that has been rinsed in cold water. Brush the surface of the strudel with milk and sprinkle thickly with sugar. Bake on the middle rack of an oven preheated to 400°-425° for 25-35 minutes until golden brown.

Remove the strudel from the oven and allow to settle a few minutes. Then slide it onto a rack to cool completely.

Note

To serve the Pear Strudel for dessert (which is recommended), serve it while still warm with a lightly sweetened or vanilla-flavored cream or crème fraîche. Whipped cream harmonizes with it well, too, especially if it is served with a few scoops of ice cream, some dark or grated chocolate or freshly grated nut chocolate.

> **Tip:** *To crumble sponge cookies and macaroons, place them in a pastic bag, close it well and then finely crush cookies with a rolling pin.*

Puff Pastry Strudel with Orange Filling

2 10-ounce packages frozen
    puff pastry
Flour for rolling

For the filling and topping:

2 ounces sponge cookies	2 tablespoons white rum
1 cup orange marmalade	4 oranges
1 tablespoon lemon juice	1 cup shelled pistachios
Juice of 2 oranges	1 egg yolk
2½ cups coconut	2 tablespoons milk
⅔ cup sugar (according to taste)	Powdered sugar for dusting

Lay out the layers of puff pastry and thaw according to package directions. On a lightly floured work surface, place puff pastry layers one on top of the other, dust again with flour and then, applying a slight amount of pressure, roll out thinly in all directions.

For the filling, place sponge cookies in a plastic bag and crush with a rolling pin. Stir marmalade with lemon and orange juice until smooth. Add coconut, sugar, rum and just enough crumbled sponge cookies to make the batter spreadable. Retain the remaining cookie crumbs. Evenly brush the marmalade mixture onto the dough leaving the edges uncoated. Sprinkle half of the remaining cookie crumbs over it. Peel and slice oranges. To do this, slide the point of a very sharp knife directly under the skins so that the individual sections fall out. Remove seeds and distribute slices over filling. Coarsely chop pistachios and sprinkle over filling together with remaining cookie crumbs. Fold the edges of the dough over the filling and then roll the strudel together as usual. Rinse a baking sheet with cold water and slide the strudel onto it. Refrigerate for 15 minutes. Whisk together egg yolk with milk, brush onto strudel and bake on the middle rack of an oven preheated to 400°-425° for about 35 minutes. Remove to a rack and allow to cool slightly. Generously dust with powdered sugar. Serve warm or cold.

> **Tip:** Puff pastry can easily be rolled and formed into a strudel when worked on lightly floured, double-strength aluminum foil. It will not stick to the work surface and can very easily be removed from the foil. Any variety of leftover sponge cake crumbs may be used instead of sponge cookies; however, be sure that whatever is used can bind the fruit juices sufficiently.

Puff
Pastries

Schiller's Curls

1 10-ounce package frozen puff pastry	Rock candy sugar for sprinkling, if desired
Flour for rolling out	1 cup whipping cream
1 egg yolk	1 teaspoon vanilla
1-2 tablespoons whipping cream or milk	

Lay out puff pastry layers next to one another and thaw according to package directions. Then place them, one on top of the other, on a lightly floured work surface. Applying gentle but even pressure, roll out a 12-inch square. Using a pizza cutter or a very sharp knife cut into 10 strips of equal breadth. Rinse a cream-curl or Schiller-curl form (available in metal at specialty shops) with cold water and also brush one of the long sides of the dough with cold water. Beginning at the tip of the form, wrap the curl around so that the wet side always overlaps slightly, which will later allow the seams of the curls to bake together. Lay the Schiller curls in their forms on a baking sheet that has been rinsed with cold water.

Whisk egg yolk with whipping cream or milk. Brush the upper surface of the curls with it and, if desired, sprinkle with rock candy sugar. Refrigerate for 10-15 minutes. Then bake on the middle rack of an oven preheated to 400°-425° for 10-15 minutes until golden brown. Immediately remove curls from their forms. If left in their forms, they will later stick to the metal and could possibly crumble. Place next to one another on a rack and allow to cool completely.

Combine cream and vanilla and whip until stiff. Fill into a pastry bag with a star spout and fill the completely cooled, but freshly baked, Schiller curls with it. These pastries taste best when fresh. Later the puff pastry becomes tender—as will any of the other pastries using this type of dough. Dust the Schiller curls generously with powdered sugar and serve immediately.

Tip: *Double strength aluminum foil can be substituted for Schiller or cream curl form. Using the bottom of a 10-inch springform pan, cut out 3 rounds and quarter them. Turn 10 of these quarters into cones and fill them with the remaining aluminum foil, torn into small pieces, in order to give them sufficient stability. These forms must also be rinsed with cold water before the strips of puff pastry can be wrapped around them.*

Chocolate Curls with Cranberry Cream

1 10-ounce package frozen puff pastry	3 ounces bittersweet chocolate
Flour for rolling out	1 cup whipping cream
1 egg yolk	1 teaspoon vanilla
2 tablespoons milk or whipping cream	3-4 tablespoons cranberry jam or preserves

Lay out layers of puff pastry next to one another and thaw according to package directions. Cut 3 to 4-inch wide strips of double-strength aluminum foil and roll these together several times until relatively stable rods are obtained. Place thawed layers of puff pastry one on top of the other on a floured work surface or on aluminum foil and, while applying gentle but even pressure, roll it out in all directions until a rectangle measuring 8 x 12 inches is formed. Using a pizza cutter or a very sharp knife, cut the dough into 1-inch strips. When cutting, be sure to cut smoothly so that the individual layers of dough are not pressed together, otherwise they will be unable to rise evenly during baking. Rinse the aluminum rods in cold water and also brush the strips of dough on one side with cold water. Wrap the strips of dough around the aluminum rods in spiral-form so that they overlap slightly on the wet side and will bake together well. Place curls on a baking sheet that has been rinsed with cold water and brush the surfaces with milk or cream whisked together with egg yolk. Bake on the middle rack of an oven preheated to 400°-425° for 12-15 minutes until golden brown. Immediately remove to a rack, take out the aluminum foil and allow to cool completely. Crumble the chocolate and, while stirring constantly, melt in a double boiler over hot, but not boiling, water. Remove from heat and allow to cool stirring repeatedly until it just begins to harden again. Very quickly brush the puff pastry curls with the chocolate and allow to cool and harden.

Whip the cream with vanilla just before serving. Drain cranberry preserves well (using a very fine sieve) and, if desired, puree them. If jam is used, stir until smooth. Spoon small portions of preserves or jam onto the stiffly whipped cream and fold in gently. Finally, place cream into a pastry bag with a very large star spout and fill the chocolate rolls with it from both sides. The rolls should be served immediately, so that the cream does not mix with the crispy dough and make it soft and disappointing.

Dutch Cherry Torte

2 10-ounce packages frozen puff pastry	2 jars sour cherries (16 ounces of fruit)
Flour for rolling	1 heaping tablespoon cornstarch
¼ cup red currant jelly	
1½ cups powdered sugar	3 cups whipping cream
2-3 tablespoons raspberry schnapps or strained lemon juice	2-3 tablespoons sugar
	1 teaspoon vanilla

Separate layers of puff pastry, lay 6 of them out one next to the other, and thaw according to package directions. Immediately refreeze the remaining layers for later use. Stack the thawed puff pastry layers on top of each other on a floured work surface or on aluminum foil and roll out three rounds each having a diameter of 11 inches. Place one piece of aluminum foil for each round on a baking sheet and rinse with cold water. Lay the dough layers on the foil and gently press a 10-inch, springform rim that has been rinsed in cold water on top of each layer to mark the dough. Pierce the bottoms repeatedly with a fork, then refrigerate for about 15 minutes. Bake the dough layers on the middle rack of an oven preheated to 400° for 15 minutes until golden brown. Remove from foil to a rack and allow to cool. Then, if necessary, cut the edges of the torte with a very sharp knife to even out the edges.

While stirring constantly, heat the red currant jelly until it is smooth and spreadable. Brush the best puff pastry layer with it. Combine powdered sugar with raspberry schnapps or lemon juice and stir to a smooth glaze. Spread over the jelly layer and allow to dry.

Drain the cherries well in a sieve and retain the juice. Measure out 1 cup and bring it to a boil in a saucepan. Combine cornstarch with some cold cherry juice or with water and stir into the boiling juice. Bring to a boil while stirring constantly, mix in cherries retaining a few particularly nice ones for decoration. Allow the cherry mixture to cool. Just before it becomes stiff, spread it evenly onto a puff pastry layer and place a second layer on top. Whip cream until stiff, sweeten with sugar and flavor with vanilla. Place part of it in a pastry bag with a star spout. Spread about ¾ of the remaining whipped cream onto the torte. Cut the glazed layer into 12-16 pieces with a sharp knife and place them on top of the cream. Brush the sides with the remaining cream. Decorate the surface of the torte with dots of cream topped with a cherry. Serve the torte as soon as possible before the whipped cream becomes runny and the puff pastry soggy.

Mango Torte with Champagne Cream

1 10-ounce package frozen
  puff pastry
Flour for rolling
2-3 ¼-ounce packages gelatin
Small bottle of champagne
  (about ⅔ cup)
5 ripe mangos
3-4 tablespoons cream sherry
3 egg yolks

½ cup sugar
Juice of 1 lemon
3 egg whites
Pinch of salt
1½ cups whipping cream
1 teaspoon vanilla
2 tablespoons chopped
  pistachios

Lay out layers of puff pastry, one next to the other, and thaw according to package directions. Then stack them on top of each other on a lightly floured work surface (or on aluminum foil) and, while applying gentle but even pressure, roll out one 12-inch round. Line a baking sheet with aluminum foil, rinse with cold water and place the puff pastry round on it. Rinse the rim of a 10-inch springform pan with cold water and place it on the dough applying only a minimal amount of pressure in order to hinder the dough from pulling up. Pierce the torte bottom repeatedly with a fork, then refrigerate for 15 minutes. Bake on the middle rack of an oven preheated to 400°-425° for about 15 minutes until golden brown. Remove the aluminum foil and cool on a rack.

Peel 4 mangos, remove pits and chop coarsely. Puree in a blender with cream sherry or press fruit through a sieve and then mix in sherry. Combine egg yolks, sugar and lemon juice and beat until sugar is dissolved and batter is foamy and white. Gradually add champagne. Then fold in mango puree. Dissolve the gelatin, allow to cool (it should be the same temperature as the mango mixture) and then stir in a little of the mango mixture. Thoroughly mix the gelatin into the cream mixture and refrigerate. Whip egg whites and salt until stiff. Separately whip cream with vanilla until stiff. Place ⅓ of the cream in a pastry bag with a star spout. Fold the remaining cream together with the egg whites into the mango cream after the latter has begun to gel.

Place a springform rim around the torte bottom and if necessary, cut the torte bottom to the appropriate size. Line the rim with aluminum foil, if preferred. Fill in the mango cream. Refrigerate until the torte is stiff. Prior to serving, remove the rim, mark 12 pieces on the surface of the torte and press out a large star of cream on each. Peel the remaining mango, remove seeds and cut into small pieces. Decorate the torte with them and sprinkle with pistachios.

Shoe Soles

1 10-ounce package frozen puff pastry	½ cup rock candy sugar 1½ cups whipping cream
Sugar for rolling out	2 teaspoons vanilla
Milk or cream for brushing	

Place layers of puff pastry, one next to the other, on a work surface and thaw according to package directions. Then brush thinly with water and stack on top of each other. Roll out, applying gentle but even pressure, a rectangle of about ½-inch thick. Cut out 2½-inch rounds and then, on a work surface that has been sprinkled with sugar, roll these out into the form of ovals or "shoe soles" 3-4 inches long. In doing this, the pieces of dough must be turned over once so that both sides will be covered with a layer of sugar. Brush one side of each shoe sole with milk or cream taking care not to get any sugar on the edges. Dampened edges could impede rising if the individual layers are glued together. Sprinkle the brushed sides with rock candy sugar. Line a baking sheet with aluminum foil and rinse with cold water. Place the shoe soles on it and allow to rest in a cool place. Bake on the middle rack of an oven that has been preheated to 400° for 10 minutes until golden brown. Immediately remove from foil onto a rack and allow to cool completely.

Just before serving, whip cream together with vanilla until stiff. Place in a pastry bag with a large star spout and generously fill cream into the half of the shoe soles without rock candy sugar.

Then place the ovals with rock candy sugar on top, press gently and serve immediately so that the pastry does not become soggy nor the cream runny. If the pastry must be served later, store unfilled in a cool, dry place to retain freshness.

> **Tip:** *For shoe soles to rise especially high, carefully spray the aluminum foil with water just before placing it in the oven. This will create a lot more steam causing the individual layers to puff up and rise. Take care not to spray the dough.*

Note

Shoe soles can be prepared with other fillings. Try fruit combined with whipped cream or slightly softened ice cream.

Twin Pretzels made of Two Kinds of Dough

⅓ cup almonds	Grated rind of ½ lemon
1¾ cups flour	1 10-ounce package frozen
Pinch of salt	puff pastry
1 egg	Flour for rolling and shaping
⅓ cup chilled butter or	3 cups powdered sugar
margarine	4-5 tablespoons lemon juice
6 tablespoons sugar	

Blanch almonds by pouring boiling water over them, leave them to soak for a brief few seconds, then remove them and slide the brown skins off. Lay skinned almonds on a towel or several layers of paper towel and allow them to dry well. Then grind twice in an almond mill. The almonds must be completely dry when ground otherwise they will clog the grinding surface. Sift flour and combine with almonds and salt. Place on a work surface and make a well in the middle. Place egg in the middle and chilled butter in flakes over the sides. Sprinkle sugar and grated lemon rind over the other ingredients and cut to a crumb-like consistency using 2 knives. With cool hands, quickly knead all ingredients into a smooth dough, working from the outside to the inside. Wrap in aluminum foil or a plastic bag and refrigerate for at least 30 minutes.

Meanwhile lay out puff pastry layers next to each other on a work surface and thaw according to package directions. Thinly brush the layers with cold water and stack on top of each other. Applying gentle but even pressure, roll out a rectangle having a width of 16 inches. Using a pizza cutter or a very sharp knife cut the rectangle into 2-inch strips. Roll the egg-tart dough to a rectangle of equal size, similarly cut into strips and form these into pencil-thick rolls. Loosely intertwine one strip of each of the doughs and form into a pretzel. Press ends together well. Lay the pretzels on a baking sheet rinsed with cold water and bake on the middle rack of an oven preheated to 400°-425° for 20-30 minutes until golden brown. Immediately, but carefully (since they crumble), remove from the baking sheet and cool on a rack. Stir together powdered sugar and lemon juice to make a glaze and cover the pretzels with it.

> **Tip:** *Both doughs are worked best when well cooled. For the inexperienced cook, it is advisable to work with small portions leaving the remaining dough in the refrigerator. The egg-tart dough may be flavored with cocoa, if variety is desired.*

Puff Pastry Cockscomb

1 10-ounce package frozen puff pastry	1 egg yolk
Flour for rolling	2 tablespoons whipping cream or milk
3 tablespoons butter	

Lay out puff pastry layers next to each other on a work surface and allow to thaw. Brush with cold water and stack. Applying gentle but even pressure, roll out the dough with a rolling pin to a rectangle measuring 10 × 16 inches. Spread butter down the length of one half of the rectangle. Whisk together egg yolk with cream or milk and brush onto the edges of the dough. Fold the second half of the rectangle over the filling and carefully press all edges with the fingertips. Cut the filled dough into 2½-inch wide strips, and cut these perpendicularly just up to the middle 3 or 4 times. Bend the strips slightly into a crescent shape, so that the incisions open up. Rinse a baking sheet with cold water and place the cockscombs on it leaving sufficient space between each one. Brush the surfaces, but not the sides, with the remaining egg. Bake on the middle rack of an oven preheated to 400°-425° for 20-25 minutes. Immediately remove from the baking sheet and allow to cool.

Marzipan Windmills

1 10-ounce package frozen puff pastry	1-2 teaspoons rum or cognac
Flour for rolling out	1 egg yolk
¼ cup marzipan	Powdered sugar for dusting
½ cup plus 2 tablespoons powdered sugar	

Thaw puff pastry as previously described and roll out to a rectangle; the dough should be ⅛th of an inch thick. Using a pizza cutter or a very sharp knife, cut the dough into 5½-inch squares. Knead the marzipan, powdered sugar and rum or cognac into a smooth dough and shape into 4 small balls. Place each slightly flattened ball into the middle of one of the squares of dough.

Make a 2-inch incision from each of the corners and fold in one of the points over the marzipan dough. Brush the points with whisked egg yolk so that they will glue together when baked. Finally brush all the surfaces of dough with whisked egg yolk taking care to leave the cut edges uncoated so that they can "puff up." Rinse a baking sheet with cold water and place the windmills on it leaving sufficient room between them. Bake on the middle rack of an oven preheated to 400°-425° for 20 minutes. Dust with powdered sugar while still warm.

Croquant Spirals

1 10-ounce package frozen puff pastry	1 egg yolk for brushing
Flour for rolling out	⅓ cup croquant

Using a pizza cutter or a very sharp knife, cut the thawed and rolled out puff pastry (see instructions above) into 2 × 5-inch strips. Make a partial incision up to about 2½ inches at one end of each strip so that the dough is still connected on the other side. Braid both ends of dough loosely so that they look like spirals. Brush the surfaces, but not the sides, with the whisked egg yolk and sprinkle with croquant. Rinse a baking sheet with cold water and place spirals on it leaving sufficient space between each one. Bake on the middle rack of an oven preheated to 400°-425° for 15-20 minutes. Remove to a rack and allow to cool.

Cinnamon Bows

1 10-ounce package frozen puff pastry	3 tablespoons sugar
Flour for rolling	2 teaspoons ground cinnamon
2 egg yolks	2 tablespoons rock candy sugar

Thaw puff pastry as previously described and roll out a 10 × 14-inch rectangle having a thickness of ⅛-inch. Cut off edges evenly. Whisk egg yolks and brush dough with it. Combine sugar with cinnamon and sprinkle ¾ of it onto the dough. Fold in half and press edges well. Using a very sharp knife or a pizza cutter, cut the dough into 2-inch wide strips. Make a 3-inch lengthwise slit down the middle of each strip.

Carefully lift one of the uncut ends and pull it through the slit. Bend the dough back until flat again and stretch slightly. Rinse a baking sheet with cold water and place the bows on it leaving sufficient space between each one. Brush surfaces with remaining whisked egg yolks.

Combine rock candy sugar with remaining cinnamon-sugar and sprinkle over bows. Bake for 15-20 minutes in an oven preheated to 400°-425°. Cool on a rack.

Apricot Pockets

1 10-ounce package frozen puff pastry	9 canned apricot halves
Flour for rolling	2 tablespoons red currant jelly
	1 egg yolk for brushing

Thaw puff pastry and roll out a 12 × 12-inch square. Divide this into squares measuring 4 × 4-inches. Drain apricots well on a paper towel.

Fold in all four corners of each square, press gently and place an apricot half, pit side up, in the middle of each pocket.

Stir jelly until smooth and place a small dot of it in the middle of each apricot. Brush all dough surfaces, but not the edges, with whisked egg yolk. Rinse a baking sheet with cold water and place apricot pockets on it leaving sufficient space between each one. Bake on the middle rack of an oven preheated to 400°-425° for 20-25 minutes.

Raspberry Squares

1 10-ounce package frozen puff pastry	3-4 tablespoons raspberry schnapps
Flour for dusting	3 tablespoons sugar
1 egg yolk	1 cup whipping cream
2 tablespoons whipping cream or milk	1 teaspoon vanilla
1 10-ounce package frozen raspberries	

Thaw puff pastry layers as usual. On a lightly floured work surface cut the pastry, without having rolled it, into small squares. To do this, halve each of the layers and then cut each half perpendicularly into 3 pieces. Brush with an egg yolk and cream mixture.

Rinse a baking sheet with cold water and place the squares on it leaving sufficient space between each one. Bake for about 10 minutes on the middle rack of an oven that has been preheated to 400°-425°. Immediately remove from the baking sheet and allow to cool. After cooling, lift a small ''lid'' off of each square.

Combine raspberries, raspberry schnapps and sugar. Cover and thaw. Whip cream with vanilla until stiff and place into a pastry bag. Drain raspberries. Press out whipped cream onto the bottoms of the squares, lay raspberries on top and cover with the lid. These squares may be dusted with powdered sugar, if desired.

Ricotta Cheese Puff Pastry Spirals

2½ cups flour	Flour for rolling
1 tablespoon baking powder	1¾ cups powdered sugar
Pinch of salt	2-3 tablespoons rum or cognac
1 cup ricotta or cottage cheese	⅓ cup chopped pistachios
1 cup plus 2 tablespoons chilled butter	

Combine flour with baking powder and salt; make a well in the middle, place ricotta or cottage cheese in it and distribute butter in flakes around the edges. Cut all ingredients to a crumb-like consistency and quickly knead into a smooth dough with cool hands. On a lightly floured work surface roll the dough into a long rectangle. Fold in ⅓ of the dough, then fold the other third on top of that and press gently. Refrigerate for 15-20 minutes. Roll again lengthwise until the dough is about 3 times

as long as wide. Fold together again, refrigerate and repeat this process once or twice more. Finally roll out the dough to a thickness of ⅛th inch, cut into strips and braid as described in the recipe for Croquant Spirals above.

Rinse a baking sheet with cold water and place the spirals on it leaving sufficient space between each. Bake on the middle rack of an oven preheated to 400°-425° for 15-20 minutes. Cool on a rack. Stir together powdered sugar and rum or cognac, glaze the spirals and sprinkle with pistachios.

Apple Crescents made of Ricotta Cheese Puff Pastry

1 recipe for ricotta cheese puff pastry	⅓ cup sliced almonds
Flour for rolling	1 egg yolk for brushing
⅓ cup thick applesauce	Powdered sugar for dusting

On a floured work surface, roll out a puff pastry to a 10 × 16-inch rectangle; Cut it into 4-inch wide strips. Divide these diagonally into two long triangles. Place some applesauce on the short side of each triangle and sprinkle with almonds. Roll up starting at the filled side and ending with the point on top. Curve into the shape of crescents. Place on a baking sheet that has been rinsed with cold water leaving sufficient space between each for expansion during baking. Brush with whisked egg yolk and bake on the middle rack of an oven preheated to 400°-425° for 20-25 minutes. Dust with powdered sugar.

Peach Lattices

1 recipe ricotta cheese puff pastry	6 canned peach halves
Flour for rolling	1 egg yolk for brushing
	Powdered sugar for dusting

Roll out the puff pastry to a thickness of ⅛ inch and divide into 5-inch squares. Cut a ½-inch wide strip off of two sides of each square. Drain peaches and blot dry with paper towel. Place pit-side down on the larger pieces of dough and cross two cut-off strips of dough over each peach. Press edges gently and brush dough with whisked egg yolk. Place on a baking sheet that has been rinsed with cold water leaving sufficient space between each pastry for expansion. Bake at 400°-425° for 20-25 minutes. Dust with powdered sugar.

> **Tip:** *Dust the apricot pockets lightly with powdered sugar before serving. To refine them even more, place an almond in the center of each apricot.*

Pig's Ears

1 10-ounce package frozen puff pastry	Flour for rolling
2 tablespoons butter or margarine	⅓ cup sugar
	Powdered sugar for dusting

Thaw puff pastry layers according to package directions. Melt butter or margarine over low heat but do not allow to brown. Remove from heat and cool to a still liquid state. Brush layers of dough thinly with cold water, stack them and applying gentle but even pressure, roll out a 8 x 12-inch rectangle having a thickness of ⅛th inch. In doing this the dough should always be rolled out in all directions so that a single area does not suffer undue stress. Evenly spread the cooled but still liquid butter over it. Sprinkle with sugar. Fold each of the long sides of the rectangle in toward the middle leaving a 1-inch wide center strip uncovered. Fold both sides of the dough so that they meet at this center and refrigerate for about 20 minutes.

Cut the dough into ¼-inch slices. It is essential to use an extremely sharp knife when cutting the dough, otherwise the individual layers could be pressed together and will not rise evenly during baking. Dip the top surface of the pig's ears into sugar or sprinkle them with sugar. Rinse a baking sheet with cold water and place them on it leaving sufficient space between each for expansion during baking. Allow the pig's ears to rest in a cool place for 15 minutes. If desired the baking sheet may be sprayed with cold water again. Bake on the middle rack of an oven

preheated to 400° for 8-10 minutes. Immediately remove from the baking sheet (they quickly stick if left for a longer period of time), and place on a large rack. Do not stack them, otherwise they will become tender and moist. Furthermore, the sides should not touch each other because they could melt causing the caramelized sugar to glue them together. Later separation would cause crumbling.

Tip: *For especially crispy caramelized pig's ears, dip both sides in sugar and, during the baking process, turn them over when they start to brown. For turning, use a thin spatula or a broad knife.*

Mirlitons

1 10-ounce package frozen puff pastry	Pinch of salt
Flour for rolling and dusting	¼ teaspoon almond extract
Butter for greasing	2 tablespoons orange liqueur
20 macaroons (about 1½ ounces)	½ cup sugar
	Grated rind of ½ orange
¾ cup ground almonds	4 tablespoons apricot jam
2 eggs	Powdered sugar for dusting
	30 skinned almond halves

Mirlitons are a particularly tender and succulent pastry that require little effort and patience in preparation. Use smooth-sided, fluted tartlet forms that widen at the top, or flaring brioche forms having a diameter of 4-inches can be used.

Lay puff pastry layers next to each other and thaw. Then cut dough into as many pieces as there are forms. Press these pieces together thoroughly, but do not actually knead them, and place on a floured work surface. Using a lightly floured rolling pin, roll each out in all directions, (from front to back and left to right) until 6-inch rounds of dough are obtained that are ¹⁄₁₂th inch thick.

Grease forms with butter and dust with flour. Fill in dough rounds and press very gently against the top rim. The dough should rise slightly above the edge of the form, because puff pastry pulls together somewhat during baking. Refrigerate for 15 minutes.

Place macaroons in a plastic bag and crush finely with a rolling pin. Combine with almonds and set aside.

Combine eggs, salt, almond extract and orange liqueur and beat until foamy. Gradually sprinkle in sugar, then add orange rind. Add dry ingredients to the egg-mixture and work into a thick batter. Stir apricot jam until smooth and drip into tartlets. Fill in almond-macaroon batter until forms are half full. Dust with powdered sugar and place 3 almonds in cloverleaf fashion on top of each.

Bake on the middle rack of an oven preheated to 425° for 25 minutes until golden brown. After about 12 minutes reduce temperature to 400°. Remove from oven and immediately loosen the edges with a pointed knife. Carefully remove from the forms and place upright on a rack to cool. Dust lightly with powdered sugar.

Peach and Cherry Pizza

1 10-ounce package frozen
  puff pastry
Flour for rolling
1 jar pitted sour cherries
½ jar cherry jelly
2-3 tablespoons Kirsch
1 small package sponge
  cookies (or ladyfingers)

1 16-ounce can peaches
1½ ¼-ounce packages gelatin
½ cup dry white wine
¼ cup sliced almonds
½ cup whipping cream
Sugar to taste
1 teaspoon vanilla

Thaw puff pastry according to package directions. Very thinly brush with water, stack and place on a lightly floured work surface. Roll out in all directions under gentle but even pressure. Rinse a pizza or paella pan with cold water. Lay dough into it so that it overlaps somewhat on all sides. Carefully moisten the edges of the pan. Pierce the dough repeatedly with a fork, then refrigerate for 15 minutes. Bake on the middle rack of an oven preheated to 400°-425° for 20 minutes until golden.

Drain the cherries in a sieve retaining the liquid. Combine cherry jelly with the Kirsch and heat while stirring constantly until smooth. Allow to cool before spreading onto the pizza. Then line pizza with sponge cookies. Drain peaches, retaining the liquid. Then decoratively distribute peach halves and cherries onto the pizza.

Dissolve the gelatin in some cold water. Measure out ½ cup of peach juice, combine it with the wine and heat, but do not boil. If desired, some sugar may be dissolved in this liquid. Add the gelatin to the wine mixture . Allow to gel in the refrigerator.

Just when it begins to stiffen, pour it over the fruit and allow to gel completely.

Brown almonds lightly in a dry pan, be sure to shake them constantly. Cool on a flat plate. Combine whipped cream and vanilla and whip until stiff; the cream may be sweetened, if desired. Place in a pastry bag. Remove torte from refrigerator after the glaze has gelled. Decorate with generous dollops of cream sprinkled with sliced almonds. Serve pizza immediately because the bottom quickly becomes soggy.

Note

Fresh peaches (or nectarines) can be used instead of canned peaches. Before use, they must be peeled and blanched.

Orange Pizza

1 10-ounce package frozen puff pastry	Pinch of salt
Flour for rolling	4 tablespoons orange liqueur
2 ounces macaroons (store bought)	1 tablespoon vanilla pudding mix
2 eggs	5 oranges
4 egg yolks	3 tablespoons bread crumbs
1 cup plus 2 tablespoons sugar	2 tablespoons ground walnuts
	1 ounce walnut halves
	2 tablespoons honey

Lay puff pastry layers next to one another and thaw according to package directions. Brush them very thinly with cold water, stack on top of each other and roll out a round of dough by applying gentle but even pressure in all directions with a rolling pin. Rinse out a paella pan or small pizza pan with cold water and lay the dough in it so that it extends over the rim. Repeatedly pierce the dough with a fork, then allow to rest in a cool place. Bake on the middle rack of an oven preheated to 400°-425° for 8-10 minutes until golden.

Place macaroons in a plastic bag and crush very finely with a rolling pin. Combine eggs and egg yolks in a bowl and add sugar, salt and orange liqueur while stirring constantly. Continue stirring until the liquid is white and foamy and the sugar is completely dissolved. Combine vanilla pudding mix with crushed macaroons and gently but thoroughly fold both into the liquid. Carefully peel oranges (white skin should no longer be visible), fillet sections by removing transparent membrane and pits. Combine bread crumbs with ground nuts. Remove the prebaked pastry shell from the oven and sprinkle evenly with the bread crumb and nut mixture. Spread egg-cream over it and then arrange orange sections in spiral fashion. Place cake on the middle rack and bake again at the same temperature for 25-30 minutes. Five minutes before the orange pizza is done, arrange walnut halves on the surface and brush the entire surface with honey. Allow surface to caramelize and honey to be absorbed into the filling somewhat before removing the cake from the oven. The cake may either be removed from the form or left in it to cool. If the latter method is chosen, it will later be necessary to lift the cake out of the form with a broad spatula in order to avoid undue damage.

> **TIP:** *If no special form is available, a springform pan or tart pan may be used. It should, however, be lined with aluminum foil and rinsed out with cold water.*

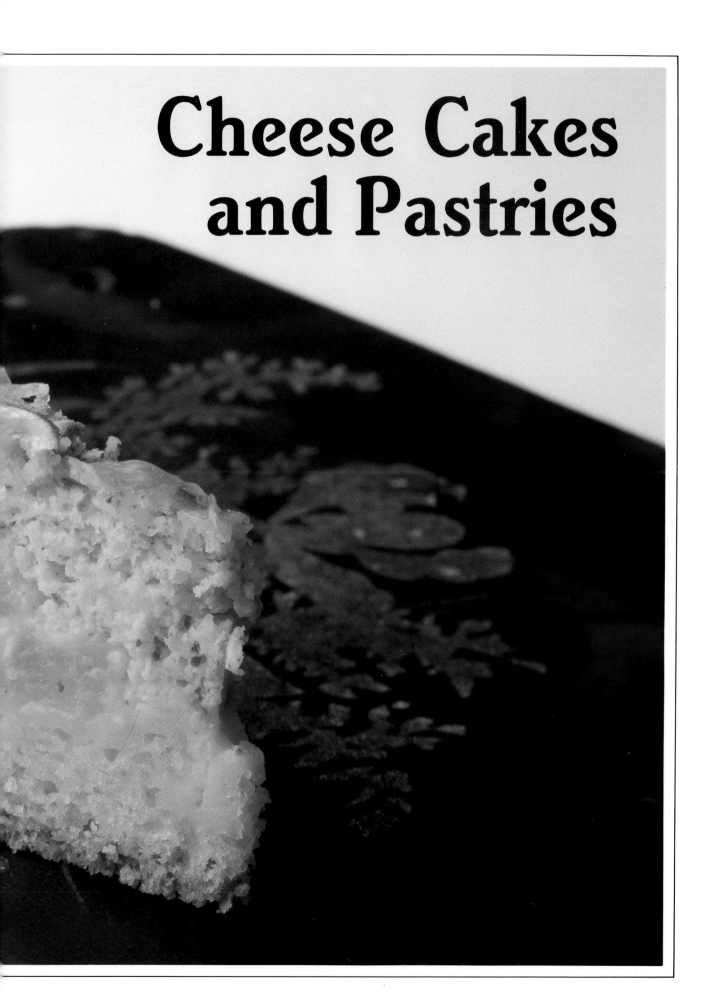

Cheese Cakes and Pastries

Fresh Cheese Rosette Cake with Apples

3½ cups sifted cake flour	1 cup ricotta or cottage
Pinch of salt	cheese
1 teaspoon baking powder	1 cup plus 2 tablespoons
	chilled butter

For the filling and topping:

½ cup raisins	Flour for rolling
1 pound tart apples	2 egg yolks
Juice of 1 lemon	3 tablespoons whipping cream
6 tablespoons sugar	Butter or margarine for
1 teaspoon ground cinnamon	greasing
1¼ cups grated coconut	2 tablespoons honey for
⅓-½ cup crumbled croquant	brushing

Combine flour, salt and baking powder. Make a well in the middle and pour cheese into it and distribute butter in flakes over the surface. Cut all ingredients until they are coarsely mixed, then, with chilled hands (rinse them in cold water and dry well), quickly knead into a smooth dough. Shape into a ball and refrigerate for at least 1 hour.

To prepare the filling, wash raisins in hot water and dry with a towel. Peel, quarter and core apples. Slice or grate them. Immediately sprinkle with lemon juice and mix well to avoid discoloration. Cover with plastic wrap. Combine sugar, cinnamon, coconut, croquant and mix well.

On a lightly floured work surface, roll out dough into a rectangle of ¼-inch thickness. Whisk together egg yolks and cream and brush onto the dough. Sprinkle with apples, raisins and sugar mixture and roll up starting on one of the long sides. Using a very sharp knife, cut into 2-inch slices and place next to each other in a 9-inch springform pan.

Bake on the lower rack of an oven preheated to 400°-425° for 30-35 minutes. Then brush surface with honey and bake another 2-3 minutes so that the honey caramelizes. Remove to a rack to cool. Serve immediately.

Variation

Bake apple turnovers using the same recipe. Divide the rolled dough into 4-inch squares. Place some filling in the middle and then fold them over diagonally after brushing the edges with some whisked egg yolk. Press edges together well and brush surfaces with honey, if desired. Or, brush with egg before baking and dust with powdered sugar before cooling.

Nougat and Hazelnut Crescents

3¾ cups sifted cake flour	1 tablespoon cognac or
½ teaspoon baking powder	brandy
Pinch of salt	1 cup ricotta or cottage
1 egg yolk	cheese
¼ teaspoon almond extract	1 cup chilled butter

For the filling and topping:

1 egg white	1 egg yolk
2 tablespoons sugar	2 tablespoons whipping cream
1⅓ cups nougat	or canned milk
1 cup ground hazelnuts	Butter or margarine for
1 tablespoon cognac or	greasing
brandy	2 tablespoons butter
Flour for rolling out	1 ounce semisweet chocolate

Combine flour, baking powder, and salt and make a well in the middle. Pour in egg yolk, almond extract, cognac or brandy and the fresh cheese. Distribute chilled butter in flakes over other ingredients and, using 1 or 2 knives, cut to a crumb-like consistency. With chilled hands, quickly knead into a smooth dough and refrigerate for 1 hour.

Shortly before the hour is over, beat egg white until foamy (it needn't be stiff), and gradually sprinkle in sugar. As soon as this mixture is very creamy, add the crumbled nougat and ground hazelnuts, then stir all ingredients into stiff dough. Flavor with cognac or brandy. On a floured work surface, roll out the dough to ¼-inch thickness. With a glass or cookie cutter having a 4-inch diameter cut out rounds of dough and place a generous dollop of the hazelnut-butter cream in the middle.

Whisk egg yolk with cream or canned milk and brush all edges with it. Fold rounds in half, press them together well and place the crescents on a greased baking sheet leaving sufficient space between each one.

Bake on the middle rack of an oven preheated to 400°-425° for 20-25 minutes until golden brown. Immediately remove to a rack. Melt butter over low heat and brush onto pastries. While stirring constantly, melt chocolate in a double boiler over hot, but not boiling, water. Remove from heat and continue stirring as it cools. As soon as it begins to stiffen, dip a fork or the tip of a knife into it and lift out some chocolate. Drip a thin stream of chocolate over the crescents in zig-zag fashion. Allow to dry, then serve the crescents as soon as possible.

Poppy Seed and Peach Snail

7½ cups flour
1⅔ cups chilled butter
1 package dry yeast
5 tablespoons sugar

1 cup lukewarm milk
1 egg yolk
Generous pinch of salt
Flour for rolling and shaping

For the filling and topping:
1 cup milk
2 tablespoons butter
1½ cups ground poppy seed
⅔ cup sugar
1 vanilla bean
Grated rind of ½ lemon
1 10-ounce can peaches

1 egg white
Pinch of salt
½ cup slivered almonds
1 egg yolk for brushing
1 tablespoon poppy seed for
    sprinkling

Pour 1½ cups flour onto a work surface and distribute 1⅓ cups butter in flakes over it. Quickly knead together, place between two pieces of waxed paper and roll out a rectangle ½ inch thick. Refrigerate for 1½ hours. Make a well in the middle of the remaining flour and add in the yeast. Stir together with 1 tablespoon sugar and some milk. Cover with a towel and allow to rise for 15 minutes. Melt remaining butter with remaining milk and cool until lukewarm. Add this liquid to the starter together with the remaining ingredients and knead into a smooth yeast dough. Knead until there are no more air bubbles and the dough no longer sticks to the sides of the bowl. Refrigerate for 1 hour.

Roll the dough into a rectangle that is at least twice the size of the prepared layer of butter. Place the butter layer on one half, brush all edges with cold water and fold the second dough half over it. Press edges well. Refrigerate for 30 minutes.

Then, while applying gentle pressure, roll out in all directions until the dough is about three times as long as it was. Prepare as shown on page 304 by folding, refrigerating and kneading three times.

For the filling bring milk and butter to a boil. Mix in poppy seed together with sugar, vanilla marrow and grated lemon rind and bring to a boil again. Drain peaches in a sieve, add 3 tablespoons of the juice to the poppy seed mixture. Simmer the mixture until creamy, then allow to cool. Whip egg white with salt until stiff and fold into the poppy-seed cream with the slivered almonds. On a floured work surface, roll out the dough to a rectangle measuring 12 × 24 inches. Spread the poppy-seed filling onto it leaving all edges free of filling. Finely chop peaches, distribute over filling and roll dough up starting from one of the long sides. Lay it onto a baking sheet in snail fashion and allow to rise in a warm place for 25 minutes. Brush with whisked egg yolk and sprinkle with poppy seed. Make several shallow slits into the surface of the dough. Place on the middle rack in an oven preheated to 400°-425°. Bake for 30-40 minutes.

Apricot Almond Cake

1 cup ricotta or cottage cheese	½ cup sugar
	Grated rind of ½ lemon
½ cup milk	5 cups sifted cake flour
½ cup oil	1 tablespoon baking powder
1 egg	Butter or oil for greasing
Pinch of salt	

For the topping:

3 pounds fresh apricots (or 2½ pounds canned apricots)	⅓ cup skinned almonds
	Powdered sugar for dusting

For the dough, combine cheese, milk, oil, egg and a pinch of salt and stir until smooth. Gradually sprinkle in sugar and stir until dissolved. Then flavor with grated lemon rind. Stir flour in by the spoonful until the dough is very stiff. Place remaining flour on a work surface, make a well in the middle and place the dough into it. Quickly knead all ingredients into a smooth dough working from the outside to the inside. Form into a ball and refrigerate for 30 minutes.

Grease a baking sheet and prepare the topping. Wash apricots and dry well. Remove stems, halve them and remove pits. Halve the almonds.

Flatten the cooled dough with hands, then roll out onto a greased baking sheet. If the baking sheet has an open end, place a piece of aluminum foil at that end so that the dough does not run off during baking. Place the apricots close to each other on the dough with pit side up. Lay a halved almond in the center where the pit should be (almonds rounded side up).

Place cake on the middle rack of an oven preheated to 400° and bake for about 45 minutes until golden brown. Remove from oven and dust with powdered sugar while still hot. After it has cooled, cut six times into 3-inch wide strips taking care that the cuts made run along the edges of the almond-filled apricots and not through the almonds. Before serving sprinkle with powdered sugar once more.

> **Tip:** *Always serve this pastry fresh. If allowed to cool completely or if serving is delayed until the next day, the cake will not taste as aromatic. To bake in advance, freeze the cake as soon as it has cooled. Before serving, freshen it a bit by placing in a hot oven for a few minutes and dusting with an additional layer of powdered sugar. In any case, it tastes delicious when served with crème fraîche or lightly whipped cream flavored with vanilla.*

Honey-Lime Torte with Pineapple

½ cup ricotta or cottage
　cheese
2 tablespoons milk or
　whipping cream
1 egg
Pinch of salt

¼ cup sugar
4 tablespoons oil
3¼ cups sifted cake flour
1 tablespoon baking powder
Oil or butter for greasing

For the filling:
1 14-ounce can pineapple
　pieces
1-2 limes
½ cup ricotta or cottage
　cheese
2 egg yolks
4 tablespoons honey

Juice of 1 lime
¼ teaspoon almond extract
2 tablespoons cornstarch
2 egg whites
Pinch of salt
½ cup whipping cream
½ cup ground almonds

For the dough, stir together ricotta or cottage cheese, milk or cream, egg, salt and sugar. Then gradually pour in oil while stirring constantly. As soon as a smooth batter is obtained, combine flour with baking powder and incorporate about half into the cheese mixture.

Place the remaining flour mixture onto a work surface, make a well in the middle and place the cheese dough in it. Working very quickly from outside to inside, knead all ingredients into a smooth, supple dough. Speed is of the essence since prolonged contact with the heat of the hands will cause the dough to become soft and sticky. Thoroughly grease a 10-inch springform pan with oil or butter and roll out the dough in it, subsequently pressing out a 1-inch high rim.

For the filling, drain the pineapple in a sieve, retaining the liquid. Brush the limes thoroughly under hot running water, then dry and cut into very thin slices. Lay the lime slices next to one another on a plate, sprinkle with sugar and allow them to absorb it.

Thoroughly stir together ricotta or cottage cheese, egg yolks, 2½ heaping tablespoons of honey, lime juice, almond extract and cornstarch. Whip egg whites with salt until stiff. Whip cream in a separate bowl until stiff. Slide both into the cheese mixture and fold the almonds and drained pineapple pieces. Fill into the prepared torte shell, smooth out the surface and cover with the lime slices laid closely next to each other. Place on the lower rack of an oven preheated to 350° and bake for 75-85 minutes. If the torte begins to darken too much, cover it with parchment paper. 5 minutes before it is done, spread remaining honey over it and allow to caramelize.

Remove from oven and allow the cake to settle on a kitchen towel for about 5 minutes, then remove springform rim and slide onto a rack. Dust the circumference with powdered sugar. Try to serve as soon as possible, later it will have lost some of its fresh flavor.

Ricotta-Rumtopf Rounds

For the topping:

1 package vanilla pudding powder	6 tablespoons sugar
1½-2 cups milk	Pinch of salt
1 vanilla bean	1 egg

For the dough:

½ cup ricotta or cottage cheese	10 tablespoons tasteless vegetable oil
3 tablespoons milk	3 cups flour
Pinch of salt	1 tablespoon baking powder
6 tablespoons sugar	Flour for rolling
Grated rind of ½ lemon	Butter or oil for greasing
1 egg	2 cups Rumtopf or brandied fruit

For the topping, whisk together the pudding powder with a few tablespoons of milk. In a saucepan, combine remaining milk, the scraped-out vanilla bean marrow and pod, sugar and salt. Bring to a boil. Pour the pudding mixture into the milk while stirring constantly and bring to a boil again. Remove the pan from the heat. Whisk the egg in a cup and stir in some of the "pudding." Add this mixture to the pan while stirring vigorously. Remove the bean pod and allow the pudding, actually a custard, to cool. Stir it quite frequently so that no skin builds up.

For the dough, stir together ricotta or cottage cheese, milk, salt, sugar, grated lemon rind, egg and oil. Incorporate a portion of the flour and the baking powder into the cheese mixture. Place the remaining flour on a work surface and knead it into the dough. Dust the work surface lightly with flour and roll out the dough to a ⅛-inch thickness. Cut out 4-inch rounds of dough with the aid of a cookie cutter, (if such a cutter is unavailable, use a saucer or small bowl as a stencil and cut around it with a knife). Brush the rounds with the pudding leaving a ½-inch rim free of pudding. Arrange the Rumtopf or brandied fruits around the rim. Then place the rounds on a greased baking sheet and bake on the middle rack of an oven preheated to 400° for 20-25 minutes.

Note

Ricotta-Apple Rounds can be baked following the same recipe. Peel, core and slice 3 tart apples. Immediately sprinkle or brush with lemon juice to avoid discoloration. Combine ¼ cup brown sugar with 3 tablespoons butter in flakes and ⅓ cup rolled oats. While stirring constantly, roast these ingredients in a frying pan until the sugar caramelizes. Then stir in about ⅓ cup slivered almonds and ⅛ teaspoon cinnamon. Arrange the apple slices on the rounds of dough, sprinkle the oat mixture over it and bake the rounds as above.

Danish Pastry Dough made with Yeast

1⅓ cups well-chilled butter	½ cup lukewarm milk
5 cups plus 2 tablespoons flour	1 egg
1 package dry yeast	Pinch of salt
¼ cup sugar	Flour for rolling and shaping

Cut 1 cup of butter into flakes. Place about ⅓ cup flour onto a work surface and very quickly knead the butter flakes into it until the mixture is homogeneous. Form into a ball, flatten it somewhat, place between two pieces of waxed paper and roll it out to a finger-thick tile measuring 9 x 10 inches. Refrigerate.

Make a well in the remaining flour. Add the yeast and stir together with some sugar, some milk and a little flour to make a starter. Cover with a towel and allow to rise in a warm place for about 15 minutes. Meanwhile, heat the remaining milk and butter until butter has melted, then allow to cool again. Add the liquid to the starter with the remaining sugar, egg and salt and knead these ingredients into a smooth, supple dough. Beat it until blisters appear and it no longer sticks to the sides of the bowl. Cover with a cloth and refrigerate for 30 minutes.

Lightly flour the work surface, place dough on it and roll out a 12 x 20-inch rectangle. Place the refrigerated butter tile on one half of the dough leaving a ½-1-inch rim uncovered. Brush the rim with cold water, fold the second half of dough over the butter tile and press all the edges firmly with a rolling pin. Refrigerate for about 30 minutes. Finally, starting from the narrower side, roll out the dough using gentle but very even pressure until the rectangle measures 12 × 24 inches. Fold, refrigerate and roll out the dough several times as described on page 307.

Pastry Strips

1 recipe danish pastry dough	2 egg whites
Flour for rolling out	⅔ cup rock candy sugar

Roll out the dough on a lightly floured work surface to a thickness of ¼ inch. Cut into rectangles measuring 2 x 4 inches. Make a 3-inch slit down the middle of each rectangle. Now pull one end of the dough through this slit so that all of the cut sides subsequently face upward again. Brush the surface with whisked egg whites and sprinkle with sugar. Place on a baking sheet and bake in a preheated oven at 400° for 20 minutes.

Jelly Pockets

1 recipe danish pastry dough	2½ cups powdered sugar
Flour for rolling	3-4 tablespoons water or lemon juice
½ jar red currant jelly	
1 egg yolk	

Roll out the dough on a lightly floured work surface and cut into 4-inch squares. Cut small, round buttons out of the remaining dough. Place a dollop of jelly in the middle of each square.

Fold the 4 corners to the middle, brush with whisked egg yolk and press a dough button into the center. Bake in a preheated oven at 400° for 20-25 minutes, then cool on a rack. Stir together powdered sugar with water or lemon juice and glaze the pockets with it.

Cock's Combs

1 recipe danish pastry dough	½ cup marzipan
Flour for rolling out	2 tablespoons candied cherries
1 egg white	2 tablespoons rum or cognac
¾ cup powdered sugar	1 egg yolk

For the glaze and trimming:
2½ cups powdered sugar	¼ cup chopped pistachios
3-4 tablespoons rum or water	

Roll out the pastry dough on a floured work surface and cut into 5-inch squares. Combine egg white with powdered sugar, crumbled marzipan, finely chopped cherries and a few drops of alcohol and mix into a stiff pastry. Spread onto half of the dough squares. Brush the edges with whisked egg yolk and fold the squares into rectangles. Press well, then make three incisions in the dough without cutting completely through. Stretch the pieces gently, brush with egg and bake for 20-25 minutes in an oven preheated to 400°. Make a frosting with the powdered sugar, rum or water. Glaze the rectangles and sprinkle with pistachios.

Windmills

1 recipe danish pastry dough	2½ cups powdered sugar
Flour for rolling out	3-4 tablespoons apricot schnapps or brandy
½ jar apricot jam	

Roll out the dough on a floured work surface and cut into 5-inch squares. From each of the four corners, make a 1½-inch diagonal incision toward the center. Place a dollop of jam in the middle of each square. Fold one half of each of the four corners in toward the center and press gently. Bake for 20-25 minutes in an oven preheated to 400°. Glaze with a sugar glaze after pastries have cooled.

Croquant Spirals

1 recipe danish pastry dough	4-5 tablespoons water or lemon juice
Flour for rolling out	⅓ cup crumbled croquant
3 cups powdered sugar	

Roll out the dough on a floured work surface and cut into 2 × 4-inch rectangles. Slit these lengthwise down the middle so that they are still connected at one end by about ½-inch. Braid both ends of dough and bake for 20 minutes in an oven preheated to 400°. Cool, then glaze with a sugar glaze and sprinkle with croquant.

Pear and Sesame Seed Cake

3 cups flour
⅔ cup well-chilled butter
1 package dry yeast
½ cup sugar
½ cup lukewarm milk

1 teaspoon vanilla
1 egg
Pinch of salt
Flour for rolling out

For the filling and topping:
⅔ cup sesame seeds
1 pound ripe, but not overly
   soft, pears
Juice of 1 lemon
4 tablespoons bread crumbs

2 tablespoons sugar
½ cup raisins
1 egg yolk for brushing
Powdered sugar for dusting

Place ¼ cup of flour onto a work surface and distribute butter in flakes over it. Quickly knead both together. Form into a tile, place between two pieces of waxed paper and roll out to a finger-thick rectangle. Refrigerate and allow to cool thoroughly. Pour the remaining flour into a bowl, make a well in the middle, add the yeast and stir together with some sugar, some milk and a little flour from the sides to make a starter. Cover with a towel and allow to rise in a warm place for about 15 minutes. Add the remaining ingredients and work into a smooth dough. Beat it until blisters appear and the dough no longer sticks to the sides of the bowl. Allow to rest in a cool place for about 15 minutes, then place on a floured work surface and roll out to a rectangle. Place the block of butter in the middle and fold the yeast dough over it from all sides. Refrigerate for 15 minutes, then roll out in one direction until it is three times as long as wide. Fold both

ends of dough in to the center so that there are 3 layers. Refrigerate again, then repeat this process 2 to 4 times, being sure to refrigerate for 15 minutes between each procedure. When rolling out, do not press too strenuously. Finally, refrigerate the dough again and prepare the filling.

While stirring constantly, roast sesame seeds in a dry pan for about 2 minutes until golden yellow. Then allow to cool. Peel, core and finely slice pears. Immediately sprinkle with lemon juice to avoid discoloration. Combine bread crumbs with sugar and raisins that have been washed in hot water and thoroughly rubbed dry. Roll the dough into a rectangle about ½-inch thick, then sprinkle with the bread-crumb mixture. Spread pear slices and sesame-seed mixture over it being sure to leave all edges uncovered. Roll up the dough and carefully press all edges and seams together. Form into a wreath or snail, place on a baking sheet and brush the surface with whisked egg. Bake for 45-50 minutes in an oven preheated to 350°-400°. Allow to cool before dusting with powdered sugar.

Nut-Filled Crescents

5 cups flour
1 cup plus 3 tablespoons chilled butter
1 package dry yeast
¼ cup sugar
½ cup lukewarm milk

Pinch of salt
1 egg
Grated rind of ½ lemon
½ teaspoon almond extract
Flour for rolling and shaping

For the filling and topping:
1 egg white
Pinch of salt
3 tablespoons sugar
¼ cup ground almonds

2 tablespoons finely chopped pistachios
1-2 teaspoons almond liqueur
2 egg yolks for brushing

For the dough, put ½ cup of flour onto a work surface, sprinkle 1 cup of butter in flakes over it. Quickly knead the two together, place between two pieces of waxed paper and roll out to an 8 x 9-inch rectangle. Refrigerate for about 1½ hours.

Make a well in the middle of the remaining flour and add the yeast with some sugar, some milk and a little flour from the sides to make a starter. Cover and allow to rise for 15 minutes.

Combine remaining milk and butter, heat until butter has melted, then cool until lukewarm. Add milk-butter liquid together with the remaining sugar, egg and flavors to the starter. Work all ingredients into a smooth dough. Beat until blisters appear and the dough no longer sticks to the sides of the bowl. Cover with a cloth and refrigerate for 45 minutes.

Knead the dough again on a lightly floured work surface, then roll out a rectangle measuring 12 × 20 inches.

Lay the chilled butter on one half of the dough, brush all edges with cold water, then fold the other dough half on top of the butter. Press edges well and refrigerate dough for 30 minutes. Subsequently give the dough three "bouts" as described in the recipe for "Danish Pastry" on page 154. Refrigerate for 30 minutes before each bout. Whip egg white and salt until stiff, then sprinkle in sugar. Fold in almonds and pistachios, and flavor with almond liqueur.

Roll out the dough on a floured work surface to a rectangle measuring 10 × 16 inches. Cut into triangles. In order to do this, cut the dough into rectangles measuring 4 × 10 inches and halve each of these diagonally making triangles. Make a ¼-inch slit on each side of the short side of the triangle. Spread some filling lengthwise on the surface of the triangle, then roll the triangle up starting from the short side. Finally, press in the the little flaps of dough on each side. Bend the crescents slightly, then place on a baking sheet and allow to rise until their volume has visibly increased. Finally, brush with egg yolk and bake for 20 minutes in an oven preheated to 425°.

Pies

Grape Pie with Chestnuts

2 cups flour	7 tablespoons chilled butter
Generous pinch of salt	2-3 tablespoons ice water

For the filling and topping:

1½ pounds red grapes	1 teaspoon vanilla
1½ pounds green grapes	3-4 tablespoons cognac
1 lemon	⅔ cup sugar
1 orange	Flour for rolling out
1 16-ounce can chestnuts	1 egg white for brushing
½ cup finely chopped walnuts	Sugar for sprinkling

For the dough, place flour on a work surface, make a well in the middle and add salt. Distribute the butter in flakes on the rim and pour the ice water into the well. Cut all ingredients until they have a crumb-like consistency. Working from the outside to the inside, quickly knead the ingredients into a smooth dough, form into a ball and refrigerate, covered, for at least 30 minutes.

Prepare the filling. Wash the grapes, dry them well and remove them from their stems. If desired, remove the pits. Carefully rind lemon and orange, be sure to remove all of the white skin since this tastes slightly bitter. Remove the segments from the membrane surrounding them. Cut segments into small pieces and remove pits at the same time. Drain the chestnuts and also cut them into small pieces. Combine with the grapes, citrus fruit and walnuts. Add vanilla, cognac and sprinkles of sugar.

Place the chilled dough on a lightly floured work surface and roll out to ⅛-inch thickness. Use a 6-7-cup oven-proof baking dish as a stencil; it should widen at the top and have a broad, unglazed rim. Place it upside-down on top of the dough. Using a pizza cutter or very sharp knife, cut out a round of dough that is about 1 inch larger than the form. Gather the leftover dough and roll out again. Now cut out one long strip that is somewhat wider than the outside rim of the form. Brush the unglazed rim with water, lay the strip of dough on it and press firmly.

Mix sugar into the fruit and carefully, without disturbing the rim, fill the fruit into the bowl. Lay the dough cover on top and carefully attach cover to rim. To do this, run the length of a finger around the rim pressing it down firmly. Then use the blunt side of a knife to press down both layers of dough so that they are firmly attached to each other.

Cut off any overlapping edges of the dough with a sharp knife; to trim the edge, hold the knife at an angle and cut upward and outward away from the edge of the bowl but following its form.

Finally, at regular intervals make numerous notches through both dough layers of the rim with the back of a knife held perpendicular to the surface of the pie. Brush the surface with whisked egg white and sprinkle with sugar. Bake on the lower rack of an oven preheated to 400° for about 45 minutes.

Immediately remove the pie from the oven and sprinkle with additional sugar, if desired. Serve hot or slightly cooled. Whipped cream or crème fraîche may be offered with the pie.

> **Tip:** *In order to simplify the procedure for placing the dough cover on the pie, roll out the dough on a large sheet of waxed paper or aluminum foil. Then invert both paper and dough and lay on top of the form. Peel off the paper or foil.*

Apple and Vanilla Pie

4 cups flour	¾ cup plus 2 tablespoons chilled butter
2 generous pinches of salt	5-6 tablespoons ice water

For the filling and topping:

2 pounds tart apples	⅔ cup grated coconut
Juice of ½ lemon	Flour for rolling out
1 teaspoon vanilla	1 egg white for brushing
1 vanilla bean	2 tablespoons butter
1⅓ cups sugar	1 egg yolk for brushing
2 tablespoons vanilla pudding powder	Powdered sugar for dusting

Prepare the dough as in the previous recipe and refrigerate.

Peel and core apples, then cut into thin slices and immediately sprinkle with lemon juice and vanilla. Slit the vanilla bean lengthwise and scrape out the marrow. Combine it with the sugar. Then add vanilla pudding powder and coconut. Finally, turn the apples in the sugar mixture so that the slices are thoroughly coated.

Roll out a little less than half the dough on a floured work surface. Place a 4-cup, inverted pie pan on it and, using it as a stencil, cut a cover out of the dough. Add the leftover dough to the remaining dough, roll out again and use it to line the pie pan. Cut off any overlapping edges. Pierce the bottom repeatedly. Whip egg white and brush on the pie shell. Fill with the apple mixture alternately layered with the butter in flakes. Cut out a round opening or ''chimney'' in the middle of the cover. Then place the cover on the pie and firmly press the rim on the form. Use thumb and index finger to press the two layers of dough together. Brush the surface with whisked egg yolk. Cut small shapes out of the leftover dough, place these on the cover and brush with egg yolk as well. Bake on the lower rack of an oven preheated to 400° for about 45 minutes. Then dust the pie with powdered sugar and allow to caramelize in the oven for another 5 minutes.

Colorful Fruit Pie

1¾ cups flour
Pinch of salt
7 tablespoons chilled butter

1 tablespoon chilled
   shortening
2-3 tablespoons ice water

For the filling and topping:
2 cups almond macaroons
⅔ cup ground almonds
½ cup sugar
4-6 oranges
1 grapefruit
2 bananas

2 kiwis
3-4 tablespoons orange
   liqueur
Flour for rolling out
1 egg white
Sugar for sprinkling

For the dough, combine flour and salt on a work surface. Sprinkle butter in flakes together with shortening, also in flakes, over the surface. Using one or two knives, cut the ingredients until they have a crumb-like consistency. Then make a well in the middle and gradually add the ice water. Working from outside to inside, knead the ingredients into a smooth dough, form into a ball and refrigerate for at least 30 minutes.

To prepare the filling, place macaroons in a plastic bag and finely crush them with a rolling pin. Combine with almonds and sugar and set aside. Carefully peel oranges and grapefruit being sure to remove all of the white skin. Remove the segments from the membrane separating them, then cut each segment into two or three pieces and remove any pits. Peel bananas and kiwis. Cut the bananas into ½-inch slices; quarter the kiwis lengthwise and then cut into 1-inch pieces. Gently combine all the fruit with the orange liqueur and the macaroon mixture.

Use a deep-dish pie pan preferably with a broad rim. Quickly knead the dough on a floured work surface (or on floured aluminum foil) and roll out to a thickness of ⅛th inch. Invert the form, place it on the dough and cut out a cover that is ¼-inch larger than the pan. Gather leftover dough, knead it and then roll out again. Cut out a strip of dough that is slightly broader than the rim of the form. Brush the rim with cold water and lay the strip of dough on it. Press very firmly so that it will continue to adhere to the pan during baking. Fill the fruit mixture into the form so that the filling is slightly higher in the center than at the edges. Lay the cover on top and firmly attach it to the strip of dough on the rim. Now cut off any overlapping dough; to do this, hold the knife at an angle with the blade pointing upward and outward. Finally, notch the edge of the dough repeatedly with the back of the knife and brush the surface with whisked egg white. Sprinkle with sugar and bake in an oven preheated to 400° for 40-45 minutes.

Pear and Ginger Pie

3¾ cups flour
Pinch of salt
⅔ cup chilled butter

3 tablespoons chilled
    shortening
3-4 tablespoons ice water

For the filling and topping:

2 pounds pears
Juice of 1 lemon
2 tablespoons butter
¼ cup sugar
4 tablespoons dry white wine
3 tablespoons pear schnapps

2 gingered plums
½ cup bread crumbs
⅔ cup finely chopped walnuts
Flour for rolling out
1 egg yolk for brushing
Powdered sugar for dusting

For the dough, combine flour and salt on a work surface. Distribute butter and shortening, both cut into flakes, over the flour-salt mixture. Cut the ingredients until they have a crumb-like consistency, then gradually add the ice water and very quickly, working from the outside to the inside, knead into a smooth dough. Form into a ball and refrigerate for about 1 hour.

Peel, quarter and core the pears. Cut the quarters into thin slices and immediately sprinkle with lemon juice. Melt the butter in a large pan, sprinkle in sugar and, as soon as it has dissolved, add the pears together with white wine and pear schnapps. Carefully turn the pears in the butter a few times and stew for 2-3 minutes. In the meantime, drain the gingered plums and add 1 teaspoon of the drained-off liquid to the pears. Remove the pan from the heat and place the contents in a bowl to avoid overcooking the pears. Cut the gingered plums into tiny slivers or

cubes and gently mix into the pear mixture together with the bread crumbs and nuts.

Roll out a little less than half of the dough on a lightly floured work surface. Invert the pie pan on it and cut out a dough cover. Knead any leftovers into the remaining dough. Roll out again and line the form. Any remaining dough can be used to make small shapes to decorate the cover.

Gently press the dough into the form, fill in the pear mixture and lay the cover on top. Firmly press the rim of the cover onto that of the shell and cut a "chimney" in the center of the cover. Brush the surface with the whisked egg yolk. Lay the decorative dough pieces on top and brush them with egg as well, then bake on the middle rack of an oven preheated to 400° for about 45 minutes. Dust the surface with powdered sugar 5 minutes before the pie is done and allow this coating to caramelize. To accomplish this more quickly, slide the pie under the broiler.

Serve the pie while still hot or just slightly cooled. It can be offered with whipped cream, if desired.

Blueberry Pie

1 10-ounce package frozen puff pastry	1 ripe pear
Flour for rolling out	1 banana
½ package sponge cookies or ladyfingers	Juice of ½ lemon
4 ounces nut or almond macaroons (commercially available)	½ cup sugar
	2-3 tablespoons rum or cognac
1 cup ground hazelnuts	1 egg yolk
½ pound blueberries	2 tablespoons whipping cream
	Powdered sugar for dusting

Separate the puff pastry layers, lay them out next to each other and thaw according to package directions. Then brush them very thinly with water and stack them on top of each other on a lightly floured work surface. While applying gentle but even pressure (the individual layers should not be squashed), thinly roll out the pastry in all directions. Place an inverted pie pan on the dough and cut out a cover. Lay this cover on a platter and refrigerate it. Roll the remaining dough onto a lightly floured rolling pin and then unroll it into the pie pan which has been rinsed out with very cold water. Loosely line the pan with the dough so that it overlaps the rim slightly. Pierce the bottom repeatedly with a fork and refrigerate. Roll out the leftover dough again and cut out small decorative shapes which will later adorn the cover. Refrigerate these as well.

For the filling, place the sponge cookies and macaroons in a plastic bag and finely crush them with a rolling pin. Combine these crumbs with the ground hazelnuts. Sort the blueberries, quickly and carefully wash them in cold water. (Do not leave them submerged in water because they will quickly soak it up.) Lay them on several layers of paper towel and allow to dry; they may be gently blotted. Peel the pear and the banana and cut both into thin slices. Immediately mix both types of fruit with lemon juice to avoid discoloration.

Remove the pie shell from the refrigerator and fill about half with the crumb-nut mixture. Combine the remainder of this mixture with the blueberries, pear and banana pieces and the sugar. Fill into the shell as well. Repeatedly add a little rum or cognac filling in the fruit mixture. Cut a small chimney in the center of the dough cover so that steam can escape during baking. Lay the cover onto the shell and carefully press the edges together. To do this effectively, gently pinch the dough between the thumb, index and middle fingers while working all the way around the pie. Whisk together egg yolk with cream and brush onto the surface. Lay the dough cut-outs on the surface and brush with the egg-yolk mixture as well. Be very careful not to brush any egg onto the outside edges of the puff pastry; if they are coated, they may not be able to rise during baking.

Place the pie on the middle rack of an oven preheated to 425° and bake for 25-35 minutes until golden brown and tender. Shortly before done, evenly dust the surface with powdered sugar and allow to caramelize. Since this process occurs very quickly, stay near the oven and observe the changing color. When the pie is done, remove it from the oven and serve piping hot or slightly cooled.

> **Tip:** *This pie can be prepared using frozen blueberries. Either thaw slightly or completely before using them and then continue as above. Note whether the fruit has been sweetened and adjust the recipe accordingly. Red currants can be used in this recipe instead of blueberries. Another variation might also be a combination of red currants, raspberries or blackberries.*

Plum Pie Flavored with Marzipan

2 cups flour	1 tablespoon sugar
Pinch of salt	3-4 tablespoons ice cold water (see note at end of recipe)
7 tablespoons chilled butter	
1 tablespoon chilled shortening	

For the filling and topping:

1 pound blue or Damson plums	1 cup ground almonds
	Flour for rolling out
½ package sponge cookies or ladyfingers	Butter or margarine for greasing
½ cup marzipan	2-3 tablespoons plum brandy
¾ cup sugar	1 egg yolk for brushing

Combine flour with salt on a work surface. Cut butter and shortening into small flakes and sprinkle over the dry ingredients together with the sugar. Using one or two knives, cut all the ingredients to a crumb-like consistency. Then starting from the outside, knead all ingredients into a smooth and supple dough. While doing this, gradually add the water by the spoonful. Work as quickly as possible so that the warmth of the hands do not raise the temperature of the dough and cause the butter to melt. Then form the dough into a ball, wrap in aluminum or in a plastic bag and refrigerate for 1-2 hours.

To prepare the filling, wash, dry and pit the plums. Chop them coarsely, if desired. Place the sponge cookies in a plastic bag and finely crush them with a rolling pin. Dice the marzipan and place in a bowl. Add the sugar, ground almonds and sponge-cookie crumbs and mix together using the fingertips.

Roll the dough out on a floured work surface, lay an inverted pie pan on it and cut out a dough cover following the outline of the pan. Then grease the pan with butter or margarine. Roll the remaining dough onto a floured rolling pin and unroll it into the pie pan. Gently press in the dough and cut off any overlapping edges. Pierce the bottom repeatedly with a fork and pour in a layer of the marzipan-crumb mixture. Combine the plums with the remaining marzipan-crumb mixture and fill into the form alternating with the liqueur, which should be dripped in. Place the cover on top and carefully pinch all the edges together. Cut a chimney into the center. (This may be done before the cover is in place.) Brush the surface with some of the whisked egg yolk. Knead together the remaining dough, roll out again and cut out small decorative shapes. Lay these on the surface and brush them with egg as well. Bake the plum pie in an oven preheated to 400° for 40-45 minutes until the crust is golden brown and the filling tender. Remove from the oven and serve lukewarm or just barely cold. Both whipped cream, either unsweetened or lightly flavored with vanilla, and vanilla ice cream are excellent accompaniments.

Note

The ice water ensures that the dough is especially light and flaky. Therefore, avoid using water straight out of the faucet. Instead, melt a few ice cubes and use them right after they have melted and before they have had a chance to warm up. This little extra will really pay off.

Pineapple Patties with Rhubarb

1⅔ cups flour	1 tablespoon sugar
Pinch of salt	7 tablespoons chilled butter

For the filling and topping:

10 ounces rhubarb	2-3 tablespoons white rum
⅔ cup sugar	1 vanilla bean
4 ounces almond macaroons	2 tablespoons flour
2 heaping tablespoons cornflakes	⅓ cup ground almonds
	Flour for rolling out
½ pineapple (about 1 pound)	1 egg yolk for brushing
1 egg	

Combine flour with salt and sugar and place on a work surface. Add the chilled butter cut into flakes. Using two knives, cut to a crumb-like consistency. Then, with chilled hands (hold them under cold running water and dry them well beforehand), very quickly knead the ingredients into a smooth dough by working from the outside to the inside. Form into a ball, wrap in aluminum foil or a plastic bag and refrigerate for at least 1 hour.

Prepare the filling. If necessary, remove the strings from the rhubarb, then cut it into ½-inch pieces. If the stalks are very broad they can also be cut lengthwise. Place some water in a pan, add about ⅔ of the sugar and bring to a boil. Add the rhubarb and stew over low heat for about 3 minutes until just barely tender. Drain into a sieve and allow to cool. Place almond macaroons and cornflakes in a plastic bag, finely and evenly crush them with a rolling pin. Carefully peel the pineapple, and remove the inner core. Cut the fruit into pieces about the same size as those of the rhubarb. Place the egg into a bowl and beat it together with the white rum, gradually sprinkle in the remaining sugar. Slit open the vanilla bean lengthwise and scrape out the marrow with a knife. Add to the egg mixture and then continue beating until the batter is very foamy and the sugar dissolved. Sift flour over it, add ground almonds with the crumb mixture and fold in gently but thoroughly.

Thinly roll out about ⅓ of the dough onto a lightly floured work surface and place small ragout-fin forms upside-down onto the dough. Cut out dough covers by following the shape of the forms, place these on a torte platter and refrigerate. Knead the leftover dough into the remaining dough, roll out again on a floured surface and use it to line the forms. Cut off overlapping edges. Fill the forms half full with the egg cream mixture. Combine the cooled rhubarb with the pineapple pieces and fill them on top. Cover with the dough covers and press all the edges together well. Cut out a chimney in the middle of each pastry. Combine this dough with any remaining dough and cut out decorative shapes to adorn the surfaces of the pastries. Brush the surface of the pastries with whisked egg yolk, lay the dough cutouts on top and brush these with egg yolk as well. Place the pastries on a baking sheet or on an oven rack and bake on the middle rack of an oven preheated to 400°-425° for 25-30 minutes until the crust is golden and the filling tender. Remove from the oven, allow to settle briefly, then either serve immediately or right after they have cooled. If desired, the pastries may be dusted with powdered sugar.

Blueberry Puff-Pastry Pie

1 10-ounce package frozen
puff pastry

For the filling:

1 pound fresh or frozen blueberries	6 tablespoons Crème de cassis
3 tart apples	½ teaspoon ground cinnamon
2 tablespoons butter	Flour for rolling
⅓ cup sugar	Water for brushing
Juice of ½ lemon	½ cup cornflakes
	Sugar for sprinkling

Lay the puff pastry layers next to each other on a work surface and thaw at room temperature. Meanwhile, prepare the filling. Sort the blueberries, rinse in cold water and drain well; if frozen blueberries are used, thaw them well. Peel, quarter and core apples. Then cut the quarters into thin slices.

Melt the butter in a frying pan or casserole dish. Turn the apple pieces in the butter until they are thoroughly coated, then sprinkle with sugar. Continue turning the apples until the sugar has caramelized and is golden in color. Then pour in the lemon juice and Crème de cassis and flavor with cinnamon. Stew the apple pieces another 2 minutes to further reduce the liquid (do not allow the apples to become too soft).

Brush the layers of puff pastry with cold water and stack them on top of each other. Then place them on a lightly floured double-strength aluminum foil and, while applying gentle but even pressure, roll out to ⅛-inch thickness. Place a 6-8-cup, deep-dish pie pan with a broad rim on the dough and use it as a stencil to cut out the cover of the pie. Cut out a chimney in the middle of the puff-pastry cover.

Cut the leftover puff pastry into 1 × 2-inch strips.

Combine the apple mixture with the blueberies and cornflakes and fill into the pie pan. Brush the inside and outside of the rim of the pan with cold water and then, one after the other, hang the strips of pastry over the rim so that they slightly overlap.

Now brush this rim of puff pastry with cold water and lay the cover on top. Firmly press the rim of the cover onto the strips of pastry and then press the overhanging strips up against the rim so that they bulge out somewhat. Finally, anchor the cover one more time by pressing in the surface of the outside rim with the backside of the prongs of a fork thereby making a slight design. Brush the surface with cold water and sprinkle with sugar. Bake on the middle rack of an oven preheated to 425° for 25-30 minutes until golden brown. Remove and serve warm or cold. Crème fraîche or lightly sweetened whipped cream are excellent accompaniments.

Variation

This pie also tastes delicious with a currant filling. Either use red currants or a mixture of red and black currants.

Peach Cups

1 10-ounce package frozen
puff pastry

For the filling and topping:

4 small peaches	Flour for rolling out
Juice of ½ lemon	Butter for greasing
2 zwieback biscuits	8 skinless almonds
⅓ cup ground almonds	Sugar for sprinkling
1 egg	Water for brushing
Pinch of salt	1 egg yolk
3 tablespoons almond liqueur	½ cup whipping cream
¼ cup sugar	2-3 ounces cream cheese

Lay the puff-pastry layers next to each other on a lightly floured work surface and thaw.

Pour boiling water over the peaches, then peel, halve and pit them. Immediately brush the cut surfaces with lemon juice to avoid discoloration.

Place the zwieback in a plastic bag and finely crush them with a rolling pin; then combine with the ground almonds. Cream the egg with salt and almond liqueur, gradually sprinkle in the sugar. Continue beating until the batter is thick and creamy and the sugar dissolved. Then fold in the zwieback mixture.

Brush the puff-pastry layers with cold water, then stack them on top of each other. Roll out to ⅛-inch thickness. Invert a 2½-inch ragout-fin form and place it on the puff pastry. Use it to cut out 8 round covers. Gather the remaining dough and form into pencil-thick rolls. Flatten the rolls slightly. Grease the forms with butter and fill in the almond cream. Fill each peach half with an almond, invert it so that the cut side faces downward and place in the bottom of the form. Sprinkle sparingly with sugar. Line the inside edge of the form with the flattened pastry rolls. Place the cover on top and press all edges together well. Using a very sharp knife, cut the cover crosswise; then refrigerate for about 10 minutes. Whisk egg yolk with 2 tablespoons cream and brush on the surface of the peach cups. Bake on the middle rack of an oven preheated to 425° for 20-25 minutes until golden brown.

Cream remaining whipping cream with the cream cheese until smooth. Remove the peach cups from the oven, open the cuts in the surface slightly and drip in the cream mixture. If desired, the surfaces can then be dusted with powdered sugar.

Short-Cut Baking

Crumb Cake with Pears

1 package crumb cake
1 egg
½ cup margarine
Margarine or butter for
    greasing

¼ cup macaroons
1 16-ounce can pear halves
½ cup chopped almonds
⅓ cup chocolate decors

Pour the package mix into a bowl and add the egg. Sprinkle margarine in flakes over it and beat or knead the ingredients for 1-2 minutes to make the crumbs. Thoroughly grease a 10-inch springform pan and pour about ⅔ of the dough into it. Press out a smooth bottom, then repeatedly pierce it with a fork. Place the macaroons in a plastic bag and crush into fine crumbs with a rolling pin. Spread evenly over the surface of the dough to hinder the absorption of moisture during baking.

Carefully drain the pear halves in a sieve, then blot them dry with a paper towel. Place them close to each other, cut-side down, on the dough and press gently. Gently fold the chopped almonds and the chocolate decors into the remaining crumb dough. Work quickly so that the chocolate has no chance to stick to the dough or melt. Sprinkle this mixture over the pears and immediately bake on the middle rack of an oven preheated to 400° for about 45 minutes. Remove from the springform pan and slide onto a rack. Allow to cool completely, then serve while still fresh.

Note

If possible, serve this "quickly made" torte immediately after it has cooled. Then it will still be quite crispy and it will taste its very best. If allowed to stand for a longer period of time, the pears could soak through in spite of the layer of macaroon crumbs. This would considerably diminish the cake's delicious taste. Of course, the fruit can be varied depending on the season.

> **Tip:** *Serve this cake with stiffly whipped cream that has been flavored with vanilla and sugar. Or combine vanilla and sugar, or sugar and rum, with crème fraîche instead of whipping cream.*
>
> *This cake tastes especially delicious when served while still warm with ice cold whipping cream which may be offered in its unwhipped state. This is how the French serve their tortes.*

Cranberry Cheese Torte

1 package almond cake
7 tablespoons softened butter
  or margarine
1 egg
1 egg white
6-7 tablespoons cold water
3-4 tablespoons almond
  liqueur
½ pound cranberries
Butter for greasing
Crumbs for sprinkling

1 cup ricotta or cottage
  cheese
2 egg yolks
Grated rind of ½ lemon
1 teaspoon almond extract
1 tablespoon cornstarch
2 egg whites
Pinch of salt
6 tablespoons sugar
⅓ cup ground almonds
Powdered sugar for dusting

Pour the contents of the package into a bowl, add the butter in flakes together with the egg, egg white and the water. Using an electric mixer, beat for 2-3 minutes at the highest speed until creamy. Combine the almond liqueur with about ⅓ of the dough. Rinse the cranberries with cold water, blot dry with a towel, and mix ⅔ into the stiffer dough and ⅓ into the moister dough.

Grease a 10-inch springform pan with butter and carefully sprinkle it with bread crumbs. Pour the larger quantity of cranberry-almond dough into it and smooth out the surface. Cream the ricotta or cottage cheese with the egg yolks, lemon rind, almond extract and cornstarch until smooth. In a separate bowl combine egg whites with salt and beat until stiff, gradually sprinkle in the sugar. Slide onto the cheese mixture, sprinkle almonds over it and gently mix all the ingredients together. Spread onto the cranberry dough and then place the remaining dough on top by the spoonful. Bake on the middle rack of an oven preheated to 400° for 80 minutes. Remove from the oven, allow to settle for a few seconds before removing from the pan, then place it on a rack. Dust with powdered sugar when cool.

> **Tip:** *Use a nut cake package mix instead of the almond mix. In this case, substitute nuts for the almonds in the cheese mixture. Any brand of package mix is suitable, however, be sure to follow the manufacturer's instructions and add the fruit only at the very end.*

Variations

Other fruit may be used instead of cranberries. Try red currants, whortleberries, chopped plums or prunes, halved cherries or coarsely grated apples. In all cases, be sure that the fruit is well dried.

Lemon Cake refined with Chocolate

6 ounces semi-sweet
   chocolate
1 package lemon cake mix
½ cup margarine
3 eggs

½-⅔ cup warm water
2 tablespoons cocoa
1-2 tablespoons cognac or
   cocoa liqueur

Coarsely grate the chocolate. Be sure it is not too warm when grated. If it has gotten too warm and begins to stick, chill it briefly in the refrigerator. Pour the lemon cake mix into a bowl, make a well in the middle and sprinkle the margarine in flakes onto the rim. Place the eggs along with the packet of lemon flavoring from the mix into the middle. Add 6-7 tablespoons of warm water and mix all the ingredients into a smooth dough by beating for about 2 minutes with an electric mixer set at the highest speed. Finally, quickly but thoroughly mix in the chocolate.

Pour the batter into a baking form and smooth out the surface. Bake on the middle rack of an oven preheated to 350° for 50-60 minutes. After about 15 minutes, open the oven and score the surface of the cake several times lengthwise with a sharp knife. After the cake is done, remove it from the oven and leave it in the baking form for about 10 minutes to settle. Then remove it to a rack. Place the cake glaze included in the package mix in a bowl. Stir in the cocoa, the remaining warm water and cognac or cocoa liqueur. Continue stirring until the glaze is smooth, then distribute it over the surface of the cake and even it out smoothly using a knife. Allow the glaze to drip over the sides in heavy drops and harden. Allow the cake to cool entirely before slicing.

Tip: *The surface of the cake may be decorated in various ways. However, be sure to add the decorations before the glaze hardens completely. Appropriate decors are chocolate wafers sprinkled with colored sugar, whole or chopped almonds (they must be blanched), coarsely grated white chocolate or thin slices of lemon or orange rind that have previously been washed in hot water and dried. Or, garnish the surface with crumbled croquant.*

Lemon Cake with Apples and Raisins

1 cup seedless raisins or
   sultanas
2 tart apples
Juice of ½ lemon
1 package lemon cake mix
⅔ cup softened margarine

2-3 eggs (depending on size)
6-7 tablespoons warm water
1-2 teaspoons ground
   cinnamon
2-3 tablespoons rum

Wash the raisins or sultanas in a sieve under hot running water, then thoroughly rub them dry with a towel. Peel, quarter and core the apples. Cut the quarters into thin slices. Immediately mix with lemon juice to avoid discoloration. Place the cake mix in a bowl, make a well in the middle and distribute the margarine in flakes around the rim. Place the eggs together with the lemon flavoring from the mix in the middle and beat all ingredients for about 2 minutes with an electric mixer set at the highest speed. Add the apples together with the raisins or sultanas and very quickly mix them into the dough with a wooden spoon or a spatula. Pour the dough into a cake form and smooth out the surface. Bake on the middle rack of an oven preheated to 350° for about 60 minutes. After about 15 minutes, score the surface of the cake lengthwise several times with a sharp knife. When done, remove the cake from the oven and allow it to settle, still in the form, for about 10 minutes.

Meanwhile, place the glaze mixture in a bowl and combine it with the cinnamon. Add the rum and stir into a smooth glaze. Remove the cake from the form and immediately pour the cinnamon glaze over it. Distribute it over the surface with a broad knife and let the excess glaze drip heavily over the sides. Allow the glaze to harden before cutting the cake.

Note

Of course, other types of fruit may be mixed into the dough. Try, for example, pear slices, pineapple pieces or pitted and coarsely chopped plums, prunes or peaches. In the case of the latter, substitute chopped nuts or almonds, or even grated coconut, either in part or completely, for the raisins.

Lemon Cake with Candied Cherries

½ pound candied cherries (in various colors)
1 package lemon cake mix
⅔ cup softened margarine

2-3 eggs
4 tablespoons warm water
4 tablespoons Kirsch

Halve or coarsely chop the candied cherries, then set aside. Place the lemon cake mix in a bowl, make a well in the middle and distribute the softened margarine cut into flakes over the rim. Place the eggs and the lemon flavoring from the mix in the well. Add 3 tablespoons warm water and 3 tablespoons Kirsch. Using an electric mixer set at the highest speed, beat all the ingredients together for about 2 minutes until a smooth dough is obtained. Add the candied cherries, and gently but thoroughly mix into the batter. They should be evenly distributed throughout the batter and care should be taken that they are not crushed. Pour the batter into a cake form and smooth out the surface. Bake on the middle rack of an oven preheated to 350° for 50-60 minutes until golden brown. After about 15 minutes of baking time, score the surface lengthwise with a sharp knife. This slit should not be deeper than ½ inch. Remove from the oven and allow the cake to settle while still in the form for about 10 minutes. During this time, prepare the glaze mixture. Place the glaze packet into a bowl, add the remaining water and remaining Kirsch, and stir until smooth. Remove the cake from the form, distribute the glaze over the surface. Using a broad knife, smooth and even out the surface. If desired, large heavy drops may drip over the sides. Allow the glaze to dry and the cake to cool.

Note

To decorate this lemon cake, halve the cherries (using all the various colors) or slice them into rings and then lay them on the surface as soon as the glaze begins to stiffen but has not yet become completely hard. Distribute the individual cherry pieces on the surface in such a way that one complete piece of cherry is on each individual slice of cake.

Drenched Lemon Cake

1 package lemon cake mix
½-⅔ cup softened margarine
2-3 eggs (depending on size)
7-8 tablespoons water
¾ cup powdered sugar

Juice of 1 orange
3-4 tablespoons orange liqueur
½ pound candied lemon and/ or orange slices

Place the lemon cake mix in a bowl and make a well in the middle. Distribute the margarine in flakes over the rim. Place the eggs and 6-7 tablespoons of water in the middle and add the enclosed lemon flavoring. Using an electric mixer set at the highest speed, beat all ingredients for about 2 minutes to obtain a smooth dough. Pour the batter into a cake form and smooth out the surface. Bake on the middle rack of an oven preheated to 350° for 50-60 minutes. After about 15 minutes of baking time, score the surface of the cake lengthwise with a sharp knife. Shortly before the cake is done, sift the powdered sugar into a bowl and stir together with the strained orange juice and 2-3 tablespoons of orange liqueur. Remove the cake from the oven, leave in the form briefly to settle, then gradually brush the powdered sugar mixture onto the surface so that it can be evenly absorbed. Remove the cake from the form, invert it on a rack, brush on the remaining sugar mixture and allow it to be absorbed as well.

Stir the glaze mixture enclosed with the remaining water and the remaining orange liqueur. Turn the cake over again and spread the glaze over the surface. Using a broad knife, spread it out evenly and, as soon as it begins to stiffen, attractively lay candied lemon and orange slices on top. Allow the glaze to harden and the cake to cool completely. The cake tastes best when first served the next day, thus allowing the flavors to develop completely. After it has cooled, it is advisable to store the cake wrapped in aluminum foil or placed under a cake cover to prevent excessive drying out.

> **Tip:** *There is a wide selection of commercially available lemon cake mixes. Any one of these mixes is acceptable, but follow the manufacturer's directions and, in the case of variations, take care not to alter the consistency of the batter too much. This will help to avoid unpleasant disasters. If uncertain as to how the various batters and doughs look (like butter cake, sponge cake and yeast dough), refer to the exact description of these doughs in the back sections of this book before starting to bake.*

Note

Package mixes cannot be stored indefinitely. Take note of the date indicating freshness when buying. It is safe to assume that all cake mixes (including those containing dry yeast) will retain their optimal baking properties for about one year. If the package has been stored in a cool and dry place, it will probably still bake up well even if this one-year period has been slightly exceeded. Cake that has been prepared from a mix will remain fresh just as long as cake made from scratch.

Fruit Bread made with Yeast Dough

½ pound dried fruit (apples, prunes, pineapple, peaches, light-colored pears)
⅓ cup raisins
4-6 tablespoons rum
Cognac or fruit brandy
½ cup dried dates
¼ cup diced candied lemon rind
1 package whole-wheat bread mix

1 cup lukewarm water
½ teaspoon ground cinnamon
½ teaspoon ground allspice
Pinch of ground nutmeg
½ cup coarsely chopped hazelnuts or almonds
Butter or margarine for greasing
1 egg yolk for brushing
⅓ cup blanched almonds

In boiling water, blanch the dried fruit together with the raisins for 3 minutes, drain and carefully blot dry. Cut into ¼-½-inch pieces. Place in a bowl, add the alcohol, cover and allow to soak. Pit the dates, dice them coarsely as well, then add them to the other fruit together with the candied lemon rind. Cover again so that the alcohol does not evaporate.

Place the yeast from the package mix in a large bowl. Add the warm water while stirring constantly, then cover and set aside for 5 minutes. Add the bread mix to the yeast mixture together with cinnamon, allspice and nutmeg. Using the kneading attachment of an electric mixer, knead the ingredients for 2-3 minutes into a dough. Cover with a towel and allow the dough to rise in a warm place for about 15 minutes.

With floured hands, punch down the dough, pour the fruit mixture and the nuts or almonds on top and quickly knead all ingredients together. Form into a ball again. Place on a greased baking sheet and, if desired, a greased rim of a springform pan may also be placed around it. Cover once again with a towel and allow to rise for 15-20 minutes. Then, brush the surface with whisked egg yolk, score the surface repeatedly with a knife and attractively decorate it with the blanched almonds. Thinly brush these with egg yolk as well. Bake on the middle rack of an oven preheated to 400°-425° for 50-60 minutes. Slide onto a rack and allow to cool thoroughly.

> **Tip:** *Alter the mixture of fruit as desired. Substitute dried figs for dates, use more apricots or pears than apples, plums and peaches, or substitute coarsely chopped walnuts for the nuts or almonds. In the case of the latter, decorate the surface with walnut halves.*

Apple Cheese Cake

1 package fruit torte mix
½ cup margarine or butter
1 egg
1 tablespoon water
Butter or margarine for
  greasing
Bread crumbs for sprinkling
1 cup ricotta or cottage
  cheese
2 egg yolks
⅔ cup sugar
3 tablespoons vanilla pudding
  mix

½ cup whipping cream
3-4 tablespoons rum or
  cognac
1½ pounds aromatic apples
Juice of 1 lemon
1 cup finely chopped or
  slivered hazelnuts or
  almonds
3 tablespoons honey
⅓ cup sliced hazelnuts or
  almonds

20 minutes before it is done, evenly spread the honey over the surface and sprinkle the sliced hazelnuts or almonds on top. Continue baking until the surface has caramelized to a golden brown and the filling is tender. Remove the cake from the oven, allow to settle briefly before sliding it onto a rack where it should cool completely before it is sliced into pieces.

Tip: *Be sure to follow the package instructions for the cake, and continue as in the recipe above. Any fruit desired may be substituted for the apples in this recipe.*

Combine the package mix with the butter or margarine, egg and water. Grease a 10-inch springform pan and carefully sprinkle it with bread crumbs. Fill in the dough and smooth out the surface. Using an electric mixer or a wire whisk, stir together the ricotta or cottage cheese, egg yolks, about ½ cup of the sugar, vanilla pudding mix and whipping cream. Continue beating until the sugar is dissolved. Flavor with the rum or cognac.

Peel, core and finely slice the apples. Immediately sprinkle with lemon juice to avoid discoloration. Fold a portion of the apples into the cheese batter together with the finely chopped or slivered hazelnuts or almonds. Spread this mixture onto the dough. Smooth out the surface and attractively arrange the remaining apples on top of it. Bake the cake on the second rack of an oven preheated to 350°-400° for 60-70 minutes. About

Tea Cakes

Punch Cake

¾ cup plus 2 tablespoons butter	6 tablespoons milk
½ cup marzipan	Butter for greasing
5 eggs	Bread crumbs for sprinkling
1 teaspoon vanilla	Juice of 2 oranges
½ cup sugar	Juice of 1 lemon
Pinch of salt	⅓ cup sugar
3 tablespoons rum	4-5 tablespoons rum
5 cups sifted cake flour	½ stick cinnamon
⅔ cup cornstarch	½ cup orange marmalade
1 teaspoon baking powder	1 egg white
⅓ cup candied lemon rind	2½ cups powdered sugar
⅔ cup ground almonds	Red and green candied cherries for decoration

Cream the butter in a bowl, gradually crumble in marzipan and continue creaming until the mixture is very soft and the marzipan completely incorporated into the butter. Alternately add the eggs and vanilla with the sugar and salt. Continue beating until the sugar is dissolved and the batter is white and very creamy. Then stir in the rum.

Combine flour, cornstarch and baking powder. Finely dice the candied lemon rind into very tiny pieces. There should be no large pieces since they will be in the way when the cake is later cut. Add the flour mixture to the creamed butter mixture along with the lemon rind and ground almonds. Stir all the ingredients together while gradually adding the milk. As soon as the ingredients are well mixed, discontinue stirring. Line a loaf pan with parchment paper, grease it and coat with bread crumbs. Fill in the dough, smooth out the surface and bake on the bottom rack of an oven preheated to 350° for 60-70 minutes. Turn the cake out onto a rack and peel off the paper. Turn the cake over again and allow to cool completely.

Squeeze the orange and lemon juice. In a saucepan, combine the juice with sugar, rum, and the cinnamon stick, which has been broken once or twice. While stirring constantly, bring to a boil and reduce to ¾ its original volume. Pour through a fine sieve and remove the spices. Stir the orange marmalade until smooth; if desired, a few drops of the hot liquid may be added to it. Then allow the punch to cool. Cut the cake into three layers. Drench the bottom layer with ⅓ of the punch, spread with marmalade and place the second cake layer on top. Drench it as well and spread with the remaining marmalade. Place the third layer on it and drench with the remaining punch.

Place the egg white in a bowl and beat it with a hand mixer. Gradually sprinkle in the powdered sugar and beat until a thick, white glaze is obtained. Glaze the cake with it and decorate the surface with sliced cherries. Do this in such a way that each slice is attractively decorated with cherries. Allow the glaze to dry completely before slicing the cake.

Raised Buns with Strawberry Cream Filling

5 cups flour	Flour for rolling
1 package dry yeast	Butter for greasing
⅓ cup sugar	1 cup whipping cream
1 cup lukewarm milk	1 teaspoon vanilla
1 egg	1 cup strawberry marmalade
Generous pinch of salt	Powdered sugar for dusting
⅓ cup softened butter	

Pour the flour into a bowl and make a well in the middle. Add the yeast, some sugar, and some milk to the middle with a little flour from the rim to make a starter. Cover with a kitchen towel and allow to rise in a warm place for about 15 minutes, or until bubbles and fissures occur. Sprinkle the remaining sugar over the flour, pour in the milk with the whisked egg and salt. Distribute the softened butter in flakes onto the rim. Vigorously stir together all the ingredients and beat the dough until bubbles occur and it no longer sticks to the sides of the bowl. Again cover with a towel and allow to rise for 20 minutes; the dough should double its volume and the surface should appear "woolly." With flat hands, press the dough together to exhaust any excess gas. Vigorously knead it and then roll it out on a lightly floured surface to finger thickness. With a cookie cutter (or a thin-rimmed glass), cut out rounds of dough measuring 3 inches in diameter. Place them on a greased baking sheet leaving sufficient room between each one for expansion during baking. Cover once more with a towel and allow to rise for 20 minutes to the shape of round balls. Bake on the middle rack of an oven preheated to 425° for about 20 minutes until golden brown. Immediately remove from the baking sheet and place the balls next to each other on a rack to cool.

Combine the whipping cream with vanilla and whip until stiff. Stir the strawberry jam until smooth. Immediately after they have cooled, cut the raised buns in half horizontally and spread strawberry jam on the bottom half. Top with whipped cream and gently press on the top half of each bun. Dust with powdered sugar and serve immediately, since they taste best while fresh.

Shortbread

1 cup plus 2 tablespoons
    butter
⅔ cup sugar
1 teaspoon vanilla or grated
    rind of ½ lemon

3¾ cups flour
Flour for shaping

Cream butter until foamy. Gradually sprinkle in sugar with vanilla or finely grated lemon rind. Continue creaming until sugar is completely dissolved. Gradually stir in part of the flour, and knead in the remaining flour. Form the dough into a ball and refrigerate for 30 minutes. Then, on a lightly floured work surface, roll out to ½-inch thickness. With a cookie cutter or a large glass cut out rounds of doughs having a diameter of 5 inches. Score these rounds diagonally. Notch the rim slightly with a fork and pierce the surface repeatedly. Knead all the leftover dough pieces together and roll out again to ½-inch thickness. Cut into ½ × 2-inch bars and pierce the surfaces of these repeatedly with a fork as well. Line a baking sheet with waxed or parchment paper, place the cookies on it and bake on the middle rack of an oven preheated to 350° for 20-25 minutes until golden brown. Remove carefully and allow to cool.

TIP: *The cookies may be lightly dusted with finely granulated sugar before baking. This results in a delicate crust and tastes delicious.*

Shortbread with Marzipan

¾ cup plus 2 tablespoons
    butter
½ cup marzipan
¼ cup sugar

1 teaspoon vanilla or grated
    rind of ½ lemon
3 cups flour
Flour for shaping

Combine butter with marzipan and stir until creamy. Gradually add the sugar with the vanilla or finely grated lemon rind. Continue creaming until the sugar is dissolved. Gradually mix in the flour, first stirring, then kneading. Form the dough into a ball and refrigerate for at least 30 minutes. Roll out on a lightly floured work surface to ½-inch thickness. Shape as in the previous recipe. These cookies may also be sprinkled with finely granulated sugar if desired. Bake just like shortbread.

Note

To knead the dough from the beginning, all ingredients, especially the butter, should be very well chilled. Cut the ingredients (butter in flakes, crumbled marzipan, sugar, flour and spices) with two knifes, then very quickly knead them into a dough.

Scones

3 cups flour	6 tablespoons milk
1 teaspoon baking powder	Flour for rolling out
Generous pinch of salt	Butter for greasing
Pinch of ground nutmeg	1 egg white for brushing
⅓ cup chilled butter	½ cup whipping cream
⅓ cup sugar	1 teaspoon vanilla
1 egg	Honey and marmalade

Combine flour with baking powder, salt and nutmeg in a bowl. Sprinkle the chilled butter in flakes and the sugar over the dry ingredients. Using the fingertips, work until ingredients are well mixed and have a crumb-like consistency. Beat the egg together with 5 tablespoons of milk until foamy. Make a well in the middle of the flour mixture and pour in the egg-milk liquid. Using the hands or a wooden spoon, stir until a stiff batter is obtained. If necessary, add more milk. Form the dough into a ball and refrigerate for 10 minutes. Then roll it out on a lightly floured work surface to a thickness of ½ inch and cut out 2-inch rounds of dough. Place them on a greased baking sheet leaving adequate space between each scone. With a fork, beat the egg white until just foamy, and brush on the surfaces of the scones. Bake in an oven preheated to 425° for 15-20 minutes until golden brown. Whip cream until stiff, flavor it with vanilla and a little sugar. Fill into a serving bowl; place the honey and marmalade in separate bowls. Remove the scones from the oven and serve while still warm. They should be cut open horizontally and filled with a dollop of whipped cream and a second dollop of honey or marmalade.

English Ginger Bars

2½ cups flour	2 preserved gingered plums
Pinch of salt	⅔ cup sugar
1 teaspoon ground ginger	¾ cup butter
½ teaspoon ground cinnamon	Butter for greasing
Grated rind of 1 orange	1½ ounces chocolate

Combine flour with salt, ginger, cinnamon and grated orange rind. Drain the gingered plums and dice them finely. Combine with the sugar and the butter in flakes, then add to the flour mixture. Quickly cut all the ingredients to a crumb-like consistency. Grease a baking sheet and roll out well over half the dough onto it. Sprinkle the remaining dough as crumbs over the rolled out half. Bake on the middle rack of an oven preheated to 425° for 20-25 minutes. Allow the cake to cool briefly, then cut into 1 × 2½-inch bars. Remove to a rack to cool further. Melt the chocolate and decorate the surfaces of the bars with very thin ribbons of chocolate.

Tartlets from Engadin

4 cups flour	Grated rind of ½ lemon
Pinch of salt	¾ cup chilled butter
1 egg	⅔ cup sugar
1 egg yolk	

For the filling:

2½ cups walnuts	2 tablespoons Kirsch
1 cup sugar	Flour for rolling
⅔ cup whipping cream	Butter for greasing
1 tablespoon honey	1 egg yolk for brushing

Make a well in the middle of the flour. Place the salt together with the egg, egg yolk and grated lemon rind in the well. Sprinkle the butter in flakes as well as the sugar onto the outside rim. Using one or two knives, cut all the ingredients to a crumb-like consistency, then quickly, with hands that are as cold as possible, knead into a smooth dough. Form into a ball and refrigerate for about 30 minutes.

To prepare the filling, coarsely chop the walnuts and set aside. Caramelize the sugar by roasting it in a frying pan while stirring constantly until it is golden in color. Remove from the heat and pour in the cream while continuing to stir. Caution is advised here since the mixture will bubble up very rapidly when the cream is added. As soon as the sugar and cream are well mixed, stir in the honey. When this has been well incorporated into the caramel, work in the chopped nuts and the Kirsch. Allow to cool briefly.

On a lightly floured work surface, roll out the dough to a thickness of 1-1½ inches. Cut out rounds 4 inches in diameter. Grease 12 tartlet forms with high rims (or brioche forms), and line each with a round of dough. Knead the leftover dough together and refrigerate.

Fill the lukewarm nut mixture into the tartlets and roll out the remaining dough to a thickness of ¹⁄₁₆th of an inch. Cut into ½-inch wide strips and either lay them lattice-fashion over the tops (so that the filling is still visible), or braid them and then pull the braids apart slightly. Lay these on top of the tartlets so that they cover the filling. Whisk the egg yolk and paint the strips of dough with it. Place the forms on a baking sheet and bake on the middle rack of an oven preheated to 400° for 30 minutes until golden brown. If the surfaces threaten to become too dark, cover them with parchment paper for the last few minutes of baking.

Remove from the oven, allow to settle briefly while still in the forms, then carefully turn them out of the forms, standing them upright again, filling facing upward, and allow to cool.

Variation

Following the same recipe, make *Engadin Nut Tidbits*: Roll out the dough to ⅛-inch thickness. Cut into 2¾-inch squares. Place some filling in the middle and fold up the dough from each of the corners. Press dough ends together firmly. Brush the surfaces with whisked egg yolk and bake the tidbits for 20 minutes until golden brown in an oven preheated to 400°. Remove from the baking sheet and allow to cool.

Florentines

⅓ cup candied cherries	⅔ cup butter
⅓ cup candied orange rind	¾ cup sugar
⅓ cup candied lemon rind	3 tablespoons honey
¾ cup sliced almonds	6 tablespoons whipping cream
1 tablespoon flour	3 ounces chocolate
½ vanilla bean	

Finely dice the candied cherries, orange and lemon rind. Crumble the sliced almonds slightly and add to the candied fruits together with the flour, refrain from mixing at this stage. Slit open the vanilla bean lengthwise and scrape out the marrow. Sprinkle it over the flour and mix in. Then mix all the ingredients together.

In a saucepan, bring the butter, sugar, honey and cream to a boil while stirring constantly. Continue stirring until heavy strings hang down from the spoon when it is lifted out of the pan.

Pour in the prepared fruit mixture and continue heating while stirring constantly. Heat until the surface of the mixture just begins to pull away from the side of the pan. Immediately remove from the heat and place in a hot, but not boiling, water bath. (This is done to keep the mixture from hardening too quickly.) Line a baking sheet with aluminum foil. Using a moistened teaspoon, drop small amounts of the batter onto the aluminum foil. With a moistened knife, spread out the batter as thinly as possible making round wafers about 2½ inches in diameter. Bake on the middle rack of an oven preheated to 350° for about 5 minutes. Cool slightly, then remove to a rack and allow to cool completely.

Crumble the chocolate and place in a double boiler. Melt it while stirring constantly, then allow to cool until lukewarm. Brush onto the bottoms of the Florentines. As soon as this chocolate layer hardens, brush on a second layer. Allow to dry only briefly before etching decorative waves into the chocolate with a fork. Invert the Florentines so that they are right-side up and allow to dry. Serve as soon as possible. If they must be stored, place them next to one another in a metal box and lay a piece of waxed paper or aluminum foil between each new layer.

Apple Pillows

3 cups flour	½ cup apple jam or jelly
2 eggs	1 tart apple
1 egg yolk	1 egg white
4 tablespoons apple brandy	Flour for rolling and shaping
¼ cup sugar	Oil for frying
2 tablespoons butter	Powdered sugar for dusting

Pour the flour onto a work surface and make a well in the middle. Pour the eggs together with the egg yolk and half the apple brandy into the well. Sprinkle with sugar and butter in flakes and, working from the outside to the inside, knead all the ingredients into a stiff dough. Form into a ball, cover and allow to rest for about 20 minutes.

Stir the apple jam or jelly together with the remaining apple brandy. Peel, core and grate the apple. Add to the jam filling. Roll out the dough to a square having a thickness of ⅛th inch. Cut into smaller rectangles measuring 2 × 4 inches. Place 1 teaspoon of the filling on one-half of each rectangle. Be sure to leave the edges of the dough free of filling. Brush the edges with whisked egg white. Fold the second half of each rectangle over the filling and carefully press together the edges. Notch them firmly with the backs of the prongs of a fork so that the two layers are securely fastened. Heat the oil to 350° and drop in the pillows a few at a time. Be sure that the pieces do not touch each other while frying. Fry for 4-5 minutes until golden brown turning them once about halfway through.

Remove from the oil with a slotted spoon and drain on a thick layer of paper towels. Then remove to a rack and thickly dust with powdered sugar. Allow to cool completely.

Egg Wreaths

8 hard-boiled egg yolks	3 cups flour
¾ cup plus 2 tablespoons butter	Flour for shaping
1 cup sugar	1 egg yolk for brushing
2 teaspoons vanilla	⅓ cup chopped almonds
1 cup sour cream	Sugar for sprinkling
2 tablespoons rum	Butter for greasing

Press the hard-boiled egg yolks through a sieve and cream together with ¼ cup of butter. Cream the remaining butter with an electric mixer and gradually sprinkle in the sugar and the vanilla. Continue beating until the batter is foamy and the sugar completely dissolved. Mix in the egg yolks together with the sour cream and rum. Gradually sprinkle in some flour. Place the

remaining flour on a work surface and make a well in the middle. Place the batter in it and, working from the outside to the inside, knead all ingredients into a stiff dough. Form into a ball and refrigerate for at least 1 hour.

On a floured work surface, shape the dough into finger-thick rolls about 6 inches long. Form into wreaths and press the ends together well. Place the rings an adequate distance apart on a greased baking sheet and bake them in an oven preheated to 400° for 15-20 minutes until golden. Remove to a rack. Brush with egg yolk and sprinkle sugar and almonds on top.

Chestnut Fingers

6 egg yolks	1 cup ground hazelnuts
¾ cup plus 2 tablespoons sugar	3 ounces ground chocolate
⅔ cup unsweetened canned chestnut puree	Butter for greasing
	Sugar for sprinkling
3 tablespoons cognac or rum	1 cup whipping cream
6 egg whites	1 teaspoon vanilla
Pinch of salt	4½ ounces chocolate

Cream the egg yolks with ¾ of the sugar until thick and white. Stir the chestnut puree with the cognac or rum until smooth and gradually fold into the egg-yolk cream. Combine the egg whites and salt with the remaining sugar and whip until stiff. Slide onto the egg-yolk cream, sprinkle the hazelnuts and chocolate on top and gently fold in.

Line a baking sheet with parchment paper. Spread the batter onto it and bake on the middle rack of an oven preheated to 350° for 15 minutes. Turn out the cake onto a kitchen towel that has been sprinkled with sugar. Moisten the parchment paper and peel off. Allow the cake to cool. Shortly before serving, cut the cake into two layers. Cut one layer in 1 × 3-inch strips. Whip the cream until stiff and sweeten it with vanilla and sugar. Melt the chocolate in a double boiler over hot, but not boiling, water; then allow to cool to lukewarm.

Spread the cream onto the uncut layer of cake. Place the cut ''fingers'' close to each other on top. With a sharp knife, cut through the second layer following the edges of the ''fingers.'' Gently press the top layers onto the cream and frost with the chocolate which may drip over the edges. Allow the chocolate layer to stiffen and serve as soon as possible.

Classic Tortes

Zuger Kirsch Torte

For the Japonais layers:

1 cup hazelnuts	½ cup sugar
4 egg whites	1 teaspoon lemon juice
Pinch of salt	⅓ cup sifted cake flour

For the Genoise layer:

¾ tablespoon butter	1¼ cups plus 2 tablespoons
5 eggs	sifted cake flour
⅔ cup sugar	Butter for greasing

For the cream and decoration:

⅓ cup sugar	Pinch cream of tartar
4 tablespoons water	1¾ cups powdered sugar
⅔ cup Kirsch	¼ cup chopped or sliced
1¼ cups butter	almonds
3 egg whites	Powdered sugar for dusting
Pinch of salt	1 teaspoon chopped pistachios

For the Japonais layer, spread out the hazelnuts on a dry baking sheet and roast in an oven preheated to 400° until the brown skins pop off. This takes about 10 minutes. Then drop the nuts into a kitchen towel and rub them against each other until all the skins are removed. Gather the nuts and allow them to cool completely. Grind them in an almond mill.

Place egg whites and salt in a bowl and beat until stiff. Gradually sprinkle in the sugar while beating continually. The mixture should be quite stiff and gleam intensely when finished and it should under no circumstances become liquid. Beat in the lemon juice. Pour the flour on top of the egg-white mixture, then sprinkle over the hazelnuts. Fold in gently. Line one large baking sheet (or two smaller ones), with aluminum foil and mark two 10-inch circles on it. Using a pastry bag with a large smooth spout, press out the Japonais batter into the circles and smooth it out with a knife or spatula. (It is also possible to distribute the batter with spoons and subsequently smooth it out.) Bake at 250°-300° for about 60 minutes, then turn out onto a rack and peel off the foil. Allow the cake layers to cool.

For the Genoise layer, melt the butter over low heat, be sure that it does not turn brown. Immediately remove from the heat and cool until lukewarm.

Whisk the eggs together in a metal bowl. Place in a hot, but not boiling, water bath and beat until foamy using an electric mixer. At the same time, gradually sprinkle in the sugar. As soon as the batter has become very foamy and thick, remove the bowl from the hot water bath. Continue to beat the egg mixture until it has cooled. To accomplish this, briefly place the bowl in a cold water bath (but never in an ice water bath). Pour the melted butter into the flour in a thin stream and continue to beat. Stop beating as soon as the butter has been mixed in. Line a 10-inch springform pan with aluminum foil or parchment paper and grease the bottom with butter. Fill in the dough and bake on the second rack from the bottom of an oven preheated to 350° for about 60 minutes. Then turn it out onto a rack and peel off the foil or paper. Allow this cake to cool, preferably overnight.

The next day, place the sugar and the water in a saucepan and bring to a boil while stirring constantly. Allow to boil vigorously for 1 minute until the sugar has dissolved and the mixture is clear. Remove from heat, allow to cool, then stir in ½ cup Kirsch.

Cream butter. In a separate bowl, beat the egg whites, salt and cream of tartar until stiff while gradually sprinkling in the powdered sugar. Stir the egg-white mixture together with the remaining Kirsch into the butter. Lay one of the Japonais layers onto a torte platter and spread about ⅓ of the Kirsch-butter cream onto it. Drench one side of the Genoise layer with half of the Kirsch-sugar liquid and lay on top of the Japonais layer. Drench the other side of the Genoise layer with the remaining Kirsch-sugar mixture and spread the second third of butter cream onto it. Lay the second Japonais bottom on top and press very gently. Spread the remaining butter cream on the sides and surface.

Roast the almonds by turning them frequently in a dry pan until they are golden brown. Generously sift powdered sugar onto the surface of the torte. Then, using a long knife or a torte palette etch a design into the surface. Sprinkle pistachios in the middle.

> **Tip:** *It is possible that the Japonais batter will run when this cake is baked. If this should occur, cut off the edges evenly after the cake has been baked but before it has cooled completely. Grind these extra pieces into crumbs after they have dried and later use them to sprinkle on the sides instead of the sliced almonds.*

Note

Surprisingly, this Kirsch torte is made without any fruit. However, this Swiss version only calls for Kirsch—and quite a bit of it at that. To include fruit, decorate the surface with candied cherries, which the Swiss quite frequently do themselves. In Switzerland, often the Zuger Kirsch Torte is made with a pink butter cream. To obtain this coloring, combine a few drops of red food coloring with the Kirsch and to the cream. In the Japonais cake, substitute ground almonds combined with some cocoa for the roasted hazelnuts.

Mozart's Pigtail

5½ cups flour	Pinch of salt
1 package dry yeast	Grated rind of 1 lemon
⅔ cup sugar	1 cup candied lemon rind
½ cup lukewarm milk	Flour for shaping
1 egg	Butter or margarine for
1 egg yolk	greasing
7 tablespoons softened butter	Milk for brushing

For the glaze:

6 tablespoons sugar	1 cup apricot marmalade
5 tablespoons water	2½ cups powdered sugar
4½ tablespoons lemon juice	

For the dough, pour the flour into a bowl, make a well in the middle and add the yeast. Stir together with some sugar, some milk and a little flour from the sides to make a starter. Cover with a cloth and allow to rise in a warm place for about 15 minutes. By then the yeast should have risen considerably and large bubbles should be visible. Add the remaining milk together with egg, egg yolk, butter in flakes and salt. Wash the lemon under hot running water or, better yet, scrub it with a brush and grate the rind. Add to the dough as well and knead until smooth. Continue to knead until blisters appear and the dough no longer sticks to the sides of the bowl. Cover again with a cloth and allow to rise in a warm place for about 20 minutes. The volume should double and the surface should appear "woolly." Finely dice the candied lemon rind.

Punch down the dough again and knead thoroughly. Then work in the candied lemon rind. On a floured work surface, divide the dough into 8 pieces of equal size. Form each piece into a thumb-thick roll. Be sure that each piece is of the same length and thickness. Lay the strands on the work surface in such a way that they are pressed together at one end and radiate out from there in one direction. Weight down the ends that are pressed together so that they do not come apart during braiding. Braid the dough into an 8-strand braid as described in the back section of this book. Press the ends together well and place the braid on a greased baking sheet. Once again, allow to rise in a warm place for 20-25 minutes. Then brush the surface with milk and bake the cake in an oven preheated to 400° for 35 minutes. Slide onto a rack.

In a saucepan, combine sugar with water and ½ tablespoon lemon juice and heat until the sugar has dissolved and the liquid is clear. Press the marmalade through a sieve and stir into the sugar mixture. Continue cooking while stirring constantly and reduce the liquid somewhat until it is quite thick. Cover the cake with this. Combine powdered sugar with the remaining lemon juice and glaze Mozart's Pigtail with it.

Mazarin's Torte

⅔ cup softened butter	3 drops almond extract
2 tablespoons sugar	2 egg yolks
1 vanilla bean	2¾ cups sifted cake flour
Pinch of salt	

For the filling and trimming:

½ cup butter	
1½ cups powdered sugar	Flour for rolling out
2 eggs	Butter or margarine for
Grated rind of 1 lemon	greasing
3 drops almond extract	Bread crumbs for coating
1 cup finely grated, blanched	Powdered sugar for dusting
almonds	

For the dough, cream the butter until it "squeaks." Then gradually add the sugar together with the scraped-out vanilla marrow, salt, almond extract and egg yolks. Beat until the sugar is completely dissolved and the batter is foamy. Stir the flour into the dough as much as possible; knead in the remainder. Form the dough into a ball, wrap in aluminum foil and refrigerate for 2 hours.

Begin preparing the filling shortly before the dough is fully refrigerated. Here, too, cream the butter until it squeaks, then gradually add powdered sugar, eggs, grated lemon rind and almond extract. Cream until sugar is completely dissolved. Then fold in the ground almonds by the spoonful. On a lightly floured work surface, roll out a 12-inch round of dough. Grease a 10-inch springform pan and coat the bottom and the sides with bread crumbs. Line the bottom of the pan with the dough making a well-formed rim. Fill in the almond batter and carefully smooth out the surface. Bake the cake on the lower rack of an oven preheated to 350° for 45 minutes until golden brown. Remove from the oven and allow the cake to cool before removing it from the springform pan. Then slide it onto a rack and dust with powdered sugar.

Tip: *Mazarin's Torte tastes especially good when served with ice cold whipped cream that has been lightly sweetened and flavored with vanilla. It is also good with ice cold crème fraîche (again combined with vanilla marrow and some powdered sugar). Also try it with vanilla ice cream for a change. In this case, glaze the torte surface with melted chocolate. When served dusted with powdered sugar, chocolate ice cream is a superb accompaniment.*

Dobosch's Torte

⅓ cup butter	7 egg yolks
7 egg whites	1¾ cups sifted cake flour
Pinch of salt	Butter or margarine for
¾ cup plus 2 tablespoons	greasing
sugar	Flour for dusting
Juice of ½ lemon	

For the trimming:

1⅓ cups sugar	Juice of ½ lemon
1 teaspoon butter	Butter for brushing

For the filling:

1 cup plus 2 tablespoons	Pinch of salt
butter	½ cup sugar
½ cup plus 2 tablespoons	⅓ cup cocoa
powdered sugar	2-4 tablespoons rum or
4 egg whites	Kirsch

Melt the butter over very low heat and then cool but do not allow to harden. Combine egg whites and salt and beat until stiff, gradually sprinkle in the sugar. Continue to beat until the mixture is very stiff and has a strong sheen. Finally mix in the strained lemon juice. Beat the egg yolks briefly, then gently fold them into the egg whites. Pour the flour over the egg mixture and fold in gently but thoroughly. Grease the bottom of a 10-inch spring-form pan and dust with flour. Spread a portion on the bottom and bake it on the middle rack of an oven preheated to 350°-400° until golden. Repeat this process until there are 6-8 thin layers. After each layer, immediately remove the cake from the pan and allow to cool on a rack. Then select the nicest one and place it on the rack. In a frying pan, combine butter and sugar, melt over low heat and allow to become golden yellow. Stir in the strained lemon juice. Then immediately remove the pan from the heat and spread the caramel smoothly onto the selected cake layer. Immediately cut it into 12-16 pieces with a knife that has been greased with butter. Speed is of the essence, since the layer of caramel hardens quickly, it is likely to splinter if cut later. Set this torte layer aside until the glaze has hardened completely.

For the filling, cream the butter. Add the powdered sugar and continue beating until it has dissolved. Beat egg whites and salt until stiff, gradually sprinkle in the sugar and continue beating until the stiff batter has a strong sheen. Stir into the butter in smaller portions, then flavor this butter cream with cocoa and rum or Kirsch. Construct the torte by alternating the cake layers with the butter cream. Spread the remaining cream onto the sides. Place the caramelized pieces on top and serve immediately or store in the refrigerator until ready to serve.

The Regent Prince's Torte

1 cup softened butter
¾ cup plus 2 tablespoons
  sugar
7 egg yolks
7 egg whites
Pinch of salt

3½ cups sifted cake flour
⅓ cup cornstarch
1½ teaspoons baking powder
Butter or margarine for
  greasing
Flour for dusting

For the filling and trimming:

4½ ounces semi-sweet
  chocolate
4 egg yolks
½-¾ cup powdered sugar

⅔ cup softened butter
Pinch of salt
6 ounces chocolate glaze

Cream the butter until it is whitish in color and begins to "squeak." Then gradually add the sugar alternating with the egg yolks. Cream until the sugar is completely dissolved and the batter is very foamy. In a separate bowl, whip the egg whites and salt until stiff, then slide them onto the egg yolk batter. Combine flour with cornstarch and baking powder and fold gently but thoroughly into the egg whites. Grease a 10-inch springform pan and dust with flour. Bake 6 very thin cake layers one after the other out of the prepared cake batter. In order to do this, spread the batter thinly and evenly onto the pan bottom with a broad spatula and bake on the middle rack of an oven preheated to 400°-425°. Immediately remove the cakes from the pan and lay them next to one another on a rack to cool.

Crumble the chocolate and melt in a hot, but not boiling, water bath while stirring constantly. Stir frequently and allow it to cool until lukewarm. Then beat the chocolate with an electric mixer until it is very light and foamy. Add egg yolks alternating with powdered sugar and beat until the sugar is dissolved. Mix in the softened butter in flakes and a pinch of salt. Continue beating until the cream is light and foamy. Construct the torte by alternating the cake layers with the cream. Do not spread cream on sides or surface. Place the torte on a wooden board and weight it so that all of the layers form evenly. Refrigerate for about 2 hours. Crumble the chocolate glaze and melt in a hot, but not boiling, water bath while stirring constantly. Allow to cool until the surface just begins to "pull in." Pour it onto the surface of the torte and spread it over the top and sides with a broad knife or a spatula. This works best when the blade has been warmed over a gas flame or rinsed in hot water and then dried again. Allow the glaze to harden completely, then cut into 12-16 pieces with a warmed knife.

Rembrandt's Torte

7½ cups sifted cake flour
1 teaspoon baking powder
7 eggs
1 cup sugar
Pinch of salt
Grated rind of 1 lemon

1⅓ cups chilled butter or
    margarine
Flour for rolling out
Butter or margarine for
    greasing

For the filling and trimming:
⅓ cup cocoa
⅓ cup cornstarch
2 cups milk
Pinch of salt
1⅓ cups butter

1½ cups powdered sugar
1-2 tablespoons rum
3 ounces shaved chocolate
Powdered sugar for dusting

For the dough, combine flour with baking powder and pour onto a work surface. Make a large well in the middle. Pour in the eggs and distribute the sugar together with the salt around the rim. Thoroughly wash the lemon under hot running water. Grate the rind very finely, then sprinkle it over the eggs. Distribute the butter in flakes onto the rim of flour. Cut all the ingredients with two knives to a crumb-like consistency, then with cool hands (hold them under cold running water for a length of time beforehand and then dry them well), very quickly knead the ingredients into a homogeneous dough working from the outside to the inside. Form into a ball and wrap in aluminum foil or a plastic bag. Refrigerate for at least one hour.

In the meantime, using carton or double-strength aluminum foil, cut out a stencil measuring 10 inches long and 8 inches wide. Remove the dough from the refrigerator and roll it out in smaller portions to a thickness of ¼ inch. Lay the stencil on top and cut out a layer of dough exactly the same size. Then decrease the size of the stencil by 1 inch. Roll out the remaining dough again and place the smaller stencil on it. Cut out a layer this size. Continue according to this "cutting plan of diminishing cake layers" until all the dough has been used. Bake the oval dough layers, one after the other, on a lightly greased baking sheet. Place them on the middle rack of an oven that has been preheated to 400° and bake for 10-12 minutes until golden brown. Immediately remove from the baking sheet and allow to cool on a rack. Never stack the layers, since they will then become soft and will stick to each other.

While the layers are baking (or while they are cooling), prepare the filling. Combine cocoa with cornstarch and whisk together with some milk. In a saucepan, combine the remaining milk with the salt and bring to a boil. Pour in the cocoa mixture while stirring constantly. Briefly allow it to boil vigorously, then remove the pan from the heat and place the chocolate pudding (which is actually a custard), in a cold water bath. Stir frequently while it is cooling so that no skin forms. A skin would later appear as tiny clots in the butter cream. Cream the butter until it "squeaks." Gradually sprinkle in the powdered sugar and stir until it is dissolved and the mixture is very light and foamy. Add the cooled custard in extremely small amounts and gradually stir in. Flavor with rum and test to ascertain the correct quantity needed.

Construct the cake as a pyramid by spreading the butter cream onto each of the cake layers and stacking them starting with the largest and working to the smallest. Place the individual layers on top of each other so that all the outside rims are equal in size, otherwise the torte might lean slightly. Place the remaining butter cream on top of the pyramid, smooth it out evenly over the surfaces. Crumble the shaved chocolate (with hands that are as cool as possible so that it does not begin to melt and stick), and generously sprinkle Rembrandt's torte with it. Refrigerate for at least 1 hour so that the flavors blend well with each other, and so they can be absorbed by the cake. This also facilitates easy slicing. Before serving, dust the torte with powdered sugar; keep the amount as small as possible, since the purpose of the sugar is merely to copy the light effects of Rembrandt's style of painting. Then cut the torte into equal-sized pieces with a sharp serrated knife (or, better yet, with an electric knife). The pieces should not be too large since this torte offers a generous number of layers. Also, because of the butter cream, the ingredients are quite rich and it's not exactly low-calorie fare.

Tip: *Such a large quantity of tart dough can certainly be cooled more quickly if it is divided into smaller portions. These can be wrapped separately and refrigerated. This cooling technique indeed proves to be quite practical since the dough is worked in smaller portions.*

An even greater "chiaroscuro" (dark-light) effect can be obtained when the torte is sprinkled with a mixture of light and dark chocolate shavings. Crumble both kinds, carefully combine and then very evenly distribute them over the exterior layer of butter cream. Here, too, the cake should be lightly dusted with powdered sugar as a finishing touch.

Bread Torte

½ pound stale bread
½ cup dried figs
¼ cup candied lemon rind
6 egg yolks
4 tablespoons orange liqueur
¾ cup plus 2 tablespoons
  sugar
Grated rind of ½ lemon

⅛ teaspoon ground coriander
½ teaspoon ground cinnamon
6 egg whites
Pinch of salt
⅓ cup chopped almonds
Butter for greasing
Bread crumbs for coating
Powdered sugar for dusting

Cut the bread into thin slices; lay them next to each other on a dry baking sheet and dry them in an oven preheated to 225° for 40 minutes. Allow to cool and then grind them in an almond mill. Dice the figs and candied lemon rind. Beat together egg yolks, orange liqueur and ¾ cup of sugar until foamy; flavor with coriander, grated lemon rind and cinnamon. Combine egg whites, salt and remaining sugar and beat until stiff. Fold into the egg yolk cream. Combine bread crumbs, figs, candied lemon rind and almonds and fold them into the egg yolk cream as well. Fill into a greased 10-inch springform pan that has been coated with bread crumbs. Bake on the lower rack of an oven preheated to 350° for about 40 minutes. Allow to cool before dusting with powdered sugar.

Potato Torte

⅔ pound boiled potatoes
⅓ cup raisins
4 tablespoons Kirsch
¼ cup candied cherries
¼ cup candied lemon rind
6 egg yolks
¾ cup plus 2 tablespoons
  sugar

1 orange
1¼ cups ground hazelnuts
⅔ cup sifted cake flour
1 teaspoon baking powder
6 egg whites
Pinch of salt
Butter for greasing
Bread crumbs for coating

For the glaze:
2½ cups powdered sugar
3½ tablespoons Kirsch

Immediately after boiling the potatoes, plunge them into cold water and peel them. Allow them to cool overnight. Grate them finely the next day. Wash the raisins in hot water, rub them dry and soak them in the Kirsch. Dice the candied cherries and lemon rind. Beat together egg yolks and ⅔ of the sugar until very foamy. Add the grated rind of the entire orange and juice of half of it. Combine hazelnuts, flour and baking powder and fold into the egg yolk mixture together with the potatoes.

Whip the egg whites and salt until stiff. Gradually sprinkle in the remaining sugar. Very gently fold into the egg yolk mixture together with the raisins, cherries and candied lemon rind. Grease a 10-inch springform pan with butter and coat the surfaces with bread crumbs. Fill in the dough and bake on the lower rack of an oven preheated to 350° for about 1 hour. Allow to cool. Combine the powdered sugar and Kirsch and glaze the torte.

Daisy Cake

½ cup butter	1 vanilla bean
4 eggs	3¼ cups sifted cake flour
6 egg yolks	½ cup potato starch
Pinch of salt	Butter for greasing
1½ cups plus 1 tablespoon	Flour or bread crumbs for
sugar	coating
Grated rind of ½ lemon	Powdered sugar for dusting

Melt the butter over very low heat, avoid browning it. Immediately remove from the heat and cool until lukewarm. In a bowl, combine the eggs with the egg yolks, add the salt and beat with an electric mixer until a thick, foamy cream is obtained. While beating, gradually sprinkle in the sugar. Continue beating until the batter is white in color, foamy and the sugar dissolved. Wash the lemon in hot water, dry it well and grate the rind. Slit open the vanilla bean lengthwise and scrape out the marrow. Beat both into the cream.

Combine the flour with the potato starch and add to the dough. Very gently fold it in, avoid stirring, otherwise the delicate structure of the dough will be disturbed. As soon as the flour has been folded in, pour in the butter in a thin stream, gently folding it in as well.

Grease a daisy form with butter and dust with flour or crumbs. Fill in the dough, smooth it out and place the cake on the lower rack of an oven preheated to 350°. Bake for 45-50 minutes, then remove the cake from the oven and allow to settle briefly

before turning out onto a rack. Remove from the form and allow the daisy cake to cool completely.

Dust with powdered sugar before serving.

> **Tip:** *Glaze the cake with a sugar glaze instead of dusting it with powdered sugar. This is the way it is served in Italy, the country from which it originates, when it is used as a birthday cake. Congratulatory wishes and/or flower motives are then painted on the surface. To make the colored glaze for painting, add a few drops of food coloring to some of the sugar glaze or use melted chocolate. Before trying this, be sure that the glaze underneath is dried before writing or drawing on it, otherwise, the colors will run together.*

Note

The Daisy Cake is usually baked in the daisy or "Margareten" form, which looks like a stylized flower. The use of such a form is by no means required. Lately, kitchen and cooking shops have been offering a wide variety of attractive fantasy forms, some of which may be equally suitable.

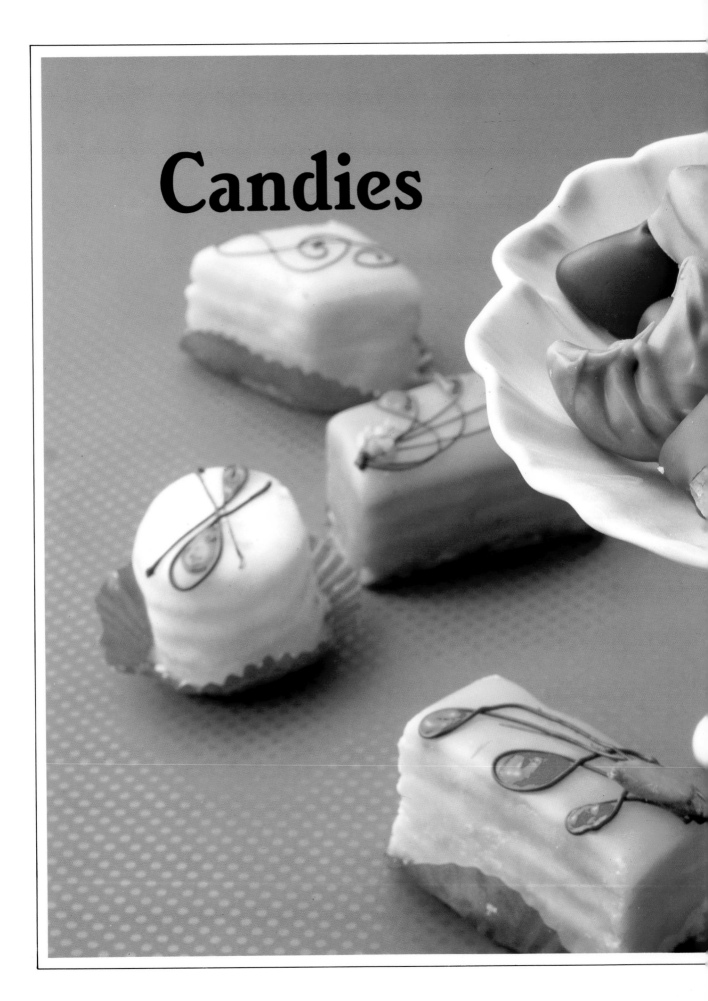

Candies

Marzipan in Koenigsberg Style

2¼ cups marzipan	1 egg yolk
2½ cups powdered sugar	Red currant jelly or raspberry
Powdered sugar for rolling	jelly for filling
and shaping	Raspberry schnapps or Crème
1 egg white	de cassis for flavoring

Crumble or coarsely dice the marzipan. Sift the powdered sugar and add it to the marzipan in small portions. Knead both together until the marzipan can absorb no more sugar. It should in any case never become hard and crumbly. Very lightly dust a work surface with powdered sugar. Place a portion of the marzipan-sugar mixture onto it and roll it out to ¼ inch thickness using a rolling pin lightly dusted with powdered sugar. Cut out the dough into any shapes desired but be sure to keep them relatively small. Cut an appropriately-sized hole in the middle of half of these shapes. Knead the cut-out marzipan with the remaining dough, roll out a portion again and continue cutting out shapes.

Whip the egg white until fluffy (not stiff or firm). Brush the marzipan pieces without a hole with this and carefully place a piece with a hole on top of each one. Decorate the edges with a marzipan pincher or pierce a delicate and attractive design in the surface with a toothpick or a small knife, or very gently apply a pastry cutter to decorate the surface. Whisk the egg yolk and thinly brush the decorated edges with it. Place the pieces on a baking sheet and bake in oven preheated to at least 425° or broil until the edges turn golden. Immediately remove from the oven since the confections can very quickly become too dark. While the edges are turning golden, stir the currant or raspberry jelly with the raspberry schnapps or Crème de cassis until it is smooth (if necessary it may be heated slightly). Fill into the holes and allow to cool.

> **Tip:** *When constructing the marzipan pieces, take care to align them exactly. It is only by paying attention to such precision that the confection will achieve its "full beauty." For variation, substitute a thick sugar glaze or candied fruit for the dot of jelly.*

Chocolate-Covered Slivered Almonds

½ cup butter	1 cup powdered sugar
1 egg yolk	2-3 tablespoons cocoa
2 tablespoons rum or cognac	1⅔ cups slivered almonds
Pinch of salt	

Dice butter and melt over low heat, avoid browning it. Remove from heat and cool until it is lukewarm. Beat together egg yolk, rum or cognac and salt. Sprinkle in powdered sugar and continue beating until the sugar has dissolved. Now carefully stir in the cocoa and finally, pour in the butter in a thin stream, followed by the slivered almonds. Using two teaspoons, drop small mounds of the mixture onto a baking sheet lined with aluminum foil. Allow to cool and harden. If desired, these may be served in paper praline cups.

Variations

To make light-colored almond splinters, reduce the amount of cocoa considerably and substitute instant coffee for the omitted quantity. Or melt light-colored chocolate then mix in the almonds and place these little mounds on foil. The same also holds for white almond splinters: melt white chocolate and mix in slivered almonds.

Florentine Marzipan Pralines

¼ cup candied cherries	½ cup whipping cream
⅛ cup candied lemon rind	2 tablespoons butter
⅛ cup candied orange rind	9 ounces marzipan
1 cup sliced almonds	1¾ cups powdered sugar
¾ cup plus 2 tablespoons sugar	A few drops of almond liqueur
Pinch of salt	1½ ounces dark chocolate
Pinch of ground ginger	1½ ounces light chocolate
1 cup flour	Blanched almonds for decoration
½ cup milk	

Finely dice candied cherries, lemon and orange rind. Crumble the almonds and mix all these ingredients together with sugar, spices and flour. Combine milk, cream and butter in a saucepan and bring to a boil, add the other ingredients and simmer, stirring constantly, for 5 minutes. Place the mixture in a hot water bath to keep it warm. Take out smaller portions and spread them not too thickly onto a baking sheet lined with aluminum foil. Either cut out small ovals or rectangles. Allow to cool and harden.

Knead together marzipan, powdered sugar and liqueur. Roll out on a work surface that has been dusted with powdered sugar and again cut out ovals or rectangles. Place two oval marzipan layers on either side of a fruit-almond layer and vice versa. Dip the rectangles into melted chocolate up to the upper edge. Coat the ovals with melted chocolate from the top down and top each with an almond.

Petits fours

5 egg yolks	¼ cup cornstarch
Pinch of salt	⅛ teaspoon baking powder
1 cup plus 2 tablespoons sugar	⅓ cup blanched, ground almonds
5 egg whites	Sugar for sprinkling
1 cup flour	

For the filling:

⅔ cup apricot preserves	Powdered sugar for rolling and dusting
7 ounces marzipan	
1¾ cups powdered sugar	

For the decorations:

3 cups powdered sugar	Candied violets, or other sugar figures; and, if desired, food coloring and sugar decors
1 egg white	
A few drops of lemon juice	
1 tablespoon butter	

For the dough, beat together egg yolks and salt until foamy, then sprinkle in ⅔ of the sugar. Continue beating until the batter is white and foamy and the sugar completely dissolved. Beat egg whites separately until stiff; continue beating while sprinkling in the remaining sugar. Slide into the egg-yolk batter. Combine flour with cornstarch and baking powder. Fold into the egg-yolk batter with the ground almonds. Line a baking sheet with parchment paper and evenly spread the dough onto it. If necessary, fold up the paper on any open sides so that the dough does not run out during baking. Bake on the middle rack of an oven preheated to 400° for 8-10 minutes until golden. Remove from the oven and turn the sponge cake out onto a kitchen towel that has been sprinkled with sugar. Immediately brush the parchment paper with water and peel it off. Cut the cake into four equal-sized pieces and allow to cool.

Place the apricot preserves in a small saucepan and stir over very low heat until smooth. Remove from heat and allow to cool, continue stirring; do not allow it to become stiff. Spread a generous ¾ of the preserves onto 3 of the cake layers, smooth out and then stack the layers. Place the 4th layer on top and thinly coat it with preserves as well.

Knead the marzipan with the powdered sugar until smooth, then roll it out on a work surface lightly dusted with powdered sugar. Place the marzipan on top of the final coating of apricot preserves as the top layer. Press gently. Sparingly dust with powdered sugar and cover with a piece of parchment paper. Lay a wooden board on top to weight it somewhat. Then allow to rest in a cool place for 24 hours so that all the layers can bond together well and become equal in thickness. The next day, remove the board and the parchment paper. Cut the sponge cake into very small pieces (squares, rectangles, triangles, trapezoids and circles).

To decorate, pour the powdered sugar into a bowl, add the egg white and stir into a thick glaze with a few drops of sparingly added lemon juice. Continue working this mixture until it is very stiff and has a strong sheen. Melt the butter over very mild heat, but do not allow it to get hot. Stir it into the sugar glaze drop by drop so that the glaze becomes supple. This mixture may now be divided as desired and colored with food coloring added drop by

drop. Be sure to add the food coloring in minimal increments since it will quickly produce intense colors. The classic Petits fours are pastel and never frosted in screaming red, blues and greens.

Place the Petits fours on a kitchen rack. Slide a piece of parchment paper or aluminum foil under it. Carefully and evenly glaze the cake pieces and smooth out all the edges. Allow the glaze to dry somewhat, then decorate with the colorful sugar flowers and other figures. All the decorations should be small and delicate so that the Petits fours are appealing to the eye.

> **Tip:** *The amount of marzipan in this recipe is generous enough to easily roll out two equal-sized layers and use one as a middle layer between the pieces of sponge cake. For completely smooth sides on the Petits fours, cover all the exposed surfaces. Roll the marzipan out to a layer double the size used above. Then cut out the desired shapes and lay them evenly over the surfaces and sides of the Petits fours. To accomplish this, the sides should also be thinly coated with apricot preserves so that the layers will stick together well.*

Note

Petits fours are especially artistic when decorations are painted on with the egg-white glaze. Take a small amount of the prepared white glaze and color it with food coloring. Fill this glaze, which should be quite tough, into a parchment-paper pastry bag with a tiny hole or spout. Place the spout directly onto the top of the Petit four and, while applying even pressure to the bag, "draw" something like a bow, wreath, flower or spiral. Make sure that the string of glaze does not break in the process. When finished, release the pressure, leave the tip of the spout on the top of the Petit four, then press down very slightly before lifting up and away from the surface. Here, too, decorate the surface with colorful sugar figures (perhaps to cover up uneven beginnings and ends of the drawing). Another possibility is to use a chocolate glaze instead of the egg-white glaze. Whenever decorating, be sure that the glaze underneath has hardened sufficiently so that it can no longer combine with the decorating glaze.

Candied Fruits

2 pounds prepared fruits like
oranges, kumquats,
pineapple slices, cherries,
Damson plums, and yellow
plums

5⅓ cups sugar
8 cups water

First prepare the fruit. Thoroughly brush oranges and kumquats under hot running water (the same applies for tangerines or lemons). Peel the pineapples, remove the eyes, cut into rings and remove the hard core with an apple corer. Thoroughly wash cherries, plums and greengages, halve and pit them. Place sufficient water in a large pot and bring to a boil. Place the fruit into it and, depending on the size and the type, allow them to soak for 5 minutes (or less) until they soften. Remove the fruit and rub dry with a towel. Cut whole fruits into slices (for instance, oranges, tangerines and lemons), halve the kumquats.

Place the sugar and 8 cups of water in a large pot and bring to a boil. Allow to boil rapidly until the sugar is completley dissolved. Using a sugar scale (see the tip) measure the sugar solution. It should measure 14 degrees on the scale. Remove the pot from the heat and allow the sugar solution to cool. As soon as it is lukewarm, lay the fruit in it and allow to soak and absorb the solution for two days. Remove the fruit and drain in a sieve. Retain the drained-off liquid and combine it with the rest of the solution. Bring to a boil again and cook until it measures 16 degrees on the sugar scale. In a wide-mouthed pot this should take about 8 minutes. Remove the pot from the heat again and allow to cool.

Lay the fruit in it again and soak for another 2 days. After this time span, boil the solution again until it measures 2 degrees higher. Allow it to cool, lay the drained fruit in it again as soon as the solution has cooled to lukewarm. Continue this procedure at regular intervals of 2 days until the sugar solution measures 33 degrees and the fruit has visibly soaked up the solution and is coated with it.

It should be noted that the cooking time constantly decreases as one proceeds. Clearly stated, this means that when reducing the solution from 14 to 16 degrees 8 minutes will be needed. To reduce the concentration from 18 to 20 degrees only 6 minutes are needed. For the last stage count on as little as 3 minutes to reach the 33 degree level. At this final stage, having reduced the solution to 33 degrees, allow it to cool until lukewarm and lay the well drained fruit into it as before. Again allow to rest for 2 days before removing it the last time and allow it to drain.

Reduce this highly concentrated sugar solution, still using an uncovered pot, until it is like honey and large, heavy bubbles form when it is boiled. Watch out for spattering; this mixture is devilishly hot and sticks to the skin. To test the consistency, stick a wooden, not plastic, spoon handle into it. Remove immediately and check to see whether the sugar on the handle is hard. If this happens right away, the solution has cooked enough. Immediately remove from the heat since the solution will caramelize and turn golden yellow or even brown if allowed to cook further. If the slightest hint of color is visible immediately add a little water; be extremely cautious because the solution will foam up hissing and spitting.

Either with a slotted spoon or skewered on a long stick, dip the pieces of fruit in individually and coat them completely with the glaze. Then lay the fruit next to each other, never touching or on top of each other since they will stick together, on parchment paper and allow to dry. Then lay the individual fruits in paper praline cups or aluminum foil and serve as soon as possible. Humidity in the air or the juice of the fruit can cause the sugar to dissolve again making the glaze soft.

Variations

Candied Fruit in a Coat of Sugar is made in this way. Candy the fruit as described above, coat it with a very thick syrup, place on parchment paper and allow to begin to dry, but not dry completely. Then turn the fruit pieces in granulated sugar and allow to dry fully. They will have an attractive, crystalline surface and will not stick together as quickly when stored.

Candied Fruit in a Coat of Chocolate is made by allowing the final thick, honey-like sugar glaze to dry completely. Then either dip the pieces in melted chocolate or coat them with it. Avoid having the chocolate too warm, otherwise the outer layer of sugar glaze could melt and the chocolate would not stick properly.

> **Tip:** *In order to get an exact measurement of the sugar in the solution, one needs a sugar scale, which is also sold under the name of sugar thermometer or degree measurer. It is generally only available in very well stocked kitchen stores and of course in bakery supply stores.*

Butter Truffles Flavored with Mocha and Cognac

½ cup butter
1 cup grated semi-sweet or mocha-flavored chocolate

2 teaspoons instant coffee
1-2 tablespoons mocha liqueur or cognac

Place the butter in a bowl and cream it with a wooden spoon or a spatula. It should squeak, just like when making a good butter cake. Then gradually sprinkle in the chocolate while stirring constantly. Alternately mix in the instant coffee with the coffee liqueur or cognac. Continue stirring after each addition until the added ingredient is fully incorporated into the butter mixture. After a homogeneous batter is obtained, it is essential to continue stirring until the cream is light and airy. If necessary, refrigerate briefly but do not allow the cream to become too hard. Then gently stir through the cream without disturbing its light consistency and fill into a pastry bag with a large star spout. Have praline cups ready. Using the pastry bag, press out a large, evenly formed dot of the cream into each cup. Place the filled praline cups on a platter and refrigerate. Serve after the pralines have cooled completely and become firm.

Whiskey Truffles

½ cup semi-sweet chocolate (or use half milk chocolate and half bittersweet chocolate)

2 tablespoons butter
½ cup powdered sugar
2 egg yolks
2-3 tablespoons whisky

Crumble the chocolate and melt in a not too hot water bath while stirring constantly. Do not allow the water to boil under any circumstances. As soon as the chocolate has melted, gradually and alternately add the butter in flakes and the powdered sugar. Stir until all the ingredients have melted and have been incorporated into the chocolate. Remove the pan from the hot water bath and carefully stir in the egg yolks one after the other. Flavor with whisky and test the taste. Fill the truffle mixture into a pastry bag with a large star spout and press out truffle cream into the praline cups. Refrigerate 3-4 hours until ice cold and stiff. Serve in the praline cups.

Note

Before refrigerating the truffle cream, shape it into small balls and roll these in powdered sugar. Here, too, they must subsequently be refrigerated and cooled well.

Layered Nougat Confection

1 cup light-colored nougat
1 cup dark-colored nougat

Cream the dark and light nougat separately. Then roll out small portions between two small pieces of parchment paper to a thickness of ⅛ inch. Cut all pieces to the same size and spread out again on new leaves of parchment paper. Refrigerate all of the nougat layers with the parchment paper and allow to become quite firm. Then remove the parchment paper from one dark and one light layer of nougat at a time and stack them on top of each other. Work quickly and carefully to avoid melting the layers with the warmth of the hands. Refrigerate the stacked nougat layers and cut them into bite-sized pieces with a very sharp knife only after they have become very firm. If desired, the surface may be lightly etched with the flat side of a serrated knife beforehand to make a waffled effect. Place the nougat confection in paper praline cups and refrigerate.

Variations

The Layered Nougat Confection can be varied in numerous ways. Coat the individual pieces with a chocolate glaze that has been melted and cooled down to lukewarm again. As soon as the glaze begins to stiffen, pull the prongs of a fork across the surface to make lines. a dark-chocolate coating decorated with a pistachio is done much more quickly, or coat the praline with light chocolate and, just as it begins to harden, swing a few lines of dark chocolate over it.

Light-colored Nougat Pralines

Cream the light-colored nougat and pour into desired praline forms or paper cups. (A pastry bag can also be used to fill the forms.) Refrigerate and allow to harden. Then carefully remove from the cups and place in new paper praline cups. Designs may be drawn on the surfaces, if desired.

Marbled Nougat Pralines

Cream dark and light nougat separately. Cool slightly. Then, with hands that are chilled or dusted with powdered sugar, shape into round or oval forms. Refrigerate well, and top with an almond, nut or coffee bean, if desired. Then coat with melted chocolate cooled until lukewarm.

Family Celebrations

Bread of Good Fortune for a Housewarming

3½ cups wheat flour
2½ cups flour
1 package dry yeast
1 tablespoon sugar
¾ cup lukewarm water
1 cup buttermilk
2 teaspoons salt
Generous pinch of 1 of the
    following ground spices:
    coriander, caraway,
    cardamom, fennel or anise
2-3 pinches ground white
    pepper

Flour for dusting and shaping
Butter or margarine for
    greasing
Oil for brushing
1 flacon salt
An attractive and, preferably,
    old bowl
3-4 tablespoons water for
    brushing
1-2 tablespoons sugar for
    brushing

Combine the flours and pour 2 cups into a bowl and make a well in the middle. Add the yeast and sprinkle with sugar. Stir in the water. Then cover this starter with a kitchen towel and allow to rise for about 30 minutes until it has doubled in size. By now large bubbles should be visible on the surface of the starter. Pour the remaining flour into a large bowl and similarly make a well in the middle. From the rim of the bowl, carefully pour in the raised starter and the buttermilk (which should not be too cold). Sprinkle the surface of the flour with pepper and distribute the spices on top. Work all the ingredients into a smooth dough and knead until bubbles appear and it no longer sticks to the sides of the bowl. It is best to do this with floured hands so that the dough does not stick so easily. Place the dough in a warm place and allow to rise until its volume has doubled. Depending on the temperature and surroundings, this may take up to 1 hour.

Dust hands with some flour, punch down the dough to exhaust any trapped air, place it on a lightly floured work surface and knead thoroughly. When finished, the dough should be completely homogeneous and very supple. Remove a small amount of the dough, cover the larger quantity with a kitchen towel and allow to rise again. Place the smaller quantity on a lightly floured work surface and roll into four thin ropes of equal length. They will later be used to form the numbers of the year and should be long enough for this purpose. Shape the larger quantity of dough into a round and very smooth loaf and place it on a greased baking sheet. Fold a piece of double-strength aluminum foil into a long strip, brush it with oil and place it around the loaf. Hold the ends together with a paper clip. This ring will serve to retain the loaf's shape. Brush the loaf's surface with lukewarm water and lay the thin ropes of dough on the surface shaped into the numbers of the appropriate year. Press gently so that they will remain attached during baking.

Mark the surface of the loaf with the aid of the salt flacon. Then, with floured fingers, make a small well in the surface. Brush this new rim of dough with oil and fill the "opening" with aluminum foil so that the dough cannot pull together during baking. Place the Bread of Good Fortune on the middle rack of an oven preheated to 425°. Immediately reduce the oven temperature to 350° and bake the bread for 1 hour until golden brown. About 20 minutes before it is done, place water in a saucepan. Dissolve the sugar in it over low heat while stirring constantly. Repeatedly brush the surface of the loaf with this solution so that it obtains a glossy sheen. After baking, leave the bread in the oven with the door slightly ajar (keep it pried open with a wooden spoon handle), and allow to settle and "steam off" briefly. Then remove to a rack and allow to cool completely. When the bread is entirely cool, carefully remove the aluminum foil and place the salt flacon in the well. Wrap the bread in foil or place it on a board wrapped in a linen cloth so that it can be served in the proper fashion.

> **Tip:** *Bread and salt are traditional housewarming, moving and wedding gifts. Therefore, be sure to present this gift "packaged" in the proper way. Garlands of flowers, small branches or colorful ribbons are especially appropriate. And the offering will be entirely authentic when presented with two schnapps glasses filled with schnapps, vodka, gin or a similar fruit liqueur. The lucky couple should then down these in one fell swoop and shatter the glasses on the floor. They can then be certain that all evil spirits have been expelled and will never be able to cross over their threshold.*

Note

Of course, other spices can be used to flavor the bread. Try allspice or ground dill seeds. It also looks very attractive when whole (that is, unground) seeds and kernels are used. However, if added, avoid getting seeds or kernels in the dough out of which the numbers are to be made. Seeds make the numbers look messy and they are not quite as easily discernible. If desired, the names or initials of the honored recipients may certainly be put on the top of the bread instead of the year.

Three-Tiered Wedding Torte

2 cups plus 3 tablespoons butter	3⅓ cups ground, blanched almonds
2½ cups plus 2 tablespoons granulated sugar	6¼ cups sifted cake flour
12 egg yolks	12 egg whites
Grated rind of 1 lemon	Pinch of salt
1 tablespoon ground mace	Parchment paper for lining the form

For the filling:

2-3 ½-ounce packages gelatin	1¾ cups finely granulated sugar
½ cup plus 1 tablespoon butter	4 cups whipping cream
6 egg yolks	6 egg whites
Juice of 4 lemons	Pinch of salt
Grated rind of 1 lemon	

For the trimming:

2 7-ounce packages marzipan	2-3 egg whites
7½ cups powdered sugar	A few drops of lemon juice
Flour for rolling and dusting	Sugar decors

For the dough, cream the butter until it is very light, then gradually add the sugar and egg yolks. As soon as the sugar is dissolved, mix in the grated lemon rind, mace and almonds. Continue beating until the batter is very foamy. In a separate bowl, beat egg whites with a pinch of salt until stiff; then gently fold into the dough together with the flour. Line three springform pans having diameters of 6, 9 and 11 inches with parchment paper or grease them. Repeat this process once in order to make 6 cakes in all. Fill in the dough and bake on the bottom rack of an oven preheated to 350°-400° until golden yellow, but not brown. Turn all 6 cakes out onto a rack to cool (preferably until the next day). Cut each cake horizontally into two layers.

For the filling, dissolve the gelatin in a small amount of water. Melt the butter in a hot, but not boiling, water bath and allow to cool until to lukewarm again. Pour the eggs together with lemon juice and rind into a large bowl and place it in a hot, but not boiling, water bath. Beat until foamy, then gradually sprinkle in the sugar. Continue beating until the mixture is thick, foamy and white and the sugar has dissolved. Slowly pour in a thin stream of melted butter, then remove the pan from the heat. While beating constantly, pour in the dissolved gelatin. Remove the bowl from the hot water bath and place it in a cold one. Continue beating the mixture until it is cold and begins to gel. In separate bowls, beat the whipping cream and egg whites combined with salt until stiff. Slide both onto the surface of the gelling mixture and fold in gently. Fill the cakes with this cream and stack them on top of each other in tiered fashion with the largest at the bottom and smallest at the top. Spread some of the cream between the individual cakes so that they adhere to each other well. Make sure that the smaller cake is always placed exactly in the middle of the next larger one otherwise the steps will not be equally broad throughout. As soon as the cakes are properly layered, trim the edges so that they are all even.

For the trimming, knead the marzipan with half the powdered sugar and roll out on a lightly floured work surface. With the aid of the springform bottoms cut a round measuring 6 inches and two rings with an outside measurement of 9 and 11 inches. Brush the cake surface and the steps with whisked egg white and "glue" the marzipan onto them. Gather the remaining marzipan, knead together, roll out and cut into strips as high as each of the steps. Brush the sides of the cake with egg white and line with the marzipan strips, press gently and allow to dry. Combine remaining powdered sugar with egg white and some lemon juice and stir into a very thick and gleaming glaze. The torte may be coated with a portion of this glaze if desired. Place the remaining glaze in a pastry bag with a very small opening (either smooth or star spout), and decorate the torte extravagantly. Brush the bottoms of sugar figures like flowers and garlands with the sugar glaze or whisked egg yolk and glue them onto the hardened glaze. Allow the completed torte to dry for a few hours before serving.

> **Tip:** *A less experienced baker may choose to brush the individual cakes with egg white and stack them on top of each other, this way avoiding the problem of spreading a cream layer between each large cake. With egg white the various layers are less likely to slip and move out of place.*

Variation

Many couples desire not only an extremely extravagant cake but also a very colorful one. In such a case, color the sugar glaze or some of the marzipan. Use food coloring which is available at supermarkets. Remember that they produce intense colors and a few drops will generally suffice.

Children's Parties

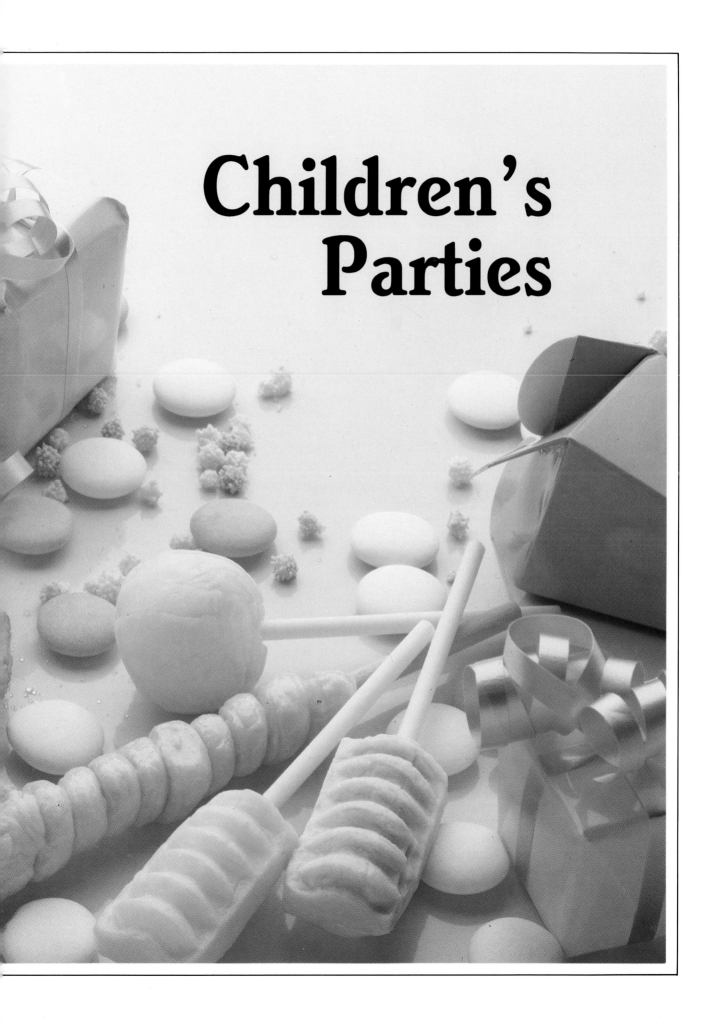

Mrs. Edith Schindel's Sweet Elephant

¾ cup plus 2 tablespoons
  butter or margarine
⅔ cup marzipan
5 egg yolks
⅔ cup sugar
Pinch of salt
3¼ cups sifted cake flour
⅛ teaspoon baking powder
⅓ cup ground almonds
3 tablespoons cocoa
1½ ounces grated chocolate
5 egg whites
Butter or margarine for
  greasing

Bread crumbs for sprinkling
1¾ cups chocolate glaze
  (about 14 ounces)
3 large triangular ice cream
  wafers
M&M's, jelly beans, sugar-
  coated chocolate wafers,
  sugar flowers or similar
  figures
If desired, 1½ cups powdered
  sugar, ½ egg white and
  food coloring

Cream butter or margarine with marzipan, gradually add egg yolks with sugar and salt. Beat until the batter is very foamy and the sugar dissolved. Combine flour, baking powder, almonds, cocoa and grated chocolate. Slide into the batter. Whip eggs until stiff, slide on top of other ingredients and gently fold everything together. Carefully grease a 10-inch springform pan and coat bottom and sides with bread crumbs. Fill in the batter, smooth out the surface and bake on the middle rack of an oven preheated to 350° for about 70 minutes. Remove to a rack and allow to cool until the next day.

Meanwhile, prepare a stencil as shown in the back section of this book. Place the stencil on the cake and, with a very sharp, thin knife, cut out the three "elephant parts." Plane the inside of the legs somewhat so that they will not stick together as the rump will. Melt the chocolate glaze in a hot, but not boiling, water bath and brush one side of both body halves. Lay on top of each other and press until well glued. Stand the elephant on its "feet" and glue on the trunk in the same way. As soon as all the parts are well fastened, thinly brush chocolate glaze on the edges of two of the ice cream wafers. Thickly and evenly coat the entire elephant with chocolate glaze. Glue the "ears" onto the head (this is somewhat easier when two slits are made to partially slide the ears). Cut "tusks" out of the third wafer and press onto the still soft glaze so that they stick on well. Finally, before the glaze is completely dry, apply the candied and sugar figures to make eyes, a saddle blanket, head ornamentation and so on. The more, the better. To further glorify this elephant with a sugar glaze, stir together powdered sugar and egg white into a thick and creamy glaze. Mix it with food coloring, if desired, and fill into a parchment paper pastry bag. Then paint away!

Crocodile made of Raised Dough

5½ cups flour
1 package dry yeast
⅔ cup sugar
2 cups lukewarm milk
2 eggs
2 egg yolks
Pinch of salt
Grated rind of ½ lemon
1 teaspoon vanilla
⅔ cup very finely diced
    candied lemon rind
⅓ cup finely diced almonds
Flour for rolling and shaping
Butter or margarine for
    greasing
Milk for whisking
2 large raisins
1¼ cups powdered sugar
1 tablespoon lemon juice

For the dough, pour the flour into a bowl and make a well in the middle. Stir the yeast into it together with some sugar, some milk and a little flour from the sides. Cover with a cloth and allow to rise for about 15 minutes. Then add the remaining milk, 1 egg, both egg yolks, salt, lemon rind and vanilla. Knead all the ingredients into a smooth dough and beat it until bubbles appear and it no longer sticks to the sides. Cover again with a cloth and allow to rise for 20-30 minutes until its volume has doubled. Punch down the dough and knead it vigorously. Knead in the finely diced candied lemon rind and the almonds and divide the dough into three portions each a little smaller than the previous one. Divide the largest piece of dough into thirds and roll into ropes or strands that are wider at one end and narrower at the other. Braid these making the smaller end into the tip of the tail and leaving the strands at the large end unbraided, it will later be used to form the mouth.

Similarly divide the next smaller portion into three strands and braid these in the same way. Whisk together the remaining egg with some milk. Brush the larger braid with it and lay the smaller one lengthwise on top of it. At the unbraided end, press together the pieces of dough and form into a head; make a deep and wide incision for the mouth. Shape the feet out of the remaining piece of dough. Brush with egg-milk as well and press into the body. Place both raisins on the head for the eyes and allow the crocodile to rise one more time. Brush all surfaces with egg-milk and bake on a greased baking sheet in an oven preheated to 400° for 40-50 minutes. Stir together powdered sugar with lemon juice and brush onto the still warm crocodile to give it a nice sheen.

Puff Pastry Swans

2 cups water	Butter for greasing
Pinch of salt	Flour for dusting
⅓ cup butter	1½ cups whipping cream
1¼ cups flour	2 teaspoons vanilla
1 teaspoon cornstarch	Powdered sugar for dusting
4-5 eggs	

Place water, salt and butter in a saucepan and bring to a boil. Remove from heat as soon as the butter has melted and the mixture begins to surge up. Immediately pour in the flour and cornstarch in one fell swoop. Stir with a wooden spoon until the flour is incorporated into the liquid, then return the pan to the stove. Continue stirring until a clump of dough forms and a white skin is visible on the bottom of the pan. Place the dough into a bowl and immediately stir in one egg. Allow to cool until lukewarm and gradually stir in the remaining eggs, first adding the next·one after the previous is completely incorporated into the dough. Depending on the size of the eggs used, the fifth one may be omitted. When finished, the dough should gleam strongly and hang down from the wooden spoon in long, firm ribbons. Discontinue stirring immediately so that the dough does not lose volume. Fill into a pastry bag with a large star spout, retaining about ¼ of the dough for the swan necks. Grease a baking sheet and dust with flour. Remove excess flour by holding the baking sheet at an angle.

Using the pastry bag, press out cream puffs onto the prepared baking sheet. They should be ovular in shape and come to a point at one end. Fill the remaining dough into a pastry bag with a smooth, medium-sized spout and press out the necks. Start with the head. Hold the spout still and press out a little extra dough, then in one smooth and quick movement draw an elongated question mark for the neck. Immediately place the baking sheet on the middle rack of an oven preheated to 425°. Place the side with the necks closest to the oven door since they bake more quickly. Bake the necks 15-20 minutes and the bodies 20-25 minutes. Do not open the door during the first 15 minutes under any circumstances, otherwise the dough will fall.

Immediately halve the bodies horizontally with a pair of scissors. Halve each upper half lengthwise to make the wings. Cool all the parts on a rack. Whip the cream and vanilla until stiff. Sweeten it if desired. Place into a pastry bag with a large star spout. Fill the bottom halves of the swans and stick the wings and necks into the cream. Dust with powdered sugar and serve immediately.

Little Mice made of Raised Dough

4 cups flour	1 teaspoon vanilla
1 package dry yeast	2 egg yolks
6 tablespoons sugar	Flour for dusting and shaping
1 cup lukewarm milk	60 raisins
½ cup raisins	60 blanched almond halves
⅓ cup candied lemon rind	Vegetable shortening or oil for
⅓ cup chopped almonds	deep frying
Pinch of salt	Powdered sugar for dusting

Pour flour into a bowl and make a well in the middle. Add the yeast and stir together with some sugar, some milk and a little flour from the sides to make a starter. Cover with a cloth and allow to rise in a warm place for 15 minutes. Wash the raisins under hot running water and dry them thoroughly with a cloth. Finely dice the candied lemon rind into tiny cubes and mix together with the chopped almonds and raisins. Set aside. Add the remaining milk and sugar to the starter together with the salt, vanilla and egg yolks. Sprinkle the prepared fruit on top and knead all ingredients together into a smooth dough. Knead until bubbles appear and it no longer sticks to the side. Cover again and allow to rise for 20 minutes. Punch down the dough, knead well and divide into 30 equal-sized pieces. To make the bodies, shape each piece into an oval; then affix two raisins for the eyes and 2 almond halves for the ears at the pointed head end. Place a sufficient distance apart on a floured board and allow to rise for 15 minutes. Meanwhile heat the oil or shortening to 325°-350°. Drop the mice, several at a time, into the hot oil and fry for about 4 minutes until golden brown. Limit the number of mice in the pot at any one time so that they each float freely without touching one another.

Fish the mice out with a slotted spoon and drain on a thick layer of paper towel. Affix the tails. To do this, make a knot at one end of a 4-inch piece of string and fray out the other end somewhat. Stick a toothpick through the knot and the string and press the tail into the body with it. Dust each mouse with a little powdered sugar and serve when cool.

> **Tip:** *For more mousy grey-brown mice instead of white ones, combine the powdered sugar with some cocoa or ground cinnamon before dusting the critters.*

Sponge-Cake Hedgehogs

5 egg yolks	Pinch of salt
5 tablespoons water	1½ cups flour
½ cup sugar	Butter for greasing
5 egg whites	Sugar for sprinkling

For the filling and trimming:

2 cups milk	½ cup plus 2 tablespoons
1 package vanilla pudding mix	powdered sugar
2 egg yolks	¼ cup cocoa
¼ cup sugar	¾ cup slivered almonds
Pinch of salt	9 ounces semi-sweet
¾ cup plus 2 tablespoons	chocolate for glazing
butter	

Combine egg yolks with water in a bowl and whisk until foamy. Gradually stir in ¾ of the sugar. In a second bowl, whip egg whites with a pinch of salt until stiff and gradually sprinkle in the remaining sugar. Slide into the egg yolk mixture, pour the flour on top and fold in gently. Line a baking sheet with parchment paper, grease it, pour in the batter and smooth out the surface. If there are any open ends, fold up the paper to keep the batter from running out. Bake on the middle rack of an oven preheated to 400° for 10-12 minutes. Turn out onto a kitchen towel sprinkled with sugar, moisten the paper with cold water and peel off. Allow the cake to cool completely.

Make a stencil for the hedgehog out of strong cardboard. For the hedgehog's body, cut out a 3-inch oval that is somewhat pointed. Place the stencil on the cake and, using a sharp knife, cut out the bodies. Gather the leftover dough, sprinkle onto a baking sheet and dry it out in an oven preheated to 400° for about 20 minutes. Cool and crumble finely.

Whisk the pudding mix with some milk and the egg yolks. Combine the remaining milk in a saucepan with the sugar and salt and bring to a boil. While stirring vigorously, pour the prepared pudding mix into the boiling milk and allow it to boil thoroughly before removing from the heat. Place it in a cold water bath to cool. Stir repeatedly to avoid the formation of a skin.

Cream the butter and gradually add the powdered sugar. Cream until the butter is very light and the sugar dissolved. When the vanilla custard and butter are at the same temperature, gradually add the custard to the butter while stirring constantly. Retain 2 heaping tablespoons of the butter cream and combine the remainder with cocoa and sponge cake crumbs. Thickly spread the butter cream onto the sponge-cake ovals in the form of a hedgehog. Immediately refrigerate and allow to harden.

Stick the almond slivers into the ovals like porcupine spikes, leaving the head free. While stirring constantly, melt the chocolate in a hot, but not boiling, water bath. Cool until it has almost hardened, then coat the hedgehogs with it. Place the remaining butter cream in a small pastry bag with a thin, smooth spout or place it in a parchment paper bag and press out the eyes and the tip of the nose onto the hedgehog's face. With the leftover chocolate, paint the pupils of the eyes. First melt the chocolate again, allow it to cool slightly, then fill it into a parchment paper pastry bag. Place a dot of butter cream in the middle of each eye. Refrigerate the hedgehogs until hard; serve chilled.

Raised Goldfish

5 cups flour	Flour for shaping
1 package dry yeast	Butter for greasing
6 tablespoons sugar	Pinch of saffron
½ cup lukewarm milk	2 tablespoons hot water
¼ cup softened butter	1 egg yolk
2 eggs	½ cup plus 2 tablespoons
Pinch of salt	powdered sugar
Grated rind of 1 lemon	Silver sugar pearls or raisins
¼ teaspoon almond extract	

Pour the flour into a bowl and make a well in the middle. Add the yeast and stir together with some sugar, some milk and a little flour from the sides to make a starter. Cover with a kitchen towel and allow to rise in a warm place for 15 minutes. Add the remaining sugar together with the remaining milk, butter in flakes, eggs, salt, lemon rind and almond extract. Knead all the ingredients together into a smooth dough. Continue kneading until bubbles appear and the dough no longer sticks to the sides of the bowl. Allow to rise for another 15-20 minutes, then punch it down and divide into pieces weighing about ⅓ pound each.

Remove a small ball of dough from each piece and roll it between the fingers into a small roll. These rolls will later be the lips. Shape the larger pieces of dough into elongated fish. Form the tails by indenting strongly from both sides and then stretching and bowing the ends outward. Brush the dough for the lips with whisked egg yolk, press together in the middle somewhat and glue onto the head. Score a few superficial slits to mark the head. Use a small pair of scissors to cut the scales into the remainder of the body. Place the fish on a greased baking sheet, being sure to leave sufficient space between each one for expansion. Allow to rise in a warm place for about 15 minutes. Dissolve saffron in hot water, cool slightly and combine with the whisked egg yolk. Brush the fish with it and bake on the middle rack of an oven preheated to 425° for 15-20 minutes. Carefully remove from the baking sheet and allow to cool completely on a rack. Combine powdered sugar with a few drops of cold water. Stir into a thick glaze and affix small dots of it onto each side of a fish's head to make the eyes. Place either a silver sugar pearl or a raisin on top for the pupil and allow to harden.

Marshmallow Morsels

1¾ cups marshmallows	2 tablespoons butter
6 ounces milk chocolate	1 cup cornflakes
2 tablespoons whipping cream	Grated coconut for sprinkling
1 teaspoon vanilla	

Coarsely cut the marshmallows and place in a saucepan. Either finely crumble or grate the chocolate and add it to the marshmallows together with the cream, vanilla and butter. While stirring constantly, melt over mild heat until a homogeneous mixture is obtained. Remove from the heat and mix in the cornflakes. Line a baking sheet with aluminum foil. Place small mounds onto the foil using two teaspoons. As quickly as possible, sprinkle the mounds with a little grated coconut so that the dark chocolate is still visible. Refrigerate for about 1 hour until the morsels have hardened. Either serve immediately or keep cold until ready to serve.

> **Tip:** *To store the morsels, place them into individual paper praline cups. Put them next to each other in a canister. To layer them, place a sheet of parchment or waxed paper between each layer so that they cannot stick together. Be sure to store them in a cool place or in the refrigerator.*

Sugar-Sprinkled Kisses

3 egg whites	½ cup finely chopped
Pinch of salt	almonds
¾ cup sugar	3 tablespoons flour
1 teaspoon lemon juice	Colored sugar sprinkles
2 cups grated coconut	

Combine egg whites with salt and beat until stiff. Then gradually sprinkle in the sugar and lemon juice. Continue beating until the sugar is dissolved and the batter gleams. Mix in the coconut, almonds and flour. Line a baking sheet with aluminum foil. Using two teaspoons, drop small macaroon-like mounds onto the foil and sprinkle with sugar sprinkles. Bake on the middle rack of an oven preheated to 325°-350° for about 30 minutes until crispy. Remove from the foil, cool and allow to dry.

Jello Ice Cream Tartlets

½ package red jello
1 cup water
3 tablespoons sugar
1 cup whipping cream
8 tartlets (commercially available)

8 scoops vanilla ice cream
3 kiwis
Colored sugar sprinkles for decorating

Stir together jello with water and allow to soak for 10 minutes. Add 2 tablespoons of sugar and prepare according to package directions; however, do not boil. Pour onto a platter and allow to cool and stiffen. Combine cream and remaining sugar and whip until stiff; brush the insides of the tartlets with some of the cream. Place the remaining whipped cream into a pastry bag with a star spout. Briefly hold the bottom of the jello platter in hot water, turn it out and dice finely. Distribute onto the tartlets and place one scoop of ice cream onto each tartlet. Cut the peeled kiwis into eighths, decorate the ice cream with 3 pieces each and then with whipped cream. Sprinkle with sugar sprinkles and serve immediately.

Banana Boats

3 egg whites
Pinch of salt
½ cup sugar
1 7-ounce package marzipan
½ cup ground almonds
¼ cup flour

1 large wafer
1½ cups powdered sugar
Lemon juice
7½ ounces chocolate
Toothpicks made of wood
5 small bananas

Whip ⅔ of the egg whites with salt until stiff, gradually sprinkle in the sugar. Continue beating until the batter is quite stiff and gleams strongly. Finely crumble the marzipan and fold into the egg white mixture together with the almonds and flour. Place this batter into a pastry bag with a large, smooth spout and press out 10 boats, each having the length of a banana, onto a baking sheet lined with parchment paper or aluminum foil. Place on the middle rack of an oven preheated to 300° and bake for 30 minutes. Immediately remove the boats from the baking sheet and slightly indent the bottoms lengthwise. Allow to cool and dry. Cut the large wafer into smaller triangles that will function as sails. Whip the remaining egg white and gradually sprinkle in the powdered sugar. Continue stirring until the mixture is thick and quite stiff. Flavor with a few drops of lemon juice; then thickly coat the sails with this glaze. Place a toothpick into the glaze on one side of the sail and allow to dry on. Peel the bananas and halve lengthwise. Trim them so that they fit onto the boats. Immediately brush bananas with lemon juice. Allow to dry, then place them onto the boats and coat with the melted, but cooled, chocolate. Stick the sails into the bananas with the aid of the toothpicks.

Holiday Baking

Bûche de Noël or Yule Log

5 egg yolks
5 tablespoons cold water
½ cup sugar
5 egg whites

Pinch of salt
1¾ cups sifted cake flour
Butter for greasing
Sugar for sprinkling

For the filling and trimming:
4½ ounces chocolate
1¼ cups powdered sugar
4 egg yolks
2 tablespoons cognac or rum
1 cup plus 2 tablespoons
    softened butter

Pinch of salt
1 tablespoon chopped
    pistachios
Powdered sugar for dusting

For the dough, combine egg yolks with water and beat until foamy, gradually sprinkle in ¾ of the sugar. Beat until the mixture is white, foamy and very creamy. In a separate bowl, combine egg whites with a pinch of salt, whip until firm, then slowly sprinkle in the remaining sugar. Slide the egg whites into the egg-yolk mixture, pour the flour on top and gently fold all ingredients together. Line a baking sheet with parchment paper and fold up any open edges so that the batter does not run out during baking. Grease the paper with butter and spread the sponge cake batter onto it. Immediately place on the middle rack of an oven preheated to 400° and bake for 10-15 minutes. Lay a kitchen towel on a work surface and sprinkle it evenly with sugar. Turn the sponge cake out onto it, remove the baking sheet and moisten the paper. Peel off immediately and roll up the sponge cake together with the towel. Allow to cool.

For the butter cream, add the chocolate and melt it while stirring constantly in a hot, but not boiling, water bath. Remove from the water bath and allow to cool down. Avoid allowing it to harden again, but at the same time cool down to no warmer than body temperature. Using a hand mixer set at the highest speed, beat it until very light and foamy, then gradually add the powdered sugar alternating with the egg yolks and cognac or rum. Mix in the softened butter in flakes and a pinch of salt. Continue beating until the mixture is very foamy and light.

Roll out the sponge cake and smoothly spread about half of the cream onto it. Now, with the aid of the cloth, form it into a roll again. Place the remaining butter cream into a pastry bag with a star spout. Refrigerate the roll and the pastry bag for about 2 hours. To make the bark, press out parallel lines down the length of the roll. Refrigerate another 3 hours, then cut off one or two slices and lay them against the log as "chopped-off boughs."

Dust the chopped pistachios with powdered sugar and sprinkle here and there on the surface of the log as "moss and snow." Refrigerate until serving.

> **Tip:** *If desired, 1-2 tablespoons of instant coffee may be added to the chocolate butter cream. Add it together with the powdered sugar and egg yolks. To forego using a pastry bag, spread the remaining cream onto the surface of the sponge cake and then etch in shallow furrows with the prongs of a fork.*

Christmas Tree Ornaments

3 egg whites
Pinch of salt
¾ cup sugar
½ teaspoon lemon juice

1½ cups flour
Various food colorings
Butter for greasing

For the trimming:
Gold and silver sugar pearls
Colorful sugar sprinkles

Chopped pistachios
Candied fruits

Combine egg whites and a pinch of salt and whip until stiff, then gradually sprinkle in sugar. Continue beating until the sugar is dissolved and the mixture is very stiff and foamy. Mix in the lemon juice. Pour the flour on top and gently but thoroughly fold in. Divide the batter into smaller portions and color them with food coloring as desired. Leave a portion uncolored. Line a baking sheet with parchment paper and grease with butter. Now, one after the other, press out forms like wreaths, stars, hearts pretzels, bows and so on. Choose only shapes through which a ribbon or string for hanging can easily be run. Sprinkle the individual cookies with sugar pearls, sugar sprinkles, chopped pistachios or finely diced candied fruits as desired. Immediately place on the middle rack of an oven preheated to 400°-425° and bake for 8-10 minutes. Carefuly remove from the baking sheet and cool on a rack. Wait until they have cooled completely before hanging on a string.

Note

The individual cookies may be decorated after baking as well. Using a cooled, still fluid glaze, paint the surfaces as desired and further sprinkle them with colorful sugar decors.

Lebkuchen Tree Decorations

Prepare half of the Gingerbread House recipe (recipe on page 234). Roll it out the next day to a thickness of ¼ inch and cut out appropriate figures. Bake them for 10-15 minutes at 400°. Immediately remove from the baking sheet and allow to cool on a rack. Paint them extravagantly with a sugar glaze (colored, as desired) and decorate with sugar decors. For hanging, pierce a small hole through the cookie and pull a string through.

Springerle

6¼ cups powdered sugar
4-5 eggs (depending on size)
Grated rind of 1 lemon
Pinch of salt
1 teaspoon ground anise
2 tablespoons white rum

5 cups flour
1 teaspoon baking powder
Flour for rolling and dusting
Butter or margarine for
    greasing

Beat together powdered sugar and eggs, then mix in grated lemon rind, salt and anise. Add the rum drop by drop and the flour combined with the baking powder. Knead together thoroughly until the dough can take in no more flour. Allow to rest up to one hour, this will help to keep the dough from sticking when it is formed. However, note that the longer it is refrigerated, the more difficult it becomes to form. It is therefore advisable to try forming a small amount immediately to find out which method works best. Roll out the dough in smaller portions to a thickness of ¾ inch. Dust the dough lightly with flour, then press a lightly floured mold onto it so that the relief is clearly imprinted. Remove the mold or tap out the dough, then use a paint brush to dust off any excess flour. Allow to dry for 24 hours on a greased and floured baking sheet. Bake on the middle rack of an oven preheated to 300° for about 30 minutes. If the Springerle begin to brown, cover them with parchment paper. Cool on a rack.

Cinnamon Stars

1-1¼ pounds almonds
    (depending on the size of
    the eggs)
5 egg whites
Pinch of salt
1 teaspoon lemon juice

5½ cups plus 2 tablespoons
    powdered sugar
3½ ounces marzipan
2 teaspoons ground cinnamon
Butter or margarine for
    greasing

Grind the almonds in a mill. Beat egg whites and salt until stiff. Gradually add the lemon juice and 4½ cups of powdered sugar. Continue beating until the batter is very thick and has a strong sheen. Remove about 5 tablespoons and set aside. Finely crumble marzipan and fold into the egg-white mixture together with almonds and cinnamon. Very carefully but thoroughly work into a stiff dough. Dust a work surface with powdered sugar and roll out small portions of the dough to a thickness of ¼ inch. Cut out stars, brush them with the remaining egg white and place on a baking sheet that has been lined with lightly greased parchment paper. Place on the middle rack of an oven preheated to 300° and allow to dry more'than bake for about 30 minutes. Remove to a rack and allow to cool completely.

Almond Speculatius

1⅓ cups butter
1⅓ cups sugar
1 teaspoon vanilla
1 egg
1 package speculatius spices
(about ⅛ teaspoon
cardamom and 2 teaspoons
cinnamon)

4½-5 cups flour (depending
on the size of the egg)
Flour for dusting
⅔-¾ cup sliced almonds
Butter for greasing

Cream butter with sugar, vanilla and egg. Continue beating until sugar is dissolved. Add speculatius spices and flour. First stir in, then knead vigorously. Wrap dough in foil and refrigerate at least 2 hours. Carefully dust speculatius molds with flour and shake out any excess. Press in the dough in small portions and cut off excess with a sharp knife. Evenly cover a work surface with sliced almonds. Remove the speculatius from the molds by hitting the backs vigorously. Gently press the almonds onto the cookies and place on a lightly greased baking sheet. Bake on the middle rack of an oven preheated to 400° for about 10 minutes. Immediately remove from the baking sheet and allow to cool on a rack.

> **Tip:** *For the speculatius to have a special sheen, brush thinly with milk before baking.*

Pfeffernüsse

4-5 eggs (depending on size)
2½ cups plus 2 tablespoons
sugar
Grated rind of 1 lemon
½ teaspoon ground cinnamon
⅛ teaspoon ground ginger
⅛ teaspoon ground allspice
⅛ teaspoon ground
cardamom
⅛ teaspoon ground coriander

⅛ teaspoon ground nutmeg
1 teaspoon freshly ground
white pepper (or slightly
less)
⅛ teaspoon salt
1 tablespoon cognac or rum
7½ cups flour
Flour for shaping
Butter or margarine for
greasing

Beat the eggs until foamy and gradually sprinkle in the sugar. Add the grated lemon rind and then mix in the spices and the salt that has been dissolved in cognac or rum. Stir in as much of the flour as possible, then knead in the remainder. Cover and set aside in a cool place overnight. The next day, shape the dough into small balls having a diameter of ¾ inch and subsequently roll them in flour. Place on a greased baking sheet and bake on the middle rack of an oven preheated to 350° for about 20 minutes until golden. Remove from the baking sheet and allow to cool.

Note

After they have cooled, the Pfeffernüsse can be brushed with a thin sugar glaze.

Gingerbread House

10 eggs
2 cups plus 2 tablespoons
   sugar
4 cups honey
5 cups ground hazelnuts
1 teaspoon salt
½ teaspoon ground cinnamon
½ teaspoon ground cloves (or
   slightly less)
Pinch of ground black pepper
4 pounds flour

¾ tablespoon baking soda
5-6 tablespoons cocoa
Flour for kneading
Butter or margarine for
   greasing
7½ cups powdered sugar
2 egg whites
A few drops of lemon juice
Colorful sugar decors for the
   trimming

Place the eggs in a very large bowl and beat until foamy with
an electric hand mixer. Gradually sprinkle in sugar and continue
beating until the mixture is white and foamy. Then, while
beating constantly, pour in the honey in a thin stream. Combine
the hazelnuts with all the spices and gently fold in. Mix flour,
baking soda and cocoa and gradually pour into the batter. Work
in as much as possible. Dust a work surface with flour, place the
dough onto it and knead vigorously. Then form into a ball and
refrigerate for 2 days (longer is even better), to allow the flavors
to blend well. Refrigeration also makes the dough more pliable
and easier to shape.

Before baking, make stencils according to the pattern on page
312. Divide the dough into thirds and vigorously knead each
third again separately. The dough should be smooth and completely homogeneous. Roll out each third finger-thick onto a
greased baking sheet and bake on the middle rack of an oven

preheated to 400° for about 15 minutes. Immediately place the
stencils on the still hot cake and cut them out exactly with a sharp
knife. The cut edges should be very smooth. Place the individual
pieces next to each other on a large rack and allow to cool
overnight.

The next day, divide the powdered sugar into two halves. To
one half, add the egg whites one after the other as well as a few
drops of lemon juice. Stir until a very smooth and gleaming glaze
is obtained. Brush all the edges of the sides with it and place these
on the "foundation." Support all the sides so that the house does
not lean and tie these walls up in some way to make certain that
they remain erect. Construct the roof in the same way after these
"walls" are well cemented. "Glue" it on and allow it to cement
well.

Prepare the second quantity of powdered sugar and begin
decorating. This glaze should be just as stiff as the first quantity.
Use it drop by drop to glue on the sugar decors and/or place it in
a small parchment paper bag and paint the house with it. It might
also be used to hang icicles from the roof.

Christmas Stollen with Almond-Kirsch Filling

6 cups flour	⅓ cup candied lemon rind
1 package dry yeast	⅓ cup candied orange rind
1 cup lukewarm milk	½ cup chopped almonds
⅔ cup sugar	⅔ cup whole blanched
1 teaspoon vanilla	almonds (3 ounces)
1 egg	½ cup candied red cherries
2 egg yolks	9 ounces marzipan
1 cup plus 2 tablespoons	2 vanilla beans
softened butter	2-3 tablespoons Kirsch
2 pinches salt	1½ cups powdered sugar
Rind of 1 orange	Flour for dusting and shaping
Pinch of ground cloves	Butter or margarine for
Pinch of mace	greasing
Pinch of cardamom	7 tablespoons-½ cup butter
½ teaspoon almond extract	for brushing
½ cup currants	Powdered sugar for dusting
½ cup raisins	

Pour flour into a large bowl and make a well in the middle. Add in the yeast and stir together with some milk, some sugar and a little flour from the sides to make a starter. Cover and allow to rise for 15-20 minutes. Then add the remaining milk, remaining sugar, vanilla, egg and egg yolks as well as the butter in flakes. Add the spices and almond extract and work all ingredients into a smooth dough. Knead until bubbles appear and the dough no longer sticks to the sides of the bowl. Allow it to rise again for another 25-30 minutes until it doubles in size.

Wash the currants and raisins in hot water and rub them dry. Combine with the very finely diced candied lemon and orange rind as well as the chopped and whole almonds. Dust fruit and almonds with a little flour. Halve or coarsely chop the candied cherries. Crumble the marzipan, add the scraped out vanilla marrow, Kirsch and powdered sugar and knead into a smooth dough. Mix in the cherries and form into a smooth roll.

Punch down the dough and knead it vigorously. Work in the fruit and almond mixture, then place it on a floured work surface and form into a thick oval. The long sides should bulge slightly. Place the marzipan roll in the middle and fold the dough in half completely covering the marzipan roll. Press down the length of the dough on either side of the marzipan roll with the sides of the hands.

Place the stollen on a greased baking sheet and allow to rise for 20-30 minutes. Then bake on the bottom rack of an oven preheated to 400° for about 1 hour. Finally, brush the stollen with melted butter until the surface will absorb no more. Dust thickly with powdered sugar.

Fruit Bread

2 pounds bread dough
  (sourdough rye bread,
  recipe page 287)
2 pounds mixed dried fruits
  (for example apples, pears,
  figs, pitted dates, prunes,
  apricots and seedless
  raisins)
½ cup robust red wine (or a
  little more)
1-2 vanilla beans
½ cup candied lemon rind
¼ cup candied orange rind
1 cup ground walnuts
⅔ cup ground blanched
  almonds

1 cup brown sugar
1-1¼ cups powdered sugar
4-6 tablespoons plum
  schnapps
1-2 teaspoons ground
  cinnamon
⅛-¼ teaspoon ground cloves
⅛-¼ teaspoon freshly ground
  black pepper
Flour for rolling and shaping
Butter or margarine for
  greasing
1 egg yolk for brushing
Blanched almonds for
  decorating

For the filling, weigh and mix together dried fruit except for the dates. Place the red wine in a saucepan together with the scraped out vanilla bean pods (retain the marrow). Bring to a boil, add the mixed fruit and simmer for 5 minutes. Remove fruit, blot dry and, except for the vanilla bean pods, dice finely together with the dates. Finely dice candied lemon and orange rind as well. Add to the fruit together with the nuts, almonds, brown sugar, powdered sugar and scraped-out vanilla marrow. Mix well and gradually work in the plum schnapps and spices. Press the mixture into the shape of a rounded loaf.

Gently knead the bread and roll it out on a lightly floured work surface to a thickness of ½ inch. The dough should be large enough to wrap up the fruit loaf. Place the fruit loaf in the middle of the dough and fold the dough over it from all sides. Brush the overlapping strips of dough with lukewarm water so that they can effortlessly bake together. Carefully press together all edges. Now, carefully turn over the fruit-bread loaf so that the seam is laying against the baking sheet. Whisk the egg yolk and brush the surface with it. Then attractively and generously decorate the surface with blanched almonds; at the same time, press the fruit together a little more. Bake on the lower rack of an oven preheated to 350° for about 2 hours. Then turn off the heat, open the door somewhat and allow to steam off a little. Remove to a rack to cool completely, if possible for 24 hours or longer.

Christmas Orange Torte

5 egg yolks
5 tablespoons cold water
1 cup plus 2 tablespoons
   sugar
1 vanilla bean
5 egg whites
Pinch of salt
1¾ cups sifted cake flour

⅓ cup cornstarch
1-2 tablespoons cocoa
½ teaspoon baking powder
½ cup ground hazelnuts or
   walnuts
Butter or margarine for
   greasing
Bread crumbs for sprinkling

For the filling and trimming:
1-2 oranges (depending on
   the size)
1 cup milk
Grated rind of 1 orange
8 egg yolks
1 cup plus 2 tablespoons
   sugar
1 teaspoon vanilla

2½ packages gelatin
2 cups whipping cream
2-3 tablespoons orange
   liqueur like Cointreau or
   Grand Marnier
Chocolate decors for
   sprinkling
Small macaroons for trimming

Combine egg yolks with water and beat until foamy. Gradually sprinkle in two-thirds of the sugar while beating constantly. Slit open the vanilla bean pod lengthwise, scrape out the marrow and add to the egg-yolk mixture. Beat egg whites with salt until stiff and slowly sprinkle in the remaining sugar. Slide into the egg-yolk mixture. Combine flour, cornstarch, cocoa and baking powder. Pour over egg mixture and gently fold in together with the ground nuts. Grease only the bottom of a 10-inch springform pan and coat it with bread crumbs. Pour the batter into it and smooth out the surface. Bake for 50-60 minutes on the second rack from the bottom of an oven preheated to 350°. Slide onto a rack and allow to cool, if possible until the next day. Then cut the cake into two layers.

For the filling and trimming, peel the oranges and carefully remove the fillets from the skin surrounding each section. Retain any juice that drips off. In a saucepan, combine milk with the grated orange rind and empty vanilla bean pod. Bring to a boil and then remove from heat. Beat egg yolks until foamy, gradually add sugar, retaining 2 tablespoons, and vanilla. Pour in the milk while beating constantly. Now place the mixture in a hot, but not boiling, water bath and allow to become thick and creamy. Avoid boiling the mixture. Add the gelatin which has been dissolved in a little water; then remove the bowl from the hot water bath and place it in a cold one. Continue beating while allowing it to cool. Place it in the refrigerator until it begins to gel.

Whip the cream and the remaining sugar until stiff. As soon as the egg-gelatin mixture begins to "streak," fold the cream into it together with the orange liqueur and any retained orange juice. Spread well over one-third of the egg-cream mixture onto the first layer of cake, place the second layer on top. Remove some of the egg-cream mixture and place it in a pastry bag with a star spout. Cover the surface and sides of the cake with the remaining egg-cream mixture and sprinkle with chocolate decors. Decorate the surface with additional dots of egg-cream mixture, macaroons and orange fillets.

More Holiday Baking

Easter Yogurt and Mango Torte

7 tablespoons butter	2 well-ripened mangos
½ cup sugar	2½ cups yogurt
2 teaspoons vanilla	1¼ cups crème fraîche
1 egg	1¼ cups powdered sugar
Pinch of salt	Juice of ½ lemon
1¼ cups sifted cake flour	1-2 tablespoons rum
½ teaspoon baking powder	1 cup whipping cream
⅓ cup ground almonds	⅓ cup finely chopped
Butter or margarine for	pistachios
greasing	12 or 16 Easter figures made
Bread crumbs for coating	of fondant, chocolate or
2 ¼-ounce packages gelatin	jelly

Cream butter in a bowl, gradually add sugar, vanilla, egg and salt. Continue beating until the batter is white, foamy and very creamy; the sugar and salt should also be dissolved. Combine flour with baking powder and fold in with the almonds.

Grease a 10-inch springform pan with butter or margarine and coat with bread crumbs. Fill in the dough and smooth out the surface. Bake on the middle rack of an oven preheated to 350°-400° for about 20 minutes until golden brown. Remove from the pan and turn the cake out onto a rack. Allow to cool completely, if possible overnight.

The next day, dissolve gelatin in some lukewarm water. Halve the mangos and remove the fruit from the seed, then peel. Finely dice the mango and then puree it in a blender. Stir together yogurt, crème fraîche, powdered sugar and lemon juice. Continue stirring until the powdered sugar has dissolved, then mix in the mango puree. Flavor with rum. Combine the gelatin with about 2 tablespoons of the yogurt mixture. Stir vigorously, and add the gelatin to the remaining yogurt mixture and refrigerate.

Place the cake on a platter. Make a ring of aluminum foil that has been folded two or three times (or use the springform rim), and place it around the cake.

As soon as the yogurt cream begins to stiffen, pour it into the prepared torte form and smooth out the surface. Refrigerate the torte in order to allow it to gel completely. Prior to serving, combine whipping cream with remaining vanilla and whip until stiff.

Remove the aluminum foil ring (or springform rim), from the torte and evenly spread whipped cream on the sides. Then sprinkle the sides with the finely chopped pistachios so that the surface appears to be light green. Place the remaining whipped cream in a pastry bag with a large star spout. Mark 12 or 16 pieces on the surface of the torte. Press out a large star of cream on the rim of each piece. Top the cream with a sugar or chocolate figure, then serve the torte as soon as possible since most of these figures quickly "leak color" when they come into contact with moisture, in this case the whipped cream.

Easter Lamb

⅓ cup butter or margarine	2 tablespoons cornstarch
3½ ounces marzipan	½ tablespoon baking powder
¼ cup sugar	½ cup ground, blanched
1 teaspoon vanilla	almonds
Pinch of salt	Butter or margarine for
2 eggs	greasing
3 drops almond extract	Bread crumbs for coating
1 teaspoon lemon juice	2 sultanas or raisins
1¼ cups plus 2 tablespoons	Powdered sugar for dusting
sifted cake flour	

Cut butter into flakes, finely crumble marzipan and place both in a bowl. Stir until creamy either by hand or with an electric mixer. Gradually add sugar alternating with vanilla, salt and eggs. Continue stirring until salt and sugar have dissolved. Flavor with almond extract and lemon juice. Combine flour, cornstarch and baking powder. Thoroughly mix into the batter with the almonds.

Carefully grease an Easter lamb form with butter or margarine (it is best to grease the form two or three times). Coat with bread crumbs. Fill in the batter and close the form according to the manufacturer's directions. Place on the middle rack of an oven preheated to 400° and bake for about 45 minutes until golden brown. To test, stick a toothpick or wooden skewer through a hole in the form or through one of the seams. The stick should be dry when removed from the cake. Remove the lamb from the oven, allow to "steam off" briefly. Remove it from its form and turn out onto a rack. Allow to cool completely.

Before serving, press both sultanas or raisins into the cake for eyes, a small toothpick or needle may be of some assistance here. Very thickly dust the lamb with powdered sugar.

Palm Thursday Pretzels

5 cups flour	¼ cup shortening
1 package dry yeast	Flour for shaping
2 tablespoons sugar	Butter or oil for greasing
½ cup milk	½ cup water
½ cup lukewarm water	1 tablespoon salt
Generous pinch of salt	Coarse salt for sprinkling

Make a well in the flour. Add yeast in the middle and stir together with sugar, milk and some flour from the sides. Cover with a cloth and allow to rise in a warm place for 20 minutes. Add the water, salt and shortening in flakes. Knead all the ingredients into a smooth dough. Continue kneading until bubbles appear and the dough no longer sticks to the sides of the bowl. Allow to rise for 30 minutes, then place on a floured work surface and knead again. Divide into 20 portions. Roll each one into a 16-inch long rope that is thicker in the middle and somewhat thinner at both ends. Form into pretzels and place on a greased baking sheet. Allow to rise for 10 minutes. Dissolve the salt in water and brush onto the pretzels. Sprinkle with coarse salt. Bake on the middle rack of an oven preheated to 425° for 30 minutes. Brush with salt water 1-2 more times after the first 20 minutes of baking time.

Swiss Lenten Rolls

5 cups flour	Flour for forming
1 package dry yeast	1 egg yolk
1 teaspoon sugar	2 tablespoons milk
1 cup milk	Caraway seeds and coarse salt
½ cup softened butter	Butter for greasing
2 generous pinches of salt	

Make a well in the flour. Add the yeast and stir together with sugar, some milk and a little flour from the sides. Cover and allow to rise for 15 minutes. Distribute the softened butter in flakes on the rim, sprinkle with salt and work all the ingredients into a smooth dough together with the milk. Knead the dough until bubbles appear and it no longer sticks to the sides of the bowl. Allow to rise for about 20 minutes.

Place on a floured work surface and knead thoroughly. Divide into about 25 pieces. Form into balls and roll out into ovals. Allow to rest and rise slightly for 15 minutes. Flatten, then make four incisions lengthwise into the dough and stretch it apart somewhat so that the cuts appear as an ''X'' in a circle. Whisk together egg yolk and milk, brush onto the pieces. Sprinkle half of them with caraway seeds and the other half with coarse salt. Place on a greased baking sheet and bake on the middle rack of an oven preheated to 475°-500° for about 5 minutes. Remove to a rack and allow to cool.

Saffron Braid

5 cups flour
1 package dry yeast
½ cup sugar
½ cup lukewarm milk
7 tablespoons butter
½ teaspoon saffron
1 vanilla bean
1 cup ground almonds
½ cup chopped almonds
2 eggs

2 egg yolks
Flour for shaping
Butter for greasing
1 egg yolk
2 tablespoons whipping cream
⅓ cup chopped almonds (or
  ¼ cup chopped pistachios
  and ¼ cup rock candy
  sugar)

Make a well in the flour. Add the yeast and stir together with some sugar, some milk and a little flour from the sides. Allow to rise for about 15 minutes. Add butter and saffron to the remaining milk. Slit open the vanilla bean, scrape out the marrow and add it to the milk together with the pod. Heat until the butter has melted, then allow to cool down. Fish out the bean pod.

Add this mixture to the starter together with the almonds, eggs and egg yolks. Knead all the ingredients into a smooth dough. Then allow to rise until its volume has doubled. Place the dough on a floured work surface, punch it down and knead thoroughly. Divide it into 3 equal pieces and shape these into 20-24-inch ropes. Braid the three strands, place on a greased baking sheet and allow to rise for 20 minutes. Whisk egg yolk together with cream and brush the braid with it. Sprinkle with chopped almonds. Place on the middle rack and bake in an oven preheated to 400°-425° for about 35 minutes. If desired, sprinkle with chopped pistachios and rock candy sugar.

Easter Nest

1 dough recipe for Saffron
  Braid
Flour for shaping
1 egg yolk
Butter for greasing

Milk for brushing
1½ cups powdered sugar
1 teaspoon lemon juice
⅓ cup chopped pistachios
¼ cup rock candy sugar

Divide the dough after it has risen the second time. Remove ⅔ and divide into four equal pieces. Roll out each of these pieces into a rope having the same diameter throughout. Braid the four strands together. Shape into a wreath and brush ends with egg yolk; press together well. Halve the remaining dough and roll each half into a rope, 20-24 inches in length. Intertwine these two strands. Place the 4-strand wreath onto a baking sheet and lay the garland on top. Brush ends with egg yolk and close this wreath as well. Allow to rise for about 20 minutes. Beat the remaining egg yolk together with some milk and thinly brush it over the entire nest. Place on the bottom rack of an oven preheated to 425° and bake for 25-30 minutes. After the nest has cooled, brush it with a sugar and lemon juice glaze and sprinkle with pistachios and rock candy sugar.

Italian Easter Dove

4 cups flour	⅓ cup candied lemon rind
2 teaspoons dry yeast	⅓ cup candied orange rind
⅓ cup sugar	Flour for shaping
½ cup lukewarm milk	Butter for greasing
⅓ cup chopped almonds	2 tablespoons sugar
4 egg yolks	2 tablespoons water
Generous pinch of salt	½ cup powdered sugar
Grated rind of ½ lemon	⅓ cup sliced almonds
½ cup softened butter	4 large raisins or sultanas

For the dough, pour flour into a large bowl and make a well in the middle. Add the yeast, then stir together with some sugar, some milk and a little flour from the sides to make a starter. Cover with a cloth and allow to rise in a warm place for 15 minutes.

Place the almonds in a dry frying pan and, while stirring constantly, roast them over mild heat until golden. Do not brown them since they then taste slightly bitter when baked. Remove from the pan to a flat plate and allow to cool.

Add the egg yolks to the starter together with the salt, lemon rind and butter in flakes. Mix all the ingredients into a smooth dough. Knead until bubbles appear and the dough no longer sticks to the sides of the bowl. Cover again and allow to rise for 20 minutes.

At the same time, finely dice the candied lemon and orange rind; combine with the cooled almonds. Punch down the dough, knead it well, then work in the dry ingredients. Allow to rise another 20 minutes. Then halve the dough and form each half into a dove. To do this, remove ⅓ from each portion of dough and form into a rope 7-8-inches long, (this rope should not be too thick). Form the larger piece of dough into a somewhat broader rope measuring about 10-11 inches in length. Grease a large baking sheet or two springform pans with butter and lay in the ropes of dough crossed into the shape of a dove. To do this, lay the smaller rope on the baking sheet, flatten it slightly in the middle and brush with water. Lay the larger rope on top perpendicular to the smaller one and press the edges together well. Use the hands to shape the dough a little better. Then place appropriately shaped strips of aluminum foil, folded one or two layers thick, around the dove in order to keep the shape. Allow to rise for 30 minutes.

Combine sugar and water. Heat it, while stirring constantly, until the sugar is dissolved and the syrup clear. Then cool it down. Brush the raised dove with it and dust with powdered sugar. Thickly distribute the sliced almonds on top as feathers. Press in two sultanas or raisins as eyes on the head end of each of the birds. Place the doves on the lower rack of an oven preheated to 350° and bake for about 45 minutes. Remove to a rack and allow to cool before removing the strips of aluminum foil.

Russian Easter Bread

7½ cups flour	Grated rind of 1 lemon
1 package dry yeast	⅛ teaspoon ground
¾ cup sugar	cardamom
1 cup lukewarm milk	1 cup raisins
¾ cup plus 2 tablespoons	½ cup currants
butter	1 cup chopped almonds
5 egg yolks	Flour for dusting and rolling
Generous pinch of salt	Butter for greasing
¼-½ teaspoon saffron	1 egg
2-3 tablespoons rum	2 tablespoons water or milk

Pour flour into a bowl and make a well in the middle. Add the yeast and stir together with some sugar, some milk and a little flour from the sides to make a starter (which should not be too wet). Dust a thin layer of flour over it from the rim, then cover with a cloth and allow to rise for 45-60 minutes.

Cream butter in a bowl and gradually add the remaining sugar, egg yolks and salt. Dissolve the saffron in rum and stir in together with lemon rind and cardamom. Work this mixture into the raised starter together with the remaining flour and knead vigorously until the dough is very supple. Wash the raisins and currants in a sieve under hot running water and throughly rub dry with a towel. Combine with well over half of the chopped almonds, lightly dust with flour and knead into the dough. Cover with a cloth again and allow to rise in a warm place for another 2 hours until its volume has doubled.

Punch down the dough and knead again, then roll it out to finger thickness on a floured work surface. With the aid of a plate (or a smaller springform pan bottom), cut out a round tile measuring about 8 inches in diameter. Cut out the next tile so that it is somewhat smaller than the first. Continue in this way until consecutively smaller circular tiles have been cut out of the remaining dough. Stack these in pyramid-fashion on a greased baking sheet.

Allow the bread to rise another 30 minutes, then brush with water or milk whisked together with the egg. Sprinkle with the remaining almonds.

Place on the lower rack of an oven preheated to 425° and bake for about 45 minutes. If the surface threatens to darken too quickly, turn down the temperature somewhat. Remove to a rack and allow to cool. To serve, cut into pie-shaped pieces. Serve with butter, if desired.

Ovenless Baking

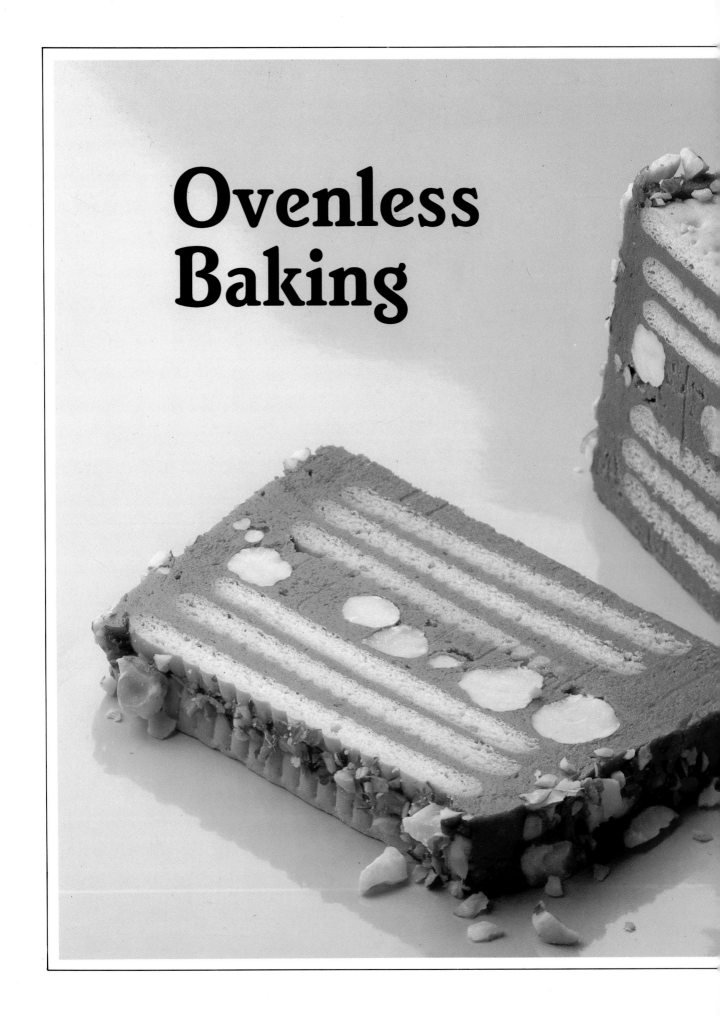

Butter Waffles

½ cup butter	3 eggs
3 tablespoons sugar	2½ cups wheat flour
1 teaspoon vanilla	1 teaspoon baking powder
Grated rind of ½ lemon	1 cup milk
Pinch of salt	Oil for greasing

Cream butter, then gradually sprinkle in sugar. Add vanilla, grated lemon rind, salt and eggs and beat the batter until smooth. Combine flour with baking powder. Add the dry ingredients by the spoonful alternating with the milk. Stir until smooth. The batter should fall from a spoon like heavy syrup. Heat the waffle iron and brush with oil. Bake the waffles 4-5 minutes at medium heat until golden.

> **Tip:** *For especially crispy waffles, substitute an equal quantity of water for the milk.*

Chocolate and Nut Waffles

½ cup butter	1 teaspoon baking powder
¼ cup sugar	1 tablespoon cocoa
4 eggs	¾ cup whipping cream
Pinch of salt	1 cup ground hazelnuts
1½ cups wheat flour	Oil for greasing

Cream butter together with sugar, eggs and a pinch of salt. Combine flour, baking powder and cocoa and add to the butter mixture alternating with the cream. Stir the dough until smooth, then fold in the ground hazelnuts. Bake in a hot and greased waffle iron for 5-7 minutes.

Wine and Yeast Waffles

3¾ cups wheat flour	½ cup white wine
2 teaspoons dry yeast	4 eggs
¼ cup sugar	Pinch of salt
1½ cups lukewarm milk	Grated rind of 1 lemon
½ cup butter	Oil for greasing

Pour flour into a bowl and make a well in the middle. Add the yeast with 1 tablespoon of sugar, ½ cup lukewarm milk and some flour from the sides. Stir together to make a starter. Cover the bowl with a kitchen towel and allow to rise in a warm place for 15 minutes until the starter has doubled in volume and blisters are visible. Melt the butter and add it together with the remaining sugar, milk, white wine, eggs, salt and grated lemon rind. Working from the middle to the outside, stir all the ingredients together well. Knead the dough until it no longer sticks to the sides and bubbles appear. Cover the bowl with a damp cloth so that no crust forms on the dough and allow to rise for another 30 minutes.

Heat the waffle iron and brush with oil. Spread the dough onto it in small portions and bake 5-7 minutes until golden.

Cinnamon Waffles

3 tablespoons butter or magarine	3 tablespoons almond liqueur
1¼ cups powdered sugar	2½ cups wheat flour
1 egg	½ teaspoon ground cinnamon

Cream butter or margarine with the sugar, egg and liqueur. Gradually work the flour into the butter mixture together with the cinnamon. Roll out the dough on a floured surface to an appropriate size for the iron. Lay the rolled-out dough into the hot, greased waffle iron and bake until golden brown.

Note

These waffles bake up best in a cast-iron waffle iron. An electric iron will work as a substitute, but it should be especially adapted for baking dry waffles or cones.

Since waffles taste best straight out of the iron, be sure to prepare filling and accompaniments in advance.

Variation

The waffle connoisseur not only has a variety of recipe choices for the waffle batter but there are also numerous possibilities available for filling and additions. For waffles that are "pure," simply sprinkle with powdered, granulated, or cinnamon sugar. Whipping cream is suitable as a filling sandwiched between two waffles. All kinds of jams and preserves are appropriate; they can be spirited onto the table without much preparation. Fruit can be served fresh, as a preserve or flambéed. Cold berry soups are especially delicious as an accompaniment; these may be flavored with a corresponding fruit schnapps. However, do thicken these soups with a little cornstarch. Augment this pastry with ice cream, for example, "Waffles à la Birne Helene," with vanilla ice cream, pears and chocolate sauce.

White-Chocolate Torte with Oranges

3 small oranges
5 tablespoons sugar
5 tablespoons water
1 cup plus 2 tablespoons
    butter
9 ounces white chocolate

3 eggs
2½ cups powdered sugar
6 tablespoons Grand Marnier
14 round, chocolate-filled
    cookies

Wash oranges and cut into ⅛-inch slices. Dissolve sugar in water and simmer the orange slices in this syrup for 5 minutes. Remove, allow to cool and then dice, reserving the smaller slices for decoration. Melt the butter, then cool it down to room temperature again. Crumble chocolate and melt in a double boiler over warm water. Beat together eggs, powdered sugar and Grand Marnier, then gradually fold in chocolate and butter.

Line an 8-inch springform pan with parchment paper and cover the bottom with 7 chocolate cookies. Spread ⅓ of the white chocolate mixture onto it. Lay the diced oranges on top for the second layer and cover with another ⅓ of the white chocolate mixture. Top with the remaining cookies and the rest of the white chocolate mixture. Cover the torte with parchment paper, place a round board on top to weight it down and refrigerate for 3-4 hours until stiff. Carefully remove the parchment paper from the torte, smooth out the surface with a knife if necessary and decorate with the remaining oranges.

Chocolate Cookie Cake

1 cup plus 2 tablespoons
    butter
4 eggs
2½ cups powdered sugar
¼ cup cocoa
5 tablespoons nut liqueur

½ cup ground hazelnuts
½ pound rectangular butter
    cookies
1 cup whole hazelnuts
½ cup chopped hazelnuts

Melt butter over low heat, then cool down to room temperature again. Beat eggs until foamy, then gradually add powdered sugar. Fold in cocoa, nut liqueur and ground hazelnuts. Carefully pour in the lukewarm butter while stirring constantly.

Line a loaf pan with parchment paper and cover the bottom with a layer of butter cookies. Pour a portion of the chocolate batter on top and then cover with another layer of cookies. Continue in this way until half of the chocolate batter and cookies have been used. Insert a layer of whole hazelnuts and cover with the chocolate. Continue alternating cookies and chocolate until the ingredients are used up. The final layer should be chocolate. Refrigerate the cake for 2 hours. Remove from the pan and peel off the paper. Roast the chopped hazelnuts in a frying pan and sprinkle over the surface and sides while still hot.

Raspberry Pancake Torte

⅓ cup almonds	1¾ cups sifted cake flour
1¼ cups milk	4 egg whites
4 egg yolks	Pinch of salt
½ cup sugar	Butter for frying

For the filling and trimming:

1 cup milk	1 pound raspberries
1 cup sugar	1 cup cottage or ricotta
Grated rind of 1 lemon	cheese
4 egg yolks	2 cups whipping cream
2 ¼-ounce packages gelatin	Pistachios for decoration

In a blender, puree almonds together with the milk, egg yolks and half the sugar. Gradually stir in the flour. In a separate bowl, beat egg whites, salt and remaining sugar until stiff, then gently fold into the batter. Melt the butter in a frying pan and fry 2½-inch pancakes. Remove and blot off excess oil with a paper towel. Place next to one another on a rack and allow to cool.

For the filling, combine milk, sugar, grated lemon rind and egg yolks in a saucepan and briefly bring to a boil. Remove from the heat. Dissolve gelatin in a little water, then add it to the hot milk. Refrigerate this mixture. Meanwhile, sort the raspberries, retaining especially nice ones for decoration. Rinse the remaining raspberries and puree in a blender. If desired, a little sugar may be added to enhance the flavor. Then stir in the cottage or ricotta

cheese. Whip cream until stiff. When the milk mixture has stiffened, stir in the cream and cheese mixture as well as the raspberry puree.

Line a springform pan with parchment paper and cover the bottom with a layer of pancakes. Pour a portion of the raspberry cream on top and cover again with pancakes. Continue until both have been exhausted. Refrigerate the torte for at least 2 hours and allow to stiffen completely. Turn out onto a platter and peel off the paper. Chop the pistachios and sprinkle the rims of the pancakes with it. Carefully rinse the retained raspberries, blot dry, then place these in the pistachio wreaths.

> **Tip:** *The filling may, of course, be prepared with other fruits. Cranberries, strawberries and blueberries are especially suitable. If sweetened cranberries are used, correct the quantity of sugar called for accordingly.*

Strawberry and Marzipan Torte

2 packages vanilla pudding
  mix
3 cups milk
6 tablespoons sugar
2 egg yolks
1 ¼-ounce package gelatin
3½ ounces marzipan

2 cups whipping cream
2 egg whites
1 pound strawberries
⅔ cup sliced almonds
4 tablespoons egg wash
3 dark layers of sponge cake

Whisk together pudding mix with some milk, sugar and the egg yolks. Bring the remaining milk to a boil, remove from the heat and stir in the pudding mix. While stirring constantly, bring to a boil again and allow to boil 2 minutes, then remove from the heat. Dissolve the gelatin in some water, then stir it into the pudding mixture. Crumble the marzipan with a fork and stir it into the pudding by the spoonful. Stir frequently as it cools in order to avoid the formation of a skin.

Rinse the strawberries, blot them dry, remove stems and halve them. Roast almonds in a dry frying pan until golden brown, then allow to cool. Place one of the cake layers onto a platter, thinly spread the marzipan cream onto it, top with half of the strawberries. Cut the next sponge cake layer so that its diameter is about 1½ inches smaller. Place it on top of the strawberries and spread the marzipan cream onto it again. Distribute half of the almonds onto it. Cut the final layer of sponge cake so that it is 3 inches smaller in diameter than the first one. Place it on top of the almonds. Cover the entire surface and sides of the torte with the remaining cream and decorate with strawberries and almonds.

Chocolate Rum Torte

6 ounces semi-sweet
  chocolate
3 cups whipping cream
1½ pounds brandied or
  Rumtopf fruit

1 tablespoon cornstarch
3 light-colored sponge cake
  layers
1 tablespoon sugar
Cocoa for dusting

Crumble the chocolate into the cream and melt in a hot water bath while stirring constantly. Allow to cool slightly, then refrigerate covered overnight. Drain the brandied fruits, retaining the liquid. Halve the brandied-fruit liquid, bring one half to a boil. From the other half, remove 2 tablespoons and combine with the cornstarch. Stir into the boiling liquid, bring to a boil again while stirring constantly. Remove from heat and allow to cool slightly, then spread onto one of the cake layers. Distribute the fruit on top and cover with the next cake layer. Whip the chocolate cream together with the sugar until stiff. Cover the second cake layer with part of it and place the final layer on top. Place some chocolate cream into a pastry bag and use it to coat the sides of the cake. Dust the surface with cocoa. Score 12 or 16 pieces on the surface of the cake and press out a dot of cream on each one.

Deep-Fried Sunday Torte

6¼ cups sifted cake flour	7 tablespoons butter
Pinch of salt	¾ cup plus 2 tablespoons
1 teaspoon vanilla	sugar
Grated rind of ½ lemon	Flour for shaping
2 eggs	Shortening or oil for frying
3 egg yolks	
2 tablespoons cognac or	
brandy	

For the filling:

½ cup water	½ cup chopped almonds
Grated rind and juice of 1	3 tablespoons orange liqueur
orange	2 tablespoons cognac or
1⅓ cups sugar	brandy
⅔ cup candied cherries	Pinch of ground cinnamon
⅓ cup candied lemon rind	Pinch of ground ginger

For the trimming:

1 tablespoon butter	¼ cup blanched almond
1 egg white	halves
3 cups powdered sugar	⅓ cup candied cherries

Combine flour with salt and pour onto a work surface, make a well in the middle. Pour in the vanilla, grated lemon rind, eggs, egg yolks and the cognac or brandy. Sprinkle the butter in flakes as well as the sugar on the rim. Cut all the ingredients to a crumb-like consistency; working from outside to inside, knead into a smooth dough. Form into a ball and refrigerate for about 30 minutes. On a lightly floured work surface, roll out the dough to ½-inch thickness and cut out 1-inch squares. Heat the shortening or oil to 325°-350°. Drop a few dough squares into the oil and fry for 4-5 minutes until golden brown. Limit the number of dough squares so that they do not touch each other while baking. Remove from the oil when done and drain on several layers of paper towels.

In a saucepan, combine water with orange juice and rind as well as the sugar. Bring to a boil while stirring constantly. Remove the pan from the heat. Finely dice the cherries and the candied lemon rind and stir them into the sugar mixture together with the almonds, alcohol and spices. Adjust the flavoring if necessary. Then mix in the deep-fried pieces of dough. Using both hands, gently toss the ingredients until the liquid is almost completely absorbed. Carefully line a 10-inch springform pan with aluminum foil, pour in the cake mixture and smooth out the surface. If desired the cake may be weighted down.

For the trimming, melt the butter, then cool it down again but do not allow it to solidify. Whip the egg white with a whisk or electric mixer and gradually sprinkle in the powdered sugar. Continue beating until the batter is very foamy and stiff. Now pour in the butter in a thin stream. Remove the torte from the foil and glaze it. Decorate with almond halves and cherries.

Rhineland Puffs

⅓ cup butter	2½ cups flour
Pinch of salt	5 tablespoons milk
¼ cup sugar	Flour for rolling
1 egg	Shortening for deep frying
2 tablespoons rum	Powdered sugar for dusting

While stirring constantly, melt butter in a saucepan over very mild heat (do not allow it to darken in color under any circumstances). Immediately remove from heat and stir in salt, sugar, egg and rum. Pour the flour into a mixing bowl and make a well in the middle. Pour in the butter mixture and stir all the ingredients together with the milk. It will not be possible to stir in all the flour, the remainder should therefore be kneaded in as quickly and thoroughly as possible.

Lightly dust a work surface with flour and heat the shortening to 325°-350°. Roll out the dough in smaller portions to a thickness of ⅛ inch. Then cut out strips with a sharp knife or a pizza cutter. Divide these into 2½-inch long rhombuses. Drop the pieces of dough into the hot oil and turn them repeatedly for about 5 minutes. (Avoid dropping too many pieces in the pot at one time. They should never touch each other, but instead should "swim" freely.) Fish out the pieces with a slotted spoon and drain on paper towels. Dust generously with powdered sugar while still warm, remove to a rack (never stack them, otherwise they will become soft), and cool completely.

Puff Pastry Fritters

1 cup water	¼-½ teaspoon almond
Pinch of salt	extract
⅓ cup butter or margarine	Shortening for deep frying
2¼ cups flour	Powdered sugar for dusting
4-5 eggs (depending on size)	

Combine water, salt and butter or margarine in a saucepan and bring to a boil. Remove from heat and drop the flour into the mixture in one fell swoop. Return to the heat and continue stirring until a smooth clump forms and the bottom of the pan is covered with a delicate white skin.

Place the puff pastry in a bowl and immediately stir in one egg. Allow to cool until lukewarm. Add the remaining eggs one after the other, first adding the next egg after the previous one has been fully incorporated into the dough.

After the fourth egg, test the dough. Using a wooden spoon, lift some dough out of the bowl. It should have a strong sheen and hang from the spoon in long, pointed ribbons. If this is not the case, add either half or all of the fifth egg. (If only half an egg is added, whisk yolk and white together before dividing.) Add the almond extract when the dough is completely mixed.

Heat the shortening to 325°-350° and fill the dough into a pastry bag with a large star spout. Be sure to avoid the creation of air bubbles, the shortening could otherwise spatter when it comes into contact with the dough. To press out the dough, hold the pastry bag perpendicular over the heated oil and press out spirals, bows, wreaths or any other desired form. Cut the strips of dough with a knife or scissors and fry until golden in color. Drain on paper towels and dust with powdered sugar. Serve as soon as possible, preferably as soon as cooled.

Pear Fritters with Currants

1 cup milk	⅓ cup currants
Pinch of salt	2 ripe, but not too soft, pears
⅓ cup butter	Juice of ½ lemon
2½ cups flour	Shortening for frying
6-7 eggs (depending on size)	Powdered sugar for dusting

Place milk, salt and butter in a saucepan and bring to a boil. Remove the pan from the heat as soon as the butter has melted and the milk begins to bubble up. Immediately pour in the flour in one fell swoop. Return the pan to the heat and stir the dough until a smooth clump forms and the bottom is covered by a delicate, white skin. Immediately remove the dough to a bowl and stir in one egg. Cool until lukewarm.

Meanwhile, place the currants in a sieve and wash under hot running water. Rub them dry in a kitchen towel. Peel, quarter and core the pears. Slice the quarters into very fine slices or ¼-inch sticks and immediately sprinkle with lemon juice to avoid discoloration. Cover with foil and set aside.

Add the remaining eggs one after the other, adding the next egg after the previous one has been fully incorporated into the dough. Make a test after the sixth egg. If the dough already has a strong sheen and hangs from a spoon in long, pointed ribbons, omit the final egg; otherwise, it should be stirred into the dough. Mix in the currants and pears when the dough is completely prepared. Heat the shortening to 325°-350°. Cut out small fritters with two spoons that have been dipped into the hot shortening. Allow the fritters to slide into the hot shortening and fry them until golden brown, turning frequently. Fish out with a slotted spoon and drain on a paper towel. Generously dust with powdered sugar while still warm.

> **Tip:** *Prepare other fritters using the recipe for Pear and Currant Fritters. Substitute apples, strips of well-dried pineapple or diced prunes for the pears. The currants may be replaced with sultanas or raisins and, if desired, almonds or nuts may be added. Additional flavors may be used to vary the fritters, for example, combine sugar with cinnamon or vanilla and dust the surface with this instead of powdered sugar. And for something extravagant, slice the fritters in half after they have cooled and fill with lightly sweetened whipped cream and/or vanilla or chocolate ice cream.*

Almond Puffs

¼ cup butter or margarine
2 eggs
2 egg yolks
Juice of ½ lemon
1 tablespoon rum
Pinch of salt
2½ cups powdered sugar
1 teaspoon vanilla

2-3 teaspoons rose water
¼ cup marzipan
3 tablespoons canned milk
5 cups flour
1 teaspoon baking powder
Flour for rolling
Oil for frying
Powdered sugar for dusting

In a saucepan, melt butter or margarine over very mild heat; do not overheat or brown. Remove from heat and set aside. Cream eggs, egg yolks, lemon juice, salt, vanilla and rum in a bowl. Gradually sprinkle in the powdered sugar. If necessary, it may be sifted prior to use since there should be no clumps in the mixture. Stir in the rose water and continue beating to a creamy batter. Crumble marzipan into another bowl, add the canned milk and stir until smooth. Combine flour with baking powder, pour onto a work surface and make a well in the middle. Pour the egg batter together with the marzipan mixture into the well and, work from outside to inside, knead all the ingredients into a smooth dough. Form into a ball, wrap in foil or a plastic bag and refrigerate for at least 30 minutes.

Roll out the dough to ¼-inch thickness on a heavily floured work surface. Cut out almond-shaped pieces of dough. Heat the oil to 350° and drop in a few almond puffs at a time. Turn frequently and fry until golden brown. This could take up to 5 minutes depending on the size of the puffs. Fish out the almond puffs with a slotted spoon and drain on a thick layer of paper towels. Generously dust with powdered sugar. Allow to cool completely in a sieve or on a rack; serve as soon as possible.

Rosettes

½ cup butter or margarine
Pinch of salt
½ cup sugar
1 teaspoon vanilla
3 eggs
2 tablespoons cognac or brandy
5 cups flour

½ teaspoon baking powder
Flour for rolling
1 egg white for brushing
Oil for frying
1 cup blackberry or black currant jelly
Powdered sugar for dusting

Cream butter or margarine in a bowl until it "squeaks." Gradually add salt and sugar alternating with the eggs and vanilla. Continue stirring until the sugar and salt are completely dissolved. Add cognac or brandy in between. Combine flour with baking powder. Stir as much as possible into the dough; then with cool hands, very quickly knead the ingredients together until no more flour is visible. To test, form the dough into a ball, cut through the middle and check to see whether both surfaces are completely homogeneous. Form the dough into a ball again and wrap in foil or a plastic bag, refrigerate for at least 45 minutes.

After refrigerating, roll the dough out onto a lightly floured work surface to a thickness of ⅛ inch and cut out rounds of three or four different sizes ranging from 1½ to 3 inches. Make several ½-inch slits on the outer rim of each of the rounds. Whisk the egg white, drip onto the middle of each round and spread out. Stack the rounds in pyramid form working from large to small. Press the rounds in the middle with the fingers or with the handle of a wooden spoon.

Heat the oil to 325°-350°. Depending on the size of the pan, drop in 2 or 3 rosettes at a time and fry, turning once, for 5-7 minutes until golden and crispy. Fish out with a slotted spoon and drain on several layers of paper towels.

Lay the rosettes next to each other on a rack and top each with a generous dollop of blackberry or black currant jelly. Generously dust the rosettes with powdered sugar, cool completely and serve as soon as possible.

Pistachio Ice Cream Torte

For the meringue bottom:

3 egg whites	¾ cup sugar
Pinch of salt	½ teaspoon lemon juice

For the ice cream layers:

¾ quart vanilla ice cream	½ cup whipping cream
½ cup croquant	1 teaspoon vanilla
½-¾ quart pistachio ice cream with pieces of pistachio	Chopped pistachios
	Sugar flowers for decoration

Whip egg whites with salt until stiff. Gradually sprinkle in sugar. Continue beating until the mixture is very stiff and has a strong sheen. Finally add the lemon juice and fill the meringue into a pastry bag with a large smooth spout. Line a 9½-inch springform pan with parchment paper and press the meringue out in spiral-fashion to make the torte bottom. Smooth out the surface if desired and place the meringue on the middle rack in the oven of an oven preheated to 250°. Dry, more than bake, for 3-4 hours, avoid browning the meringue. Peel off the paper and allow the meringue to cool and dry out further on a rack.

Thaw the vanilla ice cream somewhat. Line a 9½-inch springform pan with aluminum foil or parchment paper. Combine the soft, but not yet melted, vanilla ice cream with the croquant and fill into the springform pan. Smooth out the surface. Freeze and allow to stiffen, then place the completely cooled meringue bottom on the ice cream layer and freeze again. Thaw the pistachio ice cream somewhat. Stir it until creamy as well. Spread onto the meringue layer and freeze again allowing all three layers to harden completely. Prior to serving, combine whipping cream with vanilla and beat until stiff. Fill into a pastry bag with a large star spout. Remove the ice cream torte from the pan to a platter. Decorate the surface in lattice-fashion with the whipped cream. Sprinkle with chopped pistachios and decorate with sugar flowers. Serve immediately before the torte thaws.

Quick Mocha Ice Cream Torte

1 quart mocha ice cream	2 teaspoons vanilla
3 thin sponge cake layers	3-4 tablespoons croquant
6 tablespoons cognac or mocha liqueur	1 tablespoon colored sugar decors
2 cups whipping cream	

Chop the mocha ice cream slightly or allow to thaw somewhat. Meanwhile, dribble equal amounts of cognac or mocha liqueur on the three sponge cake layers and allow them to absorb the alcohol. Stir the ice cream until it is spreadable. Place a sponge cake layer on a platter and spread half of the ice cream onto it. Smooth out the surface and place the second cake layer on top. Press gently and spread the remaining ice cream on top.

Smooth out this surface as well and freeze the torte until it has completely frozen. Immediately before serving, whip cream until stiff. Place into a pastry bag with a large star spout and decorate the sides and surface of the torte extravagantly with stripes of cream. Sprinkle with croquant and sugar decors.

Note

If this torte is to be prepared a long time prior to serving, decorate with whipped cream as described above and freeze the torte again. In this case, however, allow the cream to thaw slightly before serving. Then sprinkle with croquant and sugar decors. If these are applied earlier, they may bleed color when the cream thaws.

Three-Colored Ice Cream Cake

¾ quart strawberry sherbert	4 tablespoons raspberry schnapps or cognac
¾ quart lemon sherbert	½ cup whipping cream
¾ quart vanilla ice cream	1 teaspoon vanilla
1 thin sponge cake	

Place a bundt form in the freezer and chill. Remove the various ice creams and allow to thaw until they are just barely spreadable. Since the different kinds of ice cream are not going to be combined but will instead be used one after the other, they should be removed from the freezer and prepared one at a time. First take out the strawberry sherbert. As soon as it is possible to stir it, remove the bundt form from the freezer and fill in the sherbert. Carefully smooth out the surface; also remove any strawberry sherbert from the sides so it will not mar the surfaces of the other layers.

Return the form to the freezer and wait until the surface of the sherbert has hardened again. At the same time, remove the lemon sherbert from the freezer and thaw until spreadable. Fill it in as the next layer, smooth out the surface and clean off the remaining sides of the form. Return the bundt form to the freezer and simultaneously thaw the vanilla ice cream. Stir until creamy and fill into the form as the last layer. Smooth out this surface and return to the freezer to freeze through completely.

Shortly before serving, place the sponge cake layer on a platter. Very briefly turn the bundt form onto the cake and mark the inner and the outer rim of the form. Return the bundt form to the freezer and cut the sponge cake into a ring. Dribble schnapps or cognac onto it and allow to soak in. Briefly dip the bundt form into hot water, turn onto the ring and remove the form. Immediately refreeze the torte. Whip the cream and vanilla until stiff. Fill into a pastry bag with a star spout and decorate the cake in a way that corresponds to the design of the form.

Broiled Layered Torte

1 cup plus 2 tablespoons butter or margarine	⅓ cup cornstarch
½ cup marzipan	7 egg whites
7 egg yolks	Pinch of salt
¾ cup plus 2 tablespoons sugar	Butter or margarine for greasing
Grated rind of 1 lemon	1 cup whipping cream
Juice of ½ lemon	1-2 teaspoons vanilla
2½ cups sifted cake flour	Slivered almonds for decoration (if desired)

Cut butter or margarine into flakes, crumble marzipan, then stir together until very creamy. Gradually add egg yolks alternating with sugar. Now and again flavor with grated lemon rind and lemon juice. Continue stirring until the sugar is completely dissolved and the batter is of a very creamy consistency. Combine flour with cornstarch and stir into the batter. Combine egg whites and salt and beat until completely stiff. Very gently, but thoroughly, fold into the batter.

Grease a 10-inch springform bottom with butter or margarine and smoothly and evenly spread 3 tablespoons of the batter onto it. Slide it under the preheated broiler, placing it as far as possible from the source of heat. Broil until the surface turns golden brown. Spread another 2-3 tablespoons of batter on it and broil in the same way. Continue until all of the batter has been used. Care should be taken that the various layers are equal in thickness and that individual layers are of the same thickness

throughout. This will insure that the cake bakes evenly rather than getting too dark in some places or even burning. Remove the finished cake from the springform bottom to a rack and allow to cool completely, if possible overnight.

The next day (or shortly before serving), whip the cream until stiff. Flavor it with vanilla and sweeten with a little sugar. Brush the sides of the torte with it. Place the remaining cream in a pastry bag with a star spout and press out 12 or 16 dots of cream on the outside rim of the surface. If desired sprinkle with sliced almonds; sliced almonds may also be sprinkled on the sides of the cake.

> **Tip:** *This torte is even more sophisticated when very carefully cut into two layers. Spread whipping cream and plum butter onto the surface and set the layers on top of each other again. Decorate as above.*

Cheese Torte with Fruit

½ pound lady fingers (sponge
   cookies)
1 cup butter or margarine
1 cup chopped hazelnuts
1 cup cream cheese
Juice of 2 lemons
¾ cup plus 1 tablespoon
   sugar

2 teaspoons vanilla
1 package lemon gelatin
½ cup water
2 cups whipping cream
1 pound strawberries

Place the cookies in a plastic bag and crush finely with a rolling pin. Retain 1 cup of crumbs. Melt butter or margarine and combine with the cookie crumbs and hazelnuts. Press this mixture into an 11-inch springform pan as the cake bottom.

For the filling, combine the cream cheese with lemon juice, sugar (retaining 2 tablespoons) and half of the vanilla. Stir these ingredients well. Pour the gelatin mix into the water together with the remaining sugar and allow to soak for 10 minutes. Then heat it and stir until well dissolved. Remove from the heat and allow to cool until just barely lukewarm. Add to the cheese mixture by the spoonful and stir in well. Refrigerate until the mixture begins to "streak." Meanwhile, combine whipping cream with vanilla and whip until stiff. Fold into the cheese mixture.

Rinse the strawberries, blot dry, remove stems and halve about ¾ of them. Fold these into the cheese mixture. Sparingly grease the springform rim, then line it with parchment paper. Fill the cheese mixture into the form and refrigerate for 3-4 hours.

Place a stencil on the surface and sprinkle with cookie crumbs. Decorate the unsprinkled area with the remaining strawberries. Finally, carefully remove the rim and peel off the paper strip.

Variation

For a change, flavor this torte with cherry gelatin supplemented by 2-4 tablespoons of cherry schnapps or liqueur. In this case, reduce the amount of lemon juice by half. Use cherries instead of strawberries for the fruit. A torte bottom containing chocolate augments the cherry filling especially well. For this, simply replace the amount of nuts called for in the above recipe with grated chocolate or chocolate decors. The butter should not be melted since this would cause the chocolate to melt as well. The torte bottom ingredients should be rubbed between the palms of the hands until they are well blended.

Reduced-Calorie Baking

Pepper and Strawberry Sponge Roll

5 egg yolks
¼ cup sugar
½ teaspoon liquid sweetener
Grated rind of 1 lemon
5 egg whites
1 cup sifted cake flour
1½ tablespoons cornstarch
Sugar for sprinkling
2 tablespoons pickled green
    peppercorns
2 pounds strawberries

2 cups cottage or ricotta
    cheese
1 cup milk
Juice and grated rind of 1
    lemon
Liquid sweetener
1½ ¼-ounce packages gelatin
1 package artificial whipping
    cream (like Dream Whip)
1 cup milk

Cream egg yolks with half the sugar. Add liquid sweetener and grated lemon rind. In a separate bowl, whip egg whites until almost stiff, slowly sprinkle in the remaining sugar and continue beating until egg whites are completely stiff. Slide egg whites into the egg-yolk mixture. Combine flour with cornstarch and pour into the egg mixture. Carefully fold in both egg whites and flour mixture with a wooden spoon. Line a baking sheet with parchment paper or aluminum foil and evenly spread the batter onto it. Bake in an oven preheated to 400° for 10-15 minutes until golden. Meanwhile, sprinkle a kitchen towel with sugar. Turn the cake out onto it and quickly but carefully peel off the paper. Immediately roll up the cake in the towel.

Remove the pickled peppercorns from the jar and drain well. Blot dry with paper towels. Retain 1 tablespoon of the peppercorns and crush the remainder in a mortar or grind them in an herb mill. Sort and wash the strawberries, remove the stems and quarter or halve the large ones. Set aside a few small strawberries for decoration. Combine strawberries with crushed peppercorns and allow the flavors to blend for about 10 minutes.

For the filling, stir together cottage or ricotta cheese with the milk, lemon juice and grated lemon rind. Flavor with sweetener. Combine the gelatin with some water and allow to soak for a few minutes. Add it to the cheese mixture and stir in evenly. Prepare the artificial whipping cream with the milk according to package directions and fold into the cheese mixture.

Unroll the sponge cake and spread it with part of the cheese mixture, retaining some of the cheese for decorating the roll. Distribute the strawberries and peppercorns onto the cheese and roll up the cake. Spread the remaining cheese onto the surface and decorate with whole peppercorns and strawberries.

Variation

If green peppercorns are not on hand, substitute black ones. Even though the black ones do not achieve the same color contrast, they do have a peppery flavor. Prepare exactly as in the recipe above. Do not, however, use whole black peppercorns for decoration, coarsely crush them instead.

Cherry Melon

3 egg whites
2 egg yolks
2 tablespoons cottage or
    ricotta cheese
Liquid sweetener
1 cup water
½ cup red wine
8 tablespoons cherry syrup
2 ¼-ounce packages red
    gelatin

1 pound cherries
1 egg yolk
⅔ cup plain yogurt
½ cup fruit juice
1 small honeydew melon
    (about ⅓ pound)
1 egg white
1½ ¼-ounce packages gelatin

Whip egg whites until stiff. In a separate bowl, cream egg yolks, cheese and sweetener and fold into the egg whites. Sparingly grease a 9-inch springform pan and fill in the batter. Bake in an oven preheated to 300° for 30 minutes. Remove from the pan and allow to cool on a rack.

Combine water, red wine and cherry syrup; flavor with sweetener. Dissolve gelatin in some water. Heat carefully while stirring constantly until gelatin powder is completely dissolved. Add to the cherry liquid and stir well. Fill ⅓ of the this into a 9-inch round bowl and refrigerate until gelled.

Meanwhile, wash and pit the cherries. As soon as the gelatin has gelled, place a second bowl, about 1 inch smaller than the first one, filled with water on top of the gelatin. Place a layer of cherries in the space between the gelatin and the smaller bowl. Heat the remaining gelatin to liquify it and pour part of it over the cherries. Refrigerate and gel again. Continue in this way until cherries and gelatin are used up.

To create the core, whisk together egg yolk and yogurt. Stir in fruit juice. Halve the honeydew melon and cut small balls out of it. Remove the remaining melon flesh and puree it in a blender with any imperfect melon balls. Fold the puree into the yogurt mixture. Sweeten with liquid sweetener, if desired. In a separate bowl, whip egg white until stiff and evenly fold into the yogurt mixture. Dissolve the gelatin according to package directions and stir into the yogurt mixture. Now carefully fold in the melon balls. Remove the cherry gelatin from the refrigerator and carefully remove the water from the smaller bowl with a ladle. Then fill the small bowl with hot water, swish it around gently and carefully remove the bowl. Fill the melon-yogurt mixture into the well. Refrigerate for 2-3 hours. Turn the gelatin melon out onto the torte bottom shortly before serving.

Almond Macaroons

4 egg whites
1¼ cups powdered sugar
⅔ cup ground almonds

3 teaspoons cocoa
⅛ teaspoon ginger
Grated rind of 1 orange

Whip egg whites until stiff. Gradually sift powdered sugar on top and continue beating until the sugar is blended in well. Fold in almonds, cocoa, ginger and orange rind. Line a baking sheet with parchment paper and, using two teaspoons, drop macaroon dough onto it. Bake on the middle rack of an oven preheated to 325° for 15-20 minutes.

Vanilla Crescents

⅔ cup ground hazelnuts
2¼ cups flour
1 teaspoon vanilla
2 tablespoons liquid
   sweetener

1 egg yolk
7 tablespoons chilled butter
2 teaspoons vanilla
2 tablespoons powdered sugar

On a work surface, combine hazelnuts and flour. Add the vanilla, sweetener, egg yolk and chilled butter in flakes. Quickly knead all the ingredients into a dough. Wrap in aluminum foil and refrigerate for 1 hour. Then form into a rope and cut into 40 pieces. Form these into little sausages and bend them into crescents. Place on a baking sheet lined with parchment paper

and bake in an oven preheated to 350° for 15 minutes. Combine vanilla with powdered sugar and sift over the crescents or turn the cookies in the sugar mixture.

Cookie-Press or Spritz Cookies

⅓ cup butter
4 teaspoons liquid sweetener
1 egg
Pinch of salt
Grated rind of 1 lemon

4 drops almond extract
4 drops rum extract
1½ cups flour
⅓ cup cornstarch
4 tablespoons milk

Cream butter together with sweetener. Add egg, salt, grated lemon rind, almond and rum extract and blend in well. Combine flour together with cornstarch and add to the butter mixture by the spoonful alternating with the milk. Fill into a pastry bag with a star spout and press S-forms or wreaths out onto a baking sheet lined with waxed paper. Bake in an oven preheated to 400° for about 20 minutes until golden. Remove to a rack and allow to cool.

Coated Cheese Cake

7 tablespoons margarine	4 tablespoons sifted cake flour
½ teaspoon liquid sweetener	Grated rind of 1 lemon
2½ cups sifted cake flour	2 cups milk
½ teaspoon baking powder	Liquid sweetener
Margarine for greasing	3 tablespoons butter
2 tablespoons butter	¼ cup sugar
3 cups cottage or ricotta	2 egg yolks
cheese	2 egg whites
1 package vanilla pudding mix	

Cream margarine with sweetener. Combine flour with baking powder and quickly knead into a smooth dough. Sparingly grease a 10-inch springform pan and line it with the dough to make 1-inch high rim.

Melt the butter and fold it into the fresh cheese. Sprinkle vanilla pudding mix and flour over it and stir in carefully avoiding the creation of lumps. Add grated lemon rind and milk. Flavor the batter with liquid sweetener and fill into the pan.

For the coating, cream butter, sugar and egg yolks. In a separate bowl, whip egg whites until stiff, then slide these into the butter mixture and fold in gently. Evenly spread the coating onto the cheese. Bake the torte in an oven preheated to 400° for 30-40 minutes. Cover with parchment paper during the last 15 minutes of baking.

Allow the cake to cool for 5-6 hours or, even better, overnight.

Cherry and Cheese Tartlets

For the tartlets:

3 egg whites	Grated rind of 1 lemon
2 cups ricotta or cottage	⅔ cup sifted cake flour
cheese	Margarine for greasing
3 egg yolks	Bread crumbs for sprinkling
Liquid sweetener	

For the filling:

1¼ cups ricotta or cottage	¼ cup ground hazelnuts
cheese	1 tablespoon sifted cake flour
1 egg	Liquid sweetener
Juice of 1 lemon	24 cherries
Grated rind of ½ lemon	

Whip egg whites until stiff. Stir together cheese with egg yolks and flavor with sweetener and lemon rind. Stir in flour and carefully fold mixture into the egg whites. Sparingly grease 6 tartlet forms, coat with bread crumbs and fill in the dough. Prebake them for 10-15 minutes at 350°. Allow to cool slightly and turn out of the forms.

For the filling, stir together the ricotta or cottage cheese with the egg and lemon juice. Stir in grated lemon rind, hazelnuts and flour. Flavor with sweetener and distribute among the 6 upright tartlets. Pit the cherries and place 3 of them on top of each tartlet. Bake for another 15 minutes at 400°.

Fresh Berry Charlotte

About 30 ladyfingers (sponge cake cookies)	Liquid sweetener
2 cups white wine	¼ pound strawberries
½ cinnamon stick	¼ pound blueberries or red currants
2 ¼-ounce packages gelatin	¼ pound green grapes
3-4 tablespoons maraschino liqueur	¼ pound raspberries
	¼ pound blackberries

Line the bottom of an 8½-inch springform pan with a portion of the ladyfingers and line the rim of the form with a strip of parchment paper. Combine ½ cup of white wine with the cinnamon stick and bring to a boil. Pour through a sieve and stir in the gelatin. Mix in the remaining wine together with the maraschino and flavor with a few drops of liquid sweetener. Allow to cool until the mixture begins to "streak."

Meanwhile, sort the berries and carefully wash them in cold water. Allow them to drip dry in a sieve. Remove the stems from the strawberries and halve or quarter the larger ones. Remove the stems from the blueberries or red currants. Skin, halve and remove pits from the grapes. Remove stems from the raspberries and blackberries without injuring the fruit. As soon as the gelatin mixture begins to harden, whip through it vigorously, then gently fold in the fruit. Fill into the prepared form and refrigerate until completely firm.

Remove the springform rim and the parchment paper prior to serving. Halve the remaining ladyfingers and heat them briefly in a dry frying pan or in a hot oven. Press them vertically onto the side of the charlotte. Place on a torte platter and cut.

> **Tip:** *Serve the Berry Charlotte with a Wine-Foam Sauce. To prepare the sauce, combine ½ cup of aromatic white wine with 3 egg yolks in a double boiler over hot, but not boiling water. Beat until the mixture is thick and creamy. Sweeten with liquid sweetener according to taste.*

Chocolate Wine Torte

4 egg yolks	Pinch of salt
⅔ cup sugar	¾ cup sifted cake flour
1 vanilla bean	3 tablespoons cornstarch
4 egg whites	2 tablespoons cocoa

For the filling and trimming:

½ pineapple (about 1 pound)	2 cups milk
⅓ pound strawberries	3 packages artificial whipping cream (like Dream Whip)
1 cup white wine	
1 package instant chocolate cream	

For the dough, whip egg yolks until foamy, then gradually sprinkle in half of the sugar. Slit the vanilla bean lengthwise, scrape out the marrow and add to the egg yolks. In a separate bowl, whip the egg whites with salt until stiff, then sprinkle in the remaining sugar and continue beating until the egg whites are completely white and have a very strong sheen. Slide into the egg yolks. Combine flour, cornstarch and cocoa. Pour over the egg mixture and gently fold all the ingredients together. Line a 10-inch springform pan with waxed paper, fill in the dough and smooth out the surface. Bake on the middle rack of an oven preheated to 350° for 25-30 minutes. Turn out onto a rack and peel off the paper. Allow the cake to cool completely.

For the filling, carefully peel the pineapple, remove the core and thinly slice the fruit. Wash strawberries briefly in cold water, blot dry, then remove stems. Halve or quarter the larger fruit. Pierce all of the fruit repeatedly with a needle. Pour the wine over the strawberries and pineapple and allow to soak.

Cut the cake into two layers, place one layer on a platter and set the other one aside. Combine the instant chocolate cream with 1½ cups of milk and beat the cream for 2-3 minutes. Drain the fruit in a sieve retaining the liquid. Measure out about 1 cup of this liquid and mix it into the chocolate cream while beating constantly. Refrigerate for about 10 minutes. Dribble the remaining liquid onto the bottom cake layer. Pour the remaining milk into a bowl, combine it with the artificial whipping cream mix and prepare according to package directions. As soon as this cream has stiffened, fold it into the chocolate cream.

Lay pineapple pieces and strawberries onto the wine-soaked cake bottom, retain a few especially nice pieces of fruit for later decoration. Spread half the cream mixture on top of the fruit, top with the second cake layer and coat the surfaces and sides of the torte with the cream. Place the remaining cream into a pastry bag with a star spout.

Mark 12 or 16 pieces on the surface of the torte and press out a large dot of cream onto each piece. Decorate with the remaining pieces of fruit and serve as soon as possible.

Kiwi Tartlets

2½ tablespoons butter or margarine	¾ cup sifted cake flour
3 tablespoons sugar	½ teaspoon baking powder
1 teaspoon vanilla	Butter or margarine for greasing
Grated rind of 1 lemon	Bread crumbs for coating
Pinch of salt	

For the meringue:

2 egg whites	½ teaspoon lemon juice
Pinch of salt	2-3 kiwis (depending on size)
2 tablespoons sugar	

Cream butter or margarine and gradually add the sugar, vanilla, lemon rind and salt. Stir until the mixture is very creamy and the sugar completely dissolved. Combine flour with baking powder, quickly but thoroughly stir it into the butter mixture.

Sparingly grease 4-6 tartlet forms (depending on the size) and coat with bread crumbs. Fill in the dough, smooth out the surface and bake on the middle rack of an oven preheated to 350° for 10-15 minutes. Turn out onto a rack and allow to cool slightly.

While the tartlets are baking, combine egg whites with salt and whip until stiff. Gradually sprinkle in the sugar and continue beating until the egg whites are very stiff and have a strong sheen. Then mix in the lemon juice and place in a pastry bag with a star spout.

Peel the kiwis and cut into slices. Halve or quarter these, if desired. Thickly fill the tartlets with kiwi slices and press out a tight spiral of meringue stars covering the surface. Bake in an oven preheated to 400°-425° until the meringue turns golden yellow. Then remove, allow to cool and serve as soon as possible. These tartlets taste best when served fresh.

Note

These Kiwi Tartlets may be served with artificial whipping cream flavored with grated lemon rind. Serve with cold, very lightly sweetened whipped cream.

Fresh Cheese Charlotte with Raspberries

3 egg yolks	Juice and grated rind of 1
3 tablespoons lukewarm water	lemon
⅓ cup sugar	¾ cup milk
3 egg whites	1-2 tablespoons liquid
Pinch of salt	sweetener
1 cup sifted cake flour	1½ ¼-ounce packages gelatin
1 tablespoon baking powder	1 package artificial whipping
Sugar for sprinkling	cream (like Dream Whip)
⅔ pound raspberries	½ cup milk
1 cup ricotta or cottage	
cheese	

Combine egg yolks with water and beat until foamy, gradually add about 3 tablespoons of the sugar. Beat until the mixture is white and foamy and the sugar dissolved. In a separate bowl, combine egg whites with salt and beat until stiff. Continue beating and gradually sprinkle in the remaining sugar. Slide the egg whites into the egg-yolk mixture. Combine flour with baking powder and gently fold into the eggs. Line a baking sheet with parchment or waxed paper and spread the batter onto it. Bake on the middle rack of an oven preheated to 400° for 10-12 minutes. Turn out onto a kitchen towel sprinkled with sugar, peel off the paper and roll up the cake together with the towel. Allow to cool.

Briefly wash the raspberries, blot them dry and remove stems. Stir cheese, lemon juice, and 2-3 tablespoons of the milk into a smooth and supple batter. Add lemon rind and flavor with liquid sweetener. In a saucepan over medium heat, dissolve the gelatin in some cold water; stir constantly. Fold evenly into the cheese mixture. Prepare the artificial whipping cream with the milk according to package directions and stir into the cheese mixture. Spread a portion of this cheese mixture onto the unrolled cake and roll it up again. Cut it into ½-inch thick slices.

Line a smooth, round bowl with the slices of cake, retaining 5-6 for the bottom. Fill in a layer of the cheese mixture into the bowl lined with sponge cake slices. Distribute a layer of raspberries onto the cheese mixture. Cover again with cheese and continue until both fruit and cheese are used up. The last layer should be the cheese mixture. Then place the retained cake slices on top. Refrigerate the Charlotte for 1 hour, then turn out onto a platter for serving.

Fresh Cheese Stollen

1 small orange	Pinch of salt
½ lemon	⅓ cup chopped almonds
5 tablespoons sugar	3 drops almond extract
¾ cup water	3 drops rum extract
2 cups ricotta or cottage	Margarine for greasing
cheese	Bread crumbs for coating
6¼ cups sifted cake flour	4 tablespoons margarine
1 tablespoon baking powder	5 tablespoons powdered sugar
2 eggs	1 teaspoon vanilla
½ cup sugar	

Wash the orange and the lemon and cut into very thin slices. Combine sugar with water and heat until the sugar has liquified. Drop in the orange and lemon slices and simmer for 3-4 minutes. Remove and drain. Allow to cool slightly, then dice finely.

Drain the cheese. This is probably done best with a cheese cloth. Combine flour with baking powder and make a well in the middle. Pour in cheese, eggs, sugar, salt, almonds, diced lemon and orange as well as the flavors. Knead all the ingredients together into a dough. Sparingly grease a baking sheet and sprinkle with bread crumbs. Form the dough into a stollen, place it on the baking sheet and bake on the middle rack of an oven preheated to 400° for 1 hour. Remove the baked stollen to a rack and brush with melted margarine while it is still hot. Sift powdered sugar combined with vanilla over the stollen.

Quince and Apple Strudel

1½ pounds quinces
1¾ cups sifted cake flour
½ teaspoon salt
1 egg
1 tablespoon shortening
¼ cup tepid water
1½ pounds apples

Juice of 1 lemon
Liquid sweetener
Flour for rolling
2 tablespoons melted butter
2 tablespoons sugar
1 teaspoon ground cinnamon

Wash quinces, place on a rack in the oven with a pan underneath and bake at 400° for 45 minutes until tender.

To prepare the strudel dough, place the flour onto a board and make a well in the middle. Pour salt, egg, shortening and the water into the well. Working from the middle outward, stir all the ingredients into a dough. Knead vigorously. Throw the ball of dough onto the work surface repeatedly and then thoroughly knead it again. Wrap it in parchment paper and allow to rest for 30 minutes in a hot, dry pot.

Wash and peel the apples. Cut out any brown spots and remove the seed housing. Slice the apple quarters into ⅛-inch slices, sprinkle with lemon juice and cover. Remove the quinces from the oven, allow them to cool slightly, then pull off the rind. Scrape the flesh of the fruit from the pit with a spoon. Press it through a sieve or puree in a blender. Generously sweeten the pureed quinces with liquid sweetener.

Roll out the dough on a floured tablecloth and pull out further until it is extremely thin and almost transparent. Brush with melted butter, retaining 1 tablespoon for the surface of the strudel. Spread the quince puree onto the dough. Equally distribute the apple slices over the entire dough surface, leaving a 1-inch rim around the edges free of filling. Combine sugar with cinnamon and sprinkle over the apple slices. Fold in the edges so that the liquid from the filling does not run out. Roll up the dough with the aid of the towel and carefully place it on a baking sheet that has previously been rinsed in cold water. Bake in an oven preheated to 425° for 45 minutes until the surface is crispy and brown.

Tip: *The taste of cold, quince-flavored whipped cream is a scrumptious contrast to warm, oven-fresh apple strudel. To prepare the cream, bake an extra quince and puree the flesh of the fruit. Prepare artificial whipping cream (for instance, Dream Whip) with 1 cup of milk according to package directions, then very gently fold in the quince puree.*

Cranberry Strudel

1½ cups sifted cake flour
½ teaspoon salt
1 tablespoon oil
⅓ cup tepid water
5 egg whites
2 tablespoons sugar

Juice of ½ lemon
1 cup canned cranberries
¼ cup chopped hazelnuts
Grated rind of 1 lemon
Flour for rolling
2 tablespoons butter

Pour the flour into a bowl and make a well in the middle. Add salt and oil, then slowly pour in the tepid water. Stir all the ingredients together, then knead thoroughly. Throw the ball of dough onto a work surface 20-30 times, then knead it again vigorously. The dough should be completely smooth when cut through with a knife. Wrap the strudel dough in parchment paper and place in a hot, dry pot (boil water in it beforehand). Allow to rest for 30 minutes.

To prepare the cranberry filling, whip egg whites until firm. Then sprinkle in sugar and beat for another minute. Add lemon juice and beat for an additional minute as well. Stir the cranberries in the jar and fold into the egg whites together with the chopped hazelnuts and grated lemon rind. Evenly dust a large tablecloth with flour. Roll out the strudel dough with a rolling pin until it is as thin as possible. With the backs of the hands, pull the dough out even farther. Melt the butter, and thinly brush onto the dough. Evenly distribute the cranberry mixture onto the dough leaving a 1-inch outside rim free of filling. Fold in the edges so that the filling does not run out during baking. Roll up the strudel with the aid of the tablecloth. Rinse a baking sheet in cold water and carefully place the strudel onto it. Bake at 350° for 40-50 minutes until golden brown.

Variation

This strudel will have even fewer calories if fresh cranberries are used. Also try red currants, in which case the amount of sugar should be increased to 3 tablespoons.

Tip: *Strudel is not only an ideal snack, but when dieting it can also serve as a substitute for a skipped meal. Two pieces will satisfy an appetite quite well and it is not more than 200-300 calories.*

Savory
Baking

Pizza

5 cups flour	Pinch of basil
1 cup plus 2 tablespoons tepid water	1 red bell pepper
	2 yellow bell peppers
½ teaspoon sugar	1-2 zucchini
1 package dry yeast	2 large onions
1 onion	½ pound cooked ham
1 tablespoon butter or margarine	1 pound mozzarella
	Oil for greasing
1-2 tablespoons oil	½ pound Hungarian salami
½ teaspoon salt	Coarsely crushed black pepper
1 large can peeled tomatoes	Pickled green peppercorns
1 6-ounce can tomato paste	Basil and oregano for sprinkling
Salt and freshly ground white pepper	4 tablespoons oil for brushing
Pinch of oregano	

Place flour in a bowl and make a well in the middle. Dissolve sugar and yeast in 4 tablespoons of water, place this mixture into the well and stir together with a little flour from the sides. Allow this starter to rise in a warm place for 15 minutes until bubbles appear on the dough.

Peel the onion, dice it finely and braise it until transparent in the melted butter or margarine. Set aside and allow to cool slightly. Add the remaining water, oil and salt to the starter and knead all ingredients into a smooth dough. Cover with a cloth and allow to rise for 30 minutes in a warm place.

To prepare the topping, drain the tomatoes and press through a sieve. Season the tomatoes with tomato paste, salt, pepper, oregano and basil. Quarter the bell peppers, remove seed housing and cut into thin strips. Wash zucchini and cut into ¼-inch slices. Peel onions and cut into rings. Cut ham into strips and mozzarella into slices. Brush a baking sheet with oil and roll out the dough. Allow to rest for 5 minutes, press the dough into the corners again. Brush with the tomato puree and top with peppers, zucchini, onion rings, ham, salami and mozzarella. Season with salt, black and green pepper, basil and oregano, brush with oil. Bake in an oven preheated to 400° for about 30 minutes.

Piroggen

7 tablespoons tepid water	2 teaspoons instant cream sauce
½ teaspoon sugar	
1½ teaspoons dry yeast	1 bunch parsley
2¼ cups flour	2 tablespoons sour cream
1 teaspoon salt	Salt and freshly ground black pepper
¼ cup shortening	
2 onions	¼ cup grated Emmenthaler
8 slices smoked ham	1 egg
2 tablespoons butter	1 tablespoon milk
1 7-ounce can mushrooms	Butter or margarine for greasing
7 tablespoons white wine	

Place the tepid water into a bowl and dissolve the sugar in it. Add the yeast and stir in a few tablespoons of flour to make a starter. Preheat the oven to warm, place the starter in the oven and allow to rise for 15 minutes. Pour the remaining flour into a bowl and place in the oven as well. Add the starter to the flour together with salt and shortening and knead into a smooth dough. Cover with a kitchen towel and allow to rise in a warm place for 30 minutes.

To prepare the filling, peel and finely dice the onions. Cut two slices of ham into thin strips and fry onions and ham in the melted butter. Drain and thinly slice the mushrooms, add them to the frying onions and simmer for 2-3 minutes. Pour in the white wine and thicken with the cream sauce. Rinse and finely chop the parsley. Cut the remaining ham into thin strips or small squares. Fold into the mixture together with the sour cream. Season with salt and pepper. Allow to cool slightly, then mix in the cheese.

Roll out the dough to a thickness of ⅛-inch and cut out rounds measuring 5-inches in diameter. Distribute the filling among the rounds and then fold them in half to make crescents. Press the edges together with a fork. Whisk together egg and milk and brush the Piroggen with this mixture. Place on a greased baking sheet and bake in an oven preheated to 400° for 15 minutes.

Olive Pockets

1 10-ounce package frozen puff pastry	Salt and freshly ground black pepper
1 can tuna fish packed in oil	Generous pinch of oregano
1 onion	Flour for rolling
1 small jar green olives stuffed with pimento	1 egg yolk
4 ounces ricotta or cottage cheese	

Lay the puff pastry layers out next to each other and allow to thaw at room temperature.

Separate the tuna fish with a fork. Peel and finely dice the onion. Slice the olives. Crush the fresh cheese with a fork and combine with the diced onion, olives and tuna fish. Season the filling with salt, black pepper and oregano.

Stack the puff pastry layers, place on a floured surface and roll out to a rectangle measuring 12 x 20 inches. Cut off a 1½-inch strip and cut the remaining dough into 6 rectangles. Distribute the filling onto the rectangles. Brush the edges with egg yolk, fold and press together well. Cut 6 small circles out of the strips of dough, brush with egg yolk and place them on top of the pockets, which have been brushed with egg yolk as well. Rinse a baking sheet with cold water and place the pockets onto it. Allow to rest for 10 minutes before baking on the middle rack of an oven preheated to 400° for 25 minutes.

Caraway Seed Sticks

2½ cups flour	7 tablespoons water
1½ cups wheat flour	1 egg yolk
4 tablespoons tepid water	2 teaspoons condensed milk
1 teaspoon sugar	2-3 tablespoons caraway
2 teaspoons dry yeast	seeds
1 teaspoon salt	2 tablespoons coarse salt
4 tablespoons sour cream	Flour for the baking sheet
2 tablespoons oil	

Place the flour in a bowl and make a well in the middle. Pour in water, sugar and yeast. Stir together with some flour from the sides and allow to rise in a warm place for 15 minutes.

Add salt, sour cream, oil and tepid water and knead all the ingredients into a smooth dough. Cover with a kitchen towel and allow to rise in a warm place for 30 minutes. Form the dough into a roll and cut it into 8 pieces. Form these pieces into sticks having a diameter of 1 inch. Make 3-4 furrows in the surface and brush with egg yolk combined with condensed milk. Sprinkle salt and caraway seeds into the furrows. Place on a floured baking sheet and bake in an oven preheated to 425° for 20-25 minutes.

Onion and Cheese Sticks

3 layers frozen puff pastry	1 egg
1 onion	½ teaspoon salt
1 tablespoon butter or	White pepper
margarine	Sweet paprika
3 ounces cheddar cheese	Flour for rolling

Lay out the puff pastry layers next to each other and allow to thaw at room temperature. Peel and very finely dice the onion. Brown in melted butter or margarine. Grate the cheese. Beat the egg with a fork and season with salt, pepper and paprika.

Place one of the puff pastry layers on a floured work surface and brush it with some whisked egg. Spread half of the diced onion and half the cheddar on it. Brush the second puff pastry layer with egg as well and lay on top of the onions and cheese, the egg-coated side should be facing downward. Brush the top surface with egg and spread with the remaining onions and cheese. Brush the final puff pastry layer with egg and lay the egg-coated side on top. Using a rolling pin, roll out the puff pastry to double its size. Cut into 1-inch wide strips and brush with egg yolk. Be sure to avoid getting egg yolk on the cut edges, otherwise the puff pastry will not rise evenly.

Wind the strips into spirals and place them on a baking sheet that has been rinsed in cold water. Allow to rest for 10 minutes.

Bake in an oven preheated to 400° for 8-10 minutes. Immediately remove to a kitchen rack, then serve as soon as possible.

Onion Rolls with Bacon

4 cups rye flour	1 tablespoon oil
1 cup wheat flour	2 large onions
1 cup sourdough (recipe on page 287)	1 teaspoon salt
	1 teaspoon caraway seeds
1 package dry yeast	6 tablespoons water
¼ pound bacon	Flour for dusting and shaping

Combine rye and wheat flour in a bowl and make a well in the middle. Pour in the sourdough and add the yeast. Stir together with a little flour from the sides and allow to rise for 15 minutes.

Dice the bacon and sauté in hot oil. Peel and dice the onion and sauté until transparent. Allow onions, bacon and fat to cool, then add to the starter together with salt, caraway seeds and water. Work all the ingredients into a smooth dough. Form into a ball, place in a bowl dusted with flour and allow to rise for 1 hour. Then, punch down the dough, form into a roll and cut it into 8 pieces. Knead these pieces again, form into balls and place them on a floured baking sheet. Cover with a kitchen towel and allow to rise for another 30 minutes. Preheat the oven to 400°, place the rolls in it and bake for 30-40 minutes.

Spring Rolls

2 cups wheat flour	3 tablespoons chopped chives
3 teaspoons baking powder	½ cup milk
⅛ teaspoon salt	Flour for shaping
2 tablespoons butter	Butter or margarine for greasing
½ cup cream cheese with herbs	2 tablespoons condensed milk

Combine flour with baking powder and stir in the salt. Place butter and cream cheese, in flakes, on top and work all the ingredients together until they have a crumb-like consistency. Rinse and chop the chives. Add to the crumbs together with the milk and knead all the ingredients into a dough. Form into a roll, then cut into 6 pieces. Knead each piece again and form into balls. Cut a deep furrow into each ball with the back of a knife and place the balls on a greased baking sheet. Brush the surfaces with condensed milk and bake in an oven preheated to 400° for 20-25 minutes.

Variation

Linseed Rolls: To make linseed rolls following the same recipe, replace the herb cream cheese with cream cheese and the chives with 4-5 tablespoons of linseed. Sprinkle the surfaces of the rolls with linseeds as well.

Peanut and Chicken Torte

2 cups flour	¼ cup peanut butter
1 egg	7 tablespoons butter
½ teaspoon salt	

For the filling:

1 pound chicken breasts	1 egg yolk
3 tablespoons flour	3 tablespoons heavy cream
1 teaspoon sweet paprika	Freshly ground white pepper
1 teaspoon curry	Ground ginger
3 tablespoons oil	Hot red paprika (or a few
2 tablespoons dry sherry	drops of Tabasco sauce)
1 can bean sprouts	Cayenne pepper
1 small can bamboo shoots	1 teaspoon soy sauce
1 small can pineapple	Butter or margarine for
½ cup salted peanuts	greasing
1 egg	

Place flour onto a work surface and make a well in the middle. Pour in egg, salt and peanut butter. Place the chilled butter in flakes on the rim and, with chilled hands, work all the ingredients into a dough as quickly as possible. Wrap in aluminum foil and refrigerate for 1 hour.

To prepare the filling, skin and bone the chicken breasts. Dice into 1-inch squares. Sift flour, paprika and curry onto a plate and turn the chicken pieces in it. Sauté in hot oil, turning frequently, then add sherry. Drain bean sprouts and bamboo shoots. Cut the bamboo shoots and pineapple into pieces and add to the chicken together with 1 tablespoon of pineapple juice and the peanuts.

Simmer these ingredients over mild heat for 10 minutes. Remove from the heat. Whisk together egg, egg yolk and cream and fold into the chicken mixture. Season with salt, pepper, curry, ginger, paprika, cayenne pepper and soy sauce.

Grease a 10-inch springform pan with butter or margarine. Press the dough into it so that there is a 1-inch rim on the sides. Repeatedly pierce the bottom with a fork. Lay a piece of parchment paper on top of the dough and weight it down with dried beans, peas or lentils. Prebake the torte shell in an oven preheated to 400° for 15-20 minutes. Then remove the beans and the paper.

Fill in the chicken mixture and bake for an additional 15-20 minutes at the same temperature.

> **Tip:** *To save time use puff pastry for the bottom. Spread peanut butter onto the puff pastry layers, then stack them and roll them out with a rolling pin.*

Rabbit Encased in a Crust

1 rabbit back
2 rabbit legs
3-4 tablespoons oil
1 large onion
1 clove garlic
2 bunches soup greens (made
 up of 1 carrot, parsley root,
 a piece of celeriac and a
 piece of leek)
1 tablespoon tomato paste
2 juniper berries
4 peppercorns
½ bay leaf
Generous pinch thyme
3 cups water
½ cup red wine
6 cups flour
1½ teaspoons salt
1⅓ cups chilled butter
1 egg

⅔ cup ice cold water
1 tablespoon butter for frying
⅔ pound shortening
½ pound lean pork
1 pound bacon
⅓ pound mushrooms
¼ pound pistachios
¼ pound pine nuts
Salt and freshly ground black
 pepper
2 tablespoons gin
2 teaspoons spices (a mixture
 of white pepper, cinnamon,
 ginger, bay leaves and
 mace)
Flour for rolling
1 egg yolk for brushing
½ cup bouillon
½ cup port
1½ ¼-ounce packages gelatin

Bone the rabbit and set aside the fillets and any other meat from the back as well as meat from the legs. Break bones and other leftover pieces down to a smaller size, place in a pot with 2-3 tablespoons of oil and, while turning frequently, roast until dark brown in an oven preheated to 475°. Peel and dice the onion and garlic, clean and trim the soup greens and brown them in the oven as well. Add tomato paste and spices, roast them as

well, then add some of the water. Allow the liquid to reduce and add additional water once or twice. Place all of the roasted ingredients in a saucepan and add the remaining water and wine. Reduce the liquid to just a few tablespoons, in the process repeatedly skim off foam.

Knead flour with salt, butter in flakes, egg and water into a smooth dough. Cover and refrigerate.

Heat the oil and butter and briefly sauté the fillets. Wrap them in some shortening. Grind the pork and rabbit meat together with the fresh bacon twice in a meat grinder using the finest blade. Press the meat through a sieve and cool it down by placing in a bowl and stirring it over·ice until it gleams. Add the cleaned and diced mushrooms together with the pistachios and pine nuts to the cold meat, also add the gin and spices.

Roll out the dough and line a loaf pan with it. Lay shortening on top of the dough, then fill in the meat mixture decoratively surrounding the rabbit fillets. Cover with bacon and place a layer of dough on top. Cut out a chimney. Use the leftover dough for decoration. Brush with egg yolk and place in an oven preheated to 425°. After about 15 minutes, reduce the temperature to 350° and bake for 60-70 minutes until done.

Dissolve the gelatin in some water. Combine the bouillon with the port and stir in the dissolved gelatin. As soon as it begins to gel, pour the liquid into the chimney. This should be done gradually in small portions so that it is distributed among all the cavities. Refrigerate until the loaf has stiffened.

Vol-au-vent

2 10-ounce packages frozen puff pastry	Juice of ½ lemon
2 egg yolks	½ pound baby shrimp
½ pound green onions	2 tablespoons crème fraîche
3 tablespoons butter	2 tablespoons whipping cream
½ pound mushrooms	1 bunch dill
½ cup white wine	3 teaspoons capers
2 cups bouillon	3 tablespoons dry vermouth
1 pound ruff fillet (similar to Atlantic butterfish)	Salt and freshly ground white pepper
	2 tablespoons cornstarch

Thaw puff pastry according to package directions.

Line a 6-inch round bowl with aluminum foil and fill with paper or aluminum foil strips. Lay aluminum foil over the filling and pinch the edges together well. Remove the resulting half circle from the bowl. Roll out ⅓ of the puff pastry to a round measuring 10-inches in diameter. Rinse a baking sheet with cold water and lay the puff pastry round on it. Place the half circle on top so that the rounded part faces upward. Roll out the remaining pastry into a round measuring at least 10-inches in diameter and lay it over the half circle. Press the edges of the pastry together well.

Cut off the excess pastry with a sharp knife so that there is a 1½-inch rim around the aluminum stencil that is equal all the way around. Roll out the leftover dough and cut a 1½-inch strip out of it. Brush with some whisked egg yolk and glue it to the edge of pastry that exceeds the aluminum stencil. Brush the entire half circle with egg yolk, retaining some for later decoration. Out of the leftover pastry, cut out stars, flowers, leaves, strips or any other desired shapes and lay them on the half circle. Brush them with egg as well. Allow the half circle to rest in a cool place for 15 minutes, then place on the middle rack of an oven preheated to 425° and bake for 20-25 minutes.

For the filling, trim onions, cut off the green parts and sauté in about 2 tablespoons of butter until translucent. Brush, wash, dry and, depending on their size, halve or quarter the mushrooms. Add to the onions and sauté as well. Pour in the white wine, wait briefly before pouring in the bouillon. Cover and simmer gently for 10 minutes.

Dice the fish into 1-inch pieces, sprinkle with lemon juice. Peel the shrimp. Sauté the fish and shrimp in the remaining butter. Stir crème fraîche and cream into the mushroom mixture, season with chopped dill, capers, salt and pepper. Add vermouth and thicken the mixture with cornstarch. Add the fish and shrimp at the end, allow them to absorb the flavors over low heat for 5 minutes, then season to taste.

When the puff pastry house has finished baking, remove it from the oven and allow to steam off briefly. With a very sharp, pointed knife, cut a small chimney into the top. Retain the lid and carefully remove the aluminum foil and any other stuffing materials, be sure to avoid injuring the puff pastry. Fill in the fish ragout, place the lid on top and serve immediately.

Gentlemen's Torte

8 egg yolks	½ cup ground nuts or almonds
4 tablespoons heavy cream	¼ cup grated Emmenthaler
½ teaspoon salt	8 egg whites
Freshly ground white pepper	Butter or margarine for greasing
Grated nutmeg	Bread crumbs for coating
1½ cups flour	
1½ teaspoons baking powder	

For the filling and trimming:

½ pound cucumber	White pepper
Salt	Sweet paprika
¾ cup plus 2 tablespoons butter	16 ounces Gorgonzola cheese
2 cups ricotta or cottage cheese	4 tablespoons whisky
8 ounces cream cheese	4 tablespoons heavy cream
1 pound baked ham	1 cup ground walnuts
½ cup milk	Coarsely crushed black pepper
	12 walnut halves

In a bowl, whisk egg yolks with cream. Add salt, pepper and ground nutmeg and beat mixture until it is as foamy as technically possible. Combine flour with baking powder, pour it over the egg mixture and add ground nuts or almonds together with the grated cheese. In a separate bowl, whip egg whites until stiff, slide into the dough and gently but thoroughly fold all the ingredients together. Grease a 10-inch springform pan with butter or margarine and coat with bread crumbs. Fill in the dough, smooth it out and bake in an oven preheated to 400° for 35 minutes. Allow to cool thoroughly on a rack. Later cut the cake into 3 layers.

For the filling, finely grate well over half of the cucumber, sprinkle with salt and set aside for 15 minutes so that the excess liquid can collect. Then press out the cucumber pieces.

Cream butter, then mix in the fresh cheese and the cream cheese. Set 2 slices of ham aside and dice the remainder. Place the diced ham in a blender and puree with the milk. Fold into the cheese mixture together with the cucumber and season with salt, pepper and paprika.

Finely crush the Gorgonzola with a fork or press it through a sieve. Stir until completely smooth together with the whisky and cream. Mix in the ground walnuts and season generously with salt and pepper.

Spread ⅓ of the ham and cheese mixture onto the first layer of cake, smooth it out and place the second layer on top. Spread this layer with the Gorgonzola cream and cover with the final layer. Evenly cover the sides and surface of the torte with the remaining ham and cheese mixture. Decorate with the retained ham, nuts and the remaining thinly sliced cucumber; refrigerate until ready to serve.

Garlic Flat Bread

1½ cups rye flour	1 teaspoon salt
1½ cups wheat flour	⅛ teaspoon allspice
5 tablespoons tepid water	2 teaspoons pickled green
1½ teaspoons dry yeast	peppercorns
1 teaspoon sugar	½ cup white wine
3 cloves garlic	Coarse salt for sprinkling
2 tablespoons butter	Flour for dusting

Combine rye and wheat flour in a bowl and make a well in the middle. Pour in the water and stir together with yeast, sugar and some flour from the sides to make a starter. Allow to rise in a warm place for 15 minutes until bubbles begin to appear.

Peel the garlic cloves, press through a garlic press or finely dice them. Melt the butter or margarine in a frying pan and sauté the garlic until golden brown. Allow to cool slightly. Add the garlic and butter together with salt, allspice, drained peppercorns and white wine to the starter. Knead all the ingredients into a dough, cover and allow to rest in a warm place for 1 hour. Roll out the dough on a floured surface to ½-inch thickness. With the back of a knife, make crisscrossing furrows in the surface of the dough and sprinkle with coarse salt. Preheat the oven to 400°-425°. While the oven is preheating, place the flat bread on a floured baking sheet and cover it with a kitchen towel. Then bake it for 30-45 minutes.

Note

This flat bread tastes especially good when served with wine. It is best when served fresh out of the oven. Allow it to cool slightly and serve with herb-garlic butter or with cream cheese.

Variation

Try flat bread rings following this recipe. Divide the dough into four pieces of equal size and roll these out. Cut out the middle using a glass with a diameter of about 2¾ inches. Use the leftover dough to make another ring. Make furrows in the surfaces radiating from one point and bake at the same temperature but about 10 minutes less than in the recipe above.

Nut and Sesame Spike

5 cups wheat flour	½ teaspoon salt
4 tablespoons tepid water	1 cup milk
1 package dry yeast	¼ cup sunflower seeds
2 tablespoons sugar	Butter or margarine for
¾ cup hazelnuts	greasing
¼ cup sesame seeds	3 tablespoons milk
¼ cup butter	1 teaspoon sugar

Warm the flour slightly in a warm oven, then place into a bowl and make a well in the middle. Pour in the tepid water, add the yeast and sprinkle in the sugar. Stir these ingredients together into a thin dough with a little flour from the sides and allow to rise in a warm place for about 15 minutes.

Slice the hazelnuts and roast them together with the sunflower seeds in about 1 tablespoon of butter. Avoid over browning or burning since this makes them taste bitter. Allow the nuts, sunflower seeds and butter to cool slightly. Place the remaining butter in flakes on the rim of the flour, sprinkle salt on top and pour milk, hazelnuts, sesame seeds and sunflower seeds, retaining some of each for decoration, into the well and knead all the ingredients together into a smooth dough. Form the dough into a ball. Place it in a bowl, cover with a kitchen towel and allow it to rise in a warm place for 1 hour.

Punch down the dough and knead it through again for 3-4 minutes. Form into a roll and cut into 10-12 pieces of equal size. Knead each of these pieces once again. Shape these pieces of dough like short carrots, but round off the pointed ends (they will otherwise become too brown when baked). Grease a baking sheet and place the pieces of dough on it in the form of a spike or ear of grain. Leave about ½-inch space between the pieces; do not lay them right next to each other because they will expand further during baking. Preheat the oven to 400°; cover the spike with a kitchen towel and allow to rise once more in a warm room. Stir together milk with sugar and brush onto the dough. Sprinkle with the remaining hazelnut slices, sesame seeds and sunflower seeds and bake for 45 minutes.

Note

This bread is suitable for breakfast and can be divided into individual rolls.

Tip: *To give away homemade things, the dough of this bread is a perfect place to start. It is especially suitable for shaping in innumerable ways. Since bread is a favorite gift at housewarming parties, bake the initials of the hosts using this dough decorated with various types of nuts and spices. It can also be worked into braids, wreaths or wheels constructed out of many tiny individual rolls. When constructing many small pieces of dough, avoid placing the individual pieces too close to each other since the dough will expand further during baking making the fancy shape harder to discern when it is done.*

Herb and Cabanossi Bread

6 cups wheat flour	¼ pound Cabanossi (Italian
1 cup milk	sausage)
1 package dry yeast	1 teaspoon salt
1 teaspoon sugar	½ teaspoon thyme
1 bunch chives	Flour for dusting
1 bunch parsley	1 10-ounce package puff
1 bunch dill	pastry

Pour the flour into a bowl and heat it slightly in the oven. Make a well in the middle and pour in 5 tablespoons of the milk, add the yeast, sprinkle in the sugar and stir together with a little flour from the sides to make a starter. Allow it to rise for 15 minutes until bubbles appear in the dough.

Rinse the herbs and blot them dry. Finely chop chives, parsley and dill. Cut the Cabanossi into slices, then halve or quarter. Add the herbs with the Cabanossi, salt, thyme and remaining milk to the flour and knead all the ingredients together into a bread dough.

Thaw the puff pastry. After the herb dough has risen, punch it down again and halve it. On a floured surface, roll out the pieces into two rectangles of equal size. Dust a rolling pin with flour as well and roll out the puff pastry. To do this, stack the layers one on top of the other and roll them out. All three rectangles should be the same size. Stack them on top of each other sandwiching the puff pastry between the herb dough. Now roll out the layers again and fold them together. Continue rolling them out to a thin layer and folding together until the two kinds of dough are well mixed with one another.

Form the dough into a long loaf; try to avoid kneading while doing this. Cover with a kitchen towel and allow to rise for another 30 minutes. Then place on a floured baking sheet and bake in an oven preheated to 400° for 80-90 minutes.

Sourdough

1 tablespoon sugar	1½ teaspoons dry yeast
2 cups water	3 cups rye flour

Dissolve the sugar in the tepid water and add the yeast. Stir in 2½ cups of rye flour, then place this mixture in a bowl (preferably one made of stoneware). Cover with a moist kitchen towel and allow to rise in a warm place for about 24 hours. Be sure to choose a bowl that is sufficiently large since sourdough expands considerably at the beginning. (It is also advisable to place the sourdough bowl in a second, slightly larger bowl as an additional insurance against overflow.) The sourdough should fill less than half of the bowl. Do not cover the bowl with a tight-fitting lid since gasses must be allowed to escape. Carbonic acid and alcohol are produced in the fermenting process, these are what cause the dough to rise. Furthermore, lactic and acetic acids are created, that is why rye breads always taste a little sour. In order to intensify this flavor, an additional ½ cup of flour is stirred in after 12 hours in order to instigate the souring process again. The sourdough should then be moved to a cooler place.

After about 1 day it will smell like apple wine. It is now ready, it has achieved its full force and flavor and can be used for baking. It can be stored in the refrigerator for 1 week.

Rye Bread

6 cups rye flour	1 cup buttermilk
2 cups wheat flour	1 cup water
2½ cups homemade	1 tablespoon salt
sourdough or 1½ cups	1 teaspoon ground caraway
commercially prepared	seeds
sourdough (plus 6	Flour for dusting and shaping
tablespoons water)	

When using commercially prepared sourdough, stir it together with the water into a smooth dough before using.

In a bowl, combine rye flour with wheat flour and make a well in the middle. Pour in the sourdough and stir it together with ¼ of the flour to make a starter. Allow to rise for 30 minutes. Then add buttermilk, water, salt and ground caraway seeds and work these ingredients into a dough. Remove from the bowl to a floured work surface and continue kneading until the dough gleams. Form into a ball, place it in a bowl dusted with flour and allow to rise for 12-18 hours. It is best to prepare this bread the evening before so that it can rise overnight.

Punch down the dough, which should have almost doubled in size. To do this, remove the dough from the bowl in such a way that part of the air can be expressed. Press the fingers into the dough and squeeze the ball together. It should be placed on a generously floured work surface and kneaded further, while incorporating some of the flour on the surface. Not all flours are the same and even if the same type is always used, the amount that can be incorporated in the kneading process may vary. Flour the work surface until the dough no longer sticks to the surface. Be sure that the flour is always kneaded in carefully. Line a bread basket with a kitchen towel, sprinkle with flour, form the dough into a loaf and lay it in the basket. Fold the ends of the towel over the loaf and allow to rise for an additional hour.

Place the loaf on a floured baking sheet and bake in an oven preheated to 425° for 70-80 minutes. Remove the bread from the oven and test it: if it is well-baked, it will sound hollow when knocking on the bottom of the loaf.

Variation

This recipe can be varied in numerous ways. Instead of or in addition to ground caraway seeds, which may of course be added as whole seeds, spices like fennel, anise, cardamom and pepper may be used. The liquid may also be replaced by water which will cause the crust to be shinier.

Quiche Fromage

2½ cups flour	½ cup heavy cream
1 egg yolk	1 tablespoon cornstarch
Pinch of salt	1 egg yolk
⅓ cup butter or margarine	Salt and freshly ground white
⅓ cup cold water	pepper
8 ounces Emmenthaler	Flour for rolling out
¼ pound Gruyère	Butter or margarine for
1 cup milk	greasing

Place the flour on a work surface and make a well in the middle. Place the egg yolk and salt in the well. Distribute the butter or margarine in flakes on the rim. With two knives, cut all the ingredients to a crumb-like consistency. Form into a ball, wrap in parchment paper or aluminum foil and refrigerate for at least 30 minutes.

To prepare the cheese filling, grate the Emmenthaler and Gruyère. Heat the milk together with the cream, retaining 2 tablespoons of the milk for preparing the cornstarch. Pour the grated cheese into the hot milk and stir until the cheese has melted. Whisk together the cornstarch with the cold milk and stir into the cheese mixture. Briefly bring to a boil, then remove from the heat. Fold in the egg yolk and season with a little salt and white pepper.

Remove the quiche dough from the refrigerator, place it on a floured work surface and roll it out to a round measuring 12 inches in diameter. Grease an 11-inch springform pan and line it with the dough so that there is a ½-inch rim. Repeatedly pierce the bottom with a fork and prebake the crust in an oven preheated to 400° for 15 minutes. Fill in the cheese batter and bake an additional 10-15 minutes.

Onion and Bacon Cake

2½ cups flour	2 pounds onions
½ cup milk	¼ pound lean bacon
1½ teaspoons dry yeast	4 tablespoons oil
½ teaspoon sugar	1⅓ cups sour cream
⅓ cup butter or margarine	2-3 eggs
Pinch of salt	1-2 teaspoons caraway seeds
Butter or margarine for	Salt and freshly ground black
greasing	pepper

Place the flour in a bowl and make a well in the middle. Heat the milk until lukewarm and pour into the well. Add the yeast, sprinkle in the sugar and stir together with some flour from the sides. Allow to rise in a warm place for 15 minutes. (Placing the dough in a 100°-125° oven works best.) After the dough has doubled in size, add the melted, but not hot, butter or margarine and the salt. Work all the ingredients into a dough and then knead it until bubbles appear. Allow to rise another 15 minutes, then roll out onto a greased baking sheet and allow to rise.

Peel and coarsely chop the onions. Dice the bacon and sauté in hot oil. Add the diced onion and sauté until translucent.

Remove from the heat and allow to cool somewhat. Combine sour cream with eggs and fold into the onion and bacon mixture. Season with caraway seeds, salt and pepper and spread onto the raised dough.

Bake on the middle rack of an oven preheated to 400° for 45 minutes.

Rustic Leek Tart

1½ teaspoons dry yeast	1 tablespoon oil
½ cup lukewarm milk	2 pounds leeks
½ teaspoon sugar	6 tablespoons white wine
1 cup wheat flour	3 eggs
1 cup rye flour	1 egg yolk
¼ cup softened butter or	1 cup sour cream
margarine	Salt
Pinch of salt	Ground allspice
⅛ teaspoon ground caraway	1 egg yolk for brushing
seeds	Ground and coarsely crushed
Butter or margarine for	black pepper
greasing	
½ pound Cabanossi (Italian	
sausage)	

Stir the yeast with the lukewarm milk, then add the sugar and about 2 tablespoons of wheat flour. Combine the rye and wheat flours in a bowl. Place both bowls, one with the flours and the other with the starter, in a 200° oven. After about 15 minutes the starter will have doubled. Add it to the flour together with ⅓ cup of softened butter or margarine, salt and ground caraway seeds. Knead all the ingredients into a smooth dough and allow to rest in a warm place for 1 hour. Grease a 10-inch springform pan. Knead the raised dough once more, roll it out and line the pan with it so that the dough extends about 1 inch over the edges.

Prepare the filling while the dough is rising. Slice the Cabanossi into ½-inch thick slices. Heat the remaining butter or margarine with the oil until quite hot and fry the sausage pieces in it. Trim, wash and cut the leeks into rings. Add the sausage and sauté as well. Pour in the white wine, cover and simmer for 10 minutes. Then allow to cool slightly. Whisk together eggs, egg yolk and sour cream and fold into the leek mixture. Season with salt, pepper and allspice. Fill the mixture into the pastry shell. Make incisions in the rim of dough to facilitate folding and gently fold the rim inward over the filling. Brush the rim thinly with whisked egg yolk and allow to rise another 10 minutes. Place on the middle rack of an oven preheated to 425°. Bake for 40-50 minutes, then sprinkle with crushed pepper.

Chinese Rolls made with Fresh Cheese Puff pastry

¾ cup plus 2 tablespoons
   butter or margarine
1 cup ricotta or cottage
   cheese
2 teaspoons yeast
Pinch of salt
Pinch of curry
Pinch of paprika
2 cups wheat flour
2½ cups flour
2 large onions
3 tablespoons oil
⅓ pound mixed ground beef
   and pork

1 large leek
½ pound cabbage
¼ pound mushrooms
½ pound bean sprouts
Salt and freshly ground black
   pepper
Soy sauce
Small pinch thyme
Flour for rolling out
¼ pound Gouda
¼ pound salted peanuts
1 egg yolk
1 tablespoon water
Oil for greasing

Cream butter or margarine with the cheese, add the yeast, salt and spices. Add the flour on top and work into the batter. Refrigerate for at least 4 hours or, better yet, overnight.

For the filling, peel, dice and sauté the onions in hot oil until translucent. Add the ground meat, sauté and simultaneously crumble with a fork. Trim, wash and finely slice the leek into rings, cut the prepared cabbage into thin strips and finely slice the mushrooms. Add to the meat together with the bean sprouts. Fry all the ingredients, then cover and steam until half tender. Season with salt, pepper, thyme and soy sauce.

Thinly roll out the dough on a floured surface. Cut out 8-10 pieces measuring 6 × 8 inches. Divide the filling among the pieces. Dice the cheese into ¼-inch squares, combine with the salted peanuts and place on top of the vegetable mixture. Whisk egg yolk with water, brush the edges of the dough with it and roll up carefully. Press the edges together firmly. Brush the rolls with the remaining egg yolk and place on an oiled baking sheet. Bake on the middle rack of an oven preheated to 425° for 30 minutes.

Variation

For a change, this recipe can also be baked up as one large roll and served as a main course with fresh salad. A salad made of endive or chinese cabbage mixed with apples and topped with a marinade of yogurt, pureed bananas and curry augments it well.

> **Tip:** *If the homemade cheese puff pastry is too much trouble or if time is short, substitute commercially-available frozen puff pastry. This requires 2, 10-ounce packages for 4 small rolls or one large roll.*

Banitza

1 10-ounce package frozen puff pastry	Black pepper
	Pinch of sugar
⅔ pound cheese	½ cup coarsely ground
2 eggs	pistachios
1 cup sour cream	Flour for rolling out
1 bunch dill	1 tablespoon butter
1 bunch parsley	1 egg yolk
½ teaspoon oregano	

Lay out the puff pastry layers next to each other and thaw at room temperature.

To prepare the cheese filling, dice the cheese and crush with a fork. Add eggs and sour cream. Using a wire whisk stir the ingredients into a supple batter. Rinse the herbs and spin or shake them dry. Finely dice the dill and parsley. Add to the cheese mixture and season with oregano, pepper and sugar. Then fold in the pistachios retaining 1 tablespoon for decoration.

Rinse a 10-inch, flat, round, casserole dish with cold water. Stack the puff pastry layers on top of one another, place on a floured work surface and roll out a rectangle measuring 12 × 24 inches. Cut out a round measuring 12-inches in diameter and line the form with it. If using an oval or rectangular form, lay it on top of the dough as a stencil and, with a sharp knife, cut out a piece of dough that is about 1 inch larger than the form. Brush the puff pastry with melted butter and fill in the cheese batter.

Cut out a second round measuring 10 inches in diameter and lay it on top of the filling. Press the edges together well and brush the surface with egg yolk. Cut strips out of the leftover dough and decorate the surface of the pastry lid with them. Brush with egg yolk, but avoid getting any egg yolk on the edges. Finely chop the remaining pistachios and sprinkle the Banitza with them.

Bake on the middle rack of an oven preheated to 400° for 40-50 minutes.

Note

The Banitza will first puff up in the oven, then it will collapse. It should be served warm as a flat pie.

> **Tip:** *The Banitza recipe may also be baked up as small, filled pockets. It is served this way in Greece. Thinly roll out the puff pastry and cut into squares. Divide the filling among them and fold diagonally into triangles. Press the edges together well.*

Shrimp Tart

3 cups flour	3-4 tablespoons port
1 egg yolk	1 teaspoon cornstarch
½ teaspoon salt	1 egg
3 tablespoons cold water	Salt and white pepper
¾ cup butter	1 pound fresh or canned
½ pound fresh or canned	shrimp
mushrooms	2½ tablespoons butter
⅓ pound Gruyère	Butter or margarine for
⅓ pound walnuts	greasing
1 cup heavy cream	

Place the flour on a work surface, make a well in the middle and pour in the egg yolk, salt and cold water. Place butter or margarine in flakes on the rim. Cut all the ingredients with a knife and then, with cool hands, quickly work ingredients into a smooth dough. Refrigerate the dough wrapped in aluminum foil or parchment paper until the filling is prepared.

Wash and trim the mushrooms. Slice half of them as thin as leaves and grind the remainder in a meat grinder or puree them in a mixer. Grate the Gruyère and half of the walnuts. Coarsely chop the remaining nuts. Heat the cream, sprinkle in the cheese and add half of the port wine. Continue stirring over mild heat until the cheese has melted. Dissolve cornstarch in cold water and stir into the sauce. Briefly bring to a boil. Fold the mushroom puree, sliced mushrooms and grated walnuts into the cheese mixture. Remove from the heat and bind with an egg. Season with some port, salt and white pepper. Fold in the chopped walnuts, retaining 1 tablespoon.

Peel the shrimp or remove them from the can and drain. Heat the butter and gently sauté. Add the remaining port.

Grease a 10-inch springform pan and press in the dough. Make a 1-inch high edge around the rim and notch using the fingertips at 1-inch intervals to make a zigzag edge. Prebake the shell for 15 minutes on the middle rack of an oven preheated to 350°. Fill in the cheese mixture and distribute the shrimp on top. Sprinkle with the remaining walnut pieces and bake an additional 15 minutes at the same temperature.

Variation

A quick variant of this can be made with puff pastry. Although the puff pastry has to thaw, the procedure is very quick after that. Thaw a 10-ounce package of frozen puff pastry by laying out the layers one next to the other. Stack them on a floured surface and roll out to a square measuring 12 inches on each side. Cut out a 10-inch round and lay it on a greased baking sheet. Cut ¾-inch strips out of the leftover pastry. Continually brush the surfaces with egg yolk, but avoid having it drip over the sides otherwise the pastry will not rise. Place the strips of pastry on the rim, 3-4 strips should be laid on top of each other until all the puff pastry is used up. Bake this pastry shell at 400° for 20 minutes. Prepare the filling as above and fill into the shell. Place in the oven for just a few minutes in order to melt and brown the surface.

Artichoke and Spinach Tart

2 cups flour	¼ pound lean bacon
1 teaspoon dry yeast	2 tablespoons butter
½ teaspoon sugar	3 tablespoons white wine
6 tablespoons tepid milk	4 tablespoons crème fraîche
6 tablespoons oil	Salt and white pepper
½ teaspoon salt	1 7-ounce can artichoke
⅛ teaspoon nutmeg	hearts
4 eggs	Butter or margarine for
1 pound fresh spinach	greasing
1 onion	2 tablespoons oil
2 cloves garlic	

Make a well in the flour. Add the yeast and sprinkle in the sugar. Pour in the milk and stir together with a little flour from the sides to make a starter. Allow to rise in a warm place for about 15 minutes. Add oil, salt and nutmeg and stir the dough until it no longer sticks to the sides of the bowl. Cover with a cloth and allow to rise for another 20 minutes.

Boil the eggs for 10 minutes until hard. Sort, wash and trim the spinach. Drain in a sieve. Peel and finely dice the onion. Peel the garlic cloves and press them through a garlic press or sprinkle with a pinch of salt and then crush them with a broad knife. Dice the bacon and sauté in hot butter. Add the diced onion and garlic and sauté until translucent, then add the white wine. Place the spinach on top and steam until it wilts, then fold in the crème fraîche and season with salt, white pepper and nutmeg. Grease a 10-inch springform pan, press in the dough and make a 1-inch rim around the edge. Allow the pastry shell to rest for 5 minutes. Then bake on the middle rack of an oven preheated to 425° for 15 minutes. Remove the artichoke hearts from the can and drain them in a sieve.

Fill the spinach mixture into the pastry shell. Slice the eggs and lay a wreath just inside the rim. Follow this with a smaller wreath of artichoke hearts, then alternate artichoke hearts and egg slices in the middle. Do not cover up the spinach completely, but allow it to show through as a green background to the colorful surface decoration. Brush egg slices and artichoke hearts with oil and heat in the hot oven for 5-10 minutes. Serve immediately.

Torta Pasqualina

5 cups flour	1 cup ricotta or cottage
1 teaspoon salt	cheese
6-7 tablespoons olive oil	2 tablespoons sour cream or
1 cup tepid water	crème fraîche
1½ pounds fresh or 1 pound	Freshly ground black pepper
frozen spinach	Grated nutmeg
Salt	2 ounces grated Parmesan
1 10-ounce can artichoke	cheese
hearts	Flour for rolling
1 onion	Butter for greasing and
1 clove garlic	brushing
2½ tablespoons butter	6 eggs

For the dough, combine flour with salt, place it on a work surface and make a well in the middle. Pour in the oil and gradually add the water. Knead all the ingredients into a smooth dough, then throw it, that is, let it fall onto the work surface with a gentle swing, until bubbles and lumps of flour are no longer visible. Form the dough into a ball, place under a hot pot (boil water in it first) and allow to rest for 30 minutes so that the flour can swell.

Trim, sort and thoroughly wash the spinach in cold water. Then drain it. Bring a generous amount of salted water to a boil and blanch the spinach in it for 2 minutes. Remove and then blanch it in ice cold water. Drain and press out thoroughly. Chop it coarsely.

Finely dice the drained artichoke hearts and the peeled onion. Crush the peeled garlic. Heat the butter or oil and sauté the onions and garlic until translucent. Add the spinach together with the artichoke hearts and, while stirring constantly, cook them until all the liquid has steamed off. Avoid burning the mixture. Remove the pot from the heat and allow the mixture to cool slightly. Stir in the cheese along with the sour cream or crème fraîche and season with salt, pepper, nutmeg and about 3 tablespoons of the Parmesan cheese.

Divide the dough into 10 pieces and roll out each of them into a round measuring about 9 inches in diameter. Grease a springform pan of the same size and lay 5 layers of dough, one on top of the other, into the pan. Brush each layer with melted butter before placing the next one on top. Distribute the spinach mixture on the stacked pastry layers and, with a spoon, make six depressions or wells in the spinach about a finger's width away from the rim of the pan. Drop one egg in each well and beat it gently, then sprinkle with the remaining Parmesan. Stack the remaining 5 rounds of dough on top. Brush each of them with butter before adding the next one and brush the top layer with an especially generous helping of melted butter. Bake on the middle rack of an oven preheated to 425° for 55 minutes. Serve hot or slightly cooled.

Baking
Encyclopedia

Types of Dough

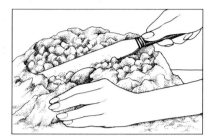

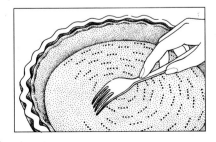

Tart Dough

The basic ingredients for tart dough: flour, fat, sugar and sometimes egg, must always be calculated in the same proportions, yet this does not in any way reduce the variety of cakes that can be made from this dough.

For the finest of all possible tart doughs, equal parts of flour and fat are worked together with half or at the most ¾ as much sugar as fat. Eggs may be omitted. This dough is ideal for fine tortes and delicate cookies.

A dough that is not quite so fine but very frequently used for fruit tarts and tartlets is made of the following proportions: 3 parts flour, 2 parts fat and 1 part sugar; egg yolk is generally added at a rate of 1 yolk per 2½ cups flour.

A third dough, which bakers like to use for small pastries, is especially crispy. It uses: 4 parts flour, 2 parts fat and 1 part sugar which, depending on the recipe, may be increased to ¾ of the quantity of fat used. A whole egg is added per 2½ cups flour. On occasion 1 additional egg yolk is added. Furthermore, there is also piquant, that is, unsweetened, tart dough.

The prerequisite for all of these tart doughs is that they must be **properly worked**. This is not at all difficult, in fact it is child's play. First, all the ingredients must be cold because the emulsified water in the fat needs to first be dissipated by the heat of the oven, thereby causing the dough to become lighter and thus making the use of baking powder unnecessary. For the same reason, tart dough must always be kneaded with chilled hands. Hold hands under cold running water for a length of time, dry them well and then knead as quickly as possible so that the dough is smooth before the hands have become warm again.

To reduce the amount of kneading time and to avoid prolonged contact of the dough with the warmth of the hands, all the ingredients should be cut together with 1 or 2 knives until they are well-blended and achieve a crumb-like consistency. If only 1 knife is used, the other hand should continually push up the wall of flour so that the egg does not run out on the work surface. When 2 knives are used it is advisable to place all the ingredients in a shallow bowl.

It is best to knead on a work surface. Spread out the fingers of both hands, place them under the sides of the dough, then pull the dough up toward the middle and press into the center of the clump with the palms of the hands. Work very quickly and only until no more flour is visible on the work surface and the exterior of the dough appears smooth. Then test it: form the dough into a ball and cut through the middle with a knife. If neither traces of flour nor air bubbles are visible, press the two halves together again, wrap in aluminum foil or a plastic bag (so that it does not dry out), and refrigerate.

An additional word about the **ingredients** themselves: the *flour* should always be sifted, on the one hand this avoids clumps of dough, and on the other it mixes in additional air. It is also recommended that cake flour be used as it is a soft, fine flour and will enhance the final outcome. It is established that the *fat* must be chilled and that holds for any kind of fat used. If kneading with the kneading attachment of a mixer or food processor, then resort to softened fat. However, this dough must be subsequently chilled as well. Both butter and margarine bake up excellently, they only differ in flavor. If shortening is substituted for part of the fat, the pastry will taste especially hearty. Oil should never be used in tart doughs.

A finely granulated *sugar* should be chosen for the tart dough since it dissolves more readily. The crystals of coarsely granulated sugars melt during baking and then sometimes remain visible as small spots or stains. Also more of the latter is needed since finer crystals sweeten more quickly and thus more intensively.

If *egg or egg yolk* is called for in the recipe, it must also be chilled. It is, of course, implied that the eggs are fresh. However, hard-boiled egg yolks may also be worked into the dough. Very fatty tart doughs can become ''crumbly,'' that means that they fall apart like crumbs for crumb cake (which is also one of the versions of cake made with tart dough). In any case, hard-boiled egg yolk is passed through a sieve, then kneaded into the dough creating the necessary bonding.

Of course, tart dough is also *seasoned or flavored*. A pinch of salt is always called for, it rounds out the flavor just as sugar does in piquant dishes. Also use grated lemon or orange rind, cinnamon, nutmeg, the marrow of vanilla bean or vanilla extract, as well as other extracts, if desired. A little rum, cognac or schnapps may also be used as flavoring. It should be noted that alcohol also makes the dough lighter. The same occurs when sour cream, ricotta or cottage cheese is mixed in. These last two are the only liquid ingredients, besides alcohol, lemon juice and egg, that are used in tart dough, with the exception of ice water which is used in meat pie doughs.

Regardless of which seasonings are used, they will always be added according to steadfast rules: all dry ingredients are mixed with the flour, all liquid or semi-liquid ingredients are added with the egg. If no egg is used, the liquid ingredients are instead added in a well made in the flour.

When preparing tart dough using *almonds or nuts,* they must be either finely chopped or ground and they should be added to the flour. If nuts are to be used, they may be substituted for up to half of the flour. If a portion of the flour is replaced by cornstarch (only up to 1/3 of the total amount of flour may be substituted with cornstarch), a very fine tart dough with a sandy texture will be obtained.

Regardless of the type of tart dough, it must always be *chilled* before shaping or rolling. It must be covered or wrapped and refrigerated for at least 30 minutes. If only small portions of the dough are worked at a time, the remainder should always be returned to the refrigerator until the time to be worked. No blisters or bubbles should appear when tart dough is baking. That is why the bottom of the pastry shell must always be repeatedly pierced with a fork, thus enabling the air to escape. When high rims are made, the bottom of the shell should be weighted down with dried peas or beans, see ''Helpful Baking Information at a Glance.''

Greasing the pan or the baking sheet is not necessary when baking very fatty tart doughs, however, these shells must be removed from the pan while still hot because cooling fat has an adhesive quality. That is why these pastry shells must be cooled on a rack.

Butter Cakes

In grandmother's day, a butter cake batter was ready only after it had been stirred in one direction for an entire hour. At that time, first-class ingredients were required for a cake just as they are in our society today with its high standard of living. Now, of course, nobody stands around stirring cake batter for an hour, since electrical appliances like the hand mixer and food processor simplify and accelerate the work, and they bring about pretty much the same result every time a cake is made. What remains the same as in yesteryear—the time of our grandmother — are the ingredients which are stirred together to make the dough.

Basically there are **4 ingredients**, which, depending on the recipe, may be supplemented. They are fat, sugar, egg and flour.

If all of the ingredients are used in the same proportion, the most noble of all butter cakes will be obtained, a <u>pound</u> or a <u>balanced cake</u>. It may be made more sophisticated by the addition of spices or flavorings and it requires no baking powder. If cornstarch is substituted for up to half of the flour, <u>finely porous sand cake</u> will be obtained.

Baking powder may be omitted in butter cakes in which the fat-sugar-egg quantity is larger than the amount of flour used; for example, no baking powder is needed in the following cake: for 1 cup fat, and 1 1/3 cups sugar, use 6-8 eggs, 5 cups flour and a few drops of liquid. If more flour is used than the combined fat-sugar-egg quantity, the batter will need baking powder in order to make it lighter. For example, for about 3/4 cup fat, 1 cup sugar, 4-5 eggs, and about 5 cups flour, 1 tablespoon baking powder and a little liquid will be needed.

Be aware of the following particulars about the ingredients: basic rule number one is that all the ingredients must be at the same temperature, and that means *room temperature*. For that reason, remove the fat and the eggs from the refrigerator and take the flour out of the pantry about 1-2 hours before baking. The same applies to the milk and all other ingredients. The *fat* may be either butter or margarine and, if desired, a portion may be replaced by shortening. Oil and coconut butter do not belong in butter cakes. The fat should be soft and supple for the butter cake, it should not however be heated or melted. If the latter is done, the fat will no longer absorb sufficient air to make the batter light. In any case, stir until the batter is creamy, that is, until it ''squeaks.'' Since the squeaking can only be heard when stirring with a wooden spoon, it is necessary to rely on the eyes. The fat should be pale white in color, very soft and extremely supple. Then very, very gradually add the *sugar* and eggs and continue stirring until the sugar has dissolved completely and the batter is once again very creamy and whitish in color. Working in as much *air* as possible at this time will help to obtain a lighter and more aromatic finished product. Put another way: the air that is not worked into the cake now, will be lacking when the cake later needs it to rise in the oven.

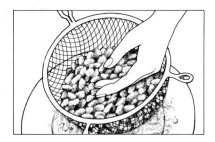

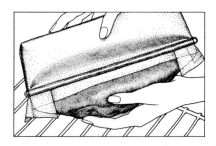

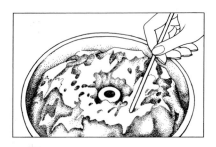

The *eggs* may only be added one at a time, which means that the next one should only be added after the prior one has been thoroughly incorporated into the fat-sugar mixture; if eggs are not added in this way the fat-sugar mixture may separate. Separation may also occur if the eggs are too cold. It is possible to make the mixture creamy again by placing it in a warm, but not hot, water bath. However, avoid melting the fat. A second trick: sprinkle a little flour onto the separated batter and stir it in thoroughly, then begin adding the remaining eggs after the dough has become completely smooth and homogeneous.

Spices, like salt, vanilla, lemon rind and others, are also added at this stage. Then the *flour* is finally mixed in. If baking powder with or without cornstarch or cocoa are called for in the recipe, these ingredients should be combined with the flour before sifting. If *liquids* are necessary, they are added in alternation with the flour. At this stage, however, only stir until all the ingredients are mixed and not longer, because this will make the dough stiff. The dough should neither be too thick nor too thin. For this reason, test the dough: lift a portion of it out of the bowl with a wooden spoon. It should ''fall heavily'' from the spoon.

To add *dried fruit, nuts, or other ingredients,* place in a sieve and coat with a little flour, (the sieve is used to allow excess flour to fall off). This procedure of ''flouring'' hinders the sinking of the fruit in the batter. If eggs are separated before they are mixed in, the stiffly beaten egg whites are folded in as the very last ingredient and they are not stirred.

And the final rule, butter cake batter should be baked immediately. This is especially important when it is prepared with baking powder, since this ingredient begins rising as soon as it comes into contact with liquid.

Butter cake is always baked in a *form* that has been greased and coated with crumbs or lined with paper. The form should be filled not more than ¾ full so that the batter does not rise over the edge. Always *test for doneness* after the prescribed baking time has been completed: stick a wooden toothpick into the cake at its highest point and check to see whether any dough sticks to it. If it comes out clean, the cake is done.

After baking, the cake should be allowed to steam off briefly.

To *turn out* a round cake, place a large round rack on top of the form and turn both upside down together, then remove the form. For a loaf pan, turn the cake out onto one hand, peel off the paper and place it upright on a rack.

Sponge Cakes

The word ''dough'' is generally used to describe the combination of eggs, sugar, flour and mostly air that makes up this very fine cake, but the baking trade describes this mixture as a ''batter'' or ''mass.'' *Air* is the leavening ingredient for sponge cake. It is distributed throughout the batter as tiny bubbles which arise when the batter is beaten, and it results in the extravagantly foamy volume of the cake. During baking, the air expands even more, it rises upward and pushes the dough increasingly higher. To achieve these results, use ''fresh eggs'' that can still take in lots of air. They should be chilled and most sponge cake recipes require that they be separated before being worked in. When separating, great care must be taken that no yolk runs into the egg whites, since the fat contained in the yolk will not allow the beaten whites to become stiff.

Normally, when making a sponge cake, egg yolk is first beaten with some water; this water may be either cold or hot, however, cold water causes fewer problems. Egg white in the egg yolk can coagulate when hot water is added and this would result in tiny specks of egg white in the final product. While beating continuously, about ¾ of the sugar is

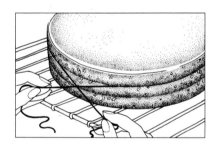

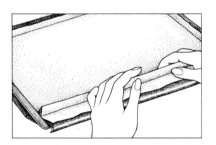

sprinkled in. Continue beating until the sugar has dissolved and the batter is thick, foamy, gleaming and very porous. Next, beat the egg whites until they are stiff. Then the remaining sugar should gradually be added. The egg whites and the sifted flour are subsequently very gently folded into the egg yolk mixture. Use pure flour or mix it with cornstarch which would result in a more porous cake. Part of the flour (sometimes the entire amount) may be replaced by ground nuts or almonds, which will make the dough especially succulent. The following utensils are suitable for folding in ingredients, a wooden spoon with a hole, a batter spatula or a wire whisk; an electric hand mixer is unsuitable. When the recipe calls for ingredients to be folded in, the dough should under no circumstances be stirred.

Equivalent quantities of ingredients are used for the simple sponge cake: for 1 egg weighing about 2 ounces, use 2 ounces (about ¼ cup) of sugar, and 2 ounces (about ⅔ cup) of sifted flour. Baking powder is not necessary if sufficient air is beaten into the mixture. However, if the dough has not been beaten thoroughly the baking powder will give added insurance that the dough will be light and airy. If more egg yolk than egg white is used, the dough will be more porous, it will have a heartier color, and will be somewhat stiffer. For a much lighter and airier sponge cake, use more egg white than yolk.

An even lighter sponge cake is made with the following quantities: 1 egg weighing about 2 ounces, 1 ounce (about 2 tablespoons) of sugar and 1 ounce (about ⅓ cup) of sifted flour.

For all sponge cake pastries that require a lot of rising, for example rolls, torte bottoms and tartlets, prepare a blitz sponge cake: beat the egg whites until very stiff, sprinkle in the sugar, then whisk the egg yolk and mix it in with the flour and bake the batter as soon as possible.

A second blitz method: beat all of the eggs together with water and sugar until they are very foamy, then sift the flour on top and gently fold it in.

If an especially soft, succulent and slightly sticky sponge cake is desired, try the next procedure for warm sponge cake: beat all the eggs together with water and sugar over a warm water bath until they are thick and creamy. Then fold in the sifted flour while all the ingredients are still on the stove. Here, too, there are variations: beat the egg yolks and sugar in a water bath, then fold in the stiffly beaten egg whites together with the flour. Or first beat the egg whites until stiff, then prepare the egg yolks over a water bath, followed by the addition of the sugar and later the flour. There are innumerable ways that all lead to a light, succulent sponge cake.

However, the most succulent of all is the butter sponge cake also known as Viennese Batter. For this, whole eggs are combined with sugar over a water bath and beaten until thick and foamy, then they are put in a cold water bath and beaten until cold. The flour is first poured into this batter, followed by the melted, lukewarm butter. Sponge cake is very frequently baked in a springform pan. Only the bottom of the pan may be greased and coated, the rim should never be greased, because the fat would melt during baking and pull down the dough of the rising cake.

Very fresh sponge cake is difficult to divide since it crumbles easily. Therefore, allow the torte to cool for at least 4-6 hours, better yet overnight. If the cake is to be divided into layers, first score the desired layers all the way around the circumference of the cake, then either use a large knife to slice the cake horizontally or separate the individual layers with a string. In the case of the latter, lay a thick string in the etched-in groove, cross the string on the front side as if making a knot and then pull the string evenly together. Lift off the resulting layer with a piece of parchment paper or with a special metal torte dividing sheet.

For a sponge cake roll, line the baking sheet with a large piece of parchment paper, fold up the ends if there is no rim in order to hinder the batter from running off. After baking, turn out the layer of cake including the paper onto a kitchen towel that has been sprinkled with sugar. Moisten the paper and peel it off, then roll up the layer of cake together with the towel so that it can be unrolled again without breaking after it has cooled.

Batter for Fritters and Beignets

Among all the different kinds of dough, this one is special because it must be cooked, or "burned" as they say in the trade, before it is baked. This batter consists of water, fat, flour and quite a few eggs, the latter enable the dough to rise or puff up. Now and then a little sugar is added to the dough, however, this amount must remain very small since sugar easily caramelizes and burns when the dough is cooked.

Exactly measure all ingredients before starting. The proportion of the various ingredients to one another is extremely important in this batter.

Place the *water* together with a pinch of salt and the *fat* which has been cut into flakes (a large piece melts very slowly by comparison) into a saucepan and bring this mixture to a boil. Do not prolong the boiling since a portion of the water will evaporate thus disturbing the proportions of the ingredients to one another. The kind of fat used, whether butter, margarine, shortening or a mixture of these fats, is merely a matter of taste and will have no other effect on the final product.

As soon as the mixture has boiled, remove the pan from the stove and pour in the entire amount of flour in one fell swoop, not gradually. Stir the flour into the liquid until it looks like thick porridge. The best utensil for this is a wooden spoon with a hole in the middle. Return the pan to the stove and stir

over medium heat until a smooth clump forms and a thin, white skin becomes visible on the bottom of the pan. Do not stop before this stage because good "burning" is the prerequisite for the later puffing up of the batter. On the other hand, do not leave the pan on the stove longer than necessary, the skin should not begin to turn brown. This would be an indication that the gluten in the flour has been exposed to too much heat.

Place this tough clump of batter in a bowl and immediately stir in *1 egg* in order to make it softer and more supple. Very experienced bakers add this egg while the pan is still on the stove. In this case, however, it is necessary to work extremely quick to avoid contact of the egg with the bottom or sides of the pan. When this happens, the egg begins to clot resulting in small white specks in the batter which do not dissolve in later stages of baking.

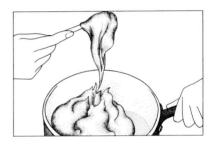

The batter must rest and cool down until lukewarm. Only when it has reached this temperature may *the remaining eggs* be mixed in and they must be added individually. That is especially important: the next egg may only be added after the prior one has been fully incorporated into the batter.

The number of eggs required depends on their size and freshness and may vary from recipe to recipe. Therefore, test the batter before the final egg is added: the batter will have achieved its proper consistency when it has a strong sheen and hangs from a wooden spoon in long, but not too soft, ribbons. If that is not yet the case, add the remaining egg or half of it. In order to add half an egg, whisk together the egg yolk and egg white and add this mixture by the spoonful. Even if this procedure seems a little cumbersome, be aware that this kind of batter should never have too much egg. If it is too soft, it will not rise upward sufficiently but instead will spread outward. As soon as the dough gleams strongly and the correct kinds of ribbons hang from the spoon, definitely stop stirring since too much stirring will also inhibit

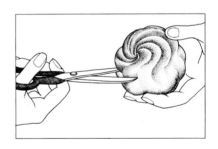

rising. A good puff pastry batter will double and possible triple its volume when baked. For this reason it is advisable to use a wooden spoon and not an electric mixer for stirring. The speed of the electrical appliance is likely to cause "overstirring."

This batter is normally "pressed into the desired form," for example cream puffs, wreaths or beignets. It may, however, be divided into portions with a spoon, but of course these will be various shapes. If it is to be baked on a flat surface (as for the flake torte), the surface will be irregular with hills and valleys made by bubbles in the dough.

The batter is baked on a greased cookie sheet that has been dusted with flour. A high temperature of 425°-450° is necessary. If the temperature is too low, the dough will not rise sufficiently, if it is too high, it will blister up at the beginning and possibly fall later on while it is still raw inside. In all cases, it is essential that the oven door is not opened during the first 10 minutes of baking, since this would certainly cause the pastries to fall.

To increase the leavening action, "vapors may be added," as the baker would say. To achieve this, a little water is poured onto the baking sheet and allowed to evaporate just after it has been put in the oven. The rising "vapors" raise the batter.

The pastries should immediately be placed on a rack after baking, so that any remaining moisture can be expressed. If the pastries are to be filled later, they should be cut with scissors at this time so that their insides can also dry out well.

To deep-fry this batter, as for beignets, press out the individual pieces onto parchment paper and slide them from the paper into the hot oil. For fritters, simply cut out a clump of dough with a spoon and drop the portions into the oil. The correct frying temperature is 325°-350°, an even temperature should be maintained throughout. If a deep-frying thermometer is unavailable, test the temperature by placing the han-

dle of a wooden spoon in the oil: the temperature is correct when small bubbles are visible on the handle when it is immersed. Or drop in a piece of white bread, the temperature is correct when it turns golden without soaking up the oil.

Raised Cakes made of Yeast Dough

In many households, store-bought yeast dough is preferred to homemade because people find the preparation of yeast doughs complicated and "risky." However, one merely has to observe a few basic rules in order to create the necessary environment in which yeast can develop. Yeast fungi are among the smallest forms of life which, like bacteria and mold, occur everywhere in nature and are able to reproduce when provided with the proper environment. For this they need moisture, food, warmth and air. **Yeast** can be obtained in various forms: fresh, formed into cubes, as bakery or compressed yeast, and as active dry yeast. *Fresh yeast* can be recognized by its even, yellowish-gray color and its firm, smooth surface. It must be crumbled in layers; it should, however, not come out of its wrapper in crumbled form and no dark edges or fissures should be visible. If either of the above phenomena should be visible, it means that the yeast is old and will have partially or completely lost its leavening properties. A dirty-looking or molded surface is also an obvious sign of tainted yeast. Smell is also an indication of age: when fresh, yeast should smell delicately sour and a little like fruit; when old, the aroma will be unpleasant and slightly musty. Fresh yeast can only be stored for a limited amount of time and must always be stored well-wrapped in the refrigerator (the best place is on the butter shelf).

Active dry yeast may be stored for months (generally up to a year) and will remain "fresh." It is sold in envelopes in

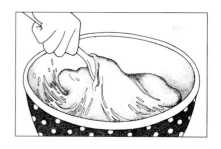

granulated or powdered form. One package is equal to about 2¾ teaspoons and one package generally suffices for 6-8 cups of flour. It may either be used to make a starter or sponge as with fresh yeast or merely be added right into the flour (this is indeed a time saver); the package instructions will indicate how to use it. The recipes in this book may be prepared with either dry or fresh yeast.

For the **preparation** of the yeast dough, warm all ingredients to body temperature (95°-98.6°), this is the optimal temperature for the yeast. Next, add the *flour* to a large bowl. Make a well in the middle and pour the yeast into it. Add the necessary moisture and food, that means, stir in the called for *liquid*, which should be lukewarm, heated to about 86°, and a pinch of *sugar* as called for in the recipe, as well as some flour from the sides of the well. This is the starter or sponge. Cover the bowl with a kitchen towel and place it in a warm, draft-free place for about 15 minutes. This may be in the vicinity of the heater or even in a slightly warmed oven. The temperature may not, however, rise above 125° otherwise the yeast cells will die. The yeast can "rise" when the yeast cells divide and give off alcohol and carbon, i.e., carbon dioxide. The alcohol is the reason for the fresh, somewhat sour smell and the delicate taste, while the carbonic acid and carbon dioxide make the dough light and cause it to rise. The gluten encircles the bubbles of gas as they attempt to work their way up and out of the dough. In this way the whole construct rises and increases in volume. The surface will clearly show bubbles, people in the trade say that it "pants." Add the remaining ingredients as soon as the dough has doubled in size. These ingredients should also be warm. Care should be taken that the fat, salt and egg yolk is never added directly to the starter but instead placed on the ring of flour. Each of these ingredients restricts the distribution of the yeast and, when placed on the rim in this way, they will gradually be mixed in

with the starter. Once the yeast cells have been combined with all the ingredients, they will need oxygen. Therefore, the dough will first have to be vigorously kneaded, then beaten until bubbles appear and it no longer sticks to the sides of the bowl. For beating, use a wooden spoon, but generally speaking it is better to use one's hands. The hands prove to be a better judge of the consistency of the dough. The dough should be elastic and, when finished, it should no longer stick between the fingers. In any case, continually lift up the dough from the bottom of the bowl to the rim and then throw it back down to the remaining dough. After it has been loosened in this way, the yeast dough should rest once more in order to rise and double its size. Here again, it will need a warm, draft-free place, since drafts will cause it to fall. Finally it is punched down so that any trapped gases can be exhausted. Then it is shaped and allowed to rise one more time before baking. The procedure described above is appropriate for simple, light yeast doughs as well as heavy ones. "Heavy" yeast doughs are like stollen, in which a large amount of fat (often combined with a lot of eggs and dried fruits) weigh down the dough, while "light" yeast doughs are used for sheet cakes, rolls and simple braids.

Now, the professional is acquainted not only with "warm" but also with two methods of **"cold dough preparation."** In the first procedure, the yeast is dissolved in cold liquid and immediately combined with the total amount of flour. This dough must then be wrapped and refrigerated for 12 hours, where it will rise in spite of the low temperatures (37.5°-45°). After this long period of rest, it is kneaded and shaped, then it must rise for about 20 minutes more.

The second procedure is very different and is appropriate for extremely rich yeast doughs. A well is made in the flour, the yeast is stirred into it together with the water. About ¾ of the flour is then worked in together with all of the fat. Next the dough is formed into a ball

and placed in a generous amount of cold water. It is left there until the ball of dough floats to the surface. When it has reached this stage the remaining flour and other ingredients are kneaded in, the dough is shaped and, without being allowed to rise again, placed in a cold oven, so that the yeast can work while the oven is warming.

Yeast doughs are generally placed on greased baking sheets or greased forms, and baked at 400°-425° as indicated in the recipe. After the baking time is finished they should immediately be removed to a rack so that they can steam off and cool down.

Food processors are especially suited for the preparation of yeast doughs, but be sure to follow the manufacturer's instructions.

Meringues and Macaroons

Egg white, sugar and air are the ingredients for this luscious, feather-light pastry. The name meringue comes from the French. The Austrians call their small meringues, little mounds of foam, Spanish wind or Merinke. And, if the sweet pastry is to be a success, it must be as light as foam.

It is essential to use *fresh egg whites*. Buy Grade A eggs and try to obtain them as fresh as possible. If their freshness is doubted, submit them to an <u>egg-float test</u>: lay an egg in a glass of water. If it sinks to the bottom of the glass and remains lying horizontally on its side perpendicular to the sides of the glass, then it is fresh and suitable for meringue. If it only slides down a part of the way and then floats at an angle or vertically, then it is definitely too old for meringue. The explanation for this is quite simple. The shell of older eggs becomes more porous allowing the liquid inside to evaporate creating a larger air chamber inside, thus making the egg lighter.

<u>The second test of freshness</u> for eggs is also very simple: crack open an egg and

1

3

5

2

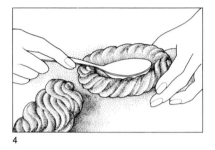

4

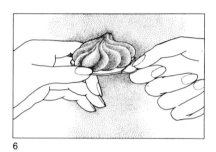

6

then allow it to slide onto a plate. If it is fresh, it will have a completely round yolk and be surrounded by a compact ring of egg white. Small, thin strings of egg white should only be visible on the external rim. As the egg grows older, the yolk will be flatter and the egg white more runny. Such eggs are no longer suitable for meringue paste.

The next requirement for whipping meringue is the careful *separation of egg yolk from egg white*. Even the slightest trace of egg yolk in the egg white will make the meringue paste creamy instead of stiff, which means that the meringues will not be hard nor will they be able to maintain their shape. Crack the eggs, which should be chilled, individually over a plate, carefully separate the white from the yolk and place the whites in one bowl and the yolks in another. This avoids the catastrophe of having one damaged egg yolk destroy the entire collection of egg whites. Of course, all the bowls and utensils must be absolutely fat free.

For the **preparation of the meringue paste**, first whip the *egg white* with a *pinch of salt* until it is so stiff that

when cut with a knife, the path of the knife still remains visible a few seconds later. Then continue whipping while gradually sprinkling in the *sugar*. The egg white foam should remain stiff throughout and a strong sheen should become visible in time. If possible, use finely granulated sugar, since large crystals dissolve too slowly and are not suitable for building an adequate "scaffolding" for the paste. Powdered sugar may be used, but it generally makes the paste somewhat sticky. A combination of granulated and powdered sugar works very well. The amount of sugar is normally twice the amount of egg whites in terms of weight, these proportions ensure a stable paste. Acid also enhances stability. For that reason a little *lemon juice* may be incorporated. An added advantage of lemon juice is that it somewhat diminishes the sweetness.

Meringues in the form of tartlets, tart shells and torte bottoms are especially well liked because these can be filled and topped with ingredients that contrast well with the sweet meringue. For **torte bottoms and tartlets**, draw one large or several small circles on ungreased

parchment paper or aluminum foil. Fill the meringue paste into a pastry bag with a large spout. For the torte bottom, press out the paste in spiral form into the circles, if desired, place dots of paste on the edge to make a ring. For tartlets, first follow the circumference of the circle with large dots of paste, then place a dollop in the middle and spread it out as the bottom. To make meringue shells, use a very large star spout and press out large spirals onto the paper.

The paste must dry more than bake. To achieve this, it is placed in a preheated oven for 4-5 hours at a temperature no higher than 215° (higher temperatures will cause the meringues to brown). The door of the oven should be held open a crack with the handle of a wooden (not plastic) spoon, thus allowing any exhausted moisture a means of escape.

After baking, the paper or foil is immediately removed (the paper may be moistened). If meringue shells have been made, their underside must immediately be pressed in with a spoon since they will crumble if indenting is left until they have cooled. For additional drying, the meringue paste should always be placed on a rack.

Subdivisions of meringue paste are macaroon and Japonais paste. Like meringue, they are made of egg white, salt, sugar and lemon juice. Subsequently almonds, nuts and/or grated coconut are mixed in. Now and again marzipan, flour or cornstarch is also added, and less frequently butter or oil as well as chocolate are called for.

To bake macaroons, use two teaspoons to drop the paste onto a baking sheet lined with waxed paper. Or fill the paste into a pastry bag and press out the cookies.

Placing them in the vicinity of the heater is the most appropriate way to warm them. If solid fats, like butter, margarine or shortening are to be used, they must either be melted and then cooled down again until lukewarm or they must be very soft and divided into small flakes or clumps so that they will blend well with the other ingredients.

Sift the warmed flour into a bowl, place salt, water and fat (and possibly an egg) in the middle and stir these ingredients working from the center toward the rim. Continue working until the dough is tough and sticky. After it has reached this stage it must be thoroughly

kneaded. This may be done in a flat, wide-mouthed bowl, however, it is easier to work on a lightly floured work surface. To knead, press the dough down with the palm of one hand and at the same time push it away from the body. Then the ball of dough is given a small turn and the procedure is repeated until the dough is completely smooth, elastic and no longer sticky. The second hand is only used now and again to re-dust the work surface with flour.

Throughout this entire working procedure it is advisable to have the dough somewhat softer when beginning to knead, and to continually re-flour the

Strudel Dough

Strudel is an ideal pastry for connoisseurs who like "lots of filling and little dough." Extremely thin dough is the secret of every good strudel. The innumerable fillings depend on region, season and personal preference, thus making one and the same dough continually appear new and different. But there are some differences in the types of dough used.

Basic ingredients for every strudel are flour, fat, water and an obligatory pinch of salt. But the question of *fat* is already controversial: some people use oil, others only butter (or margarine), and still others use shortening. Some even use a mixture of different fats. Some bakers add an *egg* to the dough and consequently reduce the water. There is no doubt that the *egg* improves the taste and makes the dough especially crispy when it is baked. Unfortunately, it makes the pulling out of the dough more difficult since the dough tends to tear more easily. If egg yolk is used, then vinegar or lemon juice should definitely be added, since the acid activates the gluten in the flour and makes the dough easier to manipulate.

For the **preparation** of an elastic dough, all ingredients must be warmed.

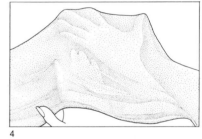

1

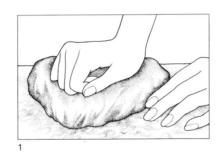

4

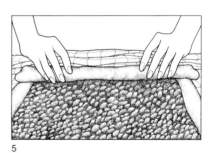

2

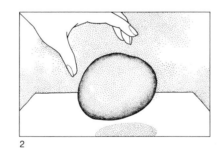

5

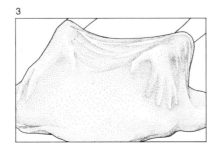

3

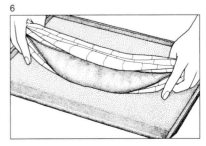

6

surface while kneading until the dough has obtained the correct consistency. Adding moisture to a stiff dough requires a great deal of effort and is seldom successful. As soon as the dough feels elastic and completely smooth, it should be "thrown" in order to remove any traces of flour and/or air bubbles. Form the dough into a ball, lift 8–12 inches in the air and repeatedly swing it down onto the work surface with gusto. Then test the dough by cutting the ball in half: if the dough inside is completely smooth and homogeneous, form into a ball again and allow to rest.

For the resting period, repeatedly rinse out a bowl with very hot water until it is quite warm, or use a saucepan in which water has been boiled. Dry the vessel and place it upside down on top of the ball of dough. Allow to rest 30 minutes so that the dough can swell. Or place the dough in a plastic bag, close it tightly, and allow to rest in a warm place for 30 minutes. This method will also keep the surface from drying out.

Next, punch down the dough and knead it again. Then *roll out* the dough. First dust an over-sized kitchen towel (or, better yet, a simple tablecloth) with some flour and place the flattened ball of dough in the middle. Roll out the dough with a rolling pin in all directions as thinly and as evenly as possible. After rolling, *pull out* the dough as much as possible. With floured hands slide, palms down, to the center of the rolled out layer of dough. Pull the hands, and along with them the dough above, toward the edge. During this process the hands should pull toward the body and simultaneously away from each other. Continue this process until the dough is so thin that it is almost transparent. It is said, that a good strudel dough should be thin enough to read a newspaper through it! If the fingernails are very long, either extend the dough with closed fists or with palms opened upward and the fingertips bending backwards away from the surface of the dough. A little tip: the dough will not tear so quickly if it is occasionally brushed with melted fat, which keeps it supple and keeps the surface from drying out.

Finally, cut off the thick edges with a sharp pair of scissors and *fill* the strudel according to the recipe. Always leave a margin at the edges free of filling. Fold over this margin in the final stage so that no filling leaks out when the strudel is rolled together. To roll up the strudel, lift the cloth at the ends closest to the body while holding the dough with the fingertips. With the palms of the hands, press gently against the cloth. Lift the fingertips away from the dough as soon as the lifting of the cloth begins to cause the filling to roll. Gradually, without jerky movements, lift the cloth at an angle until the entire strudel has rolled together. Hold the cloth by the sides and slide the strudel directly onto the baking sheet or into a pan.

Strudel tastes good both warm or just barely cooled. It should, in all cases, be served fresh because the dough becomes moist after it has stood around a while, thus diminishing its wonderful flavor.

Puff Pastry

It used to take a lot of time to prepare pastries made of fresh puff pastry. Today it is much simpler, since first-class puff pastry is available in the freezer department of most supermarkets and merely requires thawing before it is used.

The various **ingredients** of puff pastry are generally the same as those of a simple noodle dough—flour, salt, water, which must be combined with the same quantity of butter. However, this *process of working* the ingredients is the secret of puff pastry: both of the basic ingredients the flour-water dough and the butter must be bonded as extremely thin layers placed on top of each other. And this must be done repeatedly since a good puff pastry must have at least 144 layers and, depending on the type of pastry, as many as 243 individual

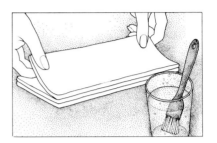

layers! In order to obtain these leafy layers, "noodle dough" is generally rolled out evenly, then a flat tile of butter is placed on top, and the noodle dough is folded over the butter tile. Both are then rolled out again under even pressure. Then this piece of dough must again be folded up according to a specific procedure and rolled out once again. These are called "rounds" in the trade. Puff pastry requires 4-5 rounds like this, however, a distinction is made between simple and double rounds. In addition to rolling and folding, the puff pastry must be refrigerated between each round so that the individual layers can bond with one another. Thus the preparation of puff pastry forces one into a procedure requiring several hours of work. That the procedure must be carried out exactly and evenly goes without saying. Therefore, it is advised to leave this tedious process to the frozen food industry, since their special machines can perform this job more quickly and evenly and the success of the final product is always ensured.

Place the **frozen puff pastry** layers next to one another and allow to thaw for about 20 minutes. Then brush them with some cold water so that they retain their uniform shape. Stack them on a lightly floured work surface and roll them out to the desired size and thickness while applying even pressure. With a rolling pin, always roll the pastry from right to left and vice versa, and later from front to back and vice versa. This way it can be assured that the pastry will not "pull up" on one side. Since puff pastry generally shrinks when baked, it is advis-

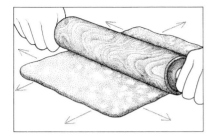

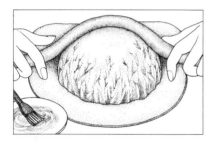

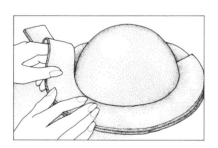

able to cut the individual pieces somewhat larger than their final size should be. If several layers are to be stacked (for example, as torte) they should be cut to the desired size before baking.

"Pulling up" can be avoided to a certain degree by refrigerating the shaped dough for 15–30 minutes (depending on the recipe) after it has been rolled out and before baking.

Puff pastry is always baked on a baking sheet that has been rinsed in cold water. The water vaporizes during baking and thus "lifts" the dough. Professionals spray additional water on the bottom of the oven. During baking, the fat in the puff pastry expands and releases the emulated water. This water as well as that on the baking sheet vaporizes and rises and simultaneously pushes the layers of dough above it upward, thus separating the leaves of dough. If these layers are squashed or kneaded, the moisture will bond with the gluten in the flour and this will inhibit the "leafing" action. For the same reason, puff pastry should only be cut with a sharp knife, pastry cutter, or cookie cutter, since here, too, the layers should not be pressed together. The egg yolk used for brushing should not run between the layers, as it would bake them together.

The oven temperature for puff pastry should be set at 400°-425°. If the temperature is too low, the fat will melt causing it to bond with the flour. Temperatures that are too high will harden the surface before the dough begins leafing.

A true feat of puff pastry is the vol-au-vent on page 282. It is more easily made than its appearance indicates. First line a round, flat bowl with aluminum foil. Then fill the foil lining with pieces of paper or strips of foil. Compress this filling material to make a sturdy half circle, then lay the construct in the middle of the rolled out dough (about ½ of the total amount of dough) and cover with the rolled-out dough. Roll out the remaining dough, brush the edge of dough covering the half circle with egg yolk and

lay the second layer of dough on top thus forming the base of the pastry house. Press the edge together and cut off any excess leaving a little dough as overlap. Brush it with egg yolk and lay additional strips of dough on top of it.

After the edges have been pressed together they can be attractively notched or small cut-outs may be made in them. A chimney should also be cut out of the top. Then the vol-au-vent can be decorated. Leftover dough is cut out into small figures and shapes, brushed with egg yolk and placed on the surface in any pattern desired. The lid of the chimney is placed on top.

After baking, remove the lid and spoon in the "filling." A little tip: when filling, protect the delicate edge of pastry with a cone made of aluminum foil.

Fresh-Cheese Dough and Yeast Puff Pastry

Here are four doughs that differ in how they are made but at the same time share numerous characteristics. When baked, they have a light and airy structure, are aromatically sour, and can be worked and shaped in various ways.

The easiest of these doughs is the Fresh Cheese Tart Dough. Nearly equal quantities of fresh cheese (ricotta or cottage cheese may be used), fat and flour are chilled and kneaded together very quickly, whereby the flour must always have previously been combined with baking powder. The dough is worked almost exactly as the classical tart dough; all ingredients are first cut to a crumb-like consistency and then quickly kneaded together with chilled hands. However, it is necessary to work this dough even more quickly so that the moisture in the cheese has no chance to combine with the gluten in the flour nor with the baking powder. Here, too, the butter should not be allowed to soften. That is why an electric mixer with a kneading attachment can be of enormous assistance for making this dough. The fresh cheese tart dough must also rest in a cool place before it is shaped and baked.

This dough can be altered to make Fresh Cheese Puff Pastry, an even more delicate dough. As soon as the dough has been kneaded until smooth, roll it out on a lightly floured work surface into a finger-thick rectangle. Then fold it into thirds as shown on the right. Refrigerate for a few minutes, then roll out and fold again. Repeat this process once or twice more, then cover and refrigerate the dough for several hours or, better yet, overnight. The fresh cheese puff pastry is then baked like real puff pastry at very high temperatures on a baking sheet rinsed with cold water which causes it to "puff up."

The simplest and quickest fresh-cheese dough is the Fresh Cheese Oil Dough.

Fresh cheese and oil are whipped together and then kneaded into flour which has been combined with baking powder. This dough does not require long resting or refrigeration. However, care should be taken that it does not become too warm when kneaded and handled. Generally twice as much flour as fresh cheese is used, depending on the amount of moisture in the cheese, additional milk may be added. An egg or egg yolk may be added to enhance the flavor and provide optimal browning. For sweet pastry, immediately add sugar to fresh cheese so that it dissolves well.

When making a fresh-cheese dough, cheeses with various fat content are available. Skim fresh cheese breaks up easily, is naturally lighter in calories and is easily digested. A creamier fresh cheese is especially "well-rounded" and ensures that cakes do not dry out quickly.

Regardless of which fresh cheese used, note that the water content may vary from package to package or batch to batch. It may be necessary to vary the amount of flour (or liquid) accordingly, since all of these doughs should be supple and elastic but should never stick to the hands.

The last dough, quite different from the above-named doughs, is the Yeast Puff Pastry. It generally does not call for fresh cheese, but there are, however, exceptions. The typical yeast puff pastry is made of a yeast dough into which layers of butter have been rolled as in a puff pastry. To do this, the well-chilled butter is first cut into flakes, then kneaded with some flour (this gives it a binding capacity), and subsequently rolled between waxed paper into a flat, rectangular block and refrigerated. After the yeast dough has risen and been kneaded, it is rolled out to a rectangle twice the original size, the butter is laid on one half and the other half folded over. The edges should be lightly moistened and carefully pressed together so that both layers bind well. It is refrigerated 30 minutes before rolled out under

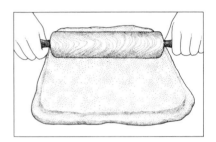

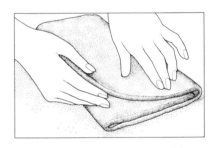

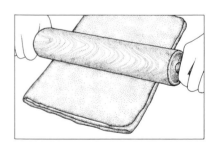

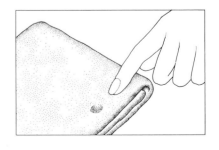

gentle but even pressure into a long, narrow rectangle. The first third is folded into the middle and the last third folded on top of that. Refrigerate again and roll out lengthwise to three times its size. Repeat these "rounds" of folding, refrigerating and rolling until the dough has finally been worked like this three or four times. The more frequently it is folded and rolled, the flakier it becomes. If worked less frequently, it may become excessively high when baked because large air pockets may form. In order to keep track of the number of rounds, it is advisable to mark the dough before each new period of refrigeration by making a slight indentation with your thumb for each completed round (see picture at left).

In executing these "rounds," and later when shaping the dough, attention should be paid to two things: the individual layers should never be disturbed and the dough must always remain cool since the layers are otherwise likely to stick together. A very sharp knife or a pastry cutter should be used when cutting the dough so that the layers are not pressed together. Before cutting, be sure to roll out the dough to the desired size and thickness. Here the same applies as for puff pastry: always roll out in all directions, since the yeast puff pastry can also "pull up." If the dough has only been rolled in one direction it is possible that round-shaped pastries could come out of the oven as ovals.

Pie Dough

Pies originated in the English kitchen where they are served warm or cold. The dough generally used is a very rich kneaded dough made of flour, fat and ice water; it is rarely sweetened.

Preparation of the dough is similar to the classic tart dough. Here, too, flour is placed onto a work surface, then quickly cut to a crumb-like consistency together with ice water and butter cut into flakes. The dough is then kneaded and refrigerated. As in the case of tart dough, the fat in this dough should not become too soft or the ice water may not bond with the gluten in the flour. Therefore, use fat directly after it has been removed from the refrigerator and "chill" the water with ice cubes. Keeping the dough cold is a prerequisite for making a light dough. Water should first vaporize and escape during baking. The use of butter, margarine, shortening or a mixture of fats only affects the flavor but not the final result of the pastry. Generally speaking, every pie dough should be covered and refrigerated for 30 minutes. Deep-dish pies may be baked with or without a pie shell underneath. For a pretty pie shell, use a low, broad pie pan. For only a lid made of dough, a higher bowl that fans out toward the top is appropriate. It should have a broad, unglazed edge so that the lid of dough does not slip into the filling.

For the pie, use about ½ of the total amount of dough, to roll out the bottom in the shape of a round. Invert the form intended for use, lay it on the dough and cut out the *pie lid* making it about ¼ inch larger than the edge of the form. Combine the leftover dough with the remaining dough, roll it out and then line the form with it. To avoid tearing, roll out both layers of dough on floured aluminum foil, cut out the foil together with the dough and first remove the foil after the dough is in place. The bottom of the pastry shell should repeatedly be pierced with a fork, so that no bubbles appear, and then filled. In order to avoid having

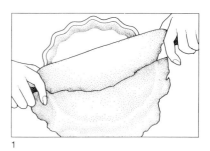

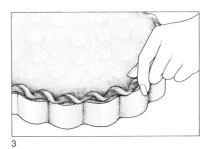

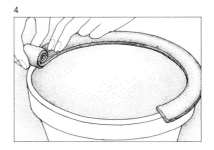

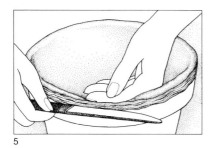

5

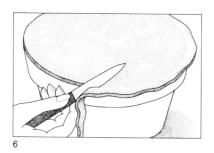

6

7

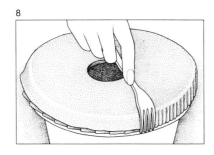

8

juicy fruit soak through the shell, coat it with a layer of bread crumbs before the fruit is filled in. Then place the lid made of dough on top and prepare the *dough edges* by pressing them with a gentle twist between the thumb and the forefinger in order to create a wavy pattern. Cut a small hole in the middle of the lid as a *chimney* to allow hot air to escape during baking.

To omit the bottom pie shell, there are two ways to *attach the lid*. The first: cut the lid about 1 inch larger than the opening of the form. Gather the leftovers and form them into a strip that is not too thin and place this strip on the moistened (unglazed) edge of the form. Fill in the fruit mixture, place the lid on top and press it against the edge of dough. Now, lay the index finger of one hand horizontally onto the edge and, with the other hand, repeatedly press the blade of a knife, also held horizontally, onto the edge so that both layers bind together completely. The blade of the knife should follow the form and be held at an angle facing diagonally upward and away from the center of the pie. Finally notch the edge repeatedly. No "chimney" is necessary in this case, since the rising vapors lift the lid and there is no pastry shell on the bottom that is likely to get wet.

The second method for attaching a lid is similar. First cut out the lid. Then divide the remaining dough into 1 x 3-inch strips and hang them over the moistened edge of the form. They should overlap a little. They may also be brushed with cold water before the lid is placed on top. This lid should also be slightly larger than the form so that the edge of the lid can be pressed together with the strips of dough onto the bowl to make a thick rim. Press the edge with the prongs of a fork against the form so that it is well attached and also so that a pattern is etched in. This lid also requires no chimney.

Helpful Baking Information at a Glance

Shaping a Stollen

Roll out the dough so that it is still quite thick and oval in shape: looking down the length of the loaf, it should be thinner in the middle than on the two outside edges. Fold the dough so that the two thicker edges on the long sides lay right next to one another. Then make shallow grooves on the right and left sides of the top surface with the sides of the hands.

In order to avoid having the heavy stollen dough spread out during baking, it is advisable to surround the long sides with strips of greased aluminum foil folded several layers thick.

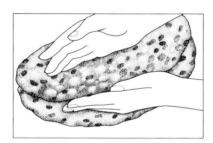

Lining Pans

Since greasing and dusting pans with flour is not always sufficient preparation, it is sometimes advisable to line the pan with parchment paper. For a *loaf pan*, first lay the paper around the pan, then make incisions diagonally toward the edges and evenly cut off the excess paper. Now grease the paper, lift it up by the corners and place it in the pan without creating folds or wrinkles.

To line the bottom of a *springform pan*, stretch a piece of parchment paper between the bottom and the rim of the pan. To line only the rim, first cut a strip of paper that is a little higher than the rim

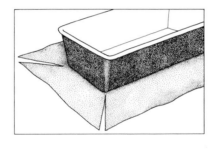

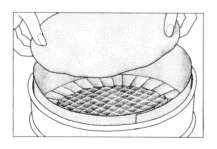

of the form. On one of its long sides, fold in about ½ inch along the entire length, make repeated incisions in this margin and place the paper into the form perpendicular to the bottom. Then cut out the bottom from parchment paper and place it on the incised margin and finally (after greasing, if required) the dough may be filled into the pan.

Blind Baking

In order to keep the tart dough rim of an unfilled tart shell from slipping down, it is baked "blind." The pan is lined with the dough, then the dough is lined with paper. For round forms, fold a square piece of parchment paper together diagonally until the outside edge is only about 1 inch wide. Then, with a pair of scissors, shorten the paper to the length of the radius of the pan. Smooth the paper out onto the dough and fill the pan up to the top edge with dried beans or peas. These dried legumes are removed after baking and can be used again after they have cooled.

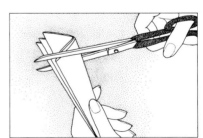

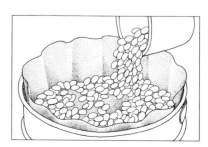

Braiding

Whether braiding hair, wool or yeast dough, the technique is always the same. In the case of dough, however, the final product can be influenced by the form of the individual strands. Strands that are the same thickness all the way through will result in very regularly shaped braids, while strands that are somewhat flattened at the ends will produce braids with thinner ends. However, for a braid that is thick at one end and thin at the other, the strands at one end will have to be rolled thinner.

The most simple braid is one that is "turned." It merely requires twisting together two strands of equal thickness.

For braiding three strands, lay the three strands over each other as shown in the drawing, in each case bending the outer most strands inward across the middle one.

A four-strand braid is worked according to the same plan, however, here the two outer strands must always be laid over the other two in the middle. Mozart's famous pigtail (recipe on page 194) requires more attention to detail. It is braided with 8 strands. For this pigtail, mark the individual strands with numbers and follow the drawing very exactly.

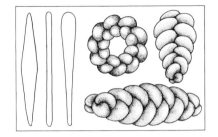

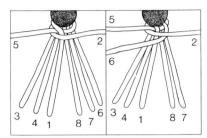

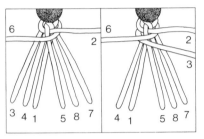

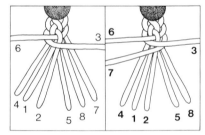

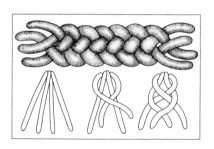

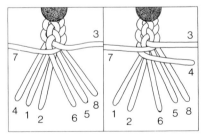

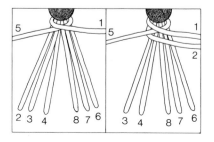

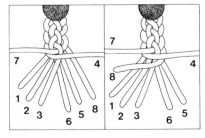

Mrs. Schindel's Sweet Elephant

(Recipe page 220)

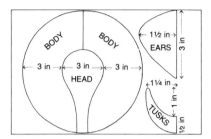

Preparation is extremely simple, since all the parts can be baked in one spring-form pan. Its diameter must be 9½ inches in order to be true to the measurements given in the drawing. The two halves are then glued to each other and the head plus trunk are attached. For the ears and tusk, cut the waffles according to the smaller drawing.

Gingerbread House

(Recipe page 234)

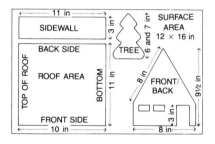

Before cutting, copy the basic pattern above and make a stencil so that all the parts will fit together exactly. Copy the measurements on the drawing and take care to make very exact right-angles. Otherwise, the house will not be a solid construction.

Ovens and other Baking Appliances

Electric and Gas Ovens

The conventional and most frequently owned ovens are electric and gas. There is relatively little difference between the two and in general both bake according to the same principle: gas and electric ovens use radiating heat that directly affect the baked good. Baking is done on one level in these ovens.

It is important to place cakes or pastries at the correct height in the oven. That is why all of these ovens have different levels at which to place the oven rack. A rule of thumb is that a space of 6 inches should remain above the expected height of the finished cake. A smaller amount of "head" space would result in heat that was too intense and would hinder the rising of the cake. Thus, all cakes baked in high pans or which rise to extreme heights should be placed on the bottom rack (examples would be the bundt cake or a yeast dough braid). The pans should always be placed on a rack and never directly on the bottom of the oven. Tortes of high or medium height, cream puffs, pastry shells for fruit tarts, cookies and sheet cakes, should all be baked on the middle rack. The highest rack is used for browning and broiling. Always place the cake in a preheated oven unless the recipe indicates otherwise. The time required for preheating varies from model to model; generally it takes 10-20 minutes for electric ovens to heat to 400° and somewhat less for gas ovens. The oven has reached the desired temperature when the indicator light goes off.

Temperature is given in Fahrenheit for electric and gas ovens. In some, usually older, models it is also possible to turn on upper and lower heat separately. In such a case, it is advisable to measure the oven temperature with a thermometer before baking to be absolutely sure that the correct temperature has been reached. In houseware shops, relatively inexpensive oven thermometers are sold with which the exact temperature can be measured. If the measured temperatures that correspond to the levels on the knob are recorded, one can easily estimate the correct level for any temperature required in these recipes. A similar procedure should be followed after the purchase of a new oven. One can almost always depend on the information provided by the manufacturer, however, it is still advisable to compare the baking times and temperatures of the recipes with those in the instruction booklet.

Convection Ovens

These use fans to evenly distribute the heat. This makes baking on different levels possible. Up to four baking sheets can be placed one above the other. It makes no difference whether the baked goods are salty or sweet, they can all be placed in the oven at the same time. There is no transference of smell or taste. Since no preheating is required in convection ovens and baking is done at low temperatures, the optimal use possible in these ovens can lead to as much as 30% reduction in energy costs. The low temperatures are also ideal for drying meringues and macaroons.

Stone Ovens

These are newly developed ovens about the size of an electric toaster oven. Bread, butter cakes, tortes and small sheet cakes can be baked in these ovens. They retain heat so well that they can be compared to the ovens in old-fashioned bakeries.

Broiler

The broiler is not only reserved for Tree-Ring Cakes and layered cakes. Today's electric broilers are conceived not only for broiling meat but also for baking cakes. The newest electric broilers also make it possible to bake with the properties of convection ovens. Here, too, the temperatures and times of the recipes must be compared to the manufacturer's instructions.

Baking Dome

This is a relatively old invention. It is a metal form in which butter cakes, torte bottoms, sponge cakes and loaf cakes can be baked. Sheet cakes will not fit. The baking dome has no thermostat, only a window through which the cake may be observed during baking. It offers small households a space-saving and economical way to bake.

Deep Fryer

Fritters, crullers and beignets attest to the fact that not everything that is baked comes from the oven. It all started with a simple pan of liquid fat on the stove and was then developed into the modern deep fryer. Several different versions of these appliances are available: they may either be square or round, with a filter for smells or with a frying basket. Their volume ranges from 1 to 4 quarts. If the appliance has no thermostat, it is advisable to obtain a fat or deep frying thermometer. The temperature of the fat should be between 325°-375°. If the temperature is too low the food to be fried will absorb fat and thus become hard to digest and overly rich. If the temperature is too high, the pastry and fat will burn. Without a thermometer, one can test the fat with a "stick or white bread test." Hold the handle of a wooden (not plastic) spoon in the hot fat. If bubbles appear on it, the fat is at the correct temperature. Or drop some small cubes of white bread into the fat. If they quickly turn golden brown, then the fat is hot enough.

Neutral oils, vegetable shortening, or a mixture of these are all suitable fats for deep frying. Butter and margarine are not suitable because they burn at high temperatures.

Waffle Iron

This is one of those small household appliances that is a desirable possession in all households, not only those with children. It always proves to be a life-saver when surprise visitors arrive because, as is well-known, waffles taste best hot off the iron. There are many different types of waffle irons available: round, square and those coated with a non-stick surface.

Other Possibilities

The simplest method is the old-fashioned frying pan on the stove. In it, large and small pancakes can be made and stacked to make fantastic tortes. It is also the best method for making sponge-cake omelettes with a large variety of fillings.

Even without any of the above equipment, it is still possible to enjoy homemade baked goods. There are ready-made torte bottoms, tartlet shells, cookies, waffles, wafers and meringues available on the market. One can always offer new "baked goods" at the table, which, depending on the recipe, have been "baked" in the refrigerator or simply filled or frosted.

Baking Pans

There is an enormous variety of pans in many colors and materials on the market. When shopping, first concentrate on the material, since that is what will determine the baking result to a greater extent than the form. Generally, these are differentiated according to smooth, light and dark, or frosted pans. The first reflects the heat, the latter absorbs it. Regardless of the choice, all metal pans must first be seasoned: after washing and drying, carefully grease the pan with oil and bake at 425° for 30 minutes.

Clay dishes are actually the fathers of our present-day baking pans. They have become "modern" again as a re-sult of the current wave of nostalgia. They are porous and are only suitable for very lightly sweetened doughs, thus, especially suitable for breads, since very sweet doughs easily bake onto the pans. Before filling, the clay dishes must always be well watered (soaked for about 15 minutes) and they may only be placed in cold ovens.

Ceramic and Earthenware dishes bake very gently and slowly, since the heat can only penetrate very slowly. Today, they are fire-proof, lead-free and covered with extremely stable glazes that hardly ever crack. Ceramic and earthenware retain heat very well, so that the oven can usually be turned off a few minutes before the end of the baking period. They should always be greased before filling and the cake should be tested with a toothpick for doneness.

Tinplate forms reflect the heat and brown less strongly. This metal requires relatively high heat and is suitable for baking in gas ovens.

Black plate pans absorb and evenly distribute the heat into the cake. They brown well and quickly.

Coated pans offer two decisive advantages. The cake can be effortlessly removed and the pans are easy to clean. Only the material and make up of the outside surface determine the result, the artificial coating does not affect the baking procedure itself.

Glass pans are extremely easy to clean and can also be washed in the dishwasher. Like ceramic dishes, they heat slowly and give off heat slowly. They therefore bake very evenly and do not brown too darkly.

Aluminum pans are available in great variation: as highly polished, often gilded fantasy shapes or as practical throw-away pans. Both types bake evenly and brown well, whereby the dark pans may be used like black plate pans. The disposable pans (in various sizes and shapes) are best suited for baking in quantity because the baked goods can be frozen and reheated in them.

Copper pans are being used more frequently today. They are not only decorative, but also produce excellent results. However, they require diligent cleaning and polishing and they are relatively expensive.

Cast-iron pans are also becoming fashionable in spite of their high price. They brown well, bake evenly and retain heat excellently. They should always be well greased and never be exposed to abrasive cleansers. To avoid rusting, they should be oiled and seasoned.

The baking pans one purchases depend on the kind of cakes one bakes. A basic set should include a tube pan and springform or loaf pan as well as a fruit tart pan and several tartlet pans. Small-sized baking pans are available especially for small households.

Baking sheets come with the stove. Every household generally has some. The same is true of broiler or fat pans.

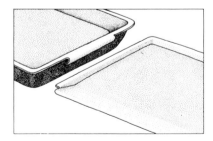

Bundt forms also bake from the middle to outside because of the chimney.

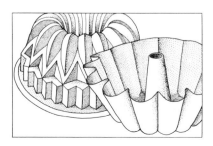

Springform pans can be obtained with an insert for Rodon cake.

Loaf pans are most versatile in lengths of 9-12 inches.

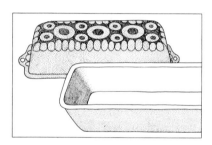

Fruit tart pans are available either round or square with smooth or fluted edges.

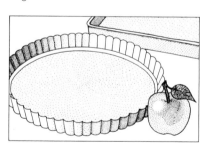

Ring-shaped pans are used for savarins and wreath cakes. They are also available in smaller sizes for individual portions.

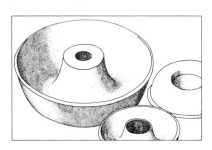

Pie pans can be round, oval or square. They may be either shallow with a low rim or deep-dish pans.

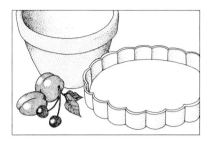

Deer's Back pan is prepared and used just like a loaf pan.

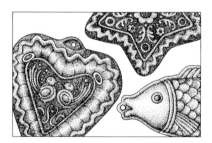

Decorative pans are available in a great variety. They come in various shapes like hearts, clovers, horseshoes, rosettes, stars, fish, etc.

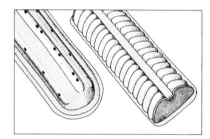

Hollow-backed pans are very rarely seen today, although they should be coming back into style. They are used for baking Easter bunnies, chicks, lambs, etc.

Baking Utensils and Accessories

Just as with cooking, the right tools are essential for baking. There are, of course, some utensils that are utterly essential and others that can be obtained later. The following list is organized with this in mind and begins, as does all baking, with weighing:

Kitchen scale is indispensible for the exact weighing of ingredients and thus for the success of a cake. The typical household scale will weigh quite exactly up to 10 pounds. Older scales measure up to 20 pounds but require balancing weights. Modern scales automatically show the weight. Scales that allow one to weigh individual ingredients are especially practical. In order to save space, choose a scale that can be mounted on the wall.

Measuring cups are necessary for measuring liquids and can also be used for measuring solid ingredients like sugar, flour, etc. They are not as exact as the kitchen scale. Measuring cups should be transparent and, of course, calibrated.

Calibrated liqueur glass is used for measuring small quantities of liquid.

Mixing bowls are a necessity. The baker should have at least two: a large, wide-mouthed one for making doughs and a smaller one with a handle for whipping cream and egg whites. It makes no difference whether the bowls are made of metal, enamel, stoneware or plastic. They should, however, be heat-resistant since some of the doughs are beaten over hot water baths. Plastic and metal bowls have the advantage of being shatter-resistant. Mixing bowls should have smooth, rounded bottoms and no grooves, since ingredients tend to get stuck in them and then do not mix well with the rest of the dough. Work will be

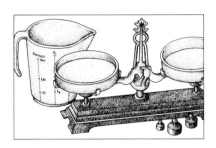

made quite a bit easier with bowls that have a rubber ring in the bottom to prevent slippage or try putting a folded kitchen towel under the bowl to keep it from slipping around.

Stirring spoons should be bought in several sizes, with and without a hole. It makes no difference whether the spoon is plastic or wood. A spoon with a hole is necessary for stirring dough and for folding in ingredients. Spoons without a hole are better for beating the dough since their surface is larger.

Wire whisk is essential for evenly mixing in creams and cheese, for stirring thin doughs and for folding in whipped egg whites and whipped cream as well as flour. Whipping cream and egg whites are rarely whipped with a whisk. The whisk should be made of rust-free metal and it should be heat-resistant so that it can be washed in the dishwasher.

Electric hand-mixer is essential in today's kitchen. It should have two beaters and a kneading attachment. The beaters are necessary for butter cakes, sponge cakes, meringues and macaroons as well as whipping cream and other cream mixtures. The kneading attachment is used for tart dough and yeast dough as well as mixing flour into very heavy butter cake batter. Always follow the manufacturer's directions when using the hand-mixer and keep in mind that these mixers achieve their results much more quickly than hand mixing does. To avoid over-beating the batter or dough, never beat longer than 8-10 minutes. Normally an electric hand-mixer can

easily manage doughs containing up to 1 pound of flour.

Sieves should be in the kitchen anyway, but at least two are needed for baking: a large one to be used for draining and straining and a very fine one for dusting with flour, cocoa and/or powdered sugar. Special flour sifters with a movable handle are available in kitchen stores; these ensure even sifting of flour. It should be used exclusively for flour and should never come into contact with moist ingredients.

Lemon press is also found in most households. It makes no difference whether the press is made of glass or plastic. If a great number of citrus fruits are pressed, an electric squeezer would probably be a worthwhile acquisition. It is often also available as an attachment to kitchen machines.

Grater is essential for grating lemon and orange rind and for other hard substances like chocolate.

Almond mill is a worthwhile acquisition because freshly grated almonds and other nuts are much more aromatic than those purchased ground. Nuts can be chopped in an electric chopper or mixer; however, the result is often more like a pastry and a great deal of the nut oil is lost because of the heat that develops in this process.

Dough scrapers and rubber spatulas are available in a variety of different kinds: the most practical is a right-angled plastic scraper that gets narrower toward one end. Somewhat more stable is a square dough scraper made of metal, which has a plastic edge as a handle on one side. Both are suitable for dividing heavy doughs onto a baking sheet or into a form and also for scraping dough off of the work surface. A rubber spatula with a wooden handle can be used to lift dough or batter as well as egg whites and whipped cream out of mixing bowls.

Rolling pin is an essential utensil. Whether it is made of the usual wood, or plastic-coated or cloth-covered makes no difference and depends on individual preference. It is always very important that it turns on its own axle. When rolling, care should be taken to roll the dough with gentle pressure; do not flatten it with force. If there is no rolling pin available, a floured wine bottle can come to the rescue in a pinch.

Pastry wheels are available with smooth or zigzag rims. Those with zigzag rims are suitable for decorating and cutting out shapes. The smooth-rimmed wheel has the same function as a sharp knife. Both are frequently used for tart doughs and puff pastry.

Pastry brushes are needed by every baker: a broad one for greasing baking sheets and cake pans and others, with soft bristles, for brushing the dough with egg, water or milk, or for glazing and "dusting off" flour, powdered sugar etc. Do not be too sparing with pastry brushes. Replace the brush as soon as bristles start to fall out; it is very difficult to remove single bristles in glazes. Choose brushes with natural bristles and heat-resistant handles, and they can be washed in the dishwasher.

Knives are extremely expensive, but nonetheless, purchase high-quality, rust-free steel knives. One needs the right sized knives in the kitchen for peeling, cutting and chopping. However, for baking one should definitely have a long torte knife (they can be obtained with

and without a serrated edge). It should be long enough to cut an entire cake into two layers: the blade should be quite thin and extremely sharp so that the cake is actually cut and the blade not shoved through. If cakes filled with whipped or other creams are to be cut with it, repeatedly dip the blade into hot water, so that the cutting edge is always clean. An electric knife is ideal for cutting these cakes into pieces, since they never crush the filling when used correctly. Use a normal everyday table knife for "cutting" tart dough.

Spoons are, of course, not only used for cooking but also for baking. They are usually already in stock in a kitchen. Tea and tablespoons are required most often for the purpose of measuring and stirring. A slotted spoon is also essential for deep frying. If a regular spoon is used, the fried pastry will not drain sufficiently.

Pancake turner is no luxury item for baking. In a pinch, use a long knife with a thin blade. It is extremely useful for lifting small pastries off of the baking sheet as well as for spreading frostings and glazes and smoothing out the sides of tortes.

Cake racks must be used to allow cakes and pastries to steam off and cool after baking. They can be obtained in round or square shapes and the spacing should be so small that pastries do not fall between the wires.

Wooden skewers or toothpicks are needed for testing baked goods for doneness. They should always be thin and, if possible, not too short.

Household scissors are also a necessary tool for every kitchen. When baking, they can be used for cutting parchment paper. They can also be used for cutting open cream puffs, since this pastry is difficult to cut with a knife while it is still hot.

Pastry bag with several different spouts is a must if one wants to serve not only good, but also attractive baked goods. They can be obtained in kitchen stores and are made of coated cloth or are available as discardable (one-time) bags. The former last a very long time. They are always sold with a set of smooth and star spouts so that they can be used to create numerous decorations. In order to press out sugar and chocolate glazes, fold a bag out of parchment paper, if necessary make a pastry bag out of a thick plastic freezer bag. To make the latter, cut off a corner and place the appropriate spout inside.

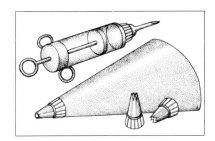

Decorating bags are available with various spouts. However, these appear to be less practical because it is difficult to guide them as well as pastry bags.

Torte divider is an inexpensive aid and is great for those who do not trust their eyes when dividing a torte. It is generally made of plastic and has two usable sides. One marks 12, the other 16 pieces, thus allowing effortless following of the lines when dividing the torte.

Wavy scraper which looks like a plastic dough scraper is etched differently on both sides and is used to decorate the edges and rims of frosted and cream-covered tortes. A knife with broad serration can be substituted for this utensil.

Wooden or marble cutting boards are usually rejected by people who do not own them and greatly prized by those who do. They are not a "must." However, they are very practical as work surfaces since cake and bread doughs do not stick to them as easily and they do not "sweat," that is, become moist. Furthermore, both, especially the marble board, keep the dough from becoming too warm.

Cookie forms and cutters are also available in an enormous selection. Picking the right cutter is often difficult.

Cookie cutters can be obtained in many different patterns and motives.

Cookie presses are available in numerous motives. A dough grinder is used in similar fashion when it has attachments for pressed cookies. There are also cookie cutters available in cooking stores, that are outfitted with special spouts like the decorating bags described above. Molds, usually made of wood

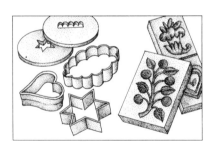

and sometimes of metal or ceramic are used for certain types of cookies (especially with Christmas motives). During the remainder of the year they are often used to decorate the walls of kitchens and they can be used for attractively molding pieces of butter.

Food processor is an appliance which should also be mentioned, although it is not really necessary for baking. However, if one frequently makes large quantities of dough (much greater than 1 pound), it would be used quite frequently. Otherwise, it would be advisable to acquire one only if it would also

regularly be used for cooking. It is not really an economical investment for baking alone.

Baking Aids

Aluminum foil can be used for lining baking sheets and pans, for covering cakes during baking and for maintaining the outer shape of cakes and breads baked on baking sheets, like stollen, strudel and braids. Tartlet pans, can be made out of doubled-layered aluminum foil shaped over the bottom of a wine bottle. Of course, these homemade forms are for one-time use only. Since aluminum foil is generally used as a wrapping material for storing and freezing, it is usually found in every household.

Parchment paper is used to line baking sheets and cake pans. It can also be used to cover baked goods that are browning too quickly, and is very practical to use when weighing ingredients; plates and bowls will not get dirty when weighing is done directly on the paper. Another use for parchment paper is as a pastry bag for decorating cakes with sugar or chocolate glazes; it can also be used for stencils that are laid on a finished product that is to be attractively dusted with powdered sugar or cocoa.

Waxed paper is actually a further development of parchment paper. It saves one the trouble of greasing the baking sheets and pans. When using it, one can be sure that cakes will not "stick." Furthermore, it saves time and trouble cleaning up.

Paper towels are not really related to baking, but they are very useful for blotting fruit dry and draining fresh cheese. They are also extremely handy for cleaning pans.

Torte doily is a decorative piece of paper placed under tortes and cakes. It simultaneously protects the torte platter when the torte is cut.

Paper frills can be obtained in various sizes and colors for petits fours, small pastries, confections and pralines.

Storing Baked Goods

There are always leftovers and it is important to store them well to maintain freshness. Also, time constraints often force one to bake a few days in advance, and it is similarly customary to make different kinds of cookies well in advance of Christmas and store them for several weeks before the big event. If each type of baked good is stored appropriately for its dough and its consistency, then freshness and flavor can be well protected.

"Dry" cakes   like butter cakes, marble cakes, etc. should be wrapped in aluminum foil. They will stay fresh for 1 week if kept in a cool, dry place. Since these cakes dry out quickly, ends of the foil should be folded over twice.

Yeast pastry   like sheet cakes with fruit, braids and unglazed bars and squares should only be stored for a very short amount of time. Wrap these in aluminum foil as well and heat them briefly before serving.

Butter and whipped cream tortes and fruit tarts   must be refrigerated. They should, however, never be stored longer than 2-3 days. It is essential to protect them against other refrigerator tastes or smells; therefore, they should be wrapped in aluminum foil or plastic wrap. A special cake cover is even better, since it usually has sufficient space so that decorations are not crushed.

Danish and puff pastry   taste best when fresh. If there are leftovers, they may be frozen, if they are not glazed, and briefly warmed up before serving.

Cookies   are usually baked "in advance" and "in quantity." Many of them require a long period of storage to become soft and tender as well as to fully develop their flavor.

Generally all cookies are immediately removed from the baking sheet, cooled on a rack and then sorted. Cookies of one kind can be stored in the same tin. Layers may, however, need to be separated by waxed paper or aluminum foil in order to avoid crumbling and sticking. Strong-flavored cookies should not be stored together in the same box, since the flavors may blend together. Similarly, soft and crispy cookies should be separated and stacked in tightly closed tins. Cookies that need to become soft and tender should remain exposed to moist air until they have reached the correct consistency. Then they should be layered in a tin and a slice of orange rind or apple should be placed inside to keep them soft.

Stollen   will retain its freshness for up to 4 weeks when wrapped in aluminum foil after it has cooled completely. It develops its best flavor when stored for this period. It should be stored in a cool but not too dry place. The best place to store a stollen is in an unglazed earthenware container covered with a damp cloth.

Pastry made of meringue or macaroon paste   must be stored in a completely dry place, so that it does not become soft. Meringues that are topped or filled with fruit, ice cream or moist glazes cannot be stored at all, since they will immediately become soft. The same applies to Strudel, which also can not be stored because of its filling.

Freezing Baked Goods

Already prepared cakes, tortes and pastry that has been stored in the freezer are a boon for unexpected guests or a ravenous appetite. In addition, a freezer allows better use of kitchen appliances and oven. A double recipe can be processed in a food processor, two loaf pans always fit into a regular oven and a convection oven can bake three baking sheets at once. Tortes, baked cakes, tartlets and pastries, breads and rolls can be frozen; meringues, macaroons and cakes with glazes cannot. The latter will become watery like marzipan or fruit glazes; croquant or cracknel softens and becomes moist. Another possibility is to freeze doughs; butter cake batter, yeast doughs, puff pastry, cream puff pastry, cheese-oil doughs, tart doughs, pie and strudel doughs are suitable for freezing. When yeast doughs are frozen, the quantity of yeast should be increased as a precaution. It should not be allowed to rise before freezing. To avoid having the surface dry out, brush it with oil. Yeast doughs can also be frozen after the topping has been applied, but before baking. It is best to freeze butter cake batter in the pan, a disposable aluminum pan, in which it is later to be baked.

For the quality of the frozen product, whether frozen as dough or already baked, it is always important to freeze at the correct temperature. A stale roll will not become fresher by warming it up after it has been frozen.

Correct wrapping is always important for whatever is frozen. It must be air-tight and waterproof in order to protect against drying out as well as against penetration by smells and flavors. The wrapping material should also be able to resist penetration by fats and acids and must be able to withstand temperatures of -40° to -75°. The following wrapping materials are suitable:

Polyethylene foil or plastic freezer wrap   can be bought as freezer bags or in rolls. One advantage of plastic wrap is that it is easy to see what is in the freezer. Furthermore, the bags and foil can be reused after washing.

Aluminum pans   are available in various sizes and shapes. Cakes that still have to be baked, like butter cakes and yeast doughs, can be frozen particularly well in aluminum pans and foil. They are then simply placed in the oven in their wrappings and baked; the wrapping material simultaneously protects against drying out.

Plastic containers are available in all sizes and shapes suitable for single pieces as well as entire cakes. Their stability makes them exceptionally appropriate for easily damaged pastry like cream tortes and puff pastry. Square boxes are also easy to stack and thus space-savers.

Other storing materials like empty yogurt, cottage cheese and margarine containers, are especially suitable for saving leftover ingredients like egg yolks or whites, cream and crumbs or streusel. Since they sometimes have no lid, they may require additional wrapping with aluminum foil.

Whatever material is chosen, it is important that a minimum of air is left in the wrapped package. Press excess air out of bags or suck out the excess with the aid of a straw. Bags can be closed with rubber bands, plastic clips or heat. If aluminum foil is used, it is advisable to fold the packages in block form or as an envelope as shown below:

For making the **block package**, place the item to be frozen in the middle of a large piece of foil, then lay the end pieces together and roll them loosely un-

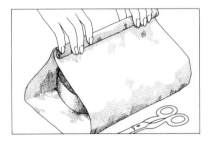

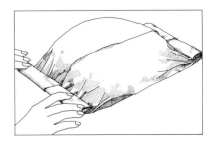

til they are directly on top of the cake. With a flat hand, press down the length of this fold, so that it is well fastened and excess air is exhausted. Now roll up the open sides in the same way and smooth them out.

The **envelope package** is especially suitable for flat pieces. The foil is smoothly laid over the item to be frozen so that both ends are on one side. Just as with the block package, these ends are rolled together and smoothed out, then the sides are similarly closed.

Doughs that still have to rise, such as yeast doughs, should not be wrapped so tightly since they will require additional space while freezing and rising. The same applies to tins and boxes. They should not be filled completely full, but instead

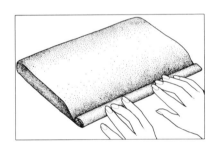

about 1 inch should be left free at the top.

Before packages are frozen, they should be labelled. This habit will save lots of time later on. The label should include a description of the contents and the quantity as well as the date on which it was frozen. The process of freezing itself should be quick, since speed will help to avoid the build-up of ice crystals. For this reason, turn the freezer to the coldest temperature. It is advisable to freeze packages containing small quantities, since this reduces freezing and thawing times.

When thawing, the baked goods should be protected against drying out. Quick heating restores freshness. Small pastries and flat sheet cakes do not have to be entirely thawed before they are reheated.

Homemade gifts

These are among the most personal of gifts. Some of these are traditional customs, like the presentation of homemade bread with salt for a housewarming, or the wedding cake or candles on a birthday cake. But, as is the case with all gifts, the wrapping is almost as important as the gift.

Whole cakes like the bundt cake, loaf cakes or fruit tarts can be placed on a stable plate and then covered with plastic wrap. A matching ribbon will round off the wrapping nicely.

Aluminum foil is also suitable and will serve to keep the cake fresh as well. Cakes presented in their baking pans are a little more elaborate. This requires removing the cake after baking, cleaning the form and then replacing the cake.

There are innumerable ways to wrap **cookies, pralines or confections**. There is a large selection of cookie tins, available in all sizes, shapes and colors. Even simple tins lend a very personal touch when filled with homemade goodies, and, if desired, these can be spray-painted or wrapped.

Light-weight wooden boxes are old-fashioned containers. These boxes are quite suitable for confections and pralines

that are presented on doilies, or are bedded in colorful paper shavings. These boxes can be purchased unadorned and then painted, lacquered or decorated with glued-on grass, flowers or torte doilies.

Aluminum foil, cellophane and doilies also offer many attractive decorative possibilities. Fold these into triangles and package the baked goods in them. These little bags can be hung from a string as party decorations and later be given away as favors. If using cellophane or aluminum foil, the package will not only look good but it will also keep well. Cute little baskets can be woven out of aluminum foil or double-strength colored foil and used for packaging individual cookies and pralines. There will be many willing takers for these gifts.

Paper plates in gold and silver covered with cellophane not only allow the contents to be seen but they protect against drying out as well.

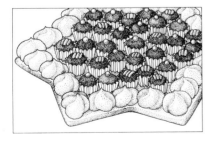

Or bake a plate out of pressed tart dough. Make a bottom and place dots or stars of dough around the edge, then fill in the confection. This way the wrapping can be eaten as well.

Pralines decoratively wrapped in doilies bound with a colored ribbon and arranged in a nest, can be kept on hand for unexpected guests or used as an attractive table decoration.

Another attractive idea is a picture made of cookies. The cookies are placed in a picture frame and covered with cellophane.

And finally, how about gifts in which the homemade sweets are simply added as an attractive filling: an attractive glass filled with pralines, a vase filled with confections, a bread basket filled with homemade bread or rolls.

Terms and Ingredients from A-Z

ABC-leavening agent Ammonium-bicarbonate is an artificial leavening agent that is predominantly used in the food industry and in bakeries. It reacts like hartshorn salt (carbonate of ammonia); it separates into ammonia, water and carbon dioxide and then decomposes.

Allspice The berries of the allspice tree are often an ingredient in spice mixtures. In baking, allspice is used in breads, pepper and honey bars.

Almond extract Oil made from almonds and also sometimes from peach and apricot seeds from which prussic acid has been removed.

Almonds There are sweet and bitter almonds. Sweet ones are used for baking since the bitter ones have a large amount of prussic acid. Almonds can be obtained blanched, unblanched, whole, slivered, chopped and grated. Because they contain a lot of fat, they can quickly become rancid and should not be stored for long periods of time. Freshly ground almonds have the greatest amount of flavor, (see hazelnuts).

Angelica The candied root of angelica is used to decorate fine tortes.

Anise This is a spice made from the seed of the plant. It is available either ground or whole. It has a very intensive flavor and can therefore seldom be combined with spices of similarly intensive flavor. It is the main ingredient in anise cookies.

Apricotizing Spreading apricot jam over a cake before glazing. Other fruit jams may be used. Apricotizing ensures good adherence of the glaze to the cake, it helps to maintain freshness and prevents the dough from penetrating and thus moistening the glaze.

Arrack   A brandy made from rice, molasses and plant juices containing sugar. It is used to flavor doughs and glazes.

Artificial honey   Similar in quality to natural honey, this is made from inverted sugar. In baking, it can be used just like honey, thus is an ingredient used in breads and honey bars.

Baking   The best temperatures for baking doughs are between 275° and 450°. During baking, the protein in the flour coagulates and creates the solid structure of the cake. The porousness is created by the carbon dioxide resulting from the leavening process.

Baking powder   An artificial leavening agent made from wine stone (the granular deposits found at the bottom of bottles of good wine), sodium and starch. When baking powder comes into contact with liquid the sodium and wine stone react to one another producing carbon dioxide as the leavening gas. Baking powder should always be stored in a dry place so that this reaction cannot take place before the substance is used.

Baking soda   Used in baking as a leavening agent. When affected by acids, carbon dioxide is released forcing the dough to rise. Baking soda is available in all supermarkets.

Beating   Beating doughs should not be confused with stirring. The dough is beaten with the hands or with a spoon. The dough is always lifted up and then thrown down onto the remaining dough (for example, in the case of yeast doughs).

Bitter chocolate   Chocolate containing at least 60% cocoa.

Blanching   The plunging of vegetables into boiling water in order to open up the cells while simultaneously retaining the color. In baking, unskinned almonds are blanched in order to remove the brown skins more easily.

"Blind" baking   The baking of doughs, usually tart doughs, without fillings. In order to avoid having the rim sink, dried legumes, peas or beans and sometimes pebbles, are baked as filling and removed after baking. Another way to achieve the same result is to press a strip of parchment paper or aluminum foil into the rim of dough. These "blind" shells can be filled with creams or fruit after they have cooled.

Block chocolate   Simple and inexpensive chocolate for baking. It can be chopped, grated or melted and folded into the dough.

Burning   The cooking of cream puff pastry before it is baked.

Butter   Made from cow's milk and containing at least 80% butter fat. It is an ideal fat for baking and has an especially delicate flavor. Butter should always be used for butter cream and butter cookies; in other cases margarine may be substituted.

Buttermilk   Liquid which results when butter is made. It has fewer calories than whole milk and can be substituted for it. It gives cakes and pastries a sour, refreshing taste and makes them somewhat lighter.

Candied lemon rind   Lemon rind that has been soaked in salt water, then cooked in a sugar solution. It is available chopped and is used for flavoring doughs.

Candied orange rind   Candied rind of bitter and other types of oranges. It is used chopped and is an important ingredient in stollen and King's Cake. It can also be used for decorating cakes and cookies.

Candied fruits   Fruits like cherries, pineapple, oranges and also spices, like ginger root or flowers like violets and lilac, that have been cooked for several days in a concentrated sugar solution. Candied orange rind and citron are the most frequently used in doughs. Whole fruits are best for decoration. (The entire process for candying fruits is described on page 208.)

Canned milk   See condensed milk.

Caramel   Heated and melted sugar that has taken on a golden brown color and a roasted taste. Caramel is used in the production of bonbons, confections and cakes. Some foods are colored with very strongly roasted caramel that has become quite dark brown in color.

Caraway   A seed used as a spice. It is available whole or ground. Caraway is used to spice hearty baked goods like rolls, bread, caraway sticks and bacon quiche.

Cardamom   The seed capsule of a ginger plant with a perfumed aroma. Cardamom is a typical Christmas spice that is used in stollen and also for flavoring bread dough.

Cashews   Fruit of the cashew tree. The white, roasted cashew nuts are slightly sweet and taste somewhat like almonds.

Chantilly   French term for whipped cream.

Charlotte   Dessert with an outside rim of sponge cookies, sponge cake or waffles and an inner core of cream, puréed fruit or ice cream.

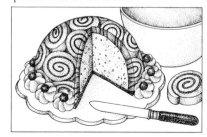

China anise   Star-shaped fruit capsule, which is ground and used for flavoring pepper cakes. China anise is more delicate and more flavorful than regular anise.

Chocolate   Made of cocoa butter, milk or cream, sugar and spices with or without nuts. In baking, chocolate can be grated, chopped and melted, then folded into the dough. It may also be used as a glaze. Grated chocolate, chocolate leaves, wafers and streusel can be used for decorating. Grated chocolate can be made by first melting chocolate, then spreading it thinly on a board and finally scraping it off with a knife.

Cinnamon   The bark of the cinnamon tree. There are varying grades of cinnamon. Cinnamon sticks are placed in boiling milk for flavoring. In baking, ground cinnamon is used. Cinnamon is an ingredient in many spice mixtures.

Coagulation   A process which occurs when ingredients for creams and dough are at different temperatures when mixed or when milk is sour. If ingredients of varying temperatures are used, the dough or batter can usually be reconstituted into a homogeneous mass if they are beaten over a hot water bath.

Coating chocolate or chocolate glaze   A chocolate coating that contains a certain amount of cocoa butter combined with either milk, semi-sweet or bitter chocolate. It is used for glazing cakes, and it can also be grated, chopped or melted and folded into doughs or creams.

Cocoa   Made from the seeds of the cocoa tree. Cocoa butter is produced by pressing out the beans. It is used in the manufacture of chocolate and cocoa powder. Cocoa beans vary in the amount of oil they contain; they may be very oily or only slightly so. Both kinds can be used as flavoring and coloring for doughs, creams and glazes. If cocoa is

mixed with other ingredients in the dough, it should first be sifted to eliminate clumps.

Coffee   Very strongly brewed coffee can be used for flavoring creams and doughs. Ground coffee cannot be sprinkled directly into doughs because it will not dissolve. Instant coffee is less complicated.

Compressed yeast   Yeast pressed into cubes (see yeast).

Condensed milk   Milk that can be stored for long periods of time. It is made through a process of condensation and sterilization. It is also called canned milk. There are several kinds ranging from 1% to 15% fat content. Condensed milk may be used for baking but should be brought down to a fat level of 5%. Whole milk is usually used when making creams because of its more pleasant taste.

Coriander   A seed used as a spice, it is available whole or ground. It is used as a spice in Christmas cookies; it is also used in bread and roll doughs. Coriander is found in spice mixtures for honey bars.

Cornstarch   Starch made from corn; a similar product is made from the potato. It is pure starch; all other substances have been removed. Starch is often mixed with flour and used as an ingredient in doughs. It can also be used for binding sauces, creams and puddings. When adding starch to hot liquids, it should always first be stirred together with a small amount of cold liquid in order to avoid clumps.

Cream   There are sweet and sour creams. In baking, sweet cream is generally used. When whipped it is used for covering and decorating tortes and it is the basic ingredient in different kinds of "creams" (these are generally a combination of pudding or butter and cream). In order to prepare whipped cream, fresh cream must be used and it should be

whipped in a cold bowl. Whipping cream should have at least 30% fat.

Creaming   This method is used for mixing high-fat cakes and butter cakes. All ingredients must be at room temperature. Put the butter in a mixing bowl and beat the fat slowly until smooth and creamy, (pale yellow in color). Add the sugar and cream at moderate speed for 8-10 minutes until the mixture is light and fluffy. Add salt and flavorings to ensure uniform incorporation; also, if using melted chocolate, add it at this stage. Add the eggs one at a time. After each addition, beat the egg until it is absorbed into the mixture before adding another egg. The addition of each egg will require about 2-3 minutes each. Scrape the sides of the bowl to ensure even mixing of all ingredients. Add the sifted dry ingredients, alternating with the addition of the liquids.

Croquant or cracknel   Made from almonds or other nuts and caramelized sugar. It can be made at home or bought in chopped or crushed form.

Currants   Raisins from dark seedless grapes. They have a delicate sour taste. They originally come from Greece as their name indicates (Corinth). They should be stored in a cool, dry place.

Deep frying   Frying pastry, meat and vegetables in hot vegetable oils.

Dried baked goods   Baked goods that can be stored for a relatively long period of time (3 months to 1 year). They include zwieback, waffles, crackers, hard cookies and cookies made with tart dough.

Dried fruit   Air-dried fruits like prunes, apricots, pears, apples, dates and figs.

Eggs   Chicken eggs are divided into Classes 1-6, which correspond to weights ranging from 2 to 3 ounces. The recipes in this book call for eggs belonging to Classes 3 and 4, having a medium weight ranging from 2-2½ ounces. If eggs of varying sizes are used, they should be weighed beforehand. Always test the freshness of eggs before baking: crack them on a flat plate, if a firm egg white rim forms around the yolk, then the egg is fresh. The thinner this ring, the older the egg. If the egg white is extremely runny, the egg should not be used for baking.

When separating egg whites from yolks, care must be taken to avoid getting any yolk in the white. If they are mixed, the egg whites will not become firm when whipped. When preparing whipped egg whites, utensils and bowls must be absolutely fat free. Egg white is sufficiently firm if a knife drawn through the peaks leaves a path that is still visible several seconds later.

Farina sugar Sugar still containing some treacle. It is therefore yellow to brown in color and slightly moist. Farina sugar is usually used for honey bars.

Fat The most ideal baking fats are butter and margarine. They may be substituted for one another except in the cases of puff pastry, butter cream and butter cookies, for which only butter should be used. Shortening is often used in hearty doughs. If vegetable oil is used, as in yeast doughs and cheese-oil doughs, neutral flavored oils should be chosen. Pure shortening is not an appropriate ingredient for doughs, but can be used for deep frying.

Flambé Briefly broiling the surface of a pastry. This is sometimes used to make the peaks of meringues turn brown.

Flavorings Extracts from various naturally occurring plants and liqueurs. Some flavors are also artificially manufactured. They are used to flavor doughs and creams. The most commonly used flavors are lemon, almond, rum, arrack, vanilla and butter. Bottles

come in various sizes. The natural flavors of lemon rind and the vanilla bean are preferable to bottled flavoring.

Flour When these recipes call for flour, they refer to all-purpose flour. Also readily available are cake and wheat flour and are recommended for some recipes. In baking, the important substance in flour is the gluten, the flour protein. Gluten coagulates at temperatures between 140° and 160° creating the structure of the baked good. Rice and corn flours do not have this gluten and that is why they are only suitable for making flat breads. Wheat flour has a great deal of gluten and therefore has excellent baking characteristics. Rye flour also has good baking characteristics; it is, however, heavier and requires more leavening power, like sourdough, in order to be made into bread. Cake flour is a fine, soft flour and is used for baking cakes and pastries to make them light and fluffy. Fresh flour should be used for the best results. It should feel smooth and cool to the touch; it should be white and have a neutral smell and taste. Flour retains its best quality up to four weeks after being milled.

Folding Slow and gentle stirring in and mixing of delicate ingredients like flour, liquids or creams into doughs with the aid of a wire whisk.

Folding under Gentle mixing in of one ingredient under another without stirring. A wooden spoon is generally used for this procedure. The term is frequently used for mixing in whipped egg whites.

Fondant Meltable sugar confection made in various shapes and colors and sometimes coated with chocolate.

Food coloring Artificially manufactured substances used for coloring foods. They mix well with glazes, creams, doughs and marzipan. They are fre-

quently available in sets of red, yellow, green and blue.

Frangipani or Franchipan Macaroon paste or almond batter that has been combined with a kind of vanilla cream. It is used as a filling for tortes and tartlets.

Fried pastry Pastry that has been deep fried.

Gateau The French term for cake or torte.

Gelatin A product made from bone glue that serves as a gelatinizing substance. Gelatin is available in sheets and as a powder; the sheets are of better quality. Clear and red gelatin are available; both work equally well, but red is generally chosen for its appearance. Gelatin sheets must be soaked before use. Gelatin in powder only needs to be mixed with water. If gelatin is to be

stirred into cold foods, it must first be dissolved in a saucepan over medium heat. Never combine gelatin with bones since this produces an awful stench. If hot spices are to be gelatinized, the pressed-out gelatin sheets can be stirred in immediately. Powder should, however, first be dissolved over heat. When gelatin is stirred into creams, it is important that the gelatin be quickly and evenly distributed. Otherwise strings of gelatin will appear and the food will not gelatinize well.

Gelling The point at which food begins to stiffen. Definite streaks remain when it is stirred.

Ginger Root of the ginger bush, it is available whole, pulverized or candied. Ginger is used to flavor Christmas cookies. Because of its intense taste it should be used sparingly. As all other candied ingredients, candied ginger can be chopped and added to the dough or used for decoration.

Glazes Coatings for baked goods that improve their appearance and taste. They also serve to keep baked goods from drying out quickly. There are glazes that are made of cold ingredients; usually powdered sugar or cocoa mixed with water, egg white, lemon juice or alcohol. Glazes made of warmed ingredients usually have a fat base, such as chocolate, nut or lemon glazes.

Glucose A syrup derived from starch that is used by the food industry in the manufacture of sweetened foods.

Graham flour This is whole-wheat meal or bruised wheat grain. Its name derives from the American medical doctor named Graham who made bread from bruised wheat grain. Today, loaves of bread are also called Graham bread when they have a large amount of bruised wheat grain in them and have been leavened with yeast.

Grated coconut or coconut flakes The grated fruit of the coconut. Grated coconut is the main ingredient in macaroons. In other recipes it is used like other nuts. Because of its high fat content it can only be stored for a short period of time.

Hartshorn salt A mixture of ammonium hydrogen carbonate and ammonium carbamate. During baking, the salt breaks down into ammonia, water and carbon dioxide which serves to make the dough lighter. Since ammonia is produced, hartshorn salt is only used in flat cookies or bars. The height of the baked good ensures that this somewhat unpleasant by-product has a chance to escape. Hartshorn salt must be stored in tightly closed containers so that moisture does not rob it of its leavening powers.

Hazelnuts Available whole, chopped or grated. Freshly grated or roasted hazelnuts are most flavorful. Hazelnuts can be roasted by placing them in a heated oven and subsequently rubbing off the skins. Nuts should be grated in an almond mill and not in a blender. In the blender, the fat causes the nut paste or butter that develops to stick to the blade.

Honey is used as a sweetener in Christmas cookies, like honey bars, because of its special flavor. Its sweetening power is less than that of sugar. There is a difference between artificial and bee honey.

Icon-shaped cake Originally this was a cake or baked good shaped in a special way for cultic purposes. Today, the term is generally used for special baking pans that represent certain figures.

Instant flour Specially treated flour that dissolves easily and has no lumps.

Instant Coffee Immediately dissolvable coffee bean extract that is prepared by a freeze-dried process. In baking it is used for flavoring creams. The powder may be added directly to the cream or first brewed as coffee and then added.

Kneading Mixing ingredients into a smooth dough. Kneading can be done with the hands or an electric mixer. It is easier to assess the consistency of the dough when kneaded with the hands, thus allowing the addition of liquid or flour.

Lemon The juice and rind have a fresh, sour flavor. Untreated fruit should be selected if the rind is to be used. The fruit should be washed before grating.

Lining Lining a baking pan with a thin layer of puff pastry or tart dough.

Macaroon paste A paste made of egg white, grated coconut, nuts, almonds and sugar. It contains no flour. Macaroon paste can be baked into macaroons or used as a filling.

Mace The dried, orange outer covering of the nutmeg seed. The spice is ground and used in the same baked goods as nutmeg.

Madeira Dessert wine made from grapes that grow in and around Madeira.

Making vapors Creating steam in the oven by pouring or spraying water into the hot oven. This process is used especially for baking bread.

Maraschino A clear, delicate cherry liqueur made from Maraca cherries.

Margarine Fat made from vegetable oils. It is less expensive than butter. It may be substituted for butter in all baking recipes except butter cream, butter cookies and puff pastry.

Marzipan Paste made from ground almonds and sugar. Marzipan is used in doughs, for fillings, as a coating and for shaping. For the latter, marzipan is kneaded together with equal parts of powdered sugar making it less sticky; then it is shaped.

Melting The liquefying of chocolate, nougat or fat usually over a hot water bath.

Meringue Dry, foam pastry made of egg white and finely granulated sugar. It may be flavored with chocolate, grated nuts or liqueurs.

Milk Milk is differentiated according to fat content: whole milk (3.5%), 2% milk and skim (0.03%). Since the amount of fat is very low, it really makes no difference what kind of milk is used for baking. Milk that has been treated with high heat in order to allow longer storage is also good for baking. Whole milk is better for puddings. Substituting buttermilk or yogurt for milk gives a slightly sour taste and the dough will be somewhat lighter because of the bacteria these liquids contain. Doughs and creams should always be prepared with fresh milk, otherwise they could coagulate or their flavor could be affected.

Mocha beans   Mocha chocolate in coffee bean form that is used for decorating cakes and cookies.

Nougat   A mixture made of roasted and grated hazelnuts or almonds, sugar, chocolate and spices. Nougat is used for making confections and pralines and also for filling tortes.

Nutmeg   The seed of the nutmeg tree. Nutmeg is available ground or as whole nuts. The spice produces the most flavor when freshly grated. It is worthwhile to invest in a nutmeg grater, since the whole nutmeg will retain its flavor for years. Nutmeg is used as a spice in Christmas cookies.

Orange rind   Only untreated fruit should be used when orange rind is called for. Orange rind has a very strong flavor and is preferred over artificial flavoring.

Pancake turner   A thin, broad metal blade with a handle. It is used for spreading glazes and creams and lifting small pastries and cookies from baking sheets.

Patisserie   French word for a cake bakery and the type of goods made there.

Peanuts   Peanuts in the shell are available commercially. They give cakes an especially sweet and hearty flavor.

Pecans   The shell of these nuts looks similar to hazelnut shells, while the kernel resembles the walnut in taste and form.

Pine nuts   White seeds of the pine tree. They are very rich and can be roasted like nuts or used ground.

Pistachio   The green nuts of the pistachio tree. They can be used chopped or whole; they can be roasted and folded into the dough or used as decoration.

Poppy seed or mohn   The seed of the poppy. It is used as a filling or topping for cakes. Poppy seeds must be crushed so that the fat is released and the flavor can develop. Poppy seed can be ground in a poppy seed mill or a blender or purchased already crushed. However, it quickly becomes rancid when exposed to air. Whole poppy seeds are used for sprinkling on rolls and braids.

Potato flour   See Cornstarch.

Preheating   Heating the oven prior to baking to the temperature called for in the recipe. Preheating usually takes 10 to 20 minutes.

Preserved fruits   Fruits, like cherries, that have been treated with sugar and are used for decorating tortes and pastries. They can also be chopped and added to doughs. These fruits are not identical to candied fruits because they have been treated only briefly with a less concentrated sugar solution and are therefore softer.

Pretzel salt   Coarse salt used for sprinkling on pretzels and other salted pastry.

Punching down   A procedure in preparing bread dough. After the dough has doubled in size the first time, it is very porous and contains a great deal of air. This air is exhausted by repeatedly punching the dough, that is, by pushing the hands into the dough and pressing them together carefully.

Raisins   Air- and sun-dried white and red grapes with seeds. Since grapes are often sprayed, the raisins should always be washed before use.

Reheating   Placing baked goods, that have been stored for a period of time, in the oven and heating them to restore freshness. The baked good should be in a pan and covered with aluminum foil in order to avoid drying out. Sugar-coated pastry should not be reheated.

Rock candy sugar   Coarse sugar crystals used for decorating baked goods.

Rose oil or rose water   Oil from rose petals used to flavor doughs and marzipan.

Rounds   Technique used for making danish pastry: cold butter is wrapped in rolled out dough, then both are rolled out together. The dough is subsequently folded again and rolled out again. This procedure is repeated 4-5 times or "rounds."

Saffron   The most expensive spice in the world. Made from the stigmas of a type of iris. It is used mainly for coloring doughs yellow and less for its flavor.

Semi-sweet chocolate   Chocolate that is at least 50% cocoa.

Sesame seeds   Seeds from the sesame plant are ground and added to bread or sprinkled whole on the top of rolls and breads. They are also used in the preparation of candies.

Sheet cakes   In general, these are sweet and hearty cakes, that are baked on a baking sheet and not in a pan.

Sifting   Coating cakes and pastries with powdered sugar or cocoa with the aid of a sieve.

Soaking   When the bottom layer of a cake or an entire cake is made to absorb fruit juice, a sugar solution or liqueurs.

Sourdough   Fermenting dough that is used in rye doughs as a leavening agent. In sourdough fermentation, not only carbon dioxide but also lactic acid and acetic acid are produced. The latter two produce the sour taste in sourdough breads. Sourdough can be ordered from the baker or made at home (see page 287).

Spices   Spices are described individually in this section. Generally speaking, the spices that are used should be as fresh as possible. They have the most flavor when just ground. Spices can be pulverized and grated on graters, in spice mills and with mortar and pestle.

Spice mixtures   Ready-made mixtures of spices.

Sponge   See starter.

Starter or sponge   A preliminary mixture of flour, yeast, sugar and lukewarm milk in which the yeast has already begun to ferment and create leavening gases.

Streusel   Crumb mixture made of butter, sugar and flour that has been rubbed between the hands. It is used as a topping on cakes.

Sugar decors   Small, colorful sugar balls used for decorating cakes and cookies.

Sugar streusel or sugar sprinkles   Colorful pellets of sugar for decorating cakes and cookies.

Sugar   Sugar can be made from sugar cane or beets and is available in granulated and powdered form. It is also available as cubes and as rock candy sugar. Granulated sugar is usually used for baking; it is available in various grinds. The finest grind is best for baking, since it dissolves quickly and sweetens most strongly. Powdered sugar is selected for sifting or dusting and for meringue pastes, because it is very fine and dissolves well in whipped egg whites.

Sultanas   Large, light-colored, dried, seedless grapes. They are sometimes treated with sulphur.

Testing for doneness   Checking the dough to see whether it has been baked completely through. The most well-known method is the toothpick or wooden skewer test. With this test all cakes baked in pans or in loaf form can be checked. A wooden skewer or toothpick is inserted into the middle of the cake. If it comes out clean, it is done. If dough sticks to the skewer, then the cake is not ready.

For cookies, the brown appearance of the surface generally indicates doneness. The color can range from deep yellow to golden brown.

Sponge cake layers are done when no indentation remains after the surface has been pressed with the fingertips.

Vanilla   The bean of the vanilla tree, which obtains its flavor through fermentation. The marrow of the bean is used for flavoring; it must be scraped out of the pod. A food that has been prepared with real vanilla can be recognized by the black dots of the marrow. The empty pod may be cooked in milk or other liquids in order to flavor them additionally. Vanilla sugar can be made by laying vanilla in the sugar tin. After a few days the sugar will absorb the vanilla

flavor. An artificially prepared vanilla-flavoring is available commercially.

Vanilla sugar   Sugar containing at least 5% real vanilla. Vanilla sugar can be recognized by the black dots it contains. Artificially produced vanilla.

Walnuts   Available in the shell or unshelled. They can be grated and folded into a dough or halved and used as decoration.

Water bath   A pan with boiling water over which sensitive creams and doughs

are beaten or over which chocolate, fat or nougat is melted. The water bath should not be kept at a rolling boil since the water could then bubble over into the cream. The bowl in which the beating or stirring is done should therefore stand tightly on the rim of the pan.

Working   Rolling and kneading of small pieces of dough in order to shape them and form a smooth surface.

Yeast   A biological leavening agent. Carbon dioxide and a little alcohol are produced during fermentation with yeast. This causes the dough to rise and become lighter. Yeast is available compressed into cakes. It should always be used fresh. Fresh yeast crumbles like cheese. Aged yeast is brownish in color and dry. It is no longer suitable as a leavening agent. Active dry yeast is the most common form available and can be stored for longer periods of time. It is granulated and can be sprinkled directly into the flour; thus it reduces preparation time normally required for making the starter.

Index